ENGLISH FOR ACADEMIC PURPOSES

Routledge Applied Linguistics is a series of comprehensive resource books, providing students and researchers with the support they need for advanced study in the core areas of English Language and Applied Linguistics.

Each book in the series guides readers through three main sections, enabling them to explore and develop major themes within the discipline.

- Section A, Introduction, establishes the key terms and concepts and extends readers' techniques of analysis through practical application.
- Section B, Extension, brings together influential articles, sets them in context, and discusses their contribution to the field.
- Section C, Exploration, builds on knowledge gained in the first two sections, setting thoughtful tasks around further illustrative material. This enables readers to engage more actively with the subject matter and encourages them to develop their own research responses.

Throughout the book, topics are revisited, extended, interwoven and deconstructed, with the reader's understanding strengthened by tasks and follow-up questions.

English for Academic Purposes:

- introduces the major theories, approaches and controversies in the field
- gathers together influential readings from key names in the discipline, including John Swales, Alistair Pennycook, Greg Myers, Brian Street and Ann Johns
- provides numerous exercises as practical study tools that encourage in students a critical approach to the subject.

Written by an experienced teacher and researcher in the field, *English for Academic Purposes* is an essential resource for students and researchers of Applied Linguistics.

Ken Hyland is Professor of Education and Head of the Centre for Academic and Professional Literacies at the Institute of Education, University of London. He has twenty-six years' experience teaching and researching academic and professional literacies.

ROUTLEDGE APPLIED LINGUISTICS

SERIES EDITORS

Christopher N. Candlin is Senior Research Professor in the Department of Linguistics at Macquarie University, Australia, and Professor of Applied Linguistics at the Open University, UK. At Macquarie, he has been Chair of the Department of Linguistics; he established and was Executive Director of the National Centre for English Language Teaching and Research (NCELTR) and foundational Director of the Centre for Language in Social Life (CLSL). He has written or edited over 150 publications and co-edits the *Journal of Applied Linguistics*. From 1996 to 2002 he was President of the International Association of Applied Linguistics (AILA). He has acted as a consultant in more than thirty-five countries and as external faculty assessor in thirty-six universities worldwide.

Ronald Carter is Professor of Modern English Language in the School of English Studies at the University of Nottingham. He has published extensively in applied linguistics, literary studies and language in education, and has written or edited over forty books and a hundred articles in these fields. He has given consultancies in the field of English language education, mainly in conjunction with the British Council, in over thirty countries worldwide, and is editor of the Routledge Interface series and advisory editor to the Routledge English Language Introduction series. He was recently elected a fellow of the British Academy of Social Sciences and is currently UK Government Advisor for ESOL and Chair of the British Association of Applied Linguistics (BAAL).

TITLES IN THE SERIES

Intercultural Communication: An advanced resource book
Adrian Holliday, Martin Hyde and John Kullman

Translation: An advanced resource book
Basil Hatim and Jeremy Munday

Grammar and Context: An advanced resource book
Ann Hewings and Martin Hewings

Second Language Acquisition: An advanced resource book
Kees de Bot, Wander Lowie and Marjolijn Verspoor

Corpus-based Language Studies: An advanced resource book
Anthony McEnery, Richard Xiao and Yukio Tono

Language and Gender: An advanced resource book
Jane Sunderland

English for Academic Purposes: An advanced resource book
Ken Hyland

English for Academic Purposes

An advanced resource book

Ken Hyland

LONDON AND NEW YORK

First published 2006
by Routledge
2 Park Square, Milton Park, Abingdon, Oxon, OX14 4RN

Simultaneously published in the USA and Canada
by Routledge
711 Third Avenue, New York, NY 10017

Routledge is an imprint of the Taylor & Francis Group, an informa business

Transferred to Digital Printing 2011

© 2006 Ken Hyland

Typeset in Akzidenz Grotesk, Minion and Novarese
by Keystroke, 28 High Street, Tettenhall, Wolverhampton

British Library Cataloguing in Publication Data
A catalogue record for this book is available from the British Library

Library of Congress Cataloguing in Publication Data
Hyland, Ken.
    English for academic purposes: an advanced resource book / Ken Hyland.
       p. cm. – (Routledge applied linguistics)
    Includes bibliographical references.
    1. English language–Study and teaching–Foreign speakers. 2. English
language–Rhetoric–Problems, exercises, etc. 3. Academic writing–Study
and teaching. 4. Language and education. 5. Applied linguistics.
    I. Title. II. Series.
    PE1128.A2H95 2006
    428.0071'1–dc22   2006002498

ISBN10: 0–415–35869–8 (hbk)
ISBN10: 0–415–35870–1 (pbk)
ISBN10: 0–203–00660–7 (ebk)

ISBN13: 978–0–415–35869–9 (hbk)
ISBN13: 978–0–415–35870–5 (pbk)
ISBN13: 978–0–203–00660–3 (ebk)

Contents

Contents

SECTION C: EXPLORATION 215

Contents cross-referenced

Series editors' preface

The Routledge Applied Linguistics series provides a comprehensive guide to a number of key areas in the field of applied linguistics. Applied linguistics is a rich, vibrant, diverse and essentially interdisciplinary field. It is now more important than ever that books in the field provide up-to-date maps of what is an ever-changing territory.

The books in this series are designed to give key insights into core areas of applied linguistics. The design of the books ensures, through key readings, that the history and development of a subject are recognized while, through key questions and tasks, integrating understandings of the topics, concepts and practices that make up its essentially interdisciplinary fabric. The pedagogic structure of each book ensures that readers are given opportunities to think, discuss, engage in tasks, draw on their own experience, reflect, research and to read and critically re-read key documents.

Each book has three main sections, each made up of approximately ten units:

A: An **Introduction** section: in which the key terms and concepts which map the field of the subject are introduced, including introductory activities and reflective tasks, designed to establish key understandings, terminology, techniques of analysis and the skills appropriate to the theme and the discipline.

B: An **Extension** section: in which selected core readings are introduced (usually edited from the original) from existing key books and articles, together with annotations and commentary, where appropriate. Each reading is introduced, annotated and commented on in the context of the whole book, and research/follow-up questions and tasks are added to enable fuller understanding of both theory and practice. In some cases, readings are short and synoptic and incorporated within a more general exposition.

C: An **Exploration** section: in which further samples and illustrative materials are provided with an emphasis, where appropriate, on more open-ended, student-centred activities and tasks, designed to support readers and users in undertaking their own locally relevant research projects. Tasks are designed for work in groups or for individuals working on their own. They can be readily included in award courses in applied linguistics, or as topics for personal study and research.

The books also contain a glossary/glossarial index, which provides a guide to the main terms used in the book, and a detailed, thematically organized Further Reading section, which lays the ground for further work in the discipline. There are also extensive bibliographies.

The target audience for the series is upper undergraduates and postgraduates on language, applied linguistics and communication studies programmes as well as teachers and researchers in professional development and distance learning programmes. High-quality applied research resources are also much needed for teachers of EFL/ESL and foreign language students at higher education colleges and universities worldwide. The books in the Routledge Applied Linguistics series are aimed at the individual reader, the student in a group and at teachers building courses and seminar programmes.

We hope that the books in this series meet these needs and continue to provide support over many years.

The Editors

Professor Christopher N. Candlin and Professor Ronald Carter are the series editors. Both have extensive experience of publishing titles in the fields relevant to this series. Between them they have written and edited over one hundred books and two hundred academic papers in the broad field of applied linguistics. Chris Candlin was president of the International Association for Applied Linguistics (AILA) from 1996 to 2002 and Ron Carter was chair of the British Association for Applied Linguistics (BAAL) from 2003 to 2006.

Professor Christopher N. Candlin
Senior Research Professor
Department of Linguistics
Division of Linguistics and Psychology
Macquarie University
Sydney NSW 2109, Australia

and

Professor of Applied Linguistics
Faculty of Education and Language Studies
The Open University
Walton Hall
Milton Keynes MK7 6AA, UK

Professor Ronald Carter
School of English Studies
University of Nottingham
Nottingham NG7 2RD, UK

Acknowledgements

The view of EAP presented in this book emerged over many years in interactions with many people, so I want to record my thanks to the students, colleagues and friends who have encouraged me, discussed ideas and provided the insights which have contributed to it. While there are too many to name individually, I have to mention my debt to Vijay Bhatia, Marina Bondi, Tim Boswood, Lesley Coles, Ann Johns and John Swales in particular for their unwavering enthusiasm, ideas, texts and conversations which have both stimulated and sustained my interest in EAP. I would also like to acknowledge the series editors, Chris Candlin and Ron Carter, for inviting me to get involved in this project, and particularly to Chris for his close reading of several drafts of the manuscript and thoughtful suggestions for revisions. Thanks too to various classes of students on MA TESOL courses in both Hong Kong and London for guinea-pigging many of the tasks and for their feedback on the ideas and approaches discussed in these pages. Finally, and as always, my gratitude goes to Fiona Hyland, for her support, her encouragement and her ideas about writing and teaching.

The author and publisher wish to express thanks to the following for use of copyright materials. Reprinted from *English for Specific Purposes*, 15 (2): Allison, D. 'Pragmatist discourse and English for Academic Purposes' pp. 85–103, copyright © 1996 with permission from Elsevier. Reprinted from *English for Specific Purposes*, 22 (3): Barron, C. 'Problem-solving and EAP: themes and issues in a collaborative teaching venture' pp. 297–314, copyright © 2002 with permission from Elsevier. Reprinted from *English for Specific Purposes*, 18: Benesch, S. 'Rights analysis: studying power relations in an academic setting' pp. 313–27, copyright © 1999 with permission from Elsevier. Reprinted from *English for Specific Purposes*, 12: Mauranen, A. 'Contrastive ESP rhetoric: metatext in Finnish–English economics texts' pp. 3–22, copyright © 1993 with permission from Elsevier. Reprinted from *English for Specific Purposes*, 16: Pennycook, A. 'Vulgar pragmatism, critical pragmatism, and EAP' pp. 253–69, copyright © 1997 with permission from Elsevier. Reprinted from *Journal of English for Academic Purposes*, 1 (1): Warschauer, M. 'Networking into academic discourse' pp. 45–58, copyright © 2002 with permission from Elsevier. Flowerdew, L. (2000) 'Using a genre-based framework to teach organisational structure in academic writing'. *ELT Journal*, 54 (4) pp. 371–5, by permission of Oxford University Press. Chin, E. (1994) 'Redefining "context" in research on writing'. *Written Communication*, II, Sage Publications, reproduced with permission. Excerpts from Johns, A. (1997) *Text, role and context*, copyright © Cambridge University Press, reproduced with permission. Reprinted from *English for Specific Purposes,* 21 (4): Hyland, K. 'Specificity revisited: how far should we go now?' pp. 385–95, copyright © 2002, with permission from Elsevier. Reprinted from *Journal of Second Language Writing,* 6 (2): Hyland, K. and Milton, J. 'Qualification and certainty in L1 and L2 students' writing' pp. 183–206, copyright © 1997, with permission of Elsevier. Excerpts from Becher, T. (1989) *Academic tribes and territories: intellectual inquiry and the cultures of disciplines,* SRHE/Open University Press, reproduced with kind permission of the Open University Press/McGraw-Hill Publishing Company. Ivanic, R., Clark, R., and Rimmershaw, R. (2000) '"What am I supposed to make of this?" The messages conveyed to students by tutors' written comments', in M. Lea and B. Stierer (eds) *Student writing in higher education: new contexts,* Open University Press, reproduced with kind permission of the Open University Press/McGraw-Hill Publishing Company. Lea, M. and Street, B. (2000) 'Student writing and staff feedback in higher education: an academic literacies approach', in M. Lea and B. Stierer (eds) *Student writing in higher education: new contexts,* Open University Press, reproduced with kind permission of the Open University Press/McGraw-Hill Publishing Company. Myers, G. (1994) 'The narratives of science and nature in popularising molecular genetics', in M. Coulthard (ed.), *Advances in written text analysis,* Routledge, reproduced with permission of the publisher. From Simpson, R. (2004) 'Stylistic features of academic speech: the role of formulaic speech', in Connor, U. and Upton, T. (eds) *Discourse in the professions,* pp. 37–64, with kind permission by John Benjamins Publishing Company, Amsterdam and Philadelphia, www.benjamins.com, and the Foundation of Language. Spack, R. (1988) 'Initiating ESL students into the academic discourse community: how far should we go?' *TESOL Quarterly,* 22 (1), pp. 29–52, reproduced with kind permission of the author. Yakhontova, T. (2002). '"Selling" or "telling"? The issue of cultural variation in research genres', in J. Flowerdew (ed.), *Academic discourse,* pp. 216–32, Longman, reproduced with kind permission of Tatyana Yakhontova. Excerpts from Swales, J. and Feak, C. (2000) *English in today's research world: a writing guide,* University of Michigan Press, reproduced with kind permission of the publisher. Swales, J. (1997) 'English as *Tyrannosaurus rex*', *World Englishes,* 16 (1), Blackwell Publishing Ltd, reproduced with permission of the publisher.

How to use this book

EAP is an activity at the forefront of language education today, and this book attempts to introduce the key elements of its theory and practice in an accessible and systematic way. *English for Academic Purposes: an advanced resource book* is designed for upper undergraduate and postgraduate students on language, applied linguistics and TESOL programmes as well as teachers and researchers in the field of language teaching. The book provides a platform for readers to engage with the main issues in the field through a series of chapters discussing the main terms and ideas, extracts from key readings, and numerous reflective and research tasks. This material therefore encourages readers to reflect on theory and practice, conduct their own research and critically evaluate the research of others.

Like other books in the Routledge Applied Linguistics series, *English for Academic Purposes* consists of three sections: an Introduction, an Extension and an Exploration:

- The Introduction units in Section A establish key terms and concepts, provide a discursive overview, develop an argument towards EAP and preview what is to come in the corresponding B and C units.

- The Extension units in Section B provide extracts from a range of original texts, some 'classic' and influential, others less known but nevertheless showcasing illustrative work and ideas. All readings include pre-reading, while-reading and post-reading tasks designed to help the reader to come to a better understanding of the texts.

- The Exploration units in Section C allow students to engage actively with the subject matter of the A and B units and take their study further by participating in a range of desk and field research tasks. The majority of these are open-ended, student-centred activities designed so that students can work with them and apply them in their own contexts.

In addition to these three sections, this book is also divided into three themes, each containing four units:

- Theme 1 addresses conceptions and controversies around the nature of EAP and its role in academic literacy education and particularly how EAP is inextricably related to wider social, cultural and institutional issues. The units focus on important topics such as the disciplinary specificity of teaching, EAP's relation to theories of situated literacy, critical pedagogy and study skills, and the expanding global role of academic English.

- Theme 2 explores key ideas and methods which inform EAP practice, looking more closely at the ways individuals participate in academic life and the theoretical and analytical tools we use to understand these forms of participation. Units in this theme concern the influence of discourse, discipline and culture on academic communication and the use of genre analysis, corpus linguistics and ethnographic methods in understanding academic texts, activities and contexts.

- Theme 3 deals with the practical issues of EAP course design and delivery, pulling together aspects of investigating, planning and teaching. In particular, these units explore different meanings of students' needs and the relationships of these needs to course design, the design and sequencing of tasks and consideration of appropriate teaching methods, working with subject teaching staff, monitoring learner progress and providing effective intervention.

Each unit in Section A concludes with an annotated list of some key texts, and a detailed glossary is supplied at the end covering central terms from EAP and applied linguistics.

There are basically two ways to use this book. The first is to go through Section A first, and then on to Sections B and C. The advantage is that, after reading Section A, students will have acquired some knowledge about the issues discussed further in the selected readings and explored in the later parts. Some of the tasks in Sections B and C are based on this approach because they refer to theories and concepts that are discussed in Section A. The other approach is to go through the same unit in each section sequentially, so first A1, B1 and C1, then A2, B2, C2 and so on. The advantage of that approach is that the issues presented in Section A are developed more deeply through the combination of theory, readings and tasks. It is, however, not necessary to work through the twelve units in order; they can be chosen according to interest and purpose, and according to the reader's experience in the field to date.

Introduction

English for Academic Purposes (EAP) has evolved rapidly over the past twenty years or so. From humble beginnings as a relatively fringe branch of English for Specific Purposes (ESP) in the early 1980s, it is today a major force in English language teaching and research around the world. Drawing its strength from a variety of theories and a commitment to research-based language education, EAP has expanded with the growth of university places in many countries and increasing numbers of international students undertaking tertiary studies in English. As a result, EAP is now situated at the front line of both theory development and innovative practice in teaching English as a second/other language.

WHAT IS EAP?

EAP is usually defined as teaching English with the aim of assisting learners' study or research in that language (e.g. Flowerdew and Peacock, 2001: 8; Jordan, 1997: 1). In this sense it is a broad term covering all areas of academic communicative practice such as:

- Pre-tertiary, undergraduate and postgraduate teaching (from the design of materials to lectures and classroom tasks).
- Classroom interactions (from teacher feedback to tutorials and seminar discussions).
- Research genres (from journal articles to conference papers and grant proposals).
- Student writing (from essays to exam papers and graduate theses).
- Administrative practice (from course documents to doctoral oral defences).

As Dudley-Evans (2001: ix) notes, EAP often tends to be a practical affair, and these areas are typically understood in terms of local contexts and the needs of particular students.

But while it involves syllabus design, needs analysis and materials development, EAP is now also a much more theoretically grounded and research informed enterprise than these kinds of characterization suggest. The communicative demands of the modern university, much like the modern workplace, involve far more than simply controlling linguistic error or polishing style. In fact, international research, experience and practice provide evidence for the heightened, complex and highly diversified nature of such demands. Supported by an expanding range of publications and research journals, there is growing awareness that students, including native English-speakers, have to take on new roles and engage with knowledge in new ways when they enter university. They find that they need to write and read unfamiliar genres and participate in novel speech events. Such broad definitions therefore fail to capture the diverse ways that EAP seeks to understand and engage learners in a critical understanding of the increasingly varied contexts and practices of academic communication.

More specifically, current EAP aims at capturing 'thicker' descriptions of language use in the academy at all age and proficiency levels, incorporating and often going beyond immediate communicative contexts to understand the nature of disciplinary knowledge itself. It employs a range of interdisciplinary influences for its research methods, theories and practices to provide insights into the structures and meanings of spoken, written, visual and electronic academic texts, into the demands placed by academic contexts on communicative behaviours, and into the pedagogic practices by which these behaviours can be developed. It is, in short, specialized English-language teaching grounded in the social, cognitive and linguistic demands of academic target situations, providing focused instruction informed by an understanding of texts and the constraints of academic contexts.

Changing contexts

The term 'English for Academic Purposes' seems to have been coined by Tim Johns in 1974 and made its first published appearance in a collection of papers edited by Cowie and Heaton in 1977 (Jordan, 2002). By the time the journal *English for Specific Purposes* began in 1980, EAP was established as one of the two main branches of ESP, together with the use of language in professional and workplace settings (sometimes referred to as EOP or English for Occupational Purposes). Since then EAP has grown steadily as English has expanded with the increasing reach of global markets. For many countries this has meant that producing an annual crop of graduates able to function in employment through English has become an economic imperative. Similarly, the parallel growth of English as the leading language for the dissemination of academic knowledge has had a major impact in binding the careers of thousands of scholars to their competence in English (e.g. Graddol, 1997).

These changes have been accompanied by a greater internationalization and globalization of higher education. Together with domestic policies advocating enhancing numbers of eligible university entrants in the UK, Australia, US and elsewhere, these factors have had a dramatic impact on universities. Student populations have become increasingly diverse, particularly in terms of their ethnic and linguistic backgrounds and educational experiences, and this presents significant challenges to university academic staff. There have also been other major changes in student demographics. With the rapid rise in refugee populations around the world, and a consequent increase in international migration, it is common for teachers to find non-native users of English in their high-school classrooms for whom the concept of 'academic language' in any language is an unfamiliar one.

The learning needs of all these student groups have a particular focus in the challenges to communicative competence presented by disciplinary-specific study, by modes of teaching and learning, and by changing communicative practices within and outside the academy. In this context, diversity takes on a particular importance. The distinctiveness of disciplinary communication, for example, presents considerable challenges to students, especially as such disciplines them-selves change and develop. There is now compelling evidence across the academic spectrum that disciplines present characteristic and changing forms of commu-nication which students must learn to master in order to succeed. At the same time, employers and professional bodies seek evidence of graduates' general workplace-relevant communication skills – skills which need increasingly to be adaptable to new, often unpredictable contexts of communication. Further, while in the past the main vehicles of academic communication were written texts, now a broad range of modalities and presentational forms confront and challenge students' com-municative competence. They must learn rapidly to negotiate a complex web of disciplinary-specific text types, assessment tasks and presentational modes (both face-to-face and online) in order first to graduate, and then to operate effectively in the workplace.

Another development pushing the expansion and increasing complexity of EAP is a concern with the English-language skills of non-native English-speaking academics, especially those working in non-English-language countries where English is used as the medium of university instruction, such as Hong Kong and Singapore. The professional and institutional expectations of these academics are closely aligned with those in the 'metropolitan' English-language-speaking countries and whether the academic is a native or non-native user of English is seen as immaterial to the roles they play and the jobs they perform. The ability to deliver lectures in English, to carry out administrative work, to participate in meetings, to present at international conferences, and, above all, to conduct and publish research in English, are all demanded as part of such lecturers' competence as academics. This group's needs and concerns are now beginning to be noticed and analysed and programmes are emerging which cater to their particular requirements.

The response of EAP

English for Academic Purposes is the language teaching profession's response to these developments, with the expansion of students studying in English leading to parallel increases in the number of EAP courses and teachers. Central to this response is the acknowledgement that the complexity and immediacy of the challenges outlined above cannot be addressed by some piecemeal remediation of individual error. Instead, EAP attempts to offer systematic, locally managed, solution-oriented approaches that address the pervasive and endemic challenges posed by academic study to a diverse student body by focusing on student needs and discipline-specific communication skills.

Course providers have recognized that teaching those who are using English for their studies differs from teaching those who are learning English for other purposes, and programmes designed to prepare non-native users of English for English-medium academic settings have grown into a multi-million-dollar enterprise around the world. For many learners, their first taste of academic study is through an EAP pre-sessional course, either in their home or in an overseas country. These courses are designed to improve students' academic communication skills in English to the level required for entry into an English-medium university or college, but there are similar developments at the other end of the educational ladder. It is increasingly understood, for instance, that children entering schooling can be helped to learn more effectively and to integrate better into the educational structure if they are taught specific academic skills and appropriate language use for such contexts.

These developments have together helped reshape the ways that English-language teaching and research are conducted in higher education, with a huge growth in research into the genres and practices of different academic contexts. This has had the result that the concept of a single, monolithic 'academic English' has been seriously undermined and disciplinary variations are acknowledged (Hyland, 2000). With the growth of interdisciplinary programmes, understanding the contributions that disciplinary cultures make to the construction, interpretation and use of academic discourses has become a central EAP enterprise.

The global growth of English in academic contexts also means that most teachers of EAP around the world are not native-speakers of English, and this has led to changes in EAP materials and teacher training courses. Many MATESOL and other postgraduate courses for teachers now include modules on EAP, for example, and there are a growing number of specialist Master's degree courses in the area available internationally. There is also increasing realization that EAP spans formal education at every level and more attention is now being given to EAP in early schooling years and to postgraduate thesis writing and dissertation supervision (Braine, 2002). Nor should we see EAP courses as exclusively directed at non-native English-speakers. Growing numbers of L1 English-speakers who enter higher education without a background in academic communication skills have made EAP a critical aspect of their learning experiences.

Continuing challenges

This expanding role for EAP has not been entirely smooth and trouble-free. Many EAP courses still lack a theoretical or research rationale and textbooks too often continue to depend on the writer's experience and intuition rather than on systematic research. This situation is changing as we see more interesting and innovative EAP courses being developed which are based on current pedagogic approaches such as consciousness raising, genre analysis and linked EAP-content modules (Benesch, 2001; Johns, 1997; Swales and Feak, 1994, 2000). These have had considerable success, but teachers are aware that a one-size-fits-all approach is vulnerable to the demands of specific teaching contexts and the needs of particular learners. As a consequence, there is substantial pedagogic and curricular creativity in local contexts in EAP and a great deal of innovative practice is unsung and not widely disseminated.

Further, the spread of EAP has often been detrimental to local languages as scholars in many countries seek to publish 'their best in the West' so that English replaces once thriving indigenous academic discourses. Equally, there is also a growing sense of disquiet concerning the socio-political implications of an 'accommodationist' view of language learning which seeks to induct learners into uncritical acceptance of disciplinary and course norms, values and discourses, particularly those connected with what Swales (*inter alia*) has referred to as the hegemony of English (see also Benesch, 2001; Canagarajah, 1999).

EAP continues to struggle with these issues, seeking to find ways of understanding and dealing with the social, cultural and ideological contexts of language use. It is in recognizing and highlighting these concerns that the field also demonstrates its vibrancy and its responsiveness to critique. EAP is a field open to self-scrutiny and change, and for these reasons it offers language teachers an ethical, reflective and fruitful field of research and professional practice and offers students a way of understanding their chosen courses and disciplines.

SECTION A
Introduction

Theme 1: Conceptions and controversies

INTRODUCTION

The applied nature of EAP, and its emergence from ESP, originally produced an agenda concerned with curriculum and instruction rather than with theory and analysis. Responding to changes in higher education, however, EAP has developed a more sophisticated appreciation of its field. From its place at the intersection of applied linguistics and education, and following a more reflective and research-oriented perspective, EAP has come to highlight some of the key features of modern academic life. Among them are that:

- Students have to take on new roles and to engage with knowledge in new ways when they enter higher education.
- Communication practices are not uniform across academic disciplines but reflect different ways of constructing knowledge and engaging in teaching and learning.
- These practices are underpinned with power and authority which work to advantage or marginalize different groups and to complicate teaching and learning.
- The growth of English as a world language of academic communication has resulted in the loss of scholarly writing in many national cultures.

These features raise interesting issues and controversies in conceptualizing EAP and determining its nature and role. In engaging with these issues EAP has matured as a field, and practitioners have come to see themselves as not simply preparing learners for study in English but as developing new kinds of literacy which will equip students to participate in new academic and cultural contexts. But these issues are by no means resolved and debates continue concerning what they mean for EAP and how we should respond to them. These issues and challenges are the topic of Theme 1.

 Task A1

> Do you agree with the four points listed above? What do you think they might mean for teaching and learning in EAP? Select one of them and consider what you believe to be its implications for the field of EAP.

Unit A1
Specific or general academic purposes?

One key issue surrounding the ways we understand and practise EAP is that of *specificity*, or the distinction between what has been called English for General Academic Purposes (EGAP) and English for Specific Academic Purposes (ESAP).

Following an EGAP approach, teachers attempt to isolate the skills, language forms and study activities thought to be common to all disciplines. Dudley-Evans and St John (1998: 41), for instance, include the following activities among such a core:

- Listening to lectures.
- Participating in supervisions, seminars and tutorials.
- Reading textbooks, articles and other material.
- Writing essays, examination answers, dissertations and reports.

This approach might encourage us to see such activities as questioning, note taking, summary writing, giving prepared presentations and so on as generic academic practices. ESAP, on the other hand, reflects the idea that, while some generalizations can be made, the differences among these skills and conventions across distinct disciplines may be greater than the similarities. ESAP therefore concerns the teaching of skills and language which are related to the demands of a particular discipline or department.

The issue of specificity therefore challenges EAP teachers to take a stance on how they view language and learning and to examine their courses in the light of this stance. It forces us to ask the question whether there are skills and features of language that are transferable across different disciplines or whether we should focus on the texts, skills and forms needed by learners in distinct disciplines.

Task A1.1

➤ Spend a few minutes to reflect on your own view of this issue. Based on your experiences as a teacher (or a student), do you think there are generic skills and language forms/functions that are useful across different fields? Or is learning more effective if it is based on the specific conventions and skills used in the student's target discipline? Is there a middle way?

This debate is not new. The idea of specificity was central to Halliday *et al.*'s (1964) original conception of ESP over forty years ago when they characterized it as centred on the language and activities appropriate to particular disciplines and occupations. They distinguished ESP from general English and set an agenda for the future development of the field. Matters are perhaps more complex now as university courses become more interdisciplinary and we learn more about the demands these courses make on students. There is, however, still a need to stress students' target goals and to prioritize the competences we want them to develop and these often relate to the particular fields in which they will mainly operate. But not everyone agrees with this view. Some EAP writers, such as Hutchison and Waters (1987), Blue (1988) and Spack (1988), argue against subject-specific teaching on the grounds that our emphasis should be on learners and learning rather than on target texts and practices. Dudley-Evans and St John (1998), on the other hand, suggest that teachers should first help students develop core academic skills with more specific work to be accomplished later.

REASONS FOR GENERAL EAP

Six main reasons have been given for taking an EGAP approach:

- Language teachers are said to lack the training, expertise and confidence to teach subject-specific conventions. Ruth Spack (1988), for instance (Text B1.1), argues that even if subject-specific conventions could be readily identified, they should be left to those who know them best, the subject teachers themselves. In other words, EAP teachers 'lack control' over specialist content and do a disservice to the disciplines and mislead students when they attempt to teach their genres.
- EAP is said to be just too hard for students with limited English proficiency. Weaker students are not ready for discipline-specific language and learning tasks and need preparatory classes to give them a good understanding of 'general English' first.
- Teaching subject-specific skills relegates EAP to a low-status service role by simply supporting academic departments rather than developing its own independent subject knowledge and skills. This leads to what Raimes (1991) calls 'the butler's stance' on the part of EAP, which acts to deprofessionalize teachers and allows universities to marginalize EAP units.
- Closely related to this is the view that by basing course content on the communicative demands of particular courses and disciplines, EAP does not prepare students for unpredictable assignments and encourages unimaginative and formulaic essays. Widdowson (1983) argues that developing skills and familiarity with specific schemata amounts to a *training* exercise. He sees this as a more restricted and mundane activity than *education*, which involves assisting learners to understand and cope with a wider range of needs. Following a similar argument, Raimes (1991) argues that academic writing at university should be part of a liberal arts curriculum teaching grammar,

literary texts and culture to add a humanities dimension to students' experience and elevate the status of the field.

- There are generic skills which are said to differ very little across the disciplines. Among those most often mentioned in this regard include skimming and scanning texts for information, paraphrasing and summarizing arguments, conducting library and Internet searches for relevant texts and ideas, taking notes from lectures and written texts, giving oral presentations and contributing to seminars and tutorials (e.g. Jordan, 1997).
- EAP courses should focus on a *common core* – a set of language forms or skills that are found in all, or nearly all, varieties and which can be transferred across contexts. Most EAP and study-skills textbooks are based on this notion, and there are numerous courses organized around themes such as 'academic writing' and 'oral presentations', or general functions like 'expressing cause and effect' or 'presenting results', and so on. Hutchison and Waters (1987: 165), for example, claim that there are insufficient variations in the grammar, functions or discourse structures of different disciplines to justify a subject-specific approach. Instead, EAP teachers are encouraged to teach 'general principles of inquiry and rhetoric' (Spack, 1988) and the common features which 'characterise all good writing' (Zamel, 1993: 35).

Task A1.2

➤ Which of these arguments in support of the wide-angle approach do you find most persuasive and why? What research data could be used as evidence to support or refute these arguments?

REASONS FOR SPECIFIC EAP

In response, there are a number of objections to the EGAP position:

- EAP teachers cannot rely on subject specialists to teach disciplinary literacy skills as they generally have neither the expertise nor the desire to do so. Rarely do lecturers have a clear understanding of the role that language plays in their discipline or the time to develop this understanding in their students. They are often too busy to address language issues in any detail and rarely have the background, training or understanding to offer a great deal of assistance. Lea and Street (1999), for instance, found that subject tutors saw academic writing conventions as largely self-evident and universal, and did not usually even spell out their expectations when setting assignments.
- The argument that weak students need to control core forms before getting on to specific, and presumably more difficult, features of language is not supported by research in second language acquisition. Students do not learn in a step-by-step fashion according to some externally imposed sequence but acquire features of the language as they need them, rather than in the order that teachers

present them. So while students may need to attend more to sentence-level features at lower proficiencies, there is no need to ignore specific language uses at any stage.

- The issue of generic skills and language also raises the question of what it is that students are actually learning. EAP professionals are concerned not simply with teaching isolated words, structures, lexical phrases and so on, but with exploring the uses of language that carry clear disciplinary values as a result of their frequency and importance to the communities that employ them. An awareness of such associations can be developed only through familiarity with the actual communicative practices of particular disciplines.

- We can dispute the view that teaching specialist discourses relegates EAP to the bottom of the academic ladder. In fact the opposite is true. The notion of a common core assumes there is a single overarching literacy and that the language used in university study is only slightly different from that found in the home and school. From this perspective, then, academic literacy can be taught to students as a set of discrete, value-free rules and technical skills usable in any situation and taught by relatively unskilled staff in special units isolated from the teaching of disciplinary competences. It therefore implies that students' difficulties with 'academic English' are simply a deficit of literacy skills created by poor schooling or lazy students which can be rectified in a few English classes. EAP then becomes a Band-aid measure to fix up deficiencies. In contrast, an ESAP view recognizes the complexities of engaging in the specific literacies of the disciplines and the specialized professional competences of those who understand and teach those literacies.

- There are serious doubts over a 'common core' of language items. A major weakness is that it focuses on a formal system and ignores the fact that any form has many possible meanings depending on its context of use. Defining what is common is relatively easy if we are just dealing with grammatical forms that comprise a finite set, but becomes impossible when we introduce meaning and use. By incorporating meaning into the common core we are led to the notion of specific varieties of academic discourse, and to the consequence that learning should take place within these varieties. As Bhatia (2002: 27) observes: 'students interacting with different disciplines need to develop communication skills that may not be an extension of general literacy to handle academic discourse, but a range of literacies to handle disciplinary variation in academic discourse'.

- EAP classes don't just focus on forms but teach a range of subject-specific communicative skills as well. Participation in these activities rarely depends on students' full control of 'common core' grammar features and few EAP teachers would want to delay instruction in such urgently demanded skills while students perfected their command of, say, the article system or noun–verb agreement.

Unfortunately for teachers and materials designers, then, it is difficult to pin down exactly what *general* academic forms and skills, what Spack calls the 'general principles of inquiry and rhetoric', actually are. Ann Johns, a prominent EAP writer, puts it like this:

At one point we thought that we had the answers, based upon a composite of pre-course needs assessments and task analyses. After completing our needs assessments, we offered instruction in notetaking, summary writing, 'general reading skills' (such as 'comprehension'), and the research paper. But as we begin to re-examine each of these areas, we find that though some generalizations can be made about the conventions and skills in academia, the differences among them may be greater than the similarities; for discipline, audience, and context significantly influence the language required. Students must therefore readjust somewhat to each academic discipline they encounter.

(Johns, 1988: 55)

Nor is it clear even if we could identify a set of common core features how these might help address students' urgent needs to operate effectively in particular courses.

Task A1.3

➤ What are the main text types and communication or learning strategies in which students are expected to engage in the course you are currently studying? Are they different from those of another discipline you have taught or know about?

ACADEMIC REGISTERS AND DISCIPLINE SPECIFICITY

This is not to say that there are *no* generalizable skills or language features of academic discourse. Most students will encounter lectures, seminars and exams, and be expected to make notes, give presentations and write assignments. In terms of language, the fact that we are able to talk about 'academic discourse' at all means that the disciplines share prominent features as a register distinct from those we are familiar with in the home or workplace. These concentrations of features, which connect language use with academic contexts, are useful for students to be aware of. One immediately obvious feature of an academic register, and one which students often find most intimidating, is what might be seen as the comparatively high degree of formality in academic texts. Essentially, this formality is achieved through the use of specialist vocabulary, impersonal voice and the ways that ideas get packed into relatively few words. These features of academic writing break down into three key areas:

■ *High lexical density.* A high proportion of content words in relation to grammar words such as prepositions, articles and pronouns which makes academic writing more tightly packed with information. Halliday (1989: 61), for example, compares a written sentence (a) (with three – italicized – grammatical words) with a conversational version (b) (with thirteen grammatical words):

(a) Investment *in a* rail facility implies *a* long-term commitment.

    (b) *If you* invest *in a* rail facility *this* implies *that you are going to be* committed *for a* long term.

■ *High nominal style.* Actions and events are presented as nouns rather than verbs to package complex phenomena as a single element of a clause. This freezes an event, such as 'The train leaves at 5.00 p.m.' and repackages it as an object: 'The train's 5.00 p.m. departure'. Turning processes into objects in this way expresses scientific perspectives that seek to show relationships between entities.

■ *Impersonal constructions.* Students are often advised to keep their academic prose as impersonal as possible, avoiding the use of 'I' and expressions of feeling. First-person pronouns are often replaced by passives ('the solution was heated'), dummy 'it' subjects ('it was possible to interview the subjects by phone'), and what are called 'abstract rhetors', where agency is attributed to things rather than people ('the data suggest', 'Table 2 shows').

The extent to which disciplines conform to these features or subject teachers expect students to use them will vary enormously. But raising students' awareness of such features helps them to see how academic fields are broadly linked and how language both helps construct, and is constructed by, features of its context.

IMPORTANCE AND IMPLICATIONS

Debates about specificity have an important impact on how practitioners in EAP see the field and carry out their work, influencing both teaching and research. Putting specificity into practice in the classroom, for instance, often involves the EAP practitioner working closely with subject specialists to gain an understanding of students' target discourses and courses. This collaboration can take various forms and can involve drawing on the subject specialist's expertise as an informant to discuss textbooks, topics and course assignments, or extend to 'linking' an EAP course with a content course (cf. Unit 10).

In classes where students are more heterogeneous in terms of discipline, specificity can be usefully exploited to highlight disciplinary differences in writing through rhetorical consciousness raising (cf. Swales and Feak, 2000). By encouraging students to explore the ways meanings are expressed in texts and compare similarities and differences, teachers can help satisfy students' demands for personal relevance while revealing to them the multi-literate nature of the academy. This helps students to understand that communication involves making choices based on the ways texts work in specific contexts and that the discourses of the academy are not based on a single set of rules. This undermines a deficit view which sees difficulties of writing and speaking in an academic register as learner weaknesses and which misrepresents these as universal, naturalized and non-contestable ways of participating in academic courses.

Equally important, the idea of specificity has encouraged EAP to adopt a strong research orientation which highlights the importance of communicative practices in particular contexts. In fact, while EAP has tended to emphasize texts, its remit is much larger, including the three dimensions underlying communication discussed by Candlin and Hyland (1999). These are the description and analysis of relevant target texts; the interpretation of the processes involved in creating and using these texts; and the connections between disciplinary texts and the institutional practices which are sustained and changed through them.

The need to inform classroom decisions with knowledge of the target language features, tasks and practices of students has led analysts to sharpen concepts and develop research methodologies to understand what is going on in particular courses and disciplines. Johns (1997: 154), for instance, urges EAP teachers to use their 'abilities to explore academic worlds: their language, their values, their genres, and their literacies, remembering at all times that these worlds are complex and evolving, conflicted and messy'. Swales (1990) shares this view that EAP should help students to become aware of the centrality of discourse and has championed a genre-based EAP, encouraging a commitment to linguistic analysis, contextual relevance, and community-relevant events in the classroom.

Moving beyond the classroom, specificity is also critical to how EAP is perceived and how it moves forward as a field of inquiry and practice. For example, placing specificity at the heart of EAP's role means that teachers are less likely to focus on decontextualized forms, less likely to see genres as concrete artefacts rather than interactive processes and less likely to emphasize a one-best-way approach to instruction.

Task A1.4

➤ Which of the pros and cons given in this unit do you see as the most persuasive? What do you see as the main challenges of discipline-specific teaching to you as an EAP teacher?

Unit A2
Study skills or academic literacy?

A second key question concerning the nature of EAP is closely related to the first. Extending the idea of specificity, it focuses on what diverse disciplinary expectations mean in practice for teachers and students. The question is whether we regard EAP as essentially skills-based, text-based or practice-based and, as a result, ask what EAP actually *is*. In other words, it touches on how we should understand EAP's role in the academy, on its status as an academic subject, on its relation to the disciplines and on the assumptions which underlie instruction. This unit surveys these three main perspectives through the changes which have led to their emergence.

EAP AND CHANGING CONTEXTS

These three conceptions, of study skills, socialization and academic literacy, have developed in succession, with later views incorporating earlier ones (Lea and Street, 2000). This represents a movement towards a more context-sensitive perspective, reflecting changes in both higher education and our understandings of academic communication. In particular, conceptions of EAP have changed because:

- We have gradually learned more about the different teaching contexts in which students find themselves and about the particular communicative demands placed on them by their studies. In the early days, EAP was largely a materials and teaching-led movement focusing on texts (e.g. Candlin *et al.*, 1975) and responding to the growing number of L2 students beginning to appear in university courses. Since then a developing research base has emphasized the rich diversity of texts, contexts and practices in which students operate in the modern university.
- There are growing numbers of students from 'non-traditional' backgrounds entering university. These students, from social groups traditionally excluded from higher education such as working-class, mature, ethnic minority and international students, mean that there is now a more culturally, socially and linguistically diverse student population in universities in many countries. In the UK, for instance, only 2 per cent of the population went to university in the 1950s compared with more than a third of the eligible age group today (HEFCE, 1999). While disparities in the participation of certain social groups continue, with individuals from working-class families still massively underrepresented,

and with provision stratified in terms of resources and status, it is nevertheless the case that undergraduate classes are no longer dominated by white middle-class monolingual school leavers in full-time enrolment. One result is that teachers can no longer assume that students' previous learning experiences will provide appropriate schemata and skills to meet course demands, while students themselves bring different identities, understandings and habits of meaning-making to their learning.

■ Students now take a broader and more heterogeneous mix of academic subjects. In addition to single-subject or joint honours degrees we now find complex modular degrees and emergent 'practice-based' courses such as nursing, management and teaching. These new course configurations are more discoursally challenging for students who have to move between genres, departments and disciplines.

The diverse learning needs of such students are therefore focused in the challenges to communicative competence presented by disciplinary-specific study, by new modes of distance and electronic teaching and learning, and by changing circumstances both within the academy and in society at large. Diversity therefore takes on a particular importance at the same time as employers demand work-ready graduates equipped with the technical and interpersonal communication skills to cope in the modern workplace. In sum, many of the old certainties about teaching and learning in higher education are slowly being undermined. This has not only given EAP greater prominence and importance in the academy, but also forced us to evolve and to ask new questions. Instead of focusing on why learners have difficulties in accessing the discourses of the academy, EAP now addresses the influence of culture and the demands of multiple literacies on students' academic experiences. The responses of EAP to these challenges are discussed below.

Task A2.1

➤ What might be the main consequences for EAP teachers of these evolving patterns of participation in higher education? What tensions might surround this expansion for students themselves?

A STUDY SKILLS APPROACH TO EAP

Study skills can be understood narrowly as the more mechanical aspects of study such as referencing, using libraries, dissertation formatting, etc. (Robinson, 1991), but they are generally seen more broadly. Richards *et al.* (1992: 359), for instance, give the following definition:

> Abilities, techniques and strategies which are used when reading, writing, or listening for study purposes. For example, study skills needed by university students studying from English language textbooks include:

adjusting reading speeds according to the type of material being read, using the dictionary, guessing word meanings from context, interpreting graphs, diagrams, and symbols, note taking and summarising.

The basis of the approach is that students need more than linguistic knowledge to be successful in their studies. Interest in study skills, in fact, emerged from a perceived over-emphasis on linguistic forms in early register-based materials. Registers refer to broad areas of activity such as communication in technical, scientific and legal fields, and early ESP materials writers, such as Herbert (1965) and Ewer and Latorre (1969), followed this approach by analysing corpora of specialist texts to establish the statistical patterns of different registers. Halliday *et al.* (1964: 88, 190) set out this programme in one of the earliest discussions of ESP:

> Registers . . . differ primarily in form . . . the crucial criteria of any given register are to be found in its grammar and lexis. . . . Every one of these specialized needs requires, before it can be met by appropriate teaching materials, detailed studies of restricted languages or special registers carried out on the basis of large samples of language used by the particular persons concerned.

When translated into the classroom this view can be seen as an early form of generic skills, but the reaction against register analysis in the 1970s moved interest away from the lexical and grammatical properties of register to the communicative tasks students had to engage in. Driven by work in education, an understanding of learning moved to examining the learners' experiences and to the actual context and situation that they learn in (e.g. Entwistle and Ramsden, 1983).

The main idea of the study skills approach is that there are common reasoning and interpreting processes underlying communication which help us to understand discourse. Rather than focusing on linguistic *form*, it is seen as being more productive to focus on interpretative *strategies* and other competences. These skills were mainly taught using general 'carrier content' which provides an academic topic to contextualize the language skills to be learnt. For example, the life cycle of plants might be used to teach biology students the language of process (Bates and Dudley-Evans, 1976).

Emerging together with a growing interest in needs analysis, the skills approach identified priorities from among the four main language skills for a particular situation. As the definition above indicates, these often involved reading, but analyses such as Munby's (1978) taxonomy suggested a wider range of skills and paved the way for more streamlined, and more empirically grounded, understandings of the competences students might need in order to engage in target behaviours (Hyland, 2003).

In particular, this auditing of skills helped clarify the relationship between teaching and target behaviours as well as itemizing the skills contributing to those behaviours, such as how library searches, note taking, lecture comprehension, etc., could be integrated to assist learners with their writing skills. Focusing on skills also highlighted the fact that students could benefit from training in learning strategies such as organizing their study time, setting study goals, memorization, exam strategies, and other study techniques. Detaching EAP from purely language issues in this way therefore meant that EAP became relevant to native English-speaking students as well as second-language learners, as many new undergraduates were unfamiliar with the requirements of the tasks they faced in this new learning context. By the late 1980s study skills was perhaps the dominant EAP approach (Jordan, 1989: 151).

One consequence of the study skills approach was a movement away from an exclusive concern with descriptions of language use towards an interest in language *learning*, a movement which reached its extreme with Hutchison and Waters's (1987) rejection of a specific academic register at all and the apparent abandonment of EAP as a distinct field of education. Despite Hutchison and Waters's attempts to emphasize the processes of learning over the distinctive nature of what was to be learnt, it became increasingly clear that the diversity of target tasks and genres which learners were forced to confront was not easily approached exclusively through a learner-centred model. Equally important, as our understanding of those target tasks and genres developed it grew increasingly obvious that they were rather more complex than first thought. Teachers came to see that many communicative activities are specific to particular disciplines, and drew the conclusion that the best way to prepare students for their learning was to provide them with an understanding of the assignments they would encounter in their academic classes, leading to an approach geared more to target genres.

Task A2.2

➤ According to Dudley-Evans and St John (1998: 95) the term 'skills' is used at two levels: five macro-skills: speaking (monologue), listening (monologue), interacting, reading and writing, each consisting of several micro-skills such as 'using cohesive markers' and 'revising a first draft'. How far do you agree with this? Does it adequately represent the main skills that EAP students must engage in? Select one skill and identify the micro-skills for it.

DISCIPLINARY SOCIALIZATION

A simple study skills model therefore gave way to a more discipline-sensitive and discourse-based approach which saw learning as an induction or *acculturation* into a new culture rather than an extension of existing skills. The language competences required by the disciplines may grow out of those which students practise in school, but require students to understand the ways language forms and strategies work to construct and represent knowledge in particular fields. A growing body of research into knowledge creation, teaching and learning began to link literacy with a more general understanding of the disciplines (e.g. Hyland, 2000; Swales, 1998). We began to see that the experiences of students, like those of academics themselves, involved interactions with others within the particular social and institutional contexts in which they studied. Like academics, learners are not independent of either each other or their contexts. As Text B1.2 suggests, attention turned to the different kinds of writing that students are asked to do and to their orientation to the particular tasks, interactions and discourses of their fields of study.

This approach draws attention to the homogeneity of disciplinary groups and practices. Each discipline might be seen as an academic tribe (Becher, 1989) with its particular norms and ways of doing things which comprise separate cultures. Within each culture students acquire specialized discourse competences that allow them to participate as group members. Wells (1992: 290) puts this succinctly:

> Each subject discipline constitutes a way of making sense of human experi-
> ence that has evolved over generations and each is dependent on its own
> particular practices: its instrumental procedures, its criteria for judging
> relevance and validity, and its conventions of acceptable forms of argument.
> In a word each has developed its own modes of discourse. To work in a
> discipline, therefore, it is necessary to be able to engage in these practices
> and, in particular, to participate in the discourses of that community.

Unlike the study skills approach, then, disciplinary socialization implies an inte-
grated view which links language, user and context. What counts as legitimate knowledge is constructed through specific teaching and learning practices in diverse disciplines. We can see, then, that this is not simply a minor shift of perspective but a basic reappraisal of EAP and its role in the academy. It suggests an important new sphere of activity which is much broader than skills teaching: it locates EAP at the heart of university teaching and learning and of students' orientation to, and success in, their fields of study.

This perspective also draws attention to the importance of *discourse* and its role in defining disciplinary groups. The term 'discourse' is widely used in the social sciences and in a variety of ways. It is often employed in a general sense to refer to different ways of representing aspects of the world, evoking the ways of thinking and talking that recur across different speakers/writers and texts. Here discourses help to scaffold the activities of social groups and their affiliations so we talk of scientific discourse or political discourse. More specifically it refers to a stretch of language, or text, that has been put to use as communication – it is language in use. These two uses are related: by engaging in certain discourses we participate in and build our communities and disciplines.

The concept of *community* will be discussed in more detail in Unit A2.5, but it is worth pointing out here that the EAP literature tends to see academic discourse communities as hierarchical with members of different rank and prestige. An important distinction is made between experts and novices in this pecking order, with newcomers socialized into the practices of members (Lave and Wenger, 1991;

Wertsch *et al.*, 1995). While undergraduates are seen as peripheral, and perhaps only temporary, members of a disciplinary community, they must nevertheless adopt the discourse practices of their professors to be accepted. To a large extent, their academic accomplishments are seen to depend on the success of this induction, shown by their ability to reproduce particular discourse forms. The emphasis here is therefore on a gradually mentored pathway to membership, or 'cognitive apprenticeship', to full induction marked by control of the genres valued by their communities.

The metaphor of *apprenticeship*, however, is not an entirely happy one, as it suggests a clear route to a well defined goal, achieving membership, which confers privileges and responsibilities (Gollin, 1998). Apprenticeship to a discipline is more vague and ill defined than apprenticeship to a trade, and lacks the same kind of implied mutual agreement between participants, with tutors willing to provide coaching and structured support and students accepting a passive and recipient role. Belcher (1994), however, points out that this was not the case in a study of three postgraduate students and Candlin and Plum (1999) found little evidence from student focus groups that undergraduates in psychology perceived their experience in this way. Introduction to the cultural world of a discipline may well take place in a situated learning context, but this is normally restricted to circumscribed pedagogic tasks, particularly writing assignments.

ACADEMIC LITERACIES

While study skills and socialization approaches have largely sought to respond to changes in tertiary education by supporting students in learning the unfamiliar demands of new kinds of discourse, the third approach, that of academic literacies, addresses some of the consequences of doing so. It does this by raising issues of relevance and legitimacy in relation to writing practices in the disciplines. Like the socialization approach, this perspective frames language as discourse practices, the ways language is used in particular contexts, rather than as a set of discrete skills. In other words it links language with action and emphasizes context. But unlike the socialization model, it sees one of the most important dimensions of these contexts as the participants' experiences of them, and, more critically, of the unequal power relations which help structure them.

This perspective takes a 'new literacies' position which rejects:

> the ways language is treated as though it were a thing, distanced from both teacher and learner and imposing on them external rules and requirements as though they were but passive recipients.
>
> (Street, 1995: 114)

Instead, literacy is something we *do*. Street characterizes literacy as a verb and Barton and Hamilton (1998: 3) see it as an activity 'located in the interactions between people'. Because literacy is integral to its contexts, it is easier to recognize the disciplinary heterogeneity which characterizes the modern university. From the student point of view a dominant feature of academic literacy practices is therefore the requirement to switch practices between one setting and another, to control a range of genres appropriate to each setting, and to handle the meanings and identities that each evokes.

Candlin and Plum (1999), for instance, show how students of business studies may be expected to confront texts from accountancy, economics, financial management, corporate organization, marketing, statistics, and so on, each giving rise to a surfeit of different text types. As an illustration, Baynham (2000: 17) asks us to think of:

> The harassed first-year nursing student, hurrying from lecture to tutorial, backpack full of photocopied journal articles, notes and guidelines for an essay on the sociology of nursing, a clinical report, a case study, a reflective journal.

Such experiences underline for students that writing and reading are not homogeneous and transferable skills which students can take with them as they move across different courses and assignments.

An academic literacies approach emphasizes that the ways we use language, referred to as 'literacy practices', are patterned by social institutions and power relationships. This means that some literacies, such as those concerned with legal, scientific and political domains, for example, become more dominant and important than others. The complexity and prestige of certain professional academic literacies work to exclude many individuals, preventing their access to academic success or membership of academic communities. For those entering the academy it forces them to make a 'cultural shift' in order to take on alien identities as members of those communities. Gee (1990: 155) stresses the importance of this shift:

> someone cannot engage in a discourse in a less than fluent manner. You are either in it or you're not. Discourses are connected with displays of identity – failing to display an identity fully is tantamount to announcing you do not have that identity – at best you are a pretender or a beginner.

Academic success means representing yourself in a way valued by your discipline, adopting the values, beliefs and identities which academic discourses embody. As a result, students often feel uncomfortable with the 'me' they portray in their academic writing, finding a conflict between the identities required to write successfully and those they bring with them.

This approach therefore builds on the socialization perspective to take a more critical view of the extent to which we can see disciplines as uncontested, homogeneous institutional practices and power as equally distributed. While the academic literacy approach lacks a clear and distinctive pedagogy, it offers a more elaborate and nuanced view of context to explain students' experiences. Drawing on Halliday's (1994) concept of *context*, it argues that we need to understand the *context of situation*, or the immediate situation in which learning and language use occur, together with the *context of culture*, a broader and more abstract notion. This concerns the ways language used in particular circumstances is influenced by the social structures, the institutional and disciplinary ideologies and the social expectations which surround those immediate circumstances. These issues will be taken up in relation to academic activity in Unit A1.4.

Finally, we can see that while each of these three perspectives on EAP addresses students' immediate needs and experiences in the academy, none explicitly refers to the post-university world of work. For most students university is a temporary experience of acquiring knowledge, more or less firmly bracketed off from other domains of life and the more urgent workplace priorities of earning a living and building a career. In those contexts activities are focused less on the individual than on the transactions and collaborations of working in teams and groups, and for second-language speakers often with less engagement with native English-speaker interlocutors and texts. One major difference between instruction for academic and workplace contexts is that there is less consensus on the skills, language and communicative behaviours required in this world (St John, 1996). It is also possible that text expectations may be linked not only with the values and conventions of particular discourse communities but with either national or corporate contexts (e.g. Garcez, 1993), so that communication strategies, status relationships and cultural differences are likely to impact far more on successful interaction (Thralls and Blyler, 1993; Pogner, 1999). These are among the key issues which are emerging as important challenges for EAP professionals.

Task A2.3

➤ What is your view? Is EAP primarily a straightforward exercise in teaching study skills, a means of socializing students into fields of study, or a way of helping students navigate their ways through conflicting issues of power and identity? Reflect on your response to this question and consider the reasons for making this choice. How might each view influence how EAP teachers carry out their role?

Unit A3
Lingua franca or *Tyrannosaurus rex*?

A third issue which shapes and confronts EAP is the consequences of the dominance that English has assumed in higher education and research throughout the world. Depending on one's perspective, English in these circumstances can be viewed as neutral lingua franca, efficiently facilitating the free exchange of knowledge, or as a *Tyrannosaurus rex*, 'a powerful carnivore gobbling up the other denizens of the academic linguistic grazing grounds' (Swales, 1997: 374).

THE GROWTH OF ACADEMIC ENGLISH

While figures are hard to come by, perhaps one in five of the world's population now speaks English with reasonable competence (Crystal, 2003) and English is now the world's predominant language of research and scholarship. This growth has, inevitably, been at the expense of other languages (Balduf and Jernudd, 1983) so that now more than 90 per cent of the journal literature in some scientific domains is printed in English and the most prestigious and cited journals are in English. Countless students and academics around the world must now gain fluency in the conventions of English-language academic discourses to understand their disciplines, to establish their careers, or to successfully navigate their learning.

These developments are largely the result of historical circumstances, particularly the legacy of US and British colonialism, the expansion of a single market across the world, and the promotion of English by US and UK governments and private companies. Phillipson (1992), for instance, has charted the role of political and economic interests in making English-language teaching a multi-billion-dollar industry. The increase in the number of world organizations, transnational corporations and the internet has accelerated this process in recent years (Gray, 2002) and its growth in higher education has been particularly dramatic, changing the conditions under which language learning takes place. Commenting on the political and economic roots of EAP, Benesch (2001: 34) argues that:

> EAP's discourse of neutrality has presented the history of this field as a consensual and inevitable chronology of pedagogical events rather than a well-crafted and organized effort on the part of governments, businesses, and foundations working together to promote English language teaching,

conferences, publications, and faculty exchanges, ensuring that markets and labor would be available to promote their economic interests.

These developments have been accompanied by an enormous expansion of second-language speakers studying academic subjects in English around the world. By the early 1990s, for example, foreign nationals outnumbered American students studying science and engineering in US graduate schools (Jenkins *et al.*, 1993), and by 2004 over one million students were studying in English outside their home countries (Ward, 2004). At the same time, the expansion of higher education in postcolonial territories such as Hong Kong, South Africa, India and Singapore has meant that more teachers are using English as a medium of instruction. More recently, countries in the former Soviet bloc, Latin America and Asia have increased their use of English in education while countries such as Germany, France and Malaysia have begun to compete for overseas students by providing courses in English in a range of disciplinary fields.

This expansion of EAP has also been fuelled by the economic imperatives of modern education provision and current 'user pays' ideologies. Fee-paying foreign students are increasingly important to universities in the anglophone world to compensate for shortfalls in government funding. There were, for instance, more than 270,000 overseas students in the UK in 2004, almost half of whom were postgraduates, contributing £23 billion to the British economy (Ward, 2004). This dependence on generating income from students has led to plans by the leading UK institutions to restrict admissions of home students to accommodate more international students (Henry, 2004), and so perhaps inevitably increasing the demand for EAP provision.

Task A3.1

➤ Reflect on this issue for a moment. Is the growth of English as the international language of academic communication a force for expanding participation in global knowledge networks or a means of restricting such access and tying it to vested corporate and academic interests? What arguments might persuade you of the opposite view to your own?

SOME CONSEQUENCES OF THE DOMINANCE OF ENGLISH

The causes and outcomes of the global spread of English in academic life are complex, but it is worth highlighting some of the effects which have dominated the debate, particularly the erosion of other academic languages and the difficulties of many non-native English speaking scholars to engage in an English-dominated academic world.

The first concern is the loss of linguistic diversity. Many European and Japanese journals, for instance, have switched to English, with Swedish, Dutch and

German-medium journals being particularly hard hit. English has superseded Russian as the academic language of the old Eastern bloc since the Cold War, Swedish has virtually disappeared in academic publications (Swales, 1997) and there is evidence that many doctoral students internationally are completing their Ph.D. theses in English where they have a choice (Wilson, 2002). With libraries increasingly encouraged to subscribe to online versions of journals, the impact of English-language journals becomes self-perpetuating as it is in these periodicals that authors will be most visible on the world stage and receive the most credit for recognition and promotion.

While this process is more pronounced in some fields than others, academics all over the world are increasingly less likely to publish in their own language. They are also likely to find their English-language publications are cited more often. References to English-language publications, for example, have reached 85 per cent in French science journals (Navarro, 1995) and, more generally, English makes up over 95 per cent of all publications in the *Science Citation Index*. Clearly a lingua franca facilitates the exchange of ideas and the dissemination of knowledge far more effectively than a polyglot system is able to, but equally there is a danger that many L2 writers may be excluded from the web of global scholarship (Gibbs, 1995), so depriving the world of knowledge developed outside the metropolitan, and anglophone, centres of research.

There is evidence, however, which strongly points in the opposite direction. The *Science Citation Index*, for instance, has been criticized for a bias towards English-language journals and, in particular, to those published in the US. Swales (2004: 40) points out that large countries with strong research traditions such as China and India are grossly underrepresented in the database, but that research communicated in English from European countries is not. Wood (2001) finds publication rates for non-native English speakers in the highly prestigious journals *Science* and *Nature* to be relatively high. Similarly, Tomkins *et al.* (2001) and Iverson (2002) show that US journals in surgery and medicine have evidenced a steady decline in US-based contributions. Swales (2004: 52) summarizes the position thus:

> In today's Anglophone research world, the status and contribution of the non-native speaker of English has become somewhat more central than it used to be and increasingly (albeit slowly) is perhaps being recognised as such by native speakers of English.

In other words, while research may be largely communicated through English, it is increasingly coming from countries where English is a foreign language.

Perhaps more serious barriers to research visibility are the structural divisions between the advantaged northern and disadvantaged southern hemispheres (Wood, 2001). Canagarajah (1996), for instance, discusses how 'non-discursive' financial and physical aspects of the research and publication process can create difficulties for periphery scholars, with access to the literature, printing quality, postal costs and editor–writer interaction posing serious difficulties. These difficulties are compounded by the need to pay for appearance in some journals, especially in the sciences. As a result, such scholars often feel themselves to be 'off-network' outsiders (Swales, 1990) in relation to work going on in the centre, although the growth of e-connections and electronic publishing may eventually make this less problematic. Indeed, the massive expansion of e-journals, the rapid access to author offprints through e-mail, the availability of paper journals on line, and the fact that international publishers offer lower-cost programs to developing countries in fields such as biomedicine or agriculture, may indicate the beginnings of a shift towards greater accessibility and participation. It is important to recognize, however, that cost is still a limiting factor for libraries in many parts of the world.

Another challenge is that of the rhetorical standards demanded by editors, referees and other gatekeepers who frequently reject non-standard varieties (Flowerdew, 2001; Gosden, 1992). Second-language academics often lack confidence in their ability to meet these standards, and in many disciplines editors insist on having submissions vetted by native English-speakers, often requiring writers to pay editors to correct or rewrite their prose before it is accepted. Clearly EAP has a major role to play here in assisting academics in developing the rhetorical skills they need to publish their work in English.

Perhaps more immediately relevant for EAP teachers, English can also have potentially negative consequences for students as they find it hard to bridge the domains of English in the classroom and their vernacular language in everyday life. Canagarajah (1999), for instance, discusses the tensions experienced by Tamil students in an EAP class in a Sri Lankan university while Flowerdew and Miller (1992) catalogue the difficulties experienced by Cantonese L1 speakers in English-medium universities in Hong Kong. Tardy (2004) similarly found that L2 postgraduate science students felt frustrated at having to spend time mastering a second language to communicate in English. The task of teachers is to bridge these linguistic worlds, not by privileging the home literacy of learners against the literacy of academic study, but by helping them to see the discourses of academic engagement as central to the study of their disciplines.

Task A3.2

➤ The problems experienced by many peripheral scholars in publishing their work in English are clearly an area which should concern EAP teachers. Identify what you see as the main difficulties for academics in the developing world and how EAP teachers can best respond to these.

PERSPECTIVES ON THE INFLUENCE OF ENGLISH

For some observers, the dominance of English in academic domains represents an impartial and inevitable development. They see it as a movement towards a common language for science which allows individuals to enter networks beyond their locality (Graddol, 2001) and which facilitates the worldwide exchange of ideas and growth of knowledge (Glaze, 2000). Global communication requires a shared linguistic code and English fits this bill owing to its already broad reach, its demonstrable value in a range of functions and domains, and its increasingly supranational character. English is said to no longer be tied to any one culture and does not emanate in a direct way from the Western metropolitan centre, so it is able to operate, in Halliday's terms, as a 'written world of secondary socialization', which performs different functions and is unthreatening to the vitality of local languages (Bisong, 1995).

For other writers, the spread of English is an insidious and destructive force, eliminating other languages, imposing the cultural dominance of the nations which speak it, and straitjacketing L2 academics into the rhetorical conventions of a single variety. Phillipson (1992) describes as 'linguistic imperialism' the process where a powerful language displaces others in some function, while Pennycook (1994) shows how its use restricts the participation of L2 academics in international forums. In Hong Kong, Singapore and India, for example, university students pursue their academic careers in a language which is not their mother tongue, and academics throughout the world are urged to publish 'their best in the West' to gain wider credit for their research.

These different perspectives reflect specific ideological orientations relating roughly to 'dependence or development'. Is English a way for countries and individual scholars to move into global academic and research forums or a Trojan horse of imperialist values and interests perpetuating reliance? While the case for diversity may seem self-evident, there are obvious problems in institutionalizing a plurality of languages as an academic lingua franca, as the majority of languages will obviously still be excluded. Nor should we assume that only native speakers of English have the expertise to participate in academic forums. Multilingualism is the norm in many countries and scholars with cultural loyalties to non-English-speaking communities are among the leading figures of their academic fields. Clearly, a more nuanced view is necessary to understand what is a complex situation.

While inevitably linked with the economic imperialism of the West, English has, at the same time, demonstrated its role outside the confines of the political and economic elites and has flourished much more demotically in such diverse areas as music, advertising and the internet. As Wallace (2002: 107) points out:

> While local language and literacies tend to serve horizontal, contingent and solidary functions, global English spans a wider range of contexts, and has universal applicability and resonance.

In academic contexts, therefore, the use of English means that language is no longer a barrier to knowledge as ever larger numbers of people can access the products of research and participate in networks which go beyond the local. As the language of globalization English can be said to empower its users (Pakir, 1999).

The fact that non-native speakers of English now outnumber native speakers (Firth, 1996: 240) means that new varieties of English emerge which do not depend on either childhood acquisition or cultural identity and which are used in contexts where no L1 English speakers are involved (Graddol, 1999). This is referred to as *English as a Lingua franca* (ELF), a variety of English which does not assume adherence to all anglo communication conventions and where traditional native-speakerness holds no advantages. Here academic users of English are no less proficient than native speakers of that language and they are not aspiring to speak a standard English variety. What matters is clarity and comprehensibility and L1 English speakers may need to adjust their language to new norms of international academic communication.

While we may be cautious of seeing English as eventually becoming a universal, culture-free language which privileges no particular group, it is not the case that languages are abstract and monolithic, imposing homogeneous ideologies and identities on passive users. Canagarajah (1999) calls such a deterministic view a *reproduction orientation*. He contrasts this with a *resistance perspective* which:

> provides for the possibility that, in everyday life, the powerless in post-colonial communities may find ways to negotiate, alter, and oppose political structures, and reconstruct their languages, cultures, and identities to their advantage. The intention is not to reject English, but to reconstitute it in more inclusive, ethical, and democratic terms . . .
>
> (Canagarajah, 1999: 2)

Precisely how this goal might be achieved remains unclear, but it is obvious that these are complex issues which demand a considered and sensitive response. We cannot see English as a hermetically sealed system unconnected with social, political and cultural issues, but equally it is unhelpful to regard EAP teachers as the unwitting agents of colonialist reconstruction.

Task A3.3

➤ Consider your own local context, or one you are familiar with. To what extent does the global spread of English seem to be a neutral or even beneficial feature supporting the inclusion of geographically peripheral scholars, and how far do you think it functions there to restrict access and promote Western interests?

Unit A4
Pragmatism or critique?

The final issue in this theme is also central to the nature of EAP, influencing how we understand and practise it. It follows closely from the themes discussed above, particularly in Unit A2 and the issue of whether EAP should be concerned with skills, disciplinary socialization or literacy practices. Here we are concerned with the *ethics* of EAP and the charge that in helping learners to develop their academic communicative competence we reinforce conformity to an unexamined educational and social order. This, then, is the issue of whether EAP is a pragmatic exercise, working to help students to fit unquestioningly into subordinate roles in their disciplines and courses, or whether it has a responsibility to help students understand the power relations of those contexts.

 Task A4.1

➤ What is your view? Is the role of EAP to help students to 'fit into roles in their disciplines and courses or to help students understand the power relations of those contexts'? What arguments might you use to persuade someone of each position?

EAP AS A PRAGMATIC ENTERPRISE

The notion of *pragmatism* can be defined in a number of ways, but in EAP it can be interpreted as meaning teaching which is 'sensitive to contexts of discourse and of action' (Allison, 1996: 87). As we have noted earlier, this has typically been seen as one of the core principles of EAP: providing targeted instruction for students which takes full account of the possibilities and constraints of local academic demands. It urges teachers to investigate contexts and learners to make decisions about what to include in their syllabus, what readings and tasks to set and how to deliver their classes. A pragmatic orientation to teaching ensures that action is informed by understanding (Widdowson, 1990), so that curricular decisions are underpinned by a sensitivity to the contexts of teaching and to the most urgent needs of learners. This, then, forms the basis of the considerable effort and commitment on the part of EAP teachers to establish students' needs, negotiate suitable goals with subject specialists and resource-conscious administrators, assemble appropriate materials and devise learning tasks.

One of the main objectives of this approach is, therefore, to empower learners by initiating them into the ways of making meanings that are valued in their target courses and disciplines, to 'help people, both native and non-native speakers, to develop their academic communicative competence' (Swales, 1990: 9). Learners commonly lack knowledge of the genres that possess 'cultural capital' in the academy, and EAP teachers are committed to more equal distribution of this knowledge to assist learners towards academic and professional success. Students and academics alike are judged by their control of the discourses of their disciplines: it is these valued discourses which determine educational life chances, regulate entry into professions, restrict passage through career pathways and have symbolic value in institutions. In other words, mastery of important disciplinary genres signifies the competence of their users in relation to their fields.

EAP teachers recognize that there are dangers in this approach. Prestigious genres are often associated with precedent and proper procedure and this means that they represent an elite of expertise and power. So by 'helping students to develop their academic communicative competence' teachers may be simultaneously stifling students' creativity and sacrificing their academic identities to the genres and discourses authorized by the academy. But while academic study privileges certain ways of making meanings and marginalizes others, this is a large part of what disciplinary engagement and participation in the work of an academic community actually mean. Ideas are negotiated within discoursal constraints which help define the boundaries of disciplines and establish valid contributions and argument.

We can also argue, however, that an understanding of the genres of the powerful not only provides access to those genres, and so redistributes valued literacy resources, but also allows users to see how they represent the interests of the powerful (Christie, 1987; Hyland, 2004). A pragmatic stance does not, therefore, exclude criticism or imply conformity (Allison, 1996). A pragmatic pedagogy has the potential for helping students to reflect on and critique the ways in which knowledge and information are organized and constructed in their disciplines. Wider understandings of influence and interests in the academy are developed not only by openly challenging existing structures but by studying texts in a comparative and questioning way which explores the relationship between disciplinary practices, institutional contexts and rhetorical preferences.

Task A4.2

➤ Ivanic (1998: 337–8) argues that the most effective teaching encourages students to be:

> active participants in social struggles, not just passively receiving knowledge and advice, but searching for understandings which will be of direct use to them, which will open up new fields of vision and new perspectives, and provide a basis for their own emancipatory and transformatory action.

Is it the role of EAP instruction to lead students in this direction? How far are you, as an EAP teacher, responsible for students to understand their learning in this way?

CRITICAL EAP

In contrast to a 'pragmatic view', critical EAP engages students in the types of activities they are asked to perform in academic classes while encouraging them to question, and perhaps even reform, those activities and the conditions they are based on. The emergence of various critical approaches to applied linguistics since the early 1980s has led to increased interest in ideas such as *ideology, identity, subjectivity* and *power* in the field of language teaching.

Of particular interest in EAP is the idea of *critical language awareness*, as this aims to:

> empower learners by providing them with a critical analytical frame-work to help them reflect on their own language experiences and practices and on the language practices of others in the institutions of which they are part and the wider society in which they live.
> (Clark and Ivanic, 1997: 217)

Critical approaches thus share an orientation with the 'academic literacies' approach to EAP by recognizing that there are various literacies, or sets of social communicative practices, in everyday life and emphasizing how access to institutionally valued literacies has the power to enhance or reduce people's life chances.

Critical theorists such as Benesch (2001) and Pennycook (1997, in Section B) argue that there is a political quietism in the EAP literature. It is too ready to conflate the needs of students with those of the disciplines and so uncritically 'accommodate' learners to the requirements of their courses. Pennycook (1997: 257), for example, argues that the *for* connecting *English* with *Academic Purposes* suggests that language is a neutral medium through which meanings pass, and that this instrumental view of language obscures the cultural, social and ideological contexts of language. He suggests that this constructs an 'unproblematic relationship between English and Academic Purposes' which can lead practitioners to accept existing conditions and to reproduce them in our classes. EAP thus constructs for itself a spurious 'neutrality' which encourages practitioners to see its goals and activities as inevitable and natural.

A critical approach thus involves questioning these goals and practices, as Benesch (2001: 41) observes:

> My critique of EAP's ideology of pragmatism is directed at its assumption that students should accommodate themselves to the demands of academic assignments, behaviours expected in academic classes, and hierarchical

arrangements within academic institutions. In addition, EAP's pragmatism assumes ESL faculty should subordinate their instruction to those demands, behaviours, and arrangements, perpetuating a service relationship to colleagues in other departments.

There are clearly two issues here: that of developing an inquiring and explanatory approach to language-mediated content, and that of establishing a credible and independent field of EAP. In some ways it might be more helpful to treat them separately as a way of moving forward to explore the most effective and nuanced ways of harnessing critical activity and creating an independent EAP.

One aspect of a critical approach is consideration of the wider *context of culture* in which EAP operates: the institutional and social structures and ideologies which intrude into local contexts of communication and the disciplinary cultures with which both students and teachers engage. Fairclough (1992) sees discourse as the link between the immediately local *context of situation* and the overarching institutional *context of culture*, as it is here where 'orders of discourse', or approved institutional practices such as assignments, seminars, essays, and so on, operate to maintain existing relations of power and authority. The practices which operate in education regulate what is worth knowing and who can know it, thus confirming the status of those who have knowledge and the position to exercise it. So by providing students with socially authorized ways of communicating, critical theorists argue that the genres we teach buttress disciplinary hierarchies and promote the values of powerful social groups by reinforcing particular social roles and relationships between writers and readers. In Benesch's words, it serves to 'accommodate' students to powerful interests.

Task A4.3

➤ Critical theorists raise several issues of direct relevance to EAP practice. What do you think are the most important of these for your own context and what kinds of tasks, topics and instructional approaches might best address them?

EAP, GENRES AND CRITICAL PEDAGOGY

It is easy to polarize the critical and pragmatist perspectives, and EAP has certainly been guilty of ignoring issues of power, but the situation is more fluid and nuanced than this at local levels. Some of the criticisms of EAP practice seem far too broad and sweeping, ignoring the fact that EAP is not a single monolithic ideology or set of assumptions but a plurality of practices and possibilities in different contexts. Many practitioners already take an inquiring attitude towards the activities of the disciplines and content courses and encourage such questioning among their students. Indeed, these issues are more often raised by teachers themselves than by students, so that critical EAP runs the danger of presuming to speak for students rather than assisting them to speak for themselves. We also need to consider the real-world consequences and pay-offs for students and how critical action might actually be harnessed to both bring about change and equip learners with a challenging and inquiring attitude to their studies and fields of practice. Clearly, such broadly theoretical arguments continue to need classroom situated exploration.

Allison (1996), for instance, points to the struggles that teachers often face in their institutions, and, despite their often vulnerable working conditions, many EAP teachers try to engage with a variety of critical issues in helping learners to understand texts and disciplines and to improve the conditions of their learning. They acknowledge that students often take a pragmatic view of their studies, yet at the same time hear them complain about the apparently arbitrary conventions of academic writing, of the vagueness of course assignments, of the obscurity of their readings and of the lack of fit between their home and academic experiences. Effective teachers therefore look at the implications of their work, attempting to avoid the unexamined, socially reproductive practices of what Cherryholmes (1988) calls 'vulgar pragmatism' in favour of a more reflective stance of 'critical pragmatism' which recognizes a variety of locally effective ways to help students demystify the academic worlds in which they find themselves so that 'critical' becomes explanatory and not only political.

Clearly critique requires understanding, and Johns (1997) suggests various ethnographic explorations that students can undertake to gain this understanding by exploring their own courses and faculty practices. Students can, for example, interview subject tutors on their reasons for selecting certain readings, textbooks, assignment topics or assessment procedures, or they can ask lecturers about their writing preferences, teaching practices, professional experiences and beliefs about the discipline. In addition, it is often possible for students to participate in the negotiation of classroom pedagogies to take greater control of their learning experience (Breen and Littlejohn, 2000; Canagarajah, 2002) or for teachers to engage learners in a critical dialogue about topics or teaching (Benesch, 2001). These issues will be taken up in Unit A3.10 in discussing *process syllabuses*.

At postgraduate level, Cadman (2002) offers ways that EAP teachers can question dominance in research education by opening discussions with supervisors, giving greater responsibility to learners and establishing a co-operative EAP classroom. These strategies rely on reconceptualizing the roles of teacher, learner and classroom through a structured process of individual and group activities to gradually take up management of their own learning. This is achieved by articulating and prioritizing their personal situations and goals and by negotiating with EAP staff, their supervisors and their classmates for an appropriate curriculum, thereby foregrounding and debating issues of power, authority and ownership of knowledge.

For others, providing learners with greater understanding of and access to valued genres is a crucial aspect of this demystification – not least because it is students from non-English-speaking backgrounds who are among the most disadvantaged by lack of such access. Learning about genres does not preclude critical analysis. In fact it provides a necessary basis for critical engagement with cultural and textual practices, as Hammond and Macken-Horarik (1999: 529) argue:

> Systematic discussion of language choices in text construction and the development of metalanguage – that is, of functional ways of talking and thinking about language – facilitates critical analysis. It helps students see written texts as constructs that can be discussed in quite precise and explicit ways and that can therefore be analysed, compared, criticised, deconstructed, and reconstructed.

Understanding how texts are socially constructed and ideologically shaped reveals the ways they work to represent some interests and perspectives and neglect others. By focusing on the literacy practices writers encounter at school, at work and at university, EAP pedagogies help them to distinguish differences and provide them with a means of understanding their educational experiences in relation to their home experiences. It undermines a view of writing as a universal, naturalized and non-contestable way of participating in communities so that what appear as dominant and superior forms of writing can be seen as simply different practices, thereby opening them to scrutiny and challenge. Providing learners with ways of talking about language and how it works as communication in particular contexts can therefore assist them with the means of both communicating effectively in writing and of analysing texts critically.

It is clearly part of every teacher's professional practice to consider these broader issues and to recognize that their work has the potential to accommodate students to the *status quo*. Teachers are responsible professionals, not simply technicians applying procedures. They constantly search for ethical ways of responding to increasingly difficult political and commercial pressures and reflect on the learning experiences of their students and whether their instruction and assessment procedures have been principled, effective and fair. They pursue wider curriculum development in the contexts in which they work and contribute their expertise to understand the social, conceptual and communicative demands that their students face. They recognize that their students often have pragmatic goals yet encourage them to greater critical awareness of the discourses they use. The greater challenge is applying this in practice – reconstructing pedagogy to engage with and promote this more critical stance. In other words, even though the educational and social issues surrounding EAP classrooms are complex and often hostile to innovation and critique, they can be places of awareness and change while meeting learning and subject course objectives.

Task A4.4

➤ Imagine you are teaching an EAP class to a group of engineering students in a university in Saudi Arabia. Bearing in mind that this is likely to be a highly constrained teaching context, how might you help students to become aware of the different ways they might respond to their learning? Are there, for instance, particular texts you might use to help learners consider the wider role of their discipline or its practices? Are there tasks or assignments which might help to encourage such a view?

INTRODUCTION

The previous theme raised the main controversies which currently engage EAP teachers and emphasized some of the ways that academic discourses are inextricably related to wider social, cultural and institutional issues. We have noted that while language is often understood, in the EGAP and skills views of EAP, for example, as a transparent and autonomous system, this fails to account for how language is actually used by individuals acting in social contexts. The concepts of *literacies*, referring to language use as something people *do* when they interact with one another, and *practices*, the idea that these language activities are bound up with routine, everyday activities in the real world, provide ways of re-establishing this link.

In this section we turn from the fundamental controversies of the field to discuss a number of key ideas and methods which inform EAP practice. This means looking more closely at the ways individuals participate in academic life and the theoretical and analytical tools we use to understand these forms of participation. The sections focus on the following key issues:

- The role of discourse in the social construction of knowledge and argument.
- The concepts of *community* and *culture* and their influence on academic communication.
- The use of genre analysis and corpus linguistics in understanding spoken and written texts.
- The importance of understanding language in relation to its contexts of use.

Task A2

➤ What do you understand by the terms literacies and practices? Why are they plural forms and what are the consequences of this plurality for EAP teachers?

Unit A5
Discourses, communities and cultures

The notion of English for *specific* Academic Purposes, and its emphasis on disciplinary-based literacies, encourages us to think about the different discourses and practices that are valued in different content fields. While disciplines are often distinguished by their specialized subject areas, the diverse topics, methodologies and ways of seeing the world which characterize them also mean that they have different discourses, different expectations of argument and different forms of verification. What counts as a worthwhile study, an effective argument and adequate evidence all depends on the disciplinary community the student is acting in. This means that writers and presenters succeed in being persuasive to the extent they can frame arguments in ways that their readers and listeners will find most convincing.

Because knowledge produced by the academy is cast largely in written language, variation in spoken genres such as lectures, seminars, peer discussions and conference presentations across disciplines has tended to be neglected until recently (Hyland, 2006). Large spoken academic corpora such as the Michigan Corpus of Academic Spoken English (MICASE) and the British Academic Spoken Corpus (BASE) are now becoming available, however (see Unit A7). This means that our understandings of disciplinary variation in spoken discourses are likely to be improved in the coming years and specific teaching materials will become increasingly available. Disciplinary variation raises a number of key issues concerning what it means to interact within a discipline, the connections between knowledge and discourse, and the influence of communities and cultures on communication. This unit introduces these issues.

DISCOURSE AND KNOWLEDGE CONSTRUCTION

Learning a discipline implies, among other goals, learning to use language in disciplinarily approved ways. It involves learning a specialized discourse for reading and writing, for presenting orally, for reasoning and problem solving, and for carrying out practical research activities. The key concepts of a discipline, its methods of persuasion, its ways of negotiating interpretations and its practices of constructing knowledge are all defined through and by language. Learning a discipline thus means learning to communicate as a member of a community. The language of science, engineering, literature or marketing is learnt in large measure by employing it for particular purposes in particular settings, and the EAP teacher's job, in part anyway, is to assist this process. Student communication is at the centre of this activity, as learning is largely mediated through written language, and control of disciplinary writing has important consequences. This is the main way that students consolidate their learning in a subject area, the means by which tutors judge the extent students have understood material, and the main instrument for assessing success or failure.

This focus on academic writing, or what Lillis (2001) calls 'essayist literacy', reflects both the gatekeeping role it plays in academic settings and the importance it has in representing academic knowledge. Essayist literacy is not a specific genre but 'institutionalized shorthand for a particular way of constructing knowledge which has come to be privileged within the academy' (Lillis, 2001: 20). This form of discourse possesses considerable 'cultural capital' (Bourdieu, 1991) as it is seen to be a guarantee of objectivity and truth: a way of representing knowledge based on impartial observation, experimental proof or faultless logic, free of the bias and interests of other forms of discourse, such as politics and commerce. But disciplinary discourses are not simply the ways that academics report their findings: just dressing the thoughts that they send into the world. They create, or *construct*, knowledge itself by securing community agreement for claims (Bruffee, 1986; Geertz, 1983).

The view that knowledge is created through the discourses of social communities has its roots in the theory of *social constructivism*. This suggests that the ways we understand the world, the categories and concepts we use, are not 'truths' proven and fixed for all time but are specific to particular cultures and periods. In other words, our knowledge does not result from objective descriptions of what the world is *really* like, but emerges in part through our perceptions of that world during our interactions. No matter how careful our experiments or rigorous our armchair reasoning, they always involve interpretation, and interpretation always depends, at least in part, on the assumptions researchers bring to the problem they are studying. Understanding is always filtered through beliefs. As the physicist Stephen Hawking (1993: 44) notes, a theory may describe a range of observations, but 'beyond that it makes no sense to ask if it corresponds to reality, because we do not know what reality is independent of a theory'. More simply, in Rorty's (1979: 170) words, knowledge is 'the social justification of belief', and in academic contexts this justification is accomplished through academic discourses.

In sum, academics cannot step outside the beliefs of their social groups to tell us 'what the world is really like' but have to draw on conventional ways of producing agreement. Persuasive potency is not grounded in rationality, exacting methodologies, dispassionate observation or informed reflection as there will always be more than one plausible interpretation of any piece of data. These competing interpretations shift attention from what happens in the lab or the library to what happens on the page. Social constructivism thus sees the agreement of community members at the heart of knowledge construction, and the language used to reach that agreement as central to the success of both students and academics. An important implication of this position for teachers is that, because it helps students to gain access to the discourses which create agreement, EAP has a central role in higher education.

Task A5.1

➤ 'Social constructivism thus sees the agreement of community members at the heart of knowledge construction, and the language used to reach that agreement as central to the success of both students and academics.' What consequences might this have for students, academics and EAP teachers? How would it influence your work as an EAP teacher?

DISCOURSE COMMUNITIES

Social constructivism tells us that the intellectual climate in which academics live and work determines the problems they investigate, the methods they employ, the results they see and the ways they write them up. This means that successful academic writing and speaking means projecting a shared context, and as we have become more sensitive to the ways language is used by individuals acting in social groups, the concept of *community* has become a key idea in EAP.

This community-based orientation to literacy focuses on the importance of writing and speaking, and learning to write and speak, as an *insider* of the community one wishes to engage with. Goffman's (1959) notion of 'membership' is crucial here as it draws attention to the importance of 'talking the talk' and the implication that academic groups might be constituted by their characteristic genres of interaction, of how they get things done, rather than existing through physical membership. An individual's engagement in disciplinary discourses can comprise membership of that discipline, an idea Swales (1998) elaborates as a 'textography of communities'.

The concept of community draws attention to the idea that we use language to communicate not only with the world at large, but with other members of our social groups, each one with its own norms, categorizations, sets of conventions and modes of inquiry (Bartholomae, 1986). Swales (1990) has defined these communities as having collective goals or purposes, while other writers have suggested a weaker connection, arguing that common interests, rather than shared goals, are essential (Johns, 1997). Barton (1994: 57), for instance, suggests they can be loose-knit groups engaged in either the reception or production of texts, or both:

> A discourse community is a group of people who have texts and practices in common, whether it is a group of academics, or the readers of teenage magazines. In fact, discourse community can refer to the people the text is aimed at; it can be the people who read a text; or it can refer to the people who participate in a set of discourse practices both by reading and writing.

Unfortunately, however, there is no clear agreement on where to actually locate discourse communities or where to draw their boundaries once we have. Is, for example, a student cohort, a university department, a specialism or a discipline the best example of a community? Are they, in other words, *local* and made up of people who regularly work together or *global* and composed of those who have a commitment to particular actions and discourses. The idea of a *disciplinary community*, for instance, suggests a relatively dispersed group of like-minded individuals, while Swales (1998) has more recently opted for a narrower version in his idea of *place discourse communities*. This draws attention to groups who regularly work together and have a sense of their common roles, purposes, discourses and history. This local–global distinction is constantly being eaten away by the advance of electronic communications which bring members in other continents closer than those in the next corridor, but the idea of a constraining system defined by a body of texts and practices is at the heart of the concept.

Discourse community therefore helps join writers, texts and readers together and, irrespective of how we define the idea, it is difficult to see how we might do without it. Essentially, it draws together a number of key aspects of context that are crucial to the ways spoken and written discourse is produced and understood. Cutting (2002: 3) points out that these are the:

- *Situational context:* what people 'know about what they can see around them'.
- *Background knowledge context:* what people know about the world, what they know about aspects of life and what they know about each other.
- *Co-textual context:* what people 'know about what they have been saying'.

Community thus provides a principled way of understanding how meaning is produced *in interaction* and so is useful in identifying how we communicate in a way that others can see as 'doing biology' or 'doing sociology'. These community conventions both restrict how something can be said and authorize the writer as someone competent to say it.

But the concept also has its critics. Some see it as a static and deterministic notion which overemphasizes conformity to shared values and practices and ignores diversity and conflict (e.g. Prior, 1998). In fact, discourse communities are not monolithic but hybrid, often inhabited by varied values and discourses and by individuals with diverse experiences, interests and influence. The experiences of many multilingual students, for example, point to the stress which can be created in shuttling between home and academic communities (Canagarajah, 1999). But this diversity is inherent in all groups and need not create antagonisms and tensions. We are typically members of several communities simultaneously – of the home, the workplace and of the academy – and so our commitment to them and participation in them can vary tremendously.

The idea of community therefore remains useful, but vague. Criticisms have sharpened the construct, however, and now we are encouraged to think of a community as more of an individual's engagement in its practices than of his or her orientations to rules and goals. Communities are not simply bundles of discourse conventions but 'ways of being' in the world, influencing the ways we act, the views we espouse, the values we hold and the identities we adopt. Nor, as Swales (1998) reminds us, does a community have to be supportive, congenial or democratic, although the most dysfunctional ones are likely to collapse. But despite difficulties, the construct helps us to see some ways that disciplines influence target texts and practices and draws attention to the fact that the discourses we teach our students are embedded in social and cultural contexts.

Task A5.2

➤ Can you identify the discourse communities you are a member of? How central is your participation in each one? Try to draw a sociometric diagram with you in the middle. This may help you to see how these communities of which you are a member overlap.

THE INFLUENCE OF CULTURE

Culture, seen ethnolinguistically and institutionally (e.g. Sarangi and Roberts, 1999), influences not only how students are expected to write and speak in the academy, but also the ways of writing and speaking they bring with them from their home environments. Through repeated experiences we develop preferred genres and patterns of communicating which come to seem natural and automatic. We gradually gain control of the genres and communicative practices we take part in by actually engaging in those genres and practices, remembering what genres are best suited to achieve which purposes and how they are set out to best say what we want to say. This kind of knowledge is sometimes referred to by literacy theorists as a *schema*, or system for storing and retrieving past knowledge. It includes knowledge about particular text features, about how a genre is used, about the contexts it occurs in, and about the roles and values associated with it. This allows us to participate in particular real-world communicative events.

The fact that cultural experiences help shape schemata means that the knowledge and expectations of our L2 students may be very different from our own and therefore influence their performance in class. While culture is a controversial notion, with no single agreed definition, one version sees it as an historically transmitted and systematic network of meanings which allow us to understand, develop and communicate our knowledge and beliefs about the world (Lantolf, 1999; Street, 1995). Language and learning are therefore closely bound up with culture. This is partly because our cultural values are carried through language, but also because cultures make available certain taken-for-granted ways of organizing our understandings, including those we use to learn and communicate. In other words, they involve interpretation as well as performance Such differences potentially include the following:

- Different linguistic proficiencies and intuitions about language.
- Different learning experiences and classroom expectations.
- Different sense of audience and self as a text producer.
- Different preferences for ways of organizing texts.
- Different writing, reading and speaking processes.
- Different understandings of text uses and the social value of different text types.

By recognizing these potential differences teachers can ensure their classroom expectations, teaching practices and assessment procedures are fair and effective.

One important, and often neglected, element in EAP classrooms is the potential for culturally divergent attitudes to knowledge to influence students' language production and how we understand students' progress. Ballard and Clanchy (1991) point out that these attitudes spread along a continuum from respecting knowledge to valuing its extension. Educational processes in Western contexts reinforce an analytical, questioning and evaluative stance to knowledge, encouraging students to criticize and recombine existing sources to dispute traditional wisdom and form their own points of view. Many Asian cultures, however, favour conserving and reproducing existing knowledge, establishing reverence for what is known through strategies such as memorization and imitation. While such strategies demonstrate respect for knowledge, they may look to Western teachers like reproducing others' ideas. So by ignoring cultural considerations, teachers may see this as plagiarism or repetition, and be misled into recasting such respect for knowledge as copying (e.g. Pennycook, 1996) or as naive and immature writing.

Culture can also intrude into learning through students' expectations about instruction and the meanings they give to classroom tasks. Students' previous learning experiences may not have adequately prepared them for the kinds of topics, teaching styles, extended writing assignments, oral presentations, analyses of real texts, and consciousness-raising tasks which often characterize EAP classes. Not all students find it easy to take a critical or combative stance towards a topic or commit themselves to a position, for example, while others may dislike asking questions or participating in groups.

One potential problem area is that of peer review. Asking students to respond to their classmates' writing is generally seen as beneficial in L2 instruction, but while it may help some learners to envisage their audience more effectively, peer evaluation has been criticized as inappropriate for learners from collectivist cultures. Carson and Nelson (1996: 1), for instance, found that Chinese students often avoided criticism of peers' work and so provided no useful feedback to them:

> Chinese students' primary goal for the groups was social – to maintain group harmony – and that this goal affected the nature and types of interaction they allowed themselves in group discussions . . . This self-monitoring led them to avoid criticism of peers' work and to avoid disagreeing with the comments of peers about their own writing.

Task A5.3

➤ In what ways are cultural factors likely to influence the ways students write and learn to write or to speak in an academic variety of English? Are these factors only likely to impact the writing of L2 students? How might you accommodate these differences in your teaching and assessments?

CONTRASTIVE RHETORIC

Perhaps the most examined influence of culture on language is the different expectations people have about academic communication. The field of *contrastive rhetoric* actively uses the notion of culture to explain differences in written texts and writing practices. Although findings are inconclusive, research suggests that the schemata of L2 and L1 writers differ in their preferred ways of organizing ideas, and that these cultural preconceptions can influence communication (e.g. Connor, 2002; Hinkel, 2002).

In a review of seventy-two studies comparing research into first- and second-language writing, for example, Silva (1993: 669) noted that 'L2 writing is strategically, rhetorically and linguistically different in important ways from L1 writing'. These conclusions have been supported by a range of studies comparing features of academic genres across cultures, producing the generalization that, compared with other languages, Anglo-American academic English tends to:

- Be more explicit about its structure and purposes.
- Employ more, and more recent, citations.
- Use fewer rhetorical questions.
- Be generally less tolerant of digressions.
- Be more tentative and cautious in making claims.
- Have stricter conventions for sub-sections and their titles.
- Use more sentence connectors (such as *therefore* and *however*).

It is unwise, however, to attribute all aspects of L2 performance to L1 writing practices. There is a tendency in this research to identify cultures with national entities, thus emphasizing a predictable sharedness *within* cultures and differences *across* them (e.g. Atkinson, 2004). Students have identities beyond the language and culture they were born into and we should avoid the tendency to stereotype them according to cultural dichotomies. We cannot simply read off cultural preferences from the surface of texts: all rhetorical patterns are available to all writers and do not allow us to predict how students from different language backgrounds will write. Spack (1997), for instance, argues that focusing on culture to explain writing differences prompts a normative, essentializing stance which leads to lumping students together on the basis of their first language. Students are not merely cultural *types* and it is perhaps a major task of EAP teachers to disabuse subject teachers of such assumptions.

This is a useful caution, but it is equally important that we should not ignore research which might help us understand the ways individuals write in a second language. Teachers can take a number of different insights from contrastive rhetoric. Most important, it helps us to recognize that student difficulties in writing or speaking may be due to the disjunction of the writer's and reader's view of what is needed in a text and that different writing styles can be the result of culturally learnt preferences. This encourages us to see the effects of different practices where we might otherwise only see individual inadequacies.

Task A5.4

➤ Consider a student or group of students you are familiar with. To what extent do you think their writing or speaking in English may have been influenced by their L1? Can such influences be positive as well as negative?

Unit A6
Genre analysis and academic texts

While social constructivism encourages us to interpret academic texts in their social contexts, genre analysis provides one of the main tools for doing so. Essentially, *genre* is a term for grouping texts together, representing how writers typically use language to respond to recurring situations. They are resources for getting things done using language, reflecting the idea that members of a community usually have little difficulty in recognizing similarities in the spoken and written texts they use frequently and are able to draw on their repeated experiences with such texts to understand and produce them relatively easily. This is because writing and speaking are based on expectations: writers, for instance, make their meanings clear by taking the trouble to anticipate what readers may be expecting based on previous texts they have read of the same kind. This unit introduces some of the key ideas of genre in EAP teaching and research, beginning with a brief characterization of the term.

 Task A6.1

➤ What genres are you familiar with from your workplace, studies and leisure? Now group them in various ways, such as whether they are spoken or written, their degree of formality, similarity of purposes, type of audience, etc.

CONCEPTIONS OF GENRE

While genres are seen as abstract, socially recognized ways of using language, theorists differ in the emphasis they give to either contexts or texts; to stability or change; and to the language used to create genres or the actions they are used to perform. Similarly, analysts have opted to examine either the actions of individuals as they create particular texts or the distribution of particular features across a range of texts to see genres as collections of rhetorical choices (Hyland, 2000).

One way of characterizing genres is in terms of the ways broad social purposes are systematically linked with context through lexical and grammatical features (Christie and Martin, 1997). Researchers working within Halliday's (1994) *Systemic Functional Linguists* (SFL) model define genres by internal linguistic criteria, grouping texts which have similar formal features. Spoken and written genres are

Table A6.1 Some university genre structures

Genre	Genre purpose	Stage	Stage purpose
Recount	To reconstruct past experiences by retelling events in original sequence	Orientation Record of events (Reorientation)	Provides information about a situation Presents events in temporal sequence Brings events into the present
Procedure	To show how something is done	Goal Materials Steps 1–n (Results)	Gives information about purpose: title or intro The equipment required Activities to achieve goal in sequence Final state or 'look' of the activity
Narrative	To entertain and instruct via reflection on experience	Orientation Complication (Evaluation) Resolution	Information about characters' situation Problems for characters to solve The major events for the characters Sorts out the problems for the characters
Report	To present information, usually by classifying and then describing characteristics	Problem Reason^n (Conclusion) Recommendations	Identification of a problem Possible reasons for or result of problem Suggestions for solving the problem Measures to be adopted from report
Explanation	To explain how and why things happen	Identification Explanation steps^n	States the topic of the text Sequence in how something occurred

Notes: Parentheses indicate an optional stage. n indicates that the stage may recur.

seen as *narratives, recounts, arguments* and *expositions,* and each genre is composed of a series of stages which contribute to the overall purpose of the genre. Table A6.1 on the previous page shows some examples.

Defining genres in this way shows how frequently recurring linguistic patterns, or *elemental genres* (Martin, 1992), combine to create more specific *macro-genres.* Thus a *research article* might comprise several elemental genres such as an *exposition,* a *discussion* and a *rebuttal.* Equally, students can use their knowledge of a single elemental genre, such as a *procedure,* to create different macro-genres, like *recipes, scientific lab reports* and *instruction manuals.* This allows teachers to gradually expose students to more complex ways of expressing a genre. Simple *procedures* such as a recipe, for example, may list the steps to be performed as a series of imperatives, but more technical examples, such as an instruction manual, may specify constraints that have to be met to carry out these instructions, perhaps expressed as conditional clauses ('If the pressure reaches 195 then open the release valve').

This classification also provides a means of understanding how genres differ in the demands they make on students. A *procedure,* for instance, consists of a series of steps which shows how to achieve a goal and may be based on simple imperative clauses using familiar action verbs and everyday objects. *Explanations,* on the other hand, are more demanding because they typically require students to use sequential, causal and conditional conjunctions. Each genre in Table 6.1 moves writers further from their own experience to more general events and objects. Not only are these kinds of meanings more highly valued in academic settings, but students need to draw on more complex resources to write them effectively.

A very different way of understanding genres is to see them as fluid and dynamic. This is the view of the *New Rhetoric* school, which represents genres as 'stabilized for now' forms of action which are open to change and subject to negotiation. Genre is seen as a form of social action which is 'centred not on the substance or the form of the discourse but on the action it is used to accomplish' (Miller, 1994: 24). As a result, research has focused on how 'expert' users exploit genres for social purposes and the ways genres are created and evolve. New Rhetoric thus widens the concept to include institutional, ideological and physical contexts, reminding us to consider the ways that genres position and influence individuals as well as the opportunities they offer for effective communication.

But because genres are seen as guiding frameworks rather than recurring linguistic structures, these theorists are sceptical about their pedagogic potential. They also see classrooms as distorting genres by transforming them into artefacts for study rather than resources for communication (Freedman and Adam, 2000). All teachers can hope to do in these circumstances is expose students to relevant genres and limit their teaching to 'overall features of format or organisation . . . and a limited set of rules regarding usage and punctuation' (Freedman, 1994: 200). New Rhetoric therefore cautions teachers against regarding genres as materially objective 'things' and against teaching methods that reduce text to fixed templates. But while we can recognize that genres evolve to meet the changing needs of communities, technologies and situations, and that individuals take liberties with text conventions, it is not usually the novice, and certainly not the L2 learner, who is best served by genre flexibility or who is able to make use of it.

Genre therefore remains an elusive term and even Swales, whose work launched the massive interest in genre in EAP, has since admitted that his original emphasis on 'communicative purpose' (Swales, 1990: 58) as a defining feature may not include all cases. Instead he suggests that genre may better be seen as a 'metaphorical endeavour' (2004: 61), identifying the following metaphors as helpful in understanding genre:

- *Frames for action:* guiding principles for achieving purposes using language.
- *Language standards:* expected conventions of layout and language.
- *Biological species:* development of genres analogous to species change.
- *Prototypes:* instances of a genre are more or less similar to 'core' exemplars.
- *Institutions:* typified and interrelated processes and values of an institution.
- *Speech acts:* the conventional actions a genre is intended to perform.

Swales argues that these metaphors offer a rich and multifaceted view of genre which captures its complex and varied nature. As we shall see below, however, views which tend towards both formal and functional ends of the continuum continue to be influential in EAP.

Task A6.2

➤ Which of Swales's metaphors seems to offer the most insightful characterization of genre for you? Can you elaborate this metaphor and say why you have chosen it? How easy do you think it would be to operationalize the metaphor in your EAP practice?

GENRE IN EAP

Some EAP theorists see genre as communicative events used by specific discourse communities. Focusing on the communicative needs of particular academic groups involves examining what these groups do with language, starting with the names members themselves give to their practices, such as *essays, dissertations* and *lectures.* These are the social/rhetorical actions routinely used by community members to achieve a particular purpose, written for a particular audience, and employed in a particular context. In this way they combine some of the aspects of the approach to genre taken by SFG, by the New Rhetoricians and by Swales. Some of these genres are shown in Table A6.2.

Table A6.2 Some academic genres

Written genres		Spoken genres	
Research articles	Book reviews	Lectures	Student presentations
Conference abstracts	Ph.D. dissertations	Seminars	Office hour sessions
Grant proposals	Textbooks	Tutorial sessions	Practicum feedback
Undergraduate essays	Reprint requests	Peer feedback	Dissertation defences
Submission letters	Editor response letters	Colloquia	Admission interviews

Swales describes the close relations between communities and their genres like this:

> discourse communities evolve their own conventions and traditions for such diverse verbal activities as running meetings, producing reports, and publicizing their activities. These recurrent classes of communicative events are the genres that orchestrate verbal life. These genres link the past and the present, and so balance forces for tradition and innovation. They structure the roles of individuals within wider frameworks, and further assist those individuals with the actualisation of their communicative plans and purposes.
>
> (Swales, 1998: 20)

While Swales admits things may be more complex than this, the idea that people acquire, use and modify genres while acting in social groups helps explain the ways we learn to become members of disciplinary communities. It therefore offers teachers a powerful way of understanding and, hopefully, addressing the communicative needs of their students.

Some genre analysis in EAP operationalizes these ideas about genre by examining representative text samples to identify salient text features, such as recurring tenses, cohesion, modality, etc., and the ways those texts are structured as a sequence of rhetorical units or *moves*. Each move is a distinct communicative act designed to achieve a particular communicative function and can be subdivided into several 'steps'. Both moves and steps may be optional, embedded in others, repeated, and may have constraints on the sequence in which they occur. Table A6.3, based on 240 postgraduate dissertation acknowledgements, shows that even the most seemingly interpersonal academic genres have a genre structure. A simple example of this structure is shown in Table A6.4.

 Task A6.3

➤ Consider the list of academic genres in Table A6.2. Which of them would be useful to your students? What would you like them to know about this genre?

Table A6.3 The structure of dissertation acknowledgements

Move		Communicative function
1 Reflecting		Introspection on the writer's research experience
2 Thanking		Mapping credit to individuals and institutions
	2.1 Presenting participants	Introducing those to be thanked
	2.2 Thanks for academic help	Thanks for intellectual support, ideas, feedback, etc.
	2.3 Thanks for resources	Thanks for data access and clerical, technical and financial support
	2.4 Thanks for moral support	Thanks for encouragement, friendship, sympathy, etc.
3 Announcing		Public statement of responsibility and inspiration
	3.1 Accepting responsibility	Asserts personal responsibility for flaws or errors
	3.2 Dedication	A formal dedication to an individual(s)

Source: Hyland (2004: 310).

Table A6.4 Example of a Ph.D. dissertation acknowledgement

1	The most rewarding achievement in my life, as I approach middle age, is the completion of my doctoral dissertation.
2:1	During the time of writing I received support and help from many people.
2:2	I am profoundly indebted to my supervisor, Dr Robert Chau, who assisted me in each step to complete the thesis.
2:3	I am grateful to the Epsom Foundation, whose research travel grant made the fieldwork possible, and to the library staff who tracked down elusive texts for me.
2:4	Finally, thanks go to my wife, who has been an important source of emotional support.
3	However, despite all this help, I am responsible for any errors in the thesis.

DISCIPLINARY DIFFERENCES

In addition to providing teachers with insights into target texts, approaches to teaching and ways of organizing their courses, genre analyses also allow us to identify the different kinds of argument and writing/speaking tasks valued by different disciplines. Previous units have noted that the writing tasks students have to do at university are specific to discipline and level and that even genres with common names, such as *laboratory reports, case studies* and *essays,* are often structured in different ways across disciplines. Coffin *et al.* (2003) (see also Unit C2), for instance, identify three genres as being pivotal to each of three main domains of knowledge: project proposals in the sciences, essays in the humanities, and reports and case studies in the social sciences. Table A6.5 summarizes the structure of two such genres.

Genres are also distinguished by the choice of features that writers in different fields use to persuade their readers. One example is the extent to which writers typically employ self-mention. While impersonality is frequently cited as a key feature of academic discourse, not all disciplines observe this convention. Science and

Table A6.5 Functional stages of two genres

Scientific project proposal		Applied social sciences case study	
Title	Concise and accurate indication of project topic	Background	Overview of the organizational or professional context of the study
Introduction	Aims and theoretical background, including literature review and rationale	Analytical framework	For academic reader, provides explanation and rationale of framework
Materials and methods	List of materials and apparatus, detailed description of methods and how these will meet aims	*or* Approach to study	For professional reader, provides explanation of the theoretical approach
Analytical methods	What data will be obtained and how they will be analysed	Findings	Main findings
		Implications	Interprets the findings and shows their relevance to the
References	List of sources the proposal refers to		organization studied
		Recommendations	Suggested action points based on the information collected

Source: Coffin *et al.* (2003: 50, 69).

engineering articles tend to suppress human agency but writers in the humanities and social sciences often make extensive use of first-person pronouns, suggesting that writers have clear promotional and interactional purposes (Hyland, 2001). Similarly, the ways research is presented orally can differ across disciplines, with different argument structures employed by engineers and biologists, for instance (Dudley-Evans, 1993). By exploring these conventions with students, teachers can help them see the options available to them when communicating in their disciplines.

MULTIMODAL DISCOURSE

While genre studies typically privilege language, many analysts claim that there is a 'visual literacy': a grammar inherent in images that we must attend to. Academic texts, particularly in the sciences, have always been multimodal, but textbooks and articles are now far more heavily influenced by graphic design than ever before and the growing challenge to the page by the screen as the dominant medium of communication means that images are ever more important in meaning making. This more integrated perspective, which deals with all the means we have of making meanings, is called multimodality. Researchers adopting this view consider the specific ways of configuring the world which different modes offer and draw attention to consequent shifts in authority, in forms of reading and in forms of human engagement with the social and natural world (Kress, 2003; Kress and Van Leeuwen 1996, 2002).

For Kress, different modes have different affordances, or potentials and limitations for meaning. Certain texts, such as novels, encourage the reader to engage in the semiotic work of imagination, following the given order of words on the line but filling the relatively 'empty' words with the reader's meaning. Contemporary electronic texts such as Web pages and the screens of CD-ROMs are more often like images in their organization and ask the reader to perform different semiotic work, offering different entry points to the 'page' and different reading paths from the order of words in a sentence, so providing opportunities to design the order of the text for themselves.

So developments in mode and media have produced changes which mean that EAP students have to be taught to 'read' visuals as much as texts. The fact that figures, tables and photographs can occupy up to a half a science research article testifies to the significance of visuals in academic genres. The examples in Figures A6.1–3 from journals in biology, maths and linguistics illustrate both the variety of visuals in academic genres and their importance in carrying key information.

Like verbal communication, visual representation is a semiotic system, or system of signs, which varies with language, culture and genre. Kress and van Leeuwen (1996) note that:

> Simplicity is . . . always based on a particular cultural orientation and ideological stance, and the result of intensive training. It is only once this training is achieved that images (and the way of looking at the world expressed by their structure) can appear 'natural' and 'simple', and hence not in need of analysis.

Miller (1998), for example, shows that while visual elements in the popular press function largely to attract the reader to the article and to explain rather than prove, visuals in academic texts are mainly arguments, following formal conventions organized for maximum persuasion and access to new information. Many scientists write their articles to highlight the visuals, and expert readers often read the visuals first. This is because while arguments are based on plausible, and well constructed, interpretations of data, they ultimately rest on findings, and these are often presented in visual form. Visuals thus buttress arguments and signal the importance of the article itself.

Some analyses take an SFL approach and claim there is a grammar inherent in images, just as there is in writing, based on choices to communicate particular meanings. Kress and Van Leeuwen (1996), for instance, show how visuals communicate meaning through such forms as point of view (whose perspective is taken), given-new structures (understood versus new information), visual transitivity (who is doing what to whom), deixis (then and now), and modality (is it true or false?). These analytical tools allow EAP teachers to explain how visuals have been organized for maximum effect and how the organization of diagrams and other visual materials may differ across cultures. In particular they encourage their students to consider:

- Which aspects of the argument are included in the visual and which omitted and why?
- What connections are drawn between the visual and the text?
- What is the relationship between the gloss of the visual and the visual itself?
- What are the connections between the visuals and their positioning on the page?

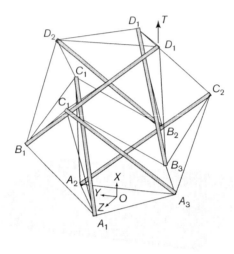

Figure A6.1 A first mathematical model of cellular tensegrity was based on this structure comprised of twenty-four linearly elastic cables (black lines) that represent actin filaments and six rigid struts (gray bars) that represent microtubules. The structure is anchored to a rigid substrate (grid) at three joints (A_1, A_2 and A_3). Force (F) is exerted at a joint (D_1) distal to the substrate [27] and [36]. A similar model in which elastic cables were replaced by linear Voigt viscoelastic elements was used by Cañadas *et al.* [43] and Sultan *et al.* [44] to simulate creep and oscillator behaviors of adherent cells, respectively (Stamenović, 2005: 258)

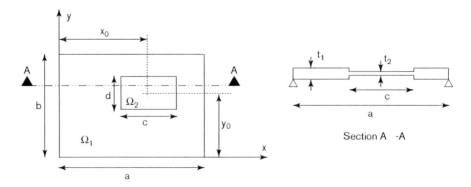

Figure A6.2 Rectangular plate with abruptly varying thickness (Azhari *et al.*, 2005: 642)

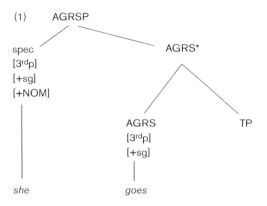

Figure A6.3 An illustration of spec–head agreement between the subject (*she*) and the verb (*goes*) in AGRSP (Curtiss and Schaeffer, 2005)

CONSTELLATIONS OF GENRES

The genres of the academy represent an enormous range which Swales (2004) refers to as a 'constellation' and Bhatia (2004) a 'colony' of academic discourse. Some of these genres display significant overlap in terms of purpose and users, while others have little in common, but all help to create a hierarchy of texts which vary in their importance to different practitioners in different disciplines. Thus writing a review article or a textbook may have little career or academic value to many academics, while writing scholarly monographs can attract credit to academics in the humanities and research articles to those working in the sciences.

Genre sets

An important aspect of such constellations is that we almost never find genres in isolation. A useful concept here, introduced by Devitt (1991), is the concept of 'genre sets' to refer to the part of the entire genre constellation that a particular individual or group engages in, either productively or receptively. Textbooks, lab reports and lectures, for instance, may be key genres for many science students while a folder of readings, extended essays and online tutorials seems to dominate the genre lives of students following distance Master's courses in TESOL and applied linguistics. Similarly, the number of genres an academic participates in appears to increase with seniority, with a wider range of occluded administrative and evaluative genres, such as course or programme appraisals, professional references and referee reports, being taken on by individuals as they climb the academic ladder. Such sets, in other words, are temporary phenomena relating to individual positionings at a given time.

Some of these genres may depend on others, some may be alternatives to others, but together they represent the full array of texts a particular group must deal with in a context. For teachers these sets and sequences are not only a useful way of contextualizing what is to be learnt by basing instruction on how genres are sequenced and used in real-world events, they also help to integrate reading, speaking and writing activities naturally in the classroom.

Genre chains

Another way of approaching genre constellations is through the idea of 'genre systems or chains', referring to how spoken and written texts cluster together in a given social context. For example, genres sometimes follow each other in a predictable chronological order, such as when applying for funding:

> Read funding announcement / information ➜
> Research funding body through Web site, etc. ➜
> Prepare research proposal ➜
> Write an application form ➜
> Read response letter ➜

Swales (2004) includes 'occluded' genres, which are unseen by outsiders, and are therefore invisible to applicants, such as the referee reports and meeting discussions which contribute to the outcome of such chains. In other circumstances one genre may be less dependent on the outcome of another, so that an activity unfolds with genres employed concurrently as a logical system. An example of this is the genres involved in writing an academic assignment (Figure A6.4).

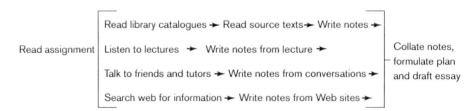

Figure A6.4 The genres involved in writing an academic assignment

Genre networks

More generally, genres are often loosely arrayed in a *network* as each interacts with, draws on, and responds to another in a particular setting. This idea refers to the notion of *intertextuality* (Bakhtin, 1986) and the fact that every utterance reacts to other utterances in that domain. We now acknowledge that little that is said is original; every utterance transforms, addresses and accommodates earlier utterances in some way. Useful here is Fairclough's distinction between *manifest intertextuality*, or the traces of earlier texts through quotes, paraphrase or citation, and *constitutive intertextuality* (or *interdiscursivity*) which involves borrowing generic or rhetorical conventions and forms to create a text, as in the use of biography in some qualitative research articles, thus merging what may be originally distinct orders of discourse to create new discourses. In other words, genre networks are the totality of genres employed in a particular domain at any one time. While this totality is constantly changing, it nevertheless links text users to a network of prior texts according to their group membership, and provides a system of coding options for making meanings.

Task A6.4

➤ Identify a genre set, chain or network in a context you are familiar with. Represent this constellation as a diagram to show the relationship of the different genres to each other, representing either their sequence or importance in that setting.

Unit A7
Corpus analysis and academic texts

Genre descriptions have to be based on sufficient text samples to ensure that the principles and regularities observed are representative of the target genre, and genre analysts have been greatly assisted in this by the use of language corpora. A *corpus* is a collection of naturally occurring texts used for linguistic study. While a corpus does not contain any new theories about language, it can offer fresh insights on familiar, but perhaps unnoticed, features of language use. This is because a corpus is a more reliable guide to what language is like than human intuition. While we all have experience of certain genres, much of this remains hidden, so that, for example, even the best teachers are often unable to explain to their students why some phrasing or expression is preferred over another in a given context. A corpus, in other words, provides an evidence-based approach to language teaching.

The idea behind a corpus is that it represents a speaker's experience of language in some domain. This makes the approach ideal for studying the features of academic genres as it means we can describe them more accurately so students can learn to use them more effectively. Using any one of a number of commercially available, and relatively inexpensive, text analysis programmes (*concordancers*), teachers can selectively examine fairly large amounts of texts to supplement their intuitions, not to confirm whether something is possible or not, but to describe whether it is frequent or not. As Sinclair (1991: 17) points out, this moves the study of language away from ideas of what is correct, towards what is typical or frequent.

 Task A7.1

➤ How might a corpus be of value to you as an EAP teacher? What kinds of texts would be most useful to your students? How would you use a corpus in your course?

CORPUS STUDIES AND FREQUENCY

The idea of *frequency* is central to corpus studies as corpora are not concerned with what can occur in a genre or register but with what frequently and typically occurs. In other words, priority is given to describing the commonest uses of the commonest words on the assumption that if something is observed to happen often enough in the past then it is likely to be significant in the future too. This allows us to predict the ways that other representative examples of the genre will be organized and the features it is likely to contain. Corpus analyses therefore often begin by automatically counting the frequency of words or grammatical patterns in order to characterize the domain under study.

Corpus studies have shown that the most frequent words in English cover an inordinate percentage of any text, with the top three words (*the, of, to*) making up some 10 per cent of the 400 million words in the Bank of English corpus, for instance, and the first 100 comprising about one-half of all written and spoken texts (e.g. Hunston, 2002). The most frequent words in any corpus are therefore grammatical words, but working down frequency lists soon reveals key items in that genre, enabling the teacher to identify and teach basic items in their classes. Table A7.1 shows differences in undergraduate course books in two disciplines.

Table A7.1 Most frequent nouns in introductory textbooks in two disciplines

Applied linguistics			Biology		
No.	% of total	Word	No.	% of total	Word
423	0.8663	language	166	0.4304	species
149	0.3052	speech	150	0.3889	DNA
128	0.2622	example	143	0.3708	spores
127	0.2601	interaction	135	0.3500	organisms
106	0.2171	act	117	0.3033	bacteria
101	0.2069	communication	116	0.3008	fungi
97	0.1987	students	95	0.2463	figure
93	0.1905	text	89	0.2307	organism
93	0.1905	acquisition	75	0.1945	RNA
91	0.1864	acts	68	0.1763	spore
90	0.1843	face	62	0.1607	cells
89	0.1823	input	59	0.1530	section
86	0.1761	rules	58	0.1504	genus
85	0.1741	communicative	55	0.1426	cell
79	0.1618	knowledge	49	0.1270	disease

One use of frequency counts in EAP is the construction of vocabulary lists such as the Academic Word List (Coxhead, 2000). These are based on the idea that vocabulary falls into three main groups (Nation, 2001):

- High-frequency words such as those included in West's (1953) General Service List of the most widely useful 2,000 word families in English, which provides coverage of about 80 per cent of most texts.
- An academic vocabulary of words which are reasonably frequent in academic writing across disciplines and genres and comprise some 8 per cent to 10 per cent of running words of academic texts.

■ A technical vocabulary which differs by subject area and covers up to 5 per cent of texts.

Students are said to find such an academic vocabulary a particularly challenging aspect of their learning (Li and Pemberton, 1994). This is because, while technical vocabulary is central to the students' specialized areas, general academic words serve a largely supportive role and are 'not likely to be glossed by the content teacher' (Flowerdew, 1993: 236). But while general academic word lists are useful for EAP materials developers, we need to be cautious about them. It remains unclear how far a single inventory can represent the vocabulary of 'academic discourse', or how far it might be useful to students irrespective of their field of study (Hyland and Tse, 2007). Individual items tend to have different frequencies and meanings in different disciplines and genres, encouraging us to look beyond common core features and the autonomous views of literacy that such lists assume to recognize that contextual factors are crucial to language choices.

More sophisticated information can be gathered using software which counts not only words, but also grammatical features. By a semi-automatic procedure known as *tagging*, codes can be added to each word indicating its part of speech, so, for instance, the word *research* is tagged as either a noun or a verb each time it occurs, allowing much more detailed analyses of target genres. Biber's (1988) research, for instance, shows how written academic prose is characterized by bundles of grammatical features such as frequent nouns, long words, attributive adjectives and prepositional phrases which function to present densely packed information. In contrast, second-person pronouns, direct questions, present-tense verbs, private verbs (*feel, think*) and *that* deletions are less frequent because of their more interactive character. A tagged corpus can assist teachers in deciding on the relative merits of recommending past or present tense when teaching report genres, for example, or whether it is more useful to focus on active or passive constructions in essay writing.

Frequency counts are also a useful way of determining the features which are over-used or under-used in the writing of L2 students in given genres. Research by Granger (1998) and Hinkel (2002) on learner corpora, for instance, shows that L2 academic essays contain a smaller range of vocabulary than L1 essays and are characterized by stylistic features more typical of informal speech than written discourse. A good example of a learner corpus informing classroom practice is Milton's (1999) study of his students' use of fixed expressions in their essays (e.g. Nattinger and De Carrico, 1998). Lacking good models of target academic genres, they seemed to fall back on a limited number of prefabricated 'lexical bundles' to avoid grammatical errors, leading them to a repetitive style of writing. By comparing a student essay corpus with a parallel corpus of L1 essays, Hong Kong school textbooks and published research articles, Milton confirmed that the L2 students used the same phrases far more often than L1 writers and was able to compile a list of alternative phrases from the L1 samples which he then included in his classes to help his students vary their academic writing (Table A7.2).

Table A7.2 Phrases in a Hong Kong learner corpus

Lexical phrases with greatest difference	Frequency of phrases per 50,000 words in each corpus			
	L2 student texts	L1 student texts	School textbooks	Published articles
Not used in L2 student texts				
In the/this case	0	9	11	16
It has also been	0	8	0	5
It can be seen that	0	8	0	4
An example of this is	0	8	0	3
This is not to say that	0	7	0	2
Overused in L2 student texts				
First of all	170	1	13	5
On the other hand	239	31	25	30
(As) we/you know	118	2	22	3
In my opinion	110	12	8	0
All in all	59	2	1	0

Source: Milton (1999: 226).

Task A7.2

➤ Why might frequency counts be useful to analysts or teachers? Do you think it would be more useful for students to discover word or pattern frequencies for themselves or to be given this information by teachers?

CONCORDANCING

In addition to frequency counts, analysts also explore corpora by examining concordances. A concordance brings together all instances of a search word or phrase in the corpus as a list of unconnected lines of text with the node word in the centre together with a sample of its linguistic environments. These lines therefore give instances of language *use* when read horizontally and evidence of *system* when read vertically. This makes it possible for the user to see regularities in its use that might otherwise be missed.

Moreover, by sorting the concordance lines by the first word to the left or to the right of the search word, frequent co-occurrences become visible. Thus in the study of dissertation acknowledgements mentioned earlier we discovered a strong tendency to use the noun *thanks* in preference to other expressions of gratitude (Hyland and Tse, 2004). By sorting concordance lines on the word to the left of this search word, we then found that this noun was modified by only three adjectives: *special, sincere* and *deep*, with *special* making up over two-thirds of all cases. Figure A7.1 is a screenshot from the program MonoConc Pro showing part of the results of this sorting.

Figure A7.1 Screenshot from MonoConc Pro, showing a left sort on the word 'thanks'

Concordancing also allows searches for word combinations, even revealing frequencies and meanings of key phrases which vary by intervening words. Thus using the * wild card by entering the expression *it * that* will search for the word *it* followed by *that* in the near vicinity, producing examples such as these in a corpus of abstracts in research papers:

it is likely that	it shows that	it is worth noting that
it seems that	it is claimed that	it is shown that
it is clear that	it is true that	it is more likely that

When these examples are studied more carefully, they show that academic writers use this phrasing extremely frequently to express their evaluation of whether the following statement is likely to be true or not. In addition, the results show that expressions of certainty occur more often than those expressing doubt. This kind of information can help student writers not only to make use of this collocation in their own writing, but to use it in effective ways. Figure A7.2 shows a screenshot of concordance lines for this structure using WordPilot 2002 with a pop-up window listing the most frequent collocations.

The analysis of potentially productive phrases such as this is particularly useful for helping student writers to see how high-frequency grammar words often occur in

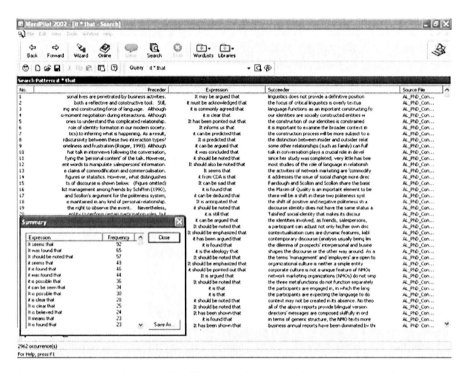

Figure A7.2 Screenshot from WordPilot, showing concordance for 'it * that' in dissertations

regular patterns, even though the lexical items within these patterns may be less frequent. Armed with this kind of information about their target genres, EAP students are able to make choices which are better informed, guided by 'expert' practice and disciplinary expectations.

In addition, corpus evidence offers a range of information for EAP teachers and learners. For instance, collocation patterns can reveal features such as the following:

- The patterns of various forms, e.g. whether first-person pronouns are associated with claims, criticisms or research procedures in academic research papers.
- The differences between words which students often confuse, e.g. *bored* versus *boring, interested* versus *interesting, possible to* versus *possible that,* etc.
- The most appropriate words to use – e.g. whether to use the preposition *in, that* or *to* with *interested* and *interesting.*
- 'Semantic prosody', or the connotative meanings a word acquires because of its regular association with other words, e.g. the word *commit* carries unfavourable implications because of its regular co-occurrence with words such as *crime, murder, mistakes,* etc. Similarly the word *rife* has unfavourable semantic prosody (Partington, 1998: 67).
- Stable lexical patterning in particular disciplines, particularly nominal groups, e.g. *critical discourse analysis* or *static electric field.*

■ The specific meanings that words take on in particular disciplines, e.g. *wall, energy, structure, concentration, body*, etc., in biology.

■ How words change their meaning as a result of the surrounding text, e.g. the word *quite* boosts the meaning of non-gradable words such as *impossible, definitely* and *agree*, and hedges gradable words such as *interesting, beautiful* and *cynical*.

To summarize, the computer analysis of text corpora is an invaluable tool for EAP teachers. It indicates the high-frequency words, phrases and grammatical structures which characterize a given genre or discipline and reveals how these are typically used in patterns of collocation, or association, with other words or phrases. This, in turn, can help teachers to better understand the texts they teach and students to become more aware of the options available to them when communicating in their disciplines.

 Task A7.3

➤ How could such concordances be built into learner exercises and tasks? Think of a task you could give to a group of students using a corpus. What problems might students have with concordancing as a classroom tool and how might you overcome those problems?

Unit A8
Ethnographically oriented analysis and EAP

Ethnography is an interpretive and qualitative approach to research based on the study of behaviour in naturally occurring settings. While acknowledging that language is always an important part of such settings, ethnographic studies take a wider view to consider the physical and experiential contexts in which language is used. This perspective therefore gives greater emphasis to what people actually *do*, locating acts of communication – of speaking, writing or listening – in the behaviour of groups and employing methods which are interpretive, contextualized and respectful of participants' views. This unit describes the broad outlines of such approaches and indicates some of the work that has been done in EAP contexts.

Task A8.1

➤ What are the advantages to studying EAP contexts? What aspects of such contexts would it be useful for EAP teachers to know about and how could the information be used?

WHAT IS ETHNOGRAPHICALLY ORIENTED RESEARCH?

Ethnography is a type of research which sets out to give a participant-, or insider-, oriented description of individuals' cultural practices (Ramanathan and Atkinson, 1999: 49). Originating in anthropology and sociology, this approach involves gathering naturally occurring data under normal conditions from numerous sources, typically over a period of time, without interfering with the context in any way. The data are then analysed to convey the participants' subjective experiences. Such approaches thus offer the possibility of rich, finely detailed descriptions of EAP contexts and how they influence the discourses of students, teachers and researchers.

My choice of *ethnographically oriented* as a title for this unit is something of a hedge, reflecting the fact that the term *ethnography* is a disputed term. While some see ethnography as the researcher's immersion in another culture, it is often used synonymously with *case study, naturalistic methods* and *qualitative research* in applied linguistics and there are few full-blown ethnographic studies in EAP.

Essentially such approaches focus on a holistic explanation of participants' behaviour and draw on the views of insiders themselves, avoiding any pre-formed interpretations to describe key incidents in functionally relevant terms in relation to the wider social context (Watson-Gegeo, 1988). Pole and Morrison (2003: 3) give five common characteristics of ethnographic studies:

- A focus on a discrete event or setting.
- A concern with the full range of social behaviour in that event or setting.
- The use of a range of research methods which may combine qualitative and quantitative but which aim at insider understandings.
- An emphasis on data and analysis which moves from detailed description to the identification of concepts and theories grounded in the data collected.
- An emphasis on rigorous research where the complexities of the event are more important than generalizations.

Clearly these features are rather loose and are perhaps not exclusive to ethnography, hence my preference for the term *ethnographically oriented*, but they point to what this kind of research seeks to do, namely:

- Offer a comprehensive, detailed and 'thick' description (Geertz, 1973).
- Portray an insider's perspective which gives precedence to the meaning of the event or situation to participants.
- Provide an account grounded in data collected from multiple sources which develops a conceptual explanatory framework.

A common criticism of such approaches is that results are not generalizable to other situations, although a deep understanding of what is specific to a particular context may be seen as a strength of such studies. In addition, research can also generate what is called *grounded theory* (Glaser and Strauss, 1967) where categories generated in the early stages of analysis are developed with multiple methods to provide analytical frameworks which may have explanatory relevance beyond the specific local situation investigated. Hammersley (2001), for example, argues that all generalizations are a matter of degree and that 'fuzzy generalizations' provide equally valuable descriptions to quantitative data.

Thus Ivanic's (1998) study of the alienation experienced by mature L1 English students in coping with the literacy demands of higher education helped illuminate Lillis's (2001) qualitative research into the experiences of her heterogeneous group of student writers. Detailed investigation of students' literacy/life history accounts informed both studies and helped to show not only how students' values and beliefs shaped their approaches to writing assignments, but also the nature of writing practices and expectations within the academy. Studies of this kind can also be on a larger scale. The 'Framing student literacy' project, for instance, investigated the spoken and written communicative experiences of students in various disciplines across four Australian universities. The study analysed a sizeable corpus of student assignments and tutor feedback together with ethnographic accounts drawn from interviews and focus group discussions with participant tutors and students in various disciplines. These addressed their views on the nature and aims of academic literacies, the conditions surrounding the writing process, and their understandings of institutional literacy demands (e.g. Plum, 1998). The textual, processual and practice-focused data not only revealed disciplinary differences in literacy practices but provided insights into how higher education proceeds through competence in an institutional form of literacy which is not shared by all students and staff.

Perhaps the best known EAP ethnography is that by Swales (1998) of his building at the University of Michigan. Through analyses of texts, systems of texts and extensive observations and interviews he reveals the lives, commitments and projects of three diverse academic cultures on the three floors of the building: the computer centre, the Herbarium and the university English language centre. The study brilliantly captures the different practices, genres and cultures of these disciplines and reveals the rich complexity which distinguishes academic activity. Through a variety of qualitative methods we get a sense of the individual voices and the kinds of insights which close observation and detailed analysis can reveal.

METHODS AND METHODOLOGY

Following Brewer (2000), we can distinguish *methods*, or the tools used to gather and analyse data, from *methodology*, or the broad theoretical framework of ethnography and the kinds of knowledge it produces. In other words, it isn't the methods or data alone which make a piece of research ethnographic, but their contribution to a wider research process. A variety of data collection methods lend themselves to ethnography as all methods, even quantitative ones, have the capacity to be ethnographic if applied with the goal of understanding the distinctions that are meaningful to the members of a given community. More commonly, methods which involve researchers getting close to the activity and which prioritize rich understandings are employed. These include:

- Detailed, longitudinal, observations of the setting and use of language.
- Interviews with participants and relevant autobiographical issues.
- Focus group discussions.
- Analyses of participants' logs and diaries.
- Questionnaire surveys.
- Biographical and literacy histories.
- Analysis of texts, documents and artefacts.

Analysis of these various kinds of data ideally occurs simultaneously and continuously as a key aspect of the research design and process. There are a range of perspectives on handling data (e.g. Richards, 2003), but Brewer's (2000) distinction between 'humanistic' and 'positivist' ethnography is helpful. The first relies more on the words of the participants, an extended story told by insiders through the use of *vignettes* (short descriptions of events) and *quotes* with minimum interference from the researcher. But it is doubtful whether the influence of the ethnographer can ever be completely removed, and the second approach admits this and employs tighter organizing frameworks, drawing on pre-structured designs and categories to capture meanings (Miles and Huberman, 1994). For instance, a researcher will bring a set of assumptions about the phenomenon under study to the design of an instrument, using a pre-coded sheet to observe behaviour, for example by simply checking pre-defined boxes at fixed intervals or every time a type of behaviour occurs rather than writing a full narrative of events as they unfold.

This helps to produce findings that seek to be both reliable (i.e. they interpret the feature consistently) and valid (they accurately reflect the feature being studied). This is achieved in three main ways:

- *Triangulation.* Conclusions are developed using a range of data sources, research methods or investigators.
- *Prolonged engagement.* The use of repeated observation and collection of sufficient data over a period of time.
- *Participant verification.* The analysis is discussed with participants and its 'reality' verified by them.

Dey (1993) emphasizes the importance of attending to patterns in ordering different sources of data as an iterative spiral which moves from collecting data to describing it, classifying it and making connections between the classifications to produce an account of the situation. So the researcher first establishes a set of rough categories to fit the data and then gradually refines them, narrowing them down, expanding and combining them to ensure that they best reflect the data:

- Conceptually useful: that they help to answer research questions.
- Empirically valid: that they are created from the data itself.
- Analytically practical: that they are easy to identify, specific and non-overlapping.

Once categorized, patterns can be looked for to determine which categories are singular, regular or variant.

Ethnographically oriented research still struggles for recognition as an appropriate research methodology in some disciplines and in EAP contexts teachers may find it hard to collect and analyse multiple data sources while engaged in a full teaching load. The methodology does, however, encourage a pragmatic approach to research where the aims and focus of a study determine the methods to be used, so the researcher adopts whatever tools seem most effective in the time available. The approach, in fact, lends itself well to educational research, providing critical insights into educational processes and practices and ways of developing theories grounded in actual investigations to achieve deeper understandings of the social influences on language use in EAP contexts.

Task A8.2

➤ Suppose you want to conduct research into the writing done in a particular setting to ensure you are providing your students with appropriate preparation for the tasks that face them. To what extent would (1) questionnaires and (2) interviews be appropriate methods of investigation? What other kinds of data might you also need?

QUALITATIVE STUDIES IN EAP

Few full-scale ethnographies have been conducted in EAP and most researchers prefer to claim that their studies have 'ethnographic elements', but there are some interesting examples of this work, much of it focusing on academic writing and the talk which surrounds such writing. Typically, this research seeks to show the effects of local settings on writers, as Prior (1998: xi) puts it:

> When seen as situated activity, writing does not stand alone as the discrete act of a writer, but emerges as a confluence of many streams of activity: reading, talking, observing, acting, making, thinking, and feeling as well as transcribing words on paper.

In this section I will briefly summarize some selected studies to illustrate how some of the principles and methods of this type of research have been applied in EAP settings.

Writing in postgraduate seminars

Prior's (1998) study is a good example of a longitudinal ethnography, exploring the contexts and processes of graduate student writing at a US university. Drawing on transcripts of seminar discussions, student texts, observations of institutional contexts, tutor feedback, and interviews with students and tutors, Prior provides an in-depth account of the ways students in four fields negotiated their writing tasks and so socialized themselves into their disciplinary communities. The interplay of these different types of data and various theories of writing allows us to see how the multiple influences of peers, mentors and students' own personal experiences all contributed to their writing and to the process of becoming academic writers. But this training of graduate students is not the induction of individuals into clearly defined disciplines, each with its own neatly configured idea and practices, but the complex production of persons whereby 'an ambiguous cast of relative newcomers and relative old-timers (re)produce themselves, their practices and their communities' (*ibid.*: xii).

University lectures in Hong Kong

Flowerdew and Miller (1996) conducted a naturalistic study into academic lectures delivered by native English-speakers to ethnic Chinese ESL students in Hong Kong. The research attempted to reveal the assumptions of lecturers and students to overcome cultural conflicts in their perceptions of lectures and improve lecture effectiveness. Data were collected by questionnaires, student and lecturer interviews and reflective diaries, observations and transcriptions of lectures, and the analysis of hand-outs and student notes. They found that while both groups recognized the importance of lectures, the students saw them as having the purpose of trans-ferring information while lecturers regarded them as vehicles for analysis and critical thinking. They also found stark differences in participatory styles, with lecturers disappointed by the reluctance of students to question or engage actively in lectures and students unwilling to risk their poor English by asking questions or be accused of 'showing off' by their classmates. On the other hand, lecturers failed to understand the noisy inattentiveness of students who were unable to adapt to the disciplinary permissiveness of these settings.

Feedback on student writing

This research investigated six ESL writers' reactions to, and uses of, teacher-written feedback in two pre-sessional courses at a New Zealand university. Fiona Hyland (1998) used a longitudinal case study approach and a variety of data sources, including class observation notes, student and tutor interview transcripts, tutor think-aloud protocols as they marked assignments, pre- and post-course question-naires, students' written drafts and revised versions and teacher-written feedback. Her results show both the value students place on feedback and the ways that they responded to and used it in their subsequent writing. Students incorporated most of the usable teacher feedback when revising, but this varied according to their individual needs and prior experiences, while a considerable amount of the revisions originated from peer or external sources. Despite different stances on feedback, the teachers tended to concentrate on *form* which encouraged formal revisions but did not appear to have a long-term developmental effect. In contrast, feedback which addressed academic issues appeared to be transferred to later essays.

Learning to read biology

Haas's (1994) longitudinal case study of the reading practices of one student through four years of undergraduate education is one of the few qualitative studies of reading. Haas used interviews, reading–writing logs, observations, student texts and think-aloud protocols to trace this student's (Eliza's) reading activities and the development of her beliefs about texts and their role in biology. She suggests that as a result of increasing subject knowledge, instruction and mentoring, Eliza's views on academic texts changed over the four years. She initially approached academic texts as authoritative and autonomous, a view which may have served her well in a school culture which emphasized the retention of information. Over time, however, she developed a richer and more rhetorically complex understanding – seeing human authors behind texts and texts as accomplishing scientific action and not just embodying knowledge. In turn, seeing knowledge as socially created led her to see herself not just as learning facts but as working 'amidst the many voices of her discipline' (*ibid.:* 74).

These brief descriptions can do no more than point to some of the ways ethnographically oriented research has contributed to our understanding of academic discourses and practices. By requiring researchers to put away their preconceptions and understand situations in their own terms, this research has produced rich, detailed descriptions of particular personal, social and institutional contexts of communication, expanding our understanding of what factors can impinge on academic practices. In turn, these insights can inform our understandings of academic contexts, how we see our students and what we do in the classroom.

Task A8.3

➤ Which of these studies seems most interesting to you and why? What feature of teaching and learning would you most like to understand in greater detail and how would you collect data to research it?

Theme 3: Design and delivery

INTRODUCTION

Having considered some key issues surrounding the nature of EAP and the methods it uses to understand its subject, this final theme pulls together some practical aspects of planning and teaching. Students cannot acquire everything they need to learn at once nor can they learn effectively from a random collection of exercises and assignments. Teachers therefore have to make a number of key decisions, about students' needs, about teaching approaches, and about the tasks, materials and assessment methods that will lead to the desired learning outcomes. So, while EAP is taught in a huge variety of settings all over the world, each with its own local constraints, available resources, teacher preferences and learner goals, any EAP course requires teachers to:

- Analyse learner needs and decide what to teach based on these needs.
- Develop a coherent course and sequence of learning.
- Decide on appropriate tasks and teaching methods.
- Monitor learner progress and provide effective intervention.

This chapter introduces these issues of planning and classroom practices.

Task A3

➤ Are EAP courses like other courses in English language teaching in the ways they are designed and organized? In what ways might they be similar and different?

Unit A9
Needs and rights

Any EAP course starts with the question 'Why are these students learning English?' It is a question which helps focus the course and make it relevant for learners by taking the world outside the language classroom into account. It means going beyond grammar and vocabulary to prepare students for their future academic experiences while, at the same time, recognizing the importance of affective, personal and social expectations of learning. For many this awareness of need is the central element of EAP course design – and the feature which distinguishes it from general language teaching (Dudley-Evans and St John, 1998; Hutchison and Waters, 1987). Until the arrival of ESP, course design in English language teaching was largely based on the teacher's intuitions about learners' needs, and for some years it meant identifying and prioritizing the discrete language items found in target texts. Today *needs* is a much broader term and also includes linguistic and learning factors as well as a sense that these should not be uncritically accepted as the sole determinant of instruction.

Task A9.1

➤ What do you think we mean by *needs* in EAP contexts and are these likely to differ from general English language teaching courses? What priority should be given to non-language needs and to the views of other interested stakeholders, such as subject disciplines, the institution, employers, funding bodies, etc.?

THE CONCEPT OF NEEDS

Needs analysis refers to the techniques for collecting and assessing information relevant to course design: it is the means of establishing the *how* and *what* of a course. It is a continuous process, since we modify our teaching as we come to learn more about our students, and in this way it actually shades into *evaluation* – the means of establishing the effectiveness of a course. *Needs* is actually an umbrella term that embraces many aspects, incorporating learners' goals and backgrounds, their language proficiencies, their reasons for taking the course, their teaching and learning preferences, and the situations they will need to communicate in. Needs can involve what learners know, don't know or want to know, and can be collected and analysed in a variety of ways (e.g. Brindley, 1989; Brown, 1995).

Needs analysis is sometimes seen as a kind of educational technology designed to measure goals with precision and accountability (Berwick, 1989). But this actually gives the process a misleading impartiality, suggesting that teachers can simply read off a course from an objective situation. But, as most teachers will know, needs are not always easy to determine and, as I shall return to below, mean different things to different participants. Essentially, needs analyses construct a picture of learning goals bringing to bear the teacher's values, beliefs and philosophies of teaching and learning. It might be more accurate, then, to see needs as jointly constructed between teachers and learners.

It is usual to distinguish between *present situation* analysis and *target situation* analysis (cf. Dudley-Evans and St John, 1998):

■ *Present situation analysis* concerns 'starting where the students are' and refers to information about learners' current proficiencies and ambitions: what they can do and what they want at the beginning of the course; their skills and perceptions; their familiarity with the specialist subject; and what they know of its demands and genres. This kind of data can be both objective (age, proficiency, prior learning experiences) and subjective (self-perceived needs, strengths and weaknesses). Essentially it refers, in Brindley's (1989) terms, to 'means needs' which enable students to learn and pursue their language goals as the course progresses, and 'ends needs', or those associated with target goals.
■ *Target situation analysis* concerns the learners' future roles and the linguistic skills and knowledge they need to perform competently in their disciplines. This relates to communication needs rather than learning needs and involves mainly objective and product-oriented data: identifying the contexts of language use, observing the language events in these contexts, and collecting and analysing target genres.

Table A9.1 summarizes the information that the course designer needs to gather about the present and target situations in the form of general questions.

Unfortunately, as we know, EAP courses rarely provide enough time to meet all identified needs, nor adequate time to collect and analyse needs data, which means that teachers typically write their courses on the basis of incomplete information. An exception to this is the classic 'communicative curriculum' (e.g. Breen and Candlin, 1980) where the course is constructed jointly by teachers and learners, such as the TalkBase programme discussed below. We should also note that needs analysis is not a 'done once then forgotten' activity. Behind every successful EAP course there is a continuous process of questioning and revision to check the original results, evaluate the effectiveness of the course and revise objectives. Needs analysis, then, is always dynamic and ongoing.

Table A9.1 A framework for needs analysis

Present situation analysis	Target situation analysis
Why are learners taking the course? Compulsory or optional Whether obvious need exists Personal/academic goals Motivation and attitude What they want to learn from the course	*Why do learners need the language?* Examination, postgraduate or undergraduate course, etc. *What genres will be used?* Lab reports, essays, seminars, lectures, etc.
How do learners learn? Learning background and experiences Concept of teaching and learning Methodological and materials preferences Preferred learning styles and strategies	*What is the typical structure of these genres?* Move analyses, salient features, genre sets, etc. *What will the content areas be?* Academic subject, specialism within discipline, secondary school subjects
Who are the learners? Age / sex / nationality / L1 Subject knowledge Interests Sociocultural background Attitudes to subject or discipline	*Who will the learner use the language with?* Native or non-native speakers Reader's knowledge – expert, beginner, etc. Relationship: peer, teacher, examiner, supervisor *Where will the learner use the language?*
What do learners know? L1 and L2 literacy abilities Proficiency in English Writing experiences and genre familiarity	Physical setting: school, university, conference Linguistic context: overseas, home country Human context: known/unknown readers

Source: after Hutchison and Waters (1987: 62–3).

Task A9.2

➤   What information do you think it is most important to collect about learners
    at the beginning of a course? Should we give priority to learners' current
    language proficiencies, their learning skills, their own perceptions of their needs,
    the target language-using context, or something else? What might be the best
    ways to collect this information and from whom should it be collected?

ANALYSING THE LEARNING CONTEXT

While we need to consider learner needs, in its various guises, every course is also a
creature of its local context. By analogy with needs analysis, deliberation on the kinds
of teaching and goals that the learning context offers is sometimes referred to as
means analysis (Holliday and Cook, 1982) and involves consideration of the teachers,
methods, materials, facilities and relationship of the course to its immediate
environment.

One important constraint is, of course, what can be realistically achieved within the
course. Intensive courses, for example, may be suitable for concentrating learners

on the textual aspects of a particular genre but lack the opportunities offered by longer courses for rewriting drafts, reflection on language use, or a more detailed analysis of the contexts in which target texts are used. Teachers also have to consider how the course relates to other courses and to the wider curriculum. There may, for instance, be opportunities for interesting collaborative work with disciplinary courses or chances to inject creativity into what seems to be an isolated and exam-driven syllabus. The availability of resources to support a proposed course may also present challenges to syllabus developers, particularly if this involves importing textbooks from overseas, and teachers may have to rely on their own materials development skills to overcome delays, plug gaps, and make texts and tasks relevant to local conditions. This, of course, highlights the key contextual resource in the success of any programme: the role of teachers and the degree of training, experience and expertise they can contribute and their attitudes towards the teaching–learning philosophy the course represents.

Institutional factors also need to be taken into account, as these differ considerably in the priority they give to EAP, so that while some schools and institutions lavish resources on language work and give credit for attending EAP courses, others treat it as a marginal and voluntary element of the curriculum. Individual institutions also vary in terms of their 'culture', influencing such issues as morale, teacher co-operation, attitudes to innovation and teacher autonomy. Poorly paid, overworked and micro-managed teachers are unlikely to inject much enthusiasm into their work or transmit positive values to learners. This is especially true as the shift in teacher education programmes in recent years from a focus on the teacher as a conduit for methods towards more autonomous roles has meant that teachers now see themselves more as self-directed and independent practitioners. Part of this involves an evaluative stance towards the elements of the teaching context over which they have control (McGrath, 2000) and an awareness that learning targets, course content, tasks and assessment methods can all be negotiated, both with institutions and with learners (Lamb, 2000). These views may sometimes conflict with those of the workplace.

More broadly, local sociocultural attitudes and practices also need to be considered to avoid imposing unwelcome methods or course content on learners. Canagarajah (1999: 5), for instance, describes how university students in Sri Lanka expressed subtle forms of resistance to the ideologies embedded in their English syllabus. By whispering, note passing and writing glosses in the margins of their textbooks the Tamil students mediated the discourses of the curriculum with their own values and practices. As Canagarajah (1999: 92) points out:

> In essence, the glosses provide evidence of a vibrant underlife in the classroom, where students collaborate in providing social, emotional and psychological sustenance and solidarity against the perceived lifelessness and reproductive tendencies of the course . . . Such comments suggest a caring community, and shared frustrations with the textbook and curriculum.

While we should not romanticize the culture of the classroom, it is important to understand the tensions which the implementation of particular approaches involves. Chick (1996), for example, offers a different angle in discussing the collusion between learners and teachers in South Africa to frustrate the implementation of methods seen as imported and culturally alien.

Holliday (1994) takes up this issue in relation to a major teaching project in Egypt, cautioning against the imposition of unfamiliar pedagogic models in non-anglo contexts. He especially points to the dangers of transferring communicative techniques such as process-oriented, task-based, inductive, collaborative methods valued by Western teachers into situations where they may conflict with students' cultural backgrounds. In a review of cultural conceptions of self, for instance, Markus and Kitayama (1991) contrast Western *independent* views, which emphasize the separateness and uniqueness of persons, with many non-Western cultures which insist on the *interdependence* of human beings. So while teachers in Western classrooms often expect writers to voice their judgements, display their knowledge and give their opinions, this can create problems for learners from more collectivist cultures where students are typically oriented by their education to group membership and to age and gender roles rather than to individual status (Ramanathan and Atkinson, 1999).

This kind of hidden 'cultural curriculum' can also be found in culturally divergent attitudes to knowledge which spread along a continuum from respecting the conservation of knowledge to valuing its extension (Ballard and Clanchy, 1991). Educational processes in Western contexts tend to reinforce an analytical, questioning and evaluative stance to knowledge, encouraging students to criticize and recombine existing sources to dispute traditional wisdom and form their own points of view, while students from many Asian cultures, for instance, may favour conserving and reproducing existing knowledge and establishing reverence for what is known through strategies such as memorization and imitation. In Bereiter and Scardamallia's (1987) terms this is 'knowledge telling' which represents immature writing, where the writer's goal is simply to say what he or she can remember based on the assignment. So, by ignoring cultural considerations, teachers may see this as plagiarism or repetition, and be misled into recasting such respect for knowledge as a developmental continuum from immaturity to maturity.

Task A9.3

➤ Consider a language teaching context you are familiar with. What factors related to the local or students' culture do you think influenced the course or student learning? What responses did you make to these and what would you do differently now?

GATHERING NEEDS DATA

To collect data on these various needs the teacher is likely to draw on a range of different sources and methods. Jordan (1997), for instance, lists fourteen different procedures for collecting needs data, including student self-assessment, class progress tests and previous research, while Brown (1995) lists twenty-four, grouping them into six main categories: existing information, tests, observations, interviews, meetings and questionnaires. Oddly, neither mentions collecting and analysing authentic texts, now regarded as a key source of information about target situations. Perhaps the most widely used approaches are:

- Questionnaires.
- Analyses of authentic spoken and written texts.
- Structured interviews.
- Observations.
- Informal consultations with faculty, learners, other EAP teachers, etc.
- Assessment results.

In practice, there has been a heavy over-reliance on questionnaires for needs analysis, despite the rather restricted reliability and one-dimensional picture that this kind of data provides. Surveys of academic writing tasks, for example, have asked both subject tutors and students to rank the tasks assigned or skills needed in particular courses but often fail to get beyond generic labels. In other words, they tend to use a set of preconceived classifications such as 'essay', 'report' or 'critical review' without recognizing that these often mean different things in different courses and disciplines.

In analysing experimental lab reports across different technical and engineering disciplines, for example, Braine (1995) found that, despite the common genre name, some fields required reports with abstracts and others didn't, some included description of apparatus but not others, some had recommendations, others had a specification of a hazards section or a heading labelled 'theory', and so on. In fact, no two disciplines had experimental report formats that were the same in their move structures. Only through such methods as examining assignment hand-outs (Horowitz, 1986), observing classes (Currie, 1993) and studying written texts themselves (Hyland, 2002) is a realistic picture of target demands likely to emerge.

The EAP and ESP literature contains numerous descriptions of the methods and outcomes of research into learner needs conducted in different parts of the world, but what is often missing is meaningful collaboration between participants who might initially approach course design with divergent or conflicting agendas. Are subject tutors, for instance, likely to hold the same views on 'needs' as EAP teachers? Do employers have a say? Will students 'buy in' to an independent characterization of their needs? For these reasons it is important to involve students as participants in any needs analysis if the course is to be useful to them. Activities which encourage student inquiry into texts, disciplinary practices or the course decisions of their tutors can feed back into a fuller, and more critical, understanding of target needs. In addition to such participatory needs analysis, the use of soft systems methodology has been suggested as a way of involving different stakeholders (Tajino *et al.*, 2005). This is an action research methodology borrowed from business contexts which recognizes explicitly that different individuals and groups have different interpretations of the world and which seeks to provide a framework to accommodate these in course design.

RIGHTS ANALYSIS

It should be clear by now that because needs analyses are necessarily limited to particular questions or issues, the framing of those issues will have an impact on the methods used, the data collected, and the conclusions drawn. As Dudley-Evans and St John (1998) point out, 'what we ask and how we interpret are dependent on a particular view of the world, on attitudes and value'. Needs analysis is influenced by the ideological preconceptions of the analyst and, as a result, 'needs' will be defined differently by different stakeholders, with university administrators, subject tutors, teachers and learners having different views. Decisions about what to teach and how to teach it are therefore not neutral professional questions but involve issues of authority in decision making with important consequences for learners. In fact, treating *need* as something existing and measurable is itself an ideological stance, and we need to reflect on whether students' needs are best served by adopting exclusively pragmatic and instrumental goals, or whether we should assist them to a more participatory and critical stance.

Benesch (2001) takes up the ways that ideology pervades needs analysis and suggests that it should include an examination of 'who sets the goals, why they were formulated, whose interests are served by them, and whether they should be challenged' (Benesch, 2001: 43). Taking a position of critical pragmatism (discussed in Unit A1.4), Benesch argues that EAP teachers should not subordinate their instruction unquestioningly to the demands of subject disciplines. Conflating students' needs and institutional demands merely perpetuates a service relationship to colleagues in other departments and upholds an unequal *status quo*. To show that teaching is more than initiating students unquestioningly into particular discourse communities, she advocates supplementing traditional needs analysis with *rights analysis*. This goes beyond target requirements to 'search for alternatives to strict adherence to those requirements' (Benesch, 2001: 45).

Rights analysis therefore involves evaluating the findings of needs analysis, recognizing the challenges that students face and interrogating the results to create more democratic and participatory involvement by students in decision making. The reading by Benesch in Text B9.1 shows one way that courses can be made more negotiable and learners helped to articulate their difficulties with their subject courses and participate more actively as members of an academic community. The notion of rights therefore encourages students to assess their options and prioritize what they need for themselves. It supports them in taking active responsibility for their learning and so resonates with the literature on autonomy in language learning (e.g. Benson and Voller, 1997).

 Task A9.4

➤ What do you think rights analysis might involve in practice? Consider what you might do to address these issues in a context you are familiar with.

Unit A10
Development and implementation

While important, needs analysis is just a means to an end: providing the basis for a course informed by an understanding of the learners, of the teaching situation and of target texts and behaviours. From rights and needs assessments a systematic course plan has to be developed by selecting and sequencing the content and tasks that will lead to desired learning outcomes. Teachers may not always have complete freedom to choose what their courses will include, and may find their syllabus handed to them by administrators or prescribed in set texts. But we always bring our own expertise and personal beliefs about teaching, learning and language to planning and implementing a course, and this not only mediates any ascribed syllabus but also allows a role for student negotiation in the process. This unit introduces some of the key issues in developing and implementing an EAP course.

Task A10.1

➤ Some teachers prefer not to use a syllabus, arguing that learning is too complex, personal and multifaceted to be organized by a formal syllabus and no syllabus can adequately cater for the needs of individual learners. One alternative is to give students control over the content and pace of their learning within a teacher-supported classroom. How successful do you think this might be in a teaching context you are familiar with?

GOALS AND OBJECTIVES

A key aspect of developing an EAP course is formulating goals and objectives from the data gathered by needs analysis. *Goals* (or aims) refer to general statements about what the course hopes to accomplish, the global target outcomes around which the course is organized. For example, these are goals taken from the Web sites of different EAP courses:

▪ The goal of this course is to help students develop the writing skills needed to successfully complete university writing assignments.
▪ This course provides practice in effective speaking skills in an academic environment.

■ This course is designed to help students improve their reading strategies for processing academic texts.
■ This course will help students improve their listening skills, diversify the strategies they use for lecture comprehension, and develop effective note-taking strategies.

While goal statements relate to needs analyses, this connection is always mediated by the judgements and views of teachers and learners about language and learning. It is the teacher (and increasingly also the student), rather than the analysis, that determines which skills and abilities are worth pursuing and achieving.

Objectives, in contrast, are more specific, describing smaller, achievable behaviours that learners will be expected to perform at the end of the course – and perhaps during it too. They facilitate planning, provide measurable outcomes and stipulate how learning will proceed. In EAP courses they often describe the competences, seen as the cluster of skills, abilities and knowledge a person must have to perform a specific task, that the learner will be expected to put into effect. The focus, in other words, is on what an individual can do rather than what is taught, as in these examples:

■ Can use a range of reference skills to access and acknowledge required information.
■ Can use a range of strategies, learning techniques and research skills to achieve tertiary study goals.
■ Can write a report based on a bar chart and a line graph.
■ Can initiate and take part in social interaction for problem solving in tertiary contexts.
■ Can apply a range of reading skills relevant to academic contexts.

Objectives, then, are useful in providing information for both teachers and learners about what will be accomplished. For teachers they contribute to a coherent teaching programme and play a key planning role for selecting and sequencing content and activities into units of work and classes, ensuring that learning will be linked to the particular teaching context. For learners they offer detailed information about the relevance of the course to their needs and a basis for explicit negotiation over what it might contain and how it might be conducted. In this way students are more likely to be involved in the course and contribute to the learning they will experience.

 Task A10.2

➤ 'Teachers who are critical of objectives, often for emotional reasons, are avoiding one tool among many that might help them become better teachers.' Do you agree with this quote from Brown (1995: 95)? What benefits do objectives have for EAP teachers?

THE EAP SYLLABUS

A syllabus is a plan of what is to be achieved through teaching and learning, identifying what will be worked on in reaching the overall course aims and providing a basis for evaluating students' progress. The literature on syllabus design draws a broad distinction between *synthetic* and *analytic types* (White, 1988; Wilkins, 1976). The former include *lexico-grammatical* and *functional* syllabuses and focus on separated bits of knowledge which students are expected to accumulate through decontextualized activities before 're-synthesizing' such knowledge in real communication. *Analytic* syllabuses, on the other hand, focus on *how* the language is to be learned and include *task-based* and *process* syllabus types. Since the emphasis here is on the *process* of acquiring the language, success is measured in terms of 'the purposes for which people are learning language and the kinds of language performance that are necessary to meet those purposes' (Wilkins, 1976: 13).

These types of syllabus constitute two ends of a continuum rather than opposing poles of a dichotomy, but while EAP courses may employ elements of both, most tend towards the analytic end of the cline. This is because they give emphasis to meaning and communication as the learner is exposed to relevant authentic target language situations and texts. Both task-based and process syllabuses present target language samples as whole chunks and encourage learners to focus on negotiating meaning, with the learner left to acquire the grammatical forms at his/her individual pace (Ellis, 2003). Students, in other words, are primarily 'users' rather than 'learners' of the language.

Breen (1987) considers that task-based and process syllabuses both represent 'how something is done' but that process syllabuses extend the focus on procedures for learning by allowing greater learner reinterpretation and decision making. *Task-based syllabuses* involve interaction between knowledge of language and using that knowledge in the solution of problems by setting up situations where the learners respond actively and engage in purposeful communication with each other. These can include real-world tasks, such as engaging in a tutorial or listening to lectures, or pedagogic tasks which facilitate learning how the language works, such as mapping how argument essays are structured. The teacher's interpretation and implementation of a syllabus, however, are usually covert and differently interpreted by students. To avoid this kind of disharmony and facilitate a shared understanding of classroom practices and greater student responsibility for learning, process syllabuses have been widely used.

Process syllabuses have a greater learning focus and are more learner-led, extending the idea of developing language learning through negotiation for meaning during tasks to negotiating aspects of the teaching–learning process itself (Breen and Littlejohn, 2000). They therefore provide a decision making framework for student–teacher collaboration in the purposes, content and ways of working in a course and offer students a voice in the management of their learning. Process syllabuses are therefore central to EAP philosophies as they can help guide students towards a relevant professional expertise through authentic opportunities to develop their knowledge and engage more meaningfully in the learning process.

One example of this more liberal development of practice at tertiary level is the innovative EAP TalkBase programme at the Asian Institute of Technology in Bangkok which offers a curriculum model for autonomous learning. While teachers co-ordinate and take part in activities, the content is supplied by students through group interaction and outcomes are not determined in advance. Hall and Kenny (1988: 29) describe three main features of the course:

■   It focuses on learners and what they want to say.
■   Tasks and content are often determined by learners.
■   The focus is on process rather than content.

Avoiding a traditional timetable, the course presents a framework of interrelated activities in weekly units, each providing input to the next, with 'a cumulative build-up for the learners in understanding and practice' (Hall and Kenny, 1988: 29). While students enter the course with little experience of speaking English, this structure appears to dramatically increase their confidence and ability.

Research is unable to confirm the direct effect of any syllabus on language learning but analytic syllabuses are more likely to offer a bridge from *declarative* knowledge, or what students know, to *procedural* knowledge, or what they can do with this knowledge. But while research into tasks and meaning negotiation continue to inform syllabus design, EAP practitioners have also continued to emphasize what is to be learned, particularly through *text-based* and *content-based* syllabuses.

Text-based syllabuses are organized around the genres that learners need and the social contexts in which they will operate (Feez, 2002; Hyland, 2004). This approach draws on the SFL tradition of genre and adopts a scaffolded pedagogy to guide learners towards control of key genres. Scaffolded learning involves active and sustained support by a teacher who models appropriate strategies for meeting particular purposes, guides students in their use of the strategies, and provides a meaningful and relevant context for using the strategies. Texts and tasks are selected according to learners' needs and sequenced according to one of a number of principles:

■   By following their use in a real-world series of interactions.
■   By perceived increasing levels of difficulty, from easiest to most complex.
■   By determining the most critical skills or functions relevant to students' immediate needs.

The planning of classroom activities in a text-based syllabus is informed by a view of learning as a series of linked stages which provide the support needed to move learners towards a critical understanding of texts. It is informed by the constructivist perspective that learning something new, or attempting to understand something familiar in greater depth, is not a linear process. In trying to make sense of things we use both our prior experience and the first-hand knowledge gained from new explorations. This is figuratively represented in the *teaching–learning cycle* shown in Figure A10.1, the key stages of which are:

1   *Setting the context:* to reveal genre purposes and the settings in which it is used.
2   *Modelling:* analysing the genre to reveal its stages and key features.
3   *Joint construction:* guided, teacher-supported practice in the genre.
4   *Independent construction:* independent writing monitored by the teacher.
5   *Comparing:* relating what has been learnt to other genres and contexts.

Each of these stages seeks to achieve a different purpose and, as we shall see in Unit A11, is associated with different types of classroom activities and teacher–learner roles.

The cycle is one way of understanding the Five Es concept long familiar in science teaching, helping learners to *engage, explore, explain, extend* and *evaluate* (e.g. Trowbridge and Bybee, 1990). The cycle is intended to be used flexibly, allowing students to enter at any stage depending on their existing knowledge of the genre and enabling teachers to return to earlier stages of the cycle for revision purposes. A key purpose of the cycle is to ensure repeated opportunities for students to engage in activities which require them to reflect on and critique their learning by developing understandings of texts, acting on these through writing or speaking, reviewing their performance and using feedback to improve their work. The model therefore allows vocabulary to be recycled and the literacy skills gained in previous cycles to be further developed by working through a new cycle at a more advanced level of expression of the genre. Learning is mediated through stages whereby

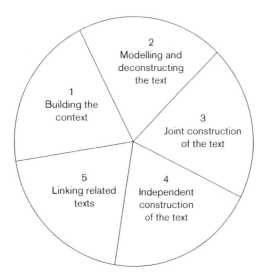

Figure A10.1 The teaching–learning cycle

teacher support is gradually withdrawn to give students increasing independence in using the genre.

Finally, *content-based syllabuses* are either thematic, sheltered or adjunct types, differing in their orientations towards language and content. Theme-based models emphasize language competence while sheltered models attempt to help students master content material and so are more discipline-specific (Brinton *et al.*, 1989: 18). In the adjunct model the language course is linked with a content course which shares the same content base, the rationale being that students will develop strategies and skills which will transfer from one course to the other. In this type of syllabus, language is also seen as functional and is integrated with the teaching of content. Pally (1999) emphasizes the 'sustained' nature of much CBI, suggesting that students can develop the rhetorical and argumentative skills associated with particular subject disciplines only through sustained, incremental practice over a period of time.

In practice, many syllabuses are hybrid, drawing on aspects of two or three different syllabus types. Generally, however, EAP syllabuses tend to be competence-based, are presented through tasks of various kinds, extend students' genre skills, involve at least some shared negotiation with learners and develop a complementary array of skills and knowledge.

 Task A10.3

➤ Which of the syllabus models mentioned above appeal to you most as an EAP teacher? Will your choice of syllabus depend on the proficiency, goals or backgrounds of your students?

ENGAGING WITH THE DISCIPLINES

The importance of well contextualized EAP instruction based on the needs of students and subject teachers has led to various ways of matching language teaching to the assignments, discourses and activities of content courses. The adjunct model described above, where an EAP course is linked with an academic content course, and team teaching, involving collaboration in the same classroom, are the most developed approach to such partnerships. The types of possible co-operative relationships with subject departments can be seen as a continuum of involvement (Baron, 1992), along which Dudley-Evans and St John (1998) identify three main types of subject–language integration: *co-operation*, *collaboration* and *team teaching*.

■ *Co-operation* refers to the use of subject teachers as specialist informants who can provide information about texts, course assignments and the conceptual and discoursal framework of the discipline. Here the teacher is proactive in gathering information about the target course and establishing what tutors and students regard as priorities. This is part of the target needs analysis where the EAP teacher finds out what is going on in the subject department and the discipline. Information is usually collected by interviews, questionnaires, observations and by studying materials and texts. Beyond this, co-operation can involve discussion with subject tutors to introduce alternative readings in the EAP course, to bring different perspectives to the content, and to analyse relevant discourse texts such as lectures, textbooks and essays.

■ *Collaboration* is further along the involvement continuum and refers to the direct working together of language and subject teacher outside the classroom. Dudley-Evans and St John (1998: 44) suggest three options here:

1   Subject tutors offer advice on readings, vocabulary preparation, etc., so that the EAP class can prepare students for a subsequent subject class. The objectives of the EAP course are thus subordinate to those of the subject course.
2   The subject department either produces or provides input into material produced for students to work with in the EAP class. This may also take the form of joint assessment. There is greater equality in this relationship than in the first option.
3   The EAP course is taken in conjunction with a subject course in an *adjunct model*. Here instruction is largely focused on addressing the study and literacy demands of the subject course, often discussing videos of lectures, set texts, and course topics from different perspectives.

The adjunct model, widely used in the US, is perhaps the most interesting of these three approaches to cross-curricular collaboration, as students enrol concurrently in two classes and study related materials. Such courses have, however, been criticized as subordinating EAP to the disciplines, an acceptance of the 'butler stance' referred to in Unit A1. But this is not an inevitable outcome by any means. It is equally possible that by focusing on learners' apparent difficulties in following subject course readings and lectures, the work of EAP teachers can wash back into the subject course and so improve learners' understandings of both language and subject content. Benesch's description of a paired EAP and Psychology class in Text B9.1, for instance, shows how an EAP adjunct course can contribute to students' critical awareness and influence how the content class is taught rather than simply complying with its requirements.

■ Finally, *team teaching* involves the closest engagement with the subject discipline as subject and EAP teachers work together in the same classroom. While costs and resources often restrict opportunities for this, pioneering work at Birmingham University in the UK on lecture comprehension shows that it can be successful. Here the subject tutor and EAP teacher together followed up each lecture with a series of questions on a recording of the lecture, including a discussion of key points and development of note-taking skills (Johns and Dudley-Evans, 1980). Commenting on the expansion of this work to the writing of examination responses, project outlines, dissertations and essays, Dudley-Evans and St John (1998) suggest three elements for their success:

1 Clearly defined and complementary roles for EAP and subject teachers.
2 Relatively few demands on the subject tutor beyond classroom responses, therefore encouraging his or her participation in the course.
3 Mutual respect for and acceptance of each other's specialist expertise.

Engagement can be a fraught enterprise, however, as participants may be suspicious and even openly critical of each other. EAP teachers may see subject tutors as unresponsive to L2 learners and regard their failure to communicate effectively as a source of student difficulties. Subject tutors might feel that EAP teachers know little about disciplinary communication and so should teach general English skills and not interfere in their classes. Barron (2002, in Text B10.1), moreover, shows how conflicts may be even more fundamental. He argues that the ontological superiority that science teachers give to their scientific facts can make them rigid when negotiating learning tasks and assignments. The divergent philosophies of functionalism in EAP and realism in science, in other words, can undermine cooperation and lead to the subordination of EAP to subject content.

Clearly some engagement with the subject discipline is essential to the development of an effective EAP course. At the minimum this should involve an understanding of the texts, tasks and forms of information delivery in the target course or discipline, and the use of tutors as informants on the literacy practices of their fields. More integrated forms of involvement are likely to bring further benefits and we are likely to see more of these pursued in the future, as content and EAP teachers gain greater understanding of each other's work and build up, over time, a working relationship of trust and respect.

 Task A10.4

➤ What kinds of engagement seem most feasible in your current situation or a context you are familiar with? What kinds of integration would you be prepared to try?

Unit A11
Methodologies and materials

Methods and materials are the interface between teaching and learning, the points at which needs, objectives and syllabuses are made tangible for both teachers and students. Both have received considerable attention in the ELT and EAP literature, often separately and with methods taking precedence, although the kinds of materials a teacher selects, as much as what he or she does with them, depend on the methodologies adopted.

Teaching methodologies are victims to fashion and a range of approaches have processed through classrooms in the past twenty-five years (e.g. Larsen-Freeman, 2000). Principled teaching is not about pre-packaged methodological products, however, but the individual teacher's construction of personal, context-specific frameworks which allow him or her to select and combine compatible procedures and materials in systematic ways for a local context. In EAP classrooms these general frameworks are influenced by the fact that students bring both specialized knowledge and learning processes from their disciplines to their EAP classes. The teacher can seek to harness and build on these to develop learners' discourse understandings in various ways, drawing on concepts such as *consciousness raising, scaffolding, collaboration, socioliteracy* and *concordancing*.

Task A11.1

➤ How might EAP methods differ from those used in EFL teaching as a result of students' specialized knowledge? Do you have a preferred method and if so how does it reflect your beliefs about teaching and learning?

CONSCIOUSNESS RAISING AND SOCIOLITERACY

EAP courses always involve attending to the texts learners will most need to use beyond the classroom. This necessarily implies a central role for genre in any methodology. Making texts and contexts a focus for analysis allows teachers to raise students' awareness of the interdependence of disciplinary valued genres, the resources used to create meaning in context and how powerful genres can be negotiated. One way of doing this is to ask students, often in small groups, to analyse, compare and manipulate representative samples of the target discourse in a process known as *rhetorical consciousness raising*. Consciousness raising is a 'top down' approach to understanding language and encourages us to see grammatical features as 'the on-line processing component of discourse and not the set of syntactic building blocks with which discourse is constructed' (Rutherford, 1987: 104). Focusing on language is not therefore an end in itself but a mean of teaching learners to use language effectively by encouraging them to experience for themselves the effect that grammatical choices have on creating meanings.

Consciousness raising is often novel for students, as it seeks to assist them to create, comprehend and reflect on the ways texts work as discourse rather than on their value as bearers of content information. It guides learners to explore key lexical, grammatical and rhetorical features and to use this knowledge to construct their own examples of the genre. Consciousness raising is therefore designed to produce better writers and speakers rather than better texts. Here the teacher's goal is to illuminate the genres that matter to students so that they understand them and use them effectively. The approach takes various forms but all address the ways meaning is constructed, and while this might mean highlighting particular text elements, these are not isolated from the overall meaning of a text. Consciousness-raising tasks are therefore holistic in looking at a feature in the context of a particular authentic text to suggest how it is used to help realize a particular writer goal.

Some common approaches involve comparisons and attention to language use through tasks where, for example, students:

- Compare spoken and written modes, such as a lecture and textbook, to raise awareness of the ways in which these differ in response to audiences and purposes.
- List the ways that reading and listening to monologue are similar and different.
- Investigate variability in academic writing by conducting mini-analyses of a feature in a text in their own discipline and then comparing the results with those of students from other fields.
- Survey the advice given on a feature in a sample of style guides and textbooks and compare its actual use in a target genre such as a student essay or research article.
- Explore the extent to which the frequency and use of a feature can be transferred across the genres students need to write or participate in.
- Reflect on how far features correspond with their use in students' first language and on their attitudes to the expectations of academic style in relation to their own needs, cultures and identities.

By exploring academic practices and discourse conventions with students, teachers can help them see the options available to them when engaging in their disciplines.

Another trajectory of consciousness raising is discussed by Johns (1997) as a 'socioliterate approach' where learners acquire academic literacies via 'exposure to discourses from a variety of social contexts' and inquiring into their own literate lives and the literacy practices of others. Johns recommends introducing students to the concepts of genre and context through familiar 'homely' genres, such as wedding invitations, then moving on to explore pedagogic genres like textbooks and exam prompts, and then less familiar academic genres. This helps students to gain an understanding of the ways register features interact with social purposes and cultural forces in known genres before they study academic genres. A key element is for students to become researchers themselves, exploring not only texts but interviewing subject tutors and more advanced students about specific classes and assignments or their own use of genres. Here, then, is both an effective and engaging task and an example of critical EAP principles in action.

SCAFFOLDING AND GRAMMATICAL COMPETENCE

Another, complementary, methodology used to build students' discourse competence in EAP classes follows the ideas of the Russian psychologist Lev Vygotsky (1978) in giving considerable recognition to the importance of *collaboration*, or peer interaction, and *scaffolding*, or teacher-supported learning. Together these concepts assist learners through two notions of learning:

- *Shared consciousness:* the idea that learners working together learn more effectively than individuals working separately.
- *Borrowed consciousness:* the idea that learners working with knowledgeable others develop greater understanding of tasks and ideas.

Scaffolding emphasizes interaction with experienced others in moving learners from their existing level of performance, what they can do now, to a level of 'potential performance', what they are able to do without assistance. Vygotsky termed this gap between current and potential performance 'the zone of proximal development' and argued that progress from one to the other is not achieved only through input, but rather through social interaction and the assistance of more skilled and experienced others.

In other words, teaching involves a dialogue between teacher and student, rather like an expert training an apprentice. Figure A11.1 (from Feez, 1998) represents the changing nature of this collaboration in response to the learner's progress. The degree of teacher intervention and the kinds of tasks selected for students to engage with therefore play a key role in scaffolding writing and speaking, representing a cline of support from closely controlled activities to autonomous extended communication, reducing direct instruction as the learner gradually assimilates the task demands and procedures for constructing the genre effectively. For those working within a Systemic Functional Linguistic approach this is done by scaffolding learners through the teaching–learning cycle described in Unit A10.

Teachers often assist this process by providing students with an explicit grammar, but this is not the decontextualized, disembodied grammar of more traditional

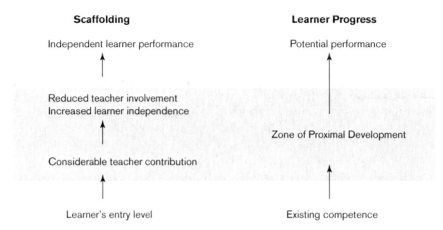

Scaffolding   **Learner Progress**

Independent learner performance   Potential performance

Reduced teacher involvement
Increased learner independence

Zone of Proximal Development

Considerable teacher contribution

Learner's entry level   Existing competence

Figure A11.1 Teacher–learner collaboration (Feez, 1998: 27)

methods. Instead of seeing texts as constructed from isolated building blocks, this starts with how grammar features represent the speaker or writer's choices for achieving certain purposes, expressing certain relationships, and conveying certain information. As Knapp and Watkins (1994: 8) point out:

> Grammar is a name for the resource available to users of a language system for producing texts. A knowledge of grammar by a speaker or a writer shifts language use from the implicit and unconscious to a conscious manipulation of language and choice of appropriate texts. A genre-based grammar focuses on the manner through which different language processes or genres in writing are codified in distinct and recognisable ways. It first considers how a text is structured and organised at the level of the whole text in relation to its purpose, audience and message. It then considers how all parts of the text, such as paragraphs and sentences, are structured, organised and coded so as to make the text effective as written communication.

Adopting methods which include an explicit understanding of spoken and written texts makes language both more relevant and immediately useful to learners in their studies.

 Task A11.2

➤ The explicit teaching of grammar is a controversial issue. Think of your own classes and practices. At what points in a lesson or unit of learning do you think it is appropriate to focus on language and how do you think this can this be done most effectively?

CORPORA AND COMPUTER-MEDIATED LEARNING

Computers are playing an increasingly important part in EAP methodologies, both in encouraging learners to actively understand target texts through data-driven learning, encouraging understanding of meanings and uses inductively via study of recurring patterns in corpora, and through computer networks.

The value of corpus work lies in the fact that it can both replace instruction with discovery and refocus attention on accuracy as an appropriate aspect of learning. This methodology not only provides an open-ended supply of language data tailored to the learner's needs rather than simply a standard set of examples, but also promotes a learner-centred approach bringing flexibility of time and place and a discovery approach to learning. Tribble and Jones (1997) discuss activities for using language corpora in L2 classes, but generally teachers have either used corpora as a basis for materials and tasks or they have trained students to explore corpora themselves. The second approach encourages an inductive understanding of language use and awareness of conventional patterns through 'data-driven learning'. Wu (1992: 32) sums up this method:

> Only when words are in their habitual environments, presented in their most frequent forms and their relational patterns and structures, can they be learnt effectively, interpreted properly and used appropriately.

This kind of direct learner access suggests two further lines of approach (Aston, 1997). Corpora can be treated as reference tools to be consulted for examples when problems arise while writing. An example of this is WordPilot 2000 (see Unit A7), which allows students to call up a concordance of a word while they are writing in MS Word (Milton, 1999; Hyland, 2003). Alternatively, they can be used as *research tools* to be systematically investigated as a means of gaining greater awareness of language use. This carries risks. Research approaches presuppose considerable motivation and a curiosity about language which is often lacking, and there is a danger that some students will be bored by an over-exposure to concordance lines. Teachers have therefore tended to guide student searches to features which are typical in target genres.

A second way that computers have contributed to EAP teaching methodologies has been in facilitating student communication via computer networks. Network-based language teaching provides teachers with a variety of ways to interpret and construct online texts and engage in both local and remote discourse communities. This is the use of computers as tools as they facilitate access to other people and to information and data via real-time chatting, e-mail, and the Web (Warschauer and Kern, 2000). The use of these approaches has not been extensively studied, but they do provide student-centred learning contexts with opportunities for 'socio-collaborative' interaction and negotiation with teachers and peers which is believed to promote language learning. Warschauer (in Text B11.3) shows how some teachers are using networked resources in their classes. The fact that students have relative autonomy and are interacting for a genuine purpose encourages participation, and the experience of participating in these modes can develop a sense of growing involvement in an academic community.

 Task A11.3

➤ How might a concordance be useful to you as an EAP teacher? Refer back to Unit A7 and consider what kinds of corpora would be most useful to your students and how you would use them in your teaching.

TYPES AND ROLES OF MATERIALS

Materials are used to stimulate and support EAP instruction and their development probably consumes most of the teacher's out-of-class work time. Materials refer to anything that can help facilitate the learning of language, and while they are predominantly paper-based, they can also include audio and visual aids, computer-mediated resources, real objects, or performance. They provide most of the input and language exposure that learners receive in the classroom and, because course outcomes significantly depend on them, teachers need to ensure that their materials relate as closely as possible to the target needs and learning profiles of their learners and to their own beliefs as teachers.

Materials are important as a means of helping teachers to understand and apply the theories of language learning, and this importance means that they have become a focus of study in their own right (e.g. Tomlinson, 1998). More directly, the kinds of materials we use are influenced by the purposes we use them for, and these provide a stimulus to writing or discussion, as a starting point for language input and analysis, and as ideas for organizing activities. Table A11.1 lists these principal roles.

The use of materials to *scaffold* learners' understandings of language use involves them in thinking about and using the language while supporting their evolving control of different texts. These materials provide learners with opportunities for

Table A11.1 The roles of materials in EAP instruction

1 *Language scaffolding.* Sources of language examples for discussion, analysis, exercises, etc.
2 *Models.* Sample texts provide exemplars of rhetorical forms and structures of target genres.
3 *Reference.* Typically text or Web-based information, explanations and examples of relevant grammatical, rhetorical or stylistic forms.
4 *Stimulus.* Sources of ideas and content to stimulate discussions and writing and to support project work. Generally texts, but can include video, graphic or audio material, items of realia, Internet material or lectures.

Source: Hyland (2003).

discussion, guided writing, analysis and manipulation of salient structures and vocabulary. Ideally these materials should provide a variety of texts and sources, not follow a rigid format, and provide learners with a sense of progression.

Models are representative samples used to illustrate particular features of a text. Typically students examine several examples of a genre to identify its structure, the ways meanings are expressed and the variations which are possible. Materials used as models thus help to increase students' awareness of how texts are organized and how purposes are realized, so, as far as possible, the texts selected should be both relevant to the students, representing the genres they will have to write in in their target contexts, and *authentic*, created to be used in real-world contexts rather than in classrooms.

Reference materials, unlike those used for modelling and scaffolding, focus on knowledge rather than practice. This category includes a range of materials including grammars, dictionaries, encyclopaedias and style guides, but all function to support the learner's understanding of language through explanations, examples and advice. This type of support is particularly useful to learners engaged in self-study with little class contact. A great deal of useful information, particularly on the conventions of academic writing, can be found on the Online Writing Labs (OWLs) of universities. Figure A11.2 gives an example of a page on writing reviews from the Institute of Education CAPLITS Web page. The advice in some reference books tends, however, to be idiosyncratic, intuitive and prescriptive, and should be treated with caution.

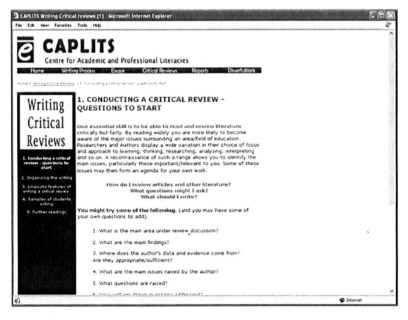

Figure A11.2 A page on writing reviews from the CAPLITS Web site of the Institute of Education, University of London

Finally, materials are commonly used to involve learners in thinking about and using language by stimulating ideas, encouraging connections with their experiences, and developing topics in ways that articulate their ideas. They provide content schemata and a reason to communicate, stimulating creativity, planning, and engagement with others. *Stimulus* materials include the full range of media, but generally, the more detailed and explicit the material, the greater support it offers learners, so that a lecture recording or a diagram can provide relatively unambiguous and structured ways of stimulating language use. In contrast, material which is open to numerous interpretations, such as a collection of divergent views on a topic or Lego bricks used to symbolize real objects, allows room for students to exercise their creativity and imagination in their responses.

 Task A11.4

➤ Where would you go to find materials to fulfil each of these four roles mentioned above? Can some materials perform more than one role? Are there any other purposes for using materials in EAP?

CREATING AND EVALUATING MATERIALS

Commercial textbooks are common in EAP classes and proponents argue that they are the most convenient form of presenting materials, that they help to achieve consistency, cohesion and progress, and that they assist teachers to prepare and learners to revise. Even where they are not set as class texts many teachers dip into them as a source of ideas for course structure, practice activities and language models. But while there are obvious advantages for teachers and institutions in using course books, opponents argue that they are inevitably reductionist and superficial, restrict teacher initiative, and cannot cater for the diverse needs of all users. Sheldon, a long-time critic of published materials, argues that:

> The whole business of the management of language learning is far too complex to be satisfactorily catered for by a pre-packaged set of decisions embodied in teaching materials. Quite simply, even with the best intentions no single textbook can possibly work in all situations.
>
> (Sheldon, 1987: 1)

The highly targeted and context-specific nature of EAP means that no textbook can ever be ideal for a particular class and so an effective teacher needs to be able to evaluate, adapt and produce suitable and effective materials. The process normally starts by evaluating the suitability of available resources or published texts against criteria of relevance, difficulty, rhetorical appropriacy, presentation, and so on, and numerous evaluation checklists exist for selecting textbooks (e.g. Cunningsworth, 1995; Harmer, 2001; Reid, 1993). But these tend to be very subjective and no set of criteria fits all situations as selection involves more than simply matching needs to available resources. It is important that teachers feel they can work with a book to achieve their goals with a particular group of learners, and this means that they cannot just accept what others recommend. More usually, teachers are evaluating not books but individual units, texts or activities, and simple criteria are more useful, determining whether the content and genre are relevant and the language focus appropriate.

Often teachers are forced to either adapt existing materials or create their own. There are five ways of adapting materials, although in practice they actually shade into each other:

- *Adding:* supplementing or extending what a textbook offers with extra readings, tasks or exercises.
- *Deleting:* omitting repetitive, irrelevant, potentially unhelpful or difficult items.
- *Modifying:* rewriting rubrics, examples, activities or explanations to improve relevance, impact or clarity.
- *Simplifying:* rewriting to reduce the difficulty of tasks, explanations or instructions.
- *Reordering:* changing the sequence of units or activities to fit course goals.

Designing new writing materials can be extremely satisfying, both professionally and creatively, as well as offering students a more tailored learning experience. It is, however, also very time-consuming. Dudley-Evans and St John (1998) estimate at least fifteen hours to produce just one hour of good learning material from authentic texts.

An important consideration in EAP materials design is whether to use authentic or contrived materials. Contrived texts are usually short dialogues or passages written to highlight a particular feature, while authentic texts are those which have not been written specifically for the classroom. Much has been written on the pros and cons of each, with authenticity providing meaningful exposure to the language but simplified texts offering 'enriched input' flooded with exemplars of the target structure (Ellis, 1999). Clearly the decision will have much to do with the role that materials are required to play, with authentic texts being more central as genre models.

While the development process can vary widely depending on local circumstances, it typically looks something like this:

- A need for materials is identified because existing resources fail to meet a course objective (determined by student need) or because students require further practice in a particular area.
- The teacher then explores this area to gain a better understanding of the particular skill or feature involved.
- The teacher, perhaps with the help of students, locates a suitable text, video, diagram or other input source.

- Activities are developed to exploit this source in a meaningful way, ensuring that these are realistic, that they work well with the text, that they relate to target needs and learner interests, and that they are clearly explained.
- The materials are produced for student use, with their physical appearance playing an important part in providing credibility and impact, arousing interest and encouraging students to engage with the activities.
- The materials are used in class and evaluated for their success in meeting the identified need, typically through teacher judgements and student questionnaires. Revising them recycles the design and development process and encourages reflection.

 Task A11.5

➤ In 1981 Allwright advised teachers to: 'use no materials, published or un-published, actually conceived or designed as materials for language teaching'. This is a central issue in EAP and has important implications for the ways we work. Do you agree with Allwright? To what extent should materials always be authentic? Does the fact that teachers use texts in ways that do not reflect their original communicative purpose make them less authentic?

Unit A12
Feedback and assessment

Assessment refers to the ways used to evaluate information about a learner's language ability or achievement. It is an integral aspect of the teaching–learning process and central to students' progress towards increasing control of their skills and understandings. It is also an everyday classroom practice, as teachers continually make judgements about the progress, strengths and weaknesses of their learners and communicate these to students. Assessment therefore has both a teaching and testing function, and a distinction is often made between *formative* and *summative* assessment. As a formative process, assessment is closely linked with teaching and with issues of teacher response, or *feedback*, allowing the teacher to advise students, monitor learning and fine-tune instruction. Summative assessment, on the other hand, is concerned with 'summing up' how much a student has learned at the end of a course. This unit will discuss these aspects of teaching and learning in relation to EAP.

Task A12.1

➤ In what ways can teachers collect information about a student's performance or progress in a course?

ISSUES IN ASSESSMENT

Assessments help teachers draw inferences about students' language abilities and make classroom decisions based on these. More specifically, there are five main reasons for evaluating learners:

■ *Diagnostic:* to identify students' strengths and weaknesses, often for needs assessment or to indicate where remedial action is needed as a course progresses.
■ *Achievement:* to enable learners to demonstrate the progress they have made in a course.
■ *Performance:* to indicate students' ability to perform target academic tasks.
■ *Proficiency:* to assess general competence for certification or university study, etc.

■ *Accountability:* to provide funding authorities with evidence that intended outcomes have been met and expenses justified.

These purposes often overlap and have additional functions such as motivating learners to feel positive about their achievements or providing practice for public exams. Writing assessment thus has clear pedagogic goals as it can directly influence teaching, promote learner progress, and inform teachers of the impact of their courses, an effect known as *washback*.

Whatever the purpose, all assessment tasks must be both *valid* and *reliable*, that is, a test should do what it is intended to do and it should do it consistently. *Validity* requires a task to assess what it claims to assess and to assess what has actually been taught, often collapsed into the idea of *construct validity* (Messick, 1996) or tests which appropriately represent the abilities being tested, such as the ability to 'write an argumentative essay' or to 'participate in a tutorial session' and so on. This implies that tasks must be based on a close analysis of target discourses to effectively elicit the appropriate rhetorical, cognitive and linguistic processes needed to participate in that discourse. A task designed to assess students' ability to write argumentative essays, for instance, should encourage them to present and support a proposition, explore points of view and weigh evidence, address an audience appropriately and draw on relevant topic material.

Weir (2004), adopting a sociocognitive approach, has stressed the importance of ensuring that assessments meet the specific needs of test takers by introducing the concept of *context validity*, or the 'extent to which the choice of tasks in a test is representative of the larger universe of tasks of which the test is assumed to be a sample' (p. 19). Weir argues that it is important to link this kind of validity, which can be determined before the test, to various kinds of *a posteriori* validity evidence. This includes what he calls *scoring validity*, or various aspects of reliability, *criterion-related validity*, referring to the relation between the test score and a relevant external performance benchmark, and *consequential validity*, which addresses the social consequences of testing and ensuring that results are used in an ethical manner. Weir argues that these types of validity should be applied at each stage of any language test design process and his discussion seems particularly relevant to EAP teachers with any involvement in testing.

Reliability is the second main element of any test. A task is considered *reliable* if it measures consistently, both in terms of the same student on different occasions and the same task across different raters.

Many factors can influence a student's test performance. These include the conditions under which tests are taken, the instructions given to students, the genre, the time of day, and so on. The complexity of these factors makes it unlikely that the same individual will perform equally well on different occasions and tasks. So while differences in the same person's scores might reveal particular strengths and weaknesses, there is a need to restrict statements about a student's writing ability to what has actually been assessed. Hughes (1989) argues that *reliability of performance* can be achieved through taking a sufficient number of samples, restricting the candidate's choice of topics and genres, giving clear task directions and ensuring students are familiar with the assessment format.

The second component of reliability concerns the consistency with which student performance is rated and this boils down to two main issues:

- All assessors should agree on the rating of the same learner performance.
- Each assessor should assess the same performance in the same way on different occasions.

Unfortunately, raters may be influenced as much by their own cultural contexts and experiences as by variations in writing quality. Even where texts are double marked, research has found that raters can differ in what they look for in writing and the standards they apply to the same text. Novice raters, for instance, tend to focus far more on grammatical accuracy and local errors, which tend to be highly visible (Weigle, 2002: 70–2). Consistency is often hard to achieve and so markers often receive training and participate in benchmarking meetings where they negotiate agreement on sample scripts using clear criteria.

Task A12.2

➤ What factors might cause variation between several teachers marking the same assignment? What might cause you to mark different students' writing on the same assignment differently and how could you minimize this variation?

DESIGN AND SCORING OF ASSESSMENT TASKS

In practical terms, designing assessment tasks involves four elements which actually shade into each other in practice:

- *Rubric:* instructions for carrying out the task. The level of detail which is provided to the students, both before the assessment in a hand-out, practice activities, and in the rubric itself, may have a considerable influence on a student's performance in the task.
- *Prompt:* the material which will stimulate the student's response. This can contain both contextual and input data. *Contextual data* establish the setting, participants, purpose, and other situational features necessary for the writer to engage in the task, while *input data* consist of the visual and/or aural material to be processed (Douglas, 2000: 55–7).
- *Expected response:* what students should do with the task; the response it seeks to elicit in terms of audience, genre, language, content, tone, etc. These form the explicit criteria against which task performance can be judged.

■ *Post-task evaluation:* assessing the effectiveness of the task in terms of its ability to discriminate among students and whether they were able to perform to their potential.

A final key issue in assessment concerns the approach to scoring. In the past a student's performance was *norm-referenced,* or judged in comparison with the performance of others, but this has largely given way to *criterion-referenced* practices where the quality of each essay is judged against explicitly stated criteria, often in terms of what the student 'can do'. Criterion-referenced techniques therefore link naturally with the principles of EAP.

Criterion-referenced scoring procedures are either holistic, analytic or trait-based. *Holistic scoring* offers a general impression of a text based on a single, integrated score, but while this is easy to use, reducing students' performance on a task to a single score cannot provide the diagnostic information which teachers can feedback into their teaching. *Analytic scoring* requires readers to judge a text against a set of criteria and give a score for each category. This provides more information than a single holistic score by separating, and sometimes weighting, individual components. In writing there may be separate scales for content, organization and grammar, for example. Finally, *primary trait scoring* involves focusing on just one feature critical to that task, such as appropriate text staging, identifying main points in a lecture, and so on. Raters often find it hard to focus exclusively on the one specified trait, however and, because it requires a new scoring guide for each task, it is a very labour-intensive method.

 Task A12.3

➤ There are three main kinds of question prompt:

■ A *base question,* e.g. 'What are the consequences of global warming for wetland birds?'
■ A *situation* to frame the task, e.g. 'Your poster proposal has been accepted at an international conference. Create the poster setting out the methods, results and implications of your research.'
■ A *text* to frame the task, e.g. 'Look at the information in the diagram and write a paragraph to describe the water cycle.'

What advantages and disadvantages might each type of prompt have for students?

TEACHER-WRITTEN FEEDBACK

An important way by which students acquire the literacy skills and epistemological understandings of their disciplines is through the written responses they receive on their writing or on their spoken presentations. Providing feedback to students is often seen as one of the teacher's most important tasks, offering the kind of individual attention that is otherwise rarely possible under classroom conditions. Not only does feedback allow students to see how others respond to their work and to learn from the responses, but the ways tutors respond reflect their beliefs about the nature of university education and the place of writing in it, so that students get a range of messages from these responses, about university values and beliefs, about the role of writing in learning, about their identity as students, about their competence as writers, and about their induction into disciplinary epistemologies.

In terms of academic literacy development, feedback emphasizes a process of writing and rewriting where the text is not seen as self-contained but points forward to other texts the student will write and to further stages of learning. Research findings over the past twenty years, however, are ambivalent about the effectiveness of teacher feedback in improving academic literacy and show that students and tutors themselves are often uncertain about what their role should be (Cohen and Cavalcanti, 1990). Some research suggests that much written feedback is of poor quality and frequently misunderstood by students. Ferris (1997), for instance, found that although three-quarters of substantive teachers' comments on drafts were used by students, only half their revisions in response to these could be considered as improvements and a third actually made matters worse. In fact Truscott (1996) summarizes this literature as suggesting that teacher feedback has little discernible effect on writing development, while Lea and Street (2000) argue that feedback fails to convey the clear disciplinary values and preferences for organizing knowledge that tutors would wish for.

Much of the research, however, focuses on error correction and reflects experimental studies which remove feedback from the real classrooms and teacher–student rela- tionships within which it occurs. Master (1995), for instance, found that grammar feedback was effective when combined with classroom discussions, while Ferris (2003) cites research that teachers' attention to form leads to a reduction in errors in later assignments when it contains comments rather than corrections. Teacher feedback should ideally respond to all aspects of student texts, but not necessarily at every stage of the teaching–writing cycle. Attention to sentence-level errors can generally be delayed to a later draft as the paper may be radically revised. Perhaps the most effective written feedback seeks to reinforce the patterns which were taught when modelling the genre so that it becomes part of the process of learning to write rather than an extemporized solution to local errors.

In fact, teacher-written feedback is generally welcomed and highly valued by second language writers (Hyland, 1998) and seems to lead to improvements in writing (Ferris, 2003). While students vary greatly in how they respond to feedback and in their ability to learn from it, it does seem to help writers resolve problems and to comprehend the social and cultural context they are working in by providing a sense of audience and an understanding of the expectations of the communities they are writing for. It is also the case, however, that subject tutors often feel uncertain and insecure about the messages they communicate in their feedback (Ivanic *et al.*, 2000).

Task A12.4

➤ How important do you think linguistic form is in writing? What strategies do you think might be effective in developing ESL students' ability to notice and correct the accuracy of their writing?

PEER FEEDBACK AND TEACHER CONFERENCING

Research indicates that for feedback to be effective it should be conveyed in a number of modes and should allow for response and interaction (e.g. Brinko, 1993). Among the most extensively employed of these modes is the writing conference, a two-way interaction between teacher and student(s) where meaning and interpretation are constantly being negotiated by participants, and which provides both teaching and learning benefits. This provides a *scaffolded* dialogue which gives teachers a chance to respond to the diverse cultural, educational and writing needs of their students, clarifying meaning and resolving ambiguities, while saving them the time spent in detailed marking of papers. For students, writing conferences can give them a clearer idea of their strengths and weaknesses, develop their autonomy, allow them to raise questions on their written feedback and help them construct a revision plan (Hyland, F., 2000).

But conferences vary considerably in the extent to which they improve student writing and the literature stresses the need for careful planning to ensure that students participate actively. Second-language students are not always in a good position to make the most of these opportunities as they may lack the experience, interactive abilities or aural comprehension skills to benefit. There is also the issue of power relations as some learners have cultural or social inhibitions about engaging informally with authority figures (Goldstein and Conrad, 1990), and this can result in students passively and unreflectively incorporating the teacher's suggestions into their work, a practice known as 'appropriation'. For teachers there are the disadvantages that conferences consume considerable amounts of time and require specialized interaction skills which have not been comprehensively defined.

An important alternative to teacher feedback is peer response. From a sociocognitive perspective, peer review can be seen as a formative developmental process which gives writers the opportunities to discuss their texts and discover others' interpretations of them. Once again the research is ambivalent and its benefits have been hard to confirm empirically, while teachers have generally been more positive than students, who tend to prefer teacher feedback.

The theoretical advantages are largely based on the fact that writing and learning are social processes. Collaborative peer review helps learners engage in a community of equals who respond to each other's work and together create an authentic social context for interaction and learning (e.g. Mittan, 1989). Practically, students are able to participate actively in learning while getting responses from real, perhaps multiple, readers in a non-threatening situation (Medonca and Johnson, 1994). Moreover, students not only benefit from seeing how readers understand their ideas and what they need to improve, but also gain the skills necessary to critically analyse and revise their own writing. On the negative side, the fact that learners are rhetorically inexperienced means that they may focus on sentence-level problems, while their lack of training means their comments may be vague and unhelpful, or even overly critical and sarcastic (Leki, 1990). There is also some concern that students from collectivist cultures may be more concerned about the need to emphasize a positive group climate than to critically appraise peers' writing, making feedback less beneficial (Carson and Nelson, 1996).

While research cautions us to avoid idealizing L2 peer group interactions as sites of constructive interaction, an important factor in the success of such groups is student training, which seems to encourage a greater level of engagement and more helpful and concrete advice (Stanley, 1992). In fact, training appears to benefit both the writer and the reader in peer dyads, with students who receive training to give peer feedback also making higher-quality revisions to their own writing (Berg, 1999). The greatest benefits, however, may be related to informal peer support mechanisms of camaraderie, empathy and concern (Hyland, F., 2000; Villamil and de Guerrero, 1996).

Task A12.5

➤ Ferris (2003: 86) summarizes research on peer response by saying, 'the evidence is fairly consistent that ESL writers are able to give one another feedback that is then utilised in revision. . . . The odds of peer feedback appear to improve even more if students are carefully trained in advance of the peer response task.' What kind of training do you think would be most helpful to make peer feedback work successfully?

SECTION B
Extension

Theme 1: Conceptions and controversies

The readings in this theme develop and flesh out the discussion in Section A of key concepts and debates surrounding the ways in which practitioners and critics understand EAP. While these debates may seem to address issues which touch on theories and ideas removed from the everyday concerns of teachers, they do, in fact, directly impact on the ways we conceptualize our classroom roles, develop our courses and practise our trade. The rapid changes in higher education in recent years have radically altered EAP teachers' relationships to their students, institutions and subject matter while wider social changes have brought a wider range of students, with diverse expectations, into their classes.

The texts in this theme represent different responses to these changes, focusing on the key issues of:

- Whether we should teach a general or specific form of academic English.
- Whether we should conceptualize our work in terms of study skills, academic socialization or academic literacy.
- Whether we see English as a neutral lingua franca facilitating international communication or as an insidious form of colonialism and commercial interest.
- Whether we see a role for critical awareness in the pragmatics of teaching EAP.

These texts bring a range of different social, political and pedagogic perspectives to these central issues which shape our conceptions of literacy, language, learning and the relationship of classroom practice to the wider world.

Unit B1
Specific or general academic purposes?

The two extracts in this section consider the importance of specificity in EAP: the extent to which it is possible to identify and teach disciplinary varieties of English. Each text takes a different view of this issue and, to some extent, draws on different arguments to make its case.

Ruth Spack (1988) 'Initiating ESL students into the academic discourse community: how far should we go?' *TESOL Quarterly*, **22 (1), 29–52.**

Text B1.1
R. Spack

This text by Ruth Spack has received considerable attention as a critique of the aims and methods of EAP. Essentially, the text emerges from an American liberal arts tradition of undergraduate education in which all first-year students are required to pass courses in essay writing. Largely hostile to 'vocational' or disciplinary-oriented writing, these courses tend to focus on personal essays, responses to reading and synthesizing information which often draw on readings from literature, history, human relations and popular culture. Writing is seen to improve through practice, revision and discussion of topics of interest to students. Here Spack argues that academic genres across disciplines share certain features. She argues that teachers of English should not be asked to teach genres of academic disciplines to which they do not belong and instead maintains that they should teach the academic writing process, focusing on 'appropriate inquiry strategies, planning, drafting, consulting, revising, and editing'. The approach is therefore based on processes of learning guided by analysing and synthesizing readings that represent a variety of genres and subjects.

Task B1.1.1: Before you read

➤ Look back at Section A (Unit A1) and review the discussion concerning specificity and the reasons for and against teaching the discourses of the disciplines.

Task B1.1.2: As you read

➤ Note the main reasons Spack gives for her view that 'we are justified in teaching general academic writing' and that 'we should leave the teaching of writing in the disciplines to the teachers of those disciplines'.

➤ Think of arguments, or examples based on your own experiences as a student or a teacher, to support or challenge these views.

➤ Consider the implications of Spack's views for teaching academic writing in EAP classes.

My concern stems from what I perceive to be a disturbing trend in L2 writing instruction, a trend that has been influenced both by the Writing Across the Curriculum (WAC) movement in L1 writing instruction and the English for specific purposes (ESP) movement in L2 instruction. This trend towards having teachers of English, including teachers of freshman composition, teach students to write in disciplines other than English may lead many in the composition field to assign papers that they are ill-equipped to handle. The purpose of this article is to remind teachers of English that we are justified in teaching general academic writing and to argue that we should leave the teaching of writing in the disciplines to the teachers of those disciplines.

Several L1 programs have been instituted to introduce students to the methods of inquiry in various disciplines. In typical programs, English teachers have collaborated with teachers in other disciplines, such as biology (Wilkinson, 1985), psychology (Faigley and Hansen, 1985), and sociology (Faigley and Hansen, 1985), linking the compositions to subject matter in another course. Investigations of these programs reveal some obvious advantages: students learn new forms of writing which as professionals they might need; they have more time to write, since there is less reading due to the fact that one subject matter is employed for two courses; and their discussions of student papers are more informative, since knowledge is shared among class members.

However, the disadvantages of such a program are equally, if not more, significant, as Wilkinson (1985) and others show, and should be of great concern to the English teacher. First of all, it is difficult for a writing course to have a carefully planned pedagogical or rhetorical rationale when it is dependent on another content course; furthermore, the timing of assignments is not always optimal. Second, the program can raise false expectations among the faculty as well as among the students. English faculty, even when they collaborate with content teachers, find they have little basis for dealing with the content. They therefore find themselves in the uncomfortable position of being less knowledgeable than their students. Students likewise can resent finding themselves in a situation in which their instructor cannot fully explain or answer questions about the subject matter. Faigley and Hansen (1985) observed collaborative courses in which completely different criteria for evaluation were applied to students' papers by the two teachers because the English teacher did not recognize when a student failed to demonstrate adequate knowledge of a discipline or showed a good grasp of new knowledge.

The same phenomenon can hold true in L2 writing instruction. Pearson (1983) finds that 'the instructor cannot always conveniently divorce the teaching of form from the understanding of content' (pp. 396–397). This drawback is often mentioned only in passing in articles recommending that English teachers use technical and scientific materials they are not familiar with (see Hill, Soppelsa, and West, 1982). But the lack of control over content on the part of English teachers who teach in the other disciplines is a serious problem.

It seems that only the rare individual teacher can learn another discipline, for each discipline offers a different system for examining experience, a different angle for looking at subject matter, a different kind of thinking (Maimon *et al.*, 1981). Furthermore, whereas the transmission of a discipline within content courses primarily requires that students comprehend, recall, and display information in examinations, writing in the disciplines

> requires a complete, active, struggling engagement with the facts and principles of a discipline, an encounter with the discipline's texts and the incorporation of them into one's own work, the framing of one's knowledge within the myriad conventions that help define a discipline, the persuading of other investigators that one's knowledge is legitimate.
>
> (Rose, 1985, p. 359)

The teaching of writing in a discipline, then, involves even more specialized knowledge and skills than does the teaching of the subject matter itself.

The difficulty of teaching writing in another discipline is compounded when we realize that within each discipline, such as the social sciences, there are subdisciplines, each with its own set of conventions. Reflection on personal events, for example, is considered legitimate evidence in sociology and anthropology, but not in behavioral psychology (Rose, 1983). Even within subdisciplines, such as anthropology, there are other subdisciplines with their own sets of conventions. The articles of physical anthropologists, for example, resemble those of natural scientists, whereas those of cultural anthropologists sometimes resemble those of literary scholars (Faigley and Hansen, 1985).

To further complicate matters, no discipline is static. In virtually all academic disciplines there is controversy concerning the validity of approaches, controversy that nonspecialists are usually unaware of until it is covered in the popular media (see, for example, Silk, 1987, for a discussion of the recent debate between political and anthropological historians). In addition, the principles of reasoning in a discipline may change over time, even in science, which is affected by the emergence of new mathematical techniques, new items of apparatus, and even new philosophical precepts (Yearley, 1981). Formal scientific papers, then, though often considered final statements of facts, are primarily contributions to scientific debate (Yearley, 1981).

Even studying a finished product – whether well written or not – cannot prepare English teachers to teach students how writers in other disciplines write. A written product such as a scientific report is merely a representation of a research process, which is finally summarized for peers; it is not a representation of a writing process. To teach writing, writing teachers should teach the writing process and to teach the writing process, they should know how to write. But English teachers are not necessarily equipped to write in other disciplines. Testimony to this truth appears in the ESP literature:

> In the author's experience, every attempt to write a passage, however satisfactory it seemed on pedagogic grounds, was promptly vetoed by the Project's scientific adviser because a technical solecism of some kind had

been committed. The ESP writer, however experienced, simply does not know when a mistake of this kind is being committed.

(1984, p. 8)

To learn to write in any discipline, students must become immersed in the subject matter; this is accomplished through reading, lectures, seminars, and so on. They learn by participating in the field, by doing, by sharing, and by talking about it with those who know more. They can also learn by observing the process through which professional academic writers produce texts or, if that is not possible, by studying that process in the type of program recommended by Swales (1987) for teaching the research paper for nonnative-speaking graduate students. They will learn efficiently from teachers who have a solid grounding in the subject matter and who have been through the process themselves.

I do not deny that programs that instruct students to write in other disciplines can work. But a review of the L1 literature (Herrington, 1985) and the L2 literature (e.g., Swales, 1987) on successful programs reveals that the teachers are immersed in the discipline. For example, Herrington's (1985) study is an observation of senior-level engineering courses taught by engineering faculty. And Swales's list of publications reveals a background in scientific discourse dating back at least to 1970.

Conclusion

It is ironic that the pressure on ESL/English teachers to teach writing of other disciplines is manifesting itself at precisely the time when influential technological institutes such as the Massachusetts Institute of Technology are funding programs to increase exposure to the humanities in an effort to produce more rounded, open-minded students. The English composition course could and should be a humanities course: a place where students are provided the enrichment of reading and writing that provoke thought and foster their intellectual and ethical development.

This approach includes exploratory writing tasks that deal with making sense of thoughts and experiences. As Rose (1983) reminds us, 'making meaning for the self, ordering experience, establishing one's own relationship to it is what informs any serious writing' (p. 118). It also includes expository writing tasks that direct students to take an evaluative and analytical stance toward what they read. Each of these processes 'makes a crucial contribution to the whole of intellectual activity' (Zeiger, 1985, p. 457).

Students will mature as writers as they receive invaluable input from numerous classroom experiences and from teachers who are conversant in other disciplines. To initiate students into the academic discourse community, we do not have to change our orientation completely, assign tasks we ourselves cannot master, or limit our assignments to prescribed, rule-governed tasks. We can instead draw on our own knowledge and abilities as we strengthen and expand the knowledge and abilities of our students.

Task B1.1.3: After you read

➤ Which of Spack's arguments do you find most compelling? Why? Does the extract convince you that EAP should abandon subject-specific writing instruction?

➤ Spack argues that the most effective way of teaching academic writing is to adopt general strategies which transcend disciplines. Do you think this removes differences between disciplines to facilitate interdisciplinary conversations about writing? Or does it remove ties between EAP and other disciplines which reduce such opportunities?

➤ 'To teach writing, writing teachers should teach the writing process and to teach the writing process, they should know how to write.' How far do you think general reading and writing academic tasks prepare ESL students to meet the cultural and linguistic difficulties they face at university? What else can be done to help students become aware of the specific demands of their target academic cultures?

Ken Hyland (2002) 'Specificity revisited: how far should we go now?' *English for Specific Purposes*, 21, 385–95.

Text B1.2
K. Hyland

As the title suggests, this text was written as a later response to, and critique of, Spack. The article challenges her view that EAP should focus on the academic writing process and ignore disciplinary differences. From a position informed by text analysis and social constructionism, this text argues that we are now in a better position to describe the literacy cultures of different academic majors more precisely and with more confidence, making subject-specific EAP more effective.

Task B1.2.1: Before you read

➤ Consider how you might respond to the views expressed in Spack's text above. Look back at your notes on Spack and think about her assertions in the light of current understandings. Do you know of any developments in theory, research or practice in English language teaching since it was written that might lead us to different conclusions?

Task B1.2.2: As you read

➤ List the reasons the author gives for taking an ESAP approach.

➤ Consider how far the arguments in this text engage with those of Spack and what further issues you would like to see addressed in this debate.

My aim here is to argue a case for specificity, that ESP involves teaching the literacy skills which are appropriate to the purposes and understandings of particular communities, and hopefully stimulate a debate through which we can critically examine our practices as teachers.

K. Hyland

Different strokes for different folks

The discourses of the academy do not form an undifferentiated, unitary mass but a variety of subject-specific literacies. Disciplines have different views of knowledge, different research practices, and different ways of seeing the world, and as a result, investigating the practices of those disciplines will inevitably take us to greater specificity.

The idea of professional communities, each with its own particular practices, genres, and communicative conventions, thus leads us towards a specific role for ESP. But this is not to deny that students also cross boundaries. They inhabit complex academic and social worlds, moving outside their disciplines to take elective courses, discussing problems and assignments with peers, lecturers and advisers, and engaging in a disparate range of spoken and written genres. We have to recognise, of course, that our students need to function in numerous social environments and that our courses should equip them with the necessary skills to do so. Such epistemological, ontological, social and discoursal border-crossings pose enormous challenges for students and teachers alike, but a good starting point is to recognise the literacy practices that help mark off these borders. The notion of specificity thus provides learners with a way of understanding the diversity they encounter at university. It shows them, in other words, that literacy is relative to the beliefs and practices of social groups and to the purposes of their individual members in accomplishing their goals.

The principle of specificity receives strong theoretical endorsement from the philosophical perspective of social constructionism (e.g. Bruffee, 1986; Rorty, 1979) and the critiques and extensions of it (e.g. Bizzell, 1992; Blyler and Thralls, 1993). This stresses that disciplines and professions are largely created and maintained through the distinctive ways that members jointly construct a view of the world through their discourses. We work within communities in a particular time and place, and these communities are created by our communicative practices; so writing is not just another aspect of what goes on in the professions or disciplines, it is seen as actually *producing* them. The model is of 'independent creativity disciplined by accountability to shared experience' (Richards, 1987: 200). As a result, the teaching of specific skills and rhetoric cannot be divorced from the teaching of a subject itself because what counts as convincing argument, appropriate tone, persuasive interaction, and so on, is managed for a particular audience (Berkenkotter and Huckin, 1985; Hyland, 2000, 2001).

Equally persuasively, we can also turn to a large, and very diverse, body of research evidence to back up this view of discipline and profession-specific variation. Once again, I will draw on academic writing to illustrate some of this research, but the point I want to make applies more widely to ESP taught in university contexts.

First, there is a considerable collection of survey results which show that the writing tasks students have to do at university are specific to discipline and related to educational level. In the humanities and social sciences, for example, analysing and synthesising multiple sources is important, while in science and technology, activity-based skills such as describing procedures, defining objects, and planning solutions are required (Casanave and Hubbard, 1992). In postgraduate programmes it seems that engineers give priority to describing charts, while business studies faculty require students to compare and ideas and take a position (Bridgeman and Carlson, 1984). In undergraduate classes, questionnaire data suggests that lab reports are common in chemistry, program documentation in computer science, and article surveys in maths (Wallace, 1995).

More interestingly, these differences begin to multiply when we move beyond the classifications of questionnaire designers. Genre categories blur when actual assignment hand-outs and essay scripts are considered, for example, and the structure of common formats such as the experimental lab report can differ completely across different technical and engineering disciplines (Braine, 1995). Ethnographic case studies of individual students and courses reinforce this picture, revealing marked diversities of task and texts in different fields (e.g. Candlin and Plum, 1999; Prior, 1998). It is not difficult to imagine how complicated this can become for students in joint degrees or interdisciplinary studies like business studies, for example, where a student may have to produce texts in fields as diverse as accountancy and corporate planning.

Overall then, this literature points to the fact that different disciplines identify different types of writing as features of academic literacy and that terms like *lab reports*, *lectures* or *memos* imply neither homogeneity nor permanence. Members' (or folk) taxonomies can, of course, be a useful first step into describing target contexts and are helpful in identifying what insiders see as similar and different (e.g. Swales, 1990: 54). It is, however, easy to be misled into believing there is greater similarity in the communicative resources of different communities than is actually the case. The expectations that a genre label calls to mind in one field may be very different to those it evokes in another, and we should hesitate before regarding such identifiers as objective and invariable descriptions of the ways members organise their communicative practices.

This view of multiple literacies is reinforced by text analysis research. While academic genres are often identified by their conventional surface features, they are actually forms of social action designed to accomplish socially recognised purposes with some hope of success. While such purposes are influenced by personal factors and subject to individual choices, these choices are likely to be relatively limited in practice. This is because successful academic writing depends on the individual writer's projection of a shared context. We are more likely to achieve our disciplinary purposes if we frame our messages in ways which appeal to appropriate culturally and institutionally legitimated relationships (e.g. Dillon, 1991; McDonald, 1994). This is why, for example, the so-called 'common core' features of academic prose often differ considerably in their frequency, expression and function across disciplines. Simply, the ways that writers present their arguments, control their rhetorical personality, and engage their readers reflect preferred disciplinary practices (Hyland, 2000).

One major reason for these differences in disciplinary discourses then, is that texts reveal generic activity (Berkenkotter and Huckin, 1995; Swales, 1990). They build on the writer's knowledge of prior texts and therefore exhibit repeated rhetorical responses to similar situations with each generic act involving some degree of innovation and judgement. This kind of typification not only offers the individual writer the resources to manage the complexities of disciplinary engagement, but also contributes to the stabilisation and reproduction of disciplines. This directs us to the ways disciplinary texts vary, not only in their content but in different appeals to background knowledge, different means of establishing truth, and different ways of engaging with readers.

In sum, this research shows that scholarly discourse is not uniform and monolithic, differentiated merely by specialist topics and vocabularies. It has to be seen as an outcome of a multitude of practices and strategies, where argument and engagement are crafted within specific communities that have different ideas about what is worth communicating, how it can be communicated, what readers are likely to know, how they might be persuaded, and so on (e.g. Faigley, 1985).

Putting the S back into ESP

Essentially ESP rests on the idea that we use language to accomplish purposes and engage with others as members of social groups. It is concerned with communication rather than language and with the processes by which texts are created and used as much as with texts themselves. What this means is that the field seeks to go beyond intuitive laundry lists of common core features and the autonomous views of literacy that such lists assume, to the practices of real people communicating in real contexts. A *specific* conception of ESP thus recognises that while generic labels such as 'academic English' or 'scientific English' may be a convenient shorthand for describing general varieties, they conceal a wealth of discursive complexity.

Unfortunately, however, such labels disguise variability and tend to misrepresent academic literacy as a naturalised, self-evident and non-contestable way of participating in academic communities. This in turn encourages the idea that there is one general 'academic English' (or 'business English', etc.) and one set of strategies for approaching reading and writing tasks that can be applied, in a painting-by-numbers fashion, across disciplines. By divorcing language from context, such an autonomous view of academic literacy misleads learners into believing that they simply have to master a set of rules which can be transferred across fields. As I noted above, many subject specialists also subscribe to this view, taking academic writing conventions to be unproblematically universal and unreflectively available. Because they are rarely provided with a means of conceptualising the varied epistemological frameworks of the academy, students (and teachers) are often unable to see the consequences these have for communication or distinguish differences in the disciplinary practices they encounter at university (Plum and Candlin, 2001).

By ignoring specificity, moreover, we also run the risk of creating an unbridgeable gulf between the everyday literacies that students bring with them from their homes and those that they find in the university. In such circumstances it is easy for both learners and teachers to reify these powerful academic and professional literacy practices; to see them as autonomous, abstract and beyond their control. Acquisition of disciplinary knowledge involves an encounter with a new and dominant literacy, and because academic ability is frequently evaluated in terms of competence in this literacy, students often find their own literacy practices to be marginalised and regarded as failed attempts to approximate these standard forms. So, by detaching academic literacy from its social consequences, it is easy to see communication difficulties as learners' own weaknesses and for ESP to become an exercise in language repair. The only way to counter this is to bring these practices back to earth by targeting specific contexts and drawing on the experiences of our learners. Only by taking the notion of specificity seriously can ESP find ways to undermine a 'single literacy' view and to replace 'remedial' approaches to teaching with those that address students' own perceptions and practices of writing.

Together all this leads to the important conclusion that expertise in a subject means being able to use its discourses in the specific ways that one's readers are likely to find effective and persuasive. While we may often talk about reports, memos, oral presentations, and so on as overarching genres and universal skills, these take on meaning only when they are situated in real contexts of use. Put simply, students do not learn in a cultural vacuum: their disciplinary activities are a central part of their engagement with others in their disciplines and they communicate effectively only by using its particular conventions appropriately.

ESP therefore involves developing new kinds of literacy, equipping students with the communicative skills to participate in particular academic and professional cultural contexts. Establishing exactly what are the specific language, skills, and genres of particular groups on which we need to base learning priorities may well be expensive, time-consuming and skill-intensive. But it is this research which both makes our teaching effective and our practices professional, and we should not give these up easily. There is, then, only one possible response to the question posed in the title of this paper: effective language teaching in the universities involves taking specificity seriously. It means that we must go as far as we can.

Task B1.2.3: After you read

➤ 'The discourses of the academy do not form an undifferentiated, unitary mass but a variety of subject-specific literacies.' What evidence does the author give for this assertion? Do you find the argument convincing?

➤ Hyland emphasizes the importance of distinct 'academic cultural contexts' as a reason for adopting a subject-specific approach. How far do you agree with the view that the disciplines comprise different 'cultures'?

➤ The text draws on different areas of research to support ESAP. Give further examples of research you know of which might contribute to this debate.

➤ Having read the two texts, do you think EAP sufficiently relates theory to practice or do you see a gap between the two?

Unit B2
Study skills or academic literacy?

The issue of an appropriate model for EAP is a central question for how we view our field, formulate our goals, construct our pedagogies and pursue our aims. The reading in this section has been influential in formulating some of the key elements involved in this debate and arguing for a particular way of viewing language instruction in higher education.

Text B2.1
M. Lea and
B. Street

Mary R. Lea and Brian V. Street (2000) 'Student writing and staff feedback in higher education: an academic literacies approach.' In M. Lea and B. Steiner (eds), *Student writing in higher education: new contexts*. Milton Keynes: Open University Press.

In this extract Mary Lea and Brian Street set out an 'academic literacies' model of writing in higher education. While neither of these authors works in EAP, they have long been concerned with student writing and with understanding textual practices in the university. Their work is situated in a British tradition known as the 'New Literacy Studies' and, indeed, Street is a leading figure in this movement (Street, 1993, 1995). This view sees literacy as something people do, an activity rather than a cognitive ability in people's heads. Instead of treating language as a thing, distanced from teacher and learner and imposing external rules on them, it is located in the interactions between people acting in particular social contexts. In this text the authors set out what this means for academic writing. They consider three conceptions of what is involved in writing within the university for students: a study skills model, a socialization model, and an academic literacies model, each successive model encapsulating the one before it to expand the contexts it applies to.

Task B2.1.1: Before you read

➤ Consider the changes in university education in your own country in recent years discussed in Unit A2 to help you contextualize the extract, particularly:

■ The increasingly different and complex courses in the modern university.

■ The growing number of students from 'non-traditional' backgrounds.

■ The developing research of the textual and communicative demands made on students.

Task B2.1.2: As you read

➤ Note Lea and Street's three models of student writing in higher education and consider how far these can be used to characterize EAP.

➤ Reflect on the divisions between teacher and student interpretations of writing requirements and what might be done to bring these together.

➤ Think about whether Lea and Street's description of undergraduate student experiences matches your own. Is this an accurate picture of how students encounter the academy?

Academic literacies

M. Lea and
B. Street

Learning in higher education involves adapting to new ways of knowing: new ways of understanding, interpreting and organizing knowledge. Academic literacy practices – reading and writing within disciplines – constitute central processes through which students learn new subjects and develop their knowledge about new areas of study. A practices approach to literacy takes account of the cultural and contextual component of writing and reading practices, and this in turn has important implications for our understanding of issues of student learning. Educational research into student learning in higher education has tended to concentrate on ways in which students can be helped to adapt their practices to those of the university (Gibbs 1994): from this perspective, the codes and conventions of academia can be taken as given. In contrast, our research is founded on the premise that in order to understand the nature of academic learning, it is important to investigate the understandings of both academic staff and students about their own literacy practices without making prior assumptions as to which practices are either appropriate or effective. This is particularly important in trying to develop a more complex analysis of what it means to become academically literate.

The notion of academic literacies has been developed from the area of 'new literacy studies' (Barton 1994; Baynham 1995a; Street 1984), as an attempt to draw out the implications of this approach for our understanding of issues of student learning. We have argued elsewhere (Lea and Street 1997a) that educational research into student writing in higher education has fallen into three main perspectives or models: study skills; academic socialization; and academic literacies (see Figure 1).

The models are not mutually exclusive, and we would not want to view them in a simple linear time dimension, whereby one model supersedes or replaces the insights provided by another. Rather, we would like to think that each model successively encapsulates those above it, so that the academic socialization perspective takes account of study skills but includes them in the broader context of the acculturation processes we describe below, and likewise the academic literacies approach encapsulates the academic socialization model, building on the insights developed there as well as the study skills view.

M. Lea and
B. Street

The academic literacies model, then, incorporates both of the other models into a more encompassing understanding of the nature of student writing within institutional practices, power relations and identities, as we explain below. We take a hierarchical view of the relationship between the three models, privileging the 'academic literacies' approach. We believe that in teaching as well as in research, addressing specific skills issues around student writing, such as how to open or close an essay or whether to use the first person, takes on an entirely different meaning if the context is solely that of study skills, if the process is seen as part of academic socialization, or if it is viewed more broadly as an aspect of the whole institutional and epistemological context. We explicate each model in turn as both a summary of our major findings in the research project and as a set of lenses through which to view the account we give of the research.

The study skills approach has assumed that literacy is a set of atomized skills which students have to learn and which are then transferable to other contexts. The focus is on attempts to 'fix' problems with student learning, which are treated as a kind of pathology. The theory of language on which it is based emphasizes surface features, grammar and spelling. Its sources lie in behavioural psychology and training programmes and it conceptualizes student writing as technical and instrumental. In recent years the crudity and insensitivity of this approach have led to refinement of the meaning of 'skills' involved and attention to broader issues of learning and social context, what we (Lea and Street 1997a) have termed the 'academic socialization' approach.

From the academic socialization perspective, the task of the tutor/adviser is to inculcate students into a new 'culture', that of the academy. The sources of this perspective lie in social psychology, in anthropology and in constructivist education. Although more sensitive both to the student as learner and to the cultural context, the approach could nevertheless be criticized on a number of grounds. It appears to assume that the academy is a relatively homogeneous culture, whose norms and practices have simply to be learnt to provide access to the whole institution. Even though at some level disciplinary and departmental difference may be acknowledged, institutional practices, including processes of change and the exercise of power, do not seem to be sufficiently theorized. Similarly, despite the fact that contextual factors in student writing are recognized as important (Hounsell 1988; Taylor *et al.* 1988), this approach tends to treat writing as a transparent medium of representation and so fails to address the deep language, literacy and discourse issues involved in the institutional production and representation of meaning.

The third approach, the one most closely allied to the 'new literacy studies', we refer to as academic literacies. This approach sees literacies as social practices, in the way we have suggested above. It views student writing and learning as issues at the level of epistemology and identities rather than skill or socialization. An academic literacies approach views the institutions in which academic practices take place as constituted in, and as sites of, discourse and power. It sees the literacy demands of the curriculum as involving a variety of communicative practices, including genres, fields and disciplines. From the student point of view a dominant feature of academic literacy practices is the requirement to switch practices between one setting and another, to deploy a repertoire of linguistic practices appropriate to each setting, and to handle the social meanings and identities that each evokes. This emphasis on identities and social meanings draws attention to deep affective and ideological conflicts in such switching and use of the linguistic repertoire. A student's personal identity – who am 'I'? – may be challenged by the forms of writing required in different

M. Lea and
B. Street

Study skills

Student deficit

- 'fix it': atomized skills; surface language, grammar, spelling
- sources: behavioural and experimental psychology; programmed learning

Student writing as technical and instrumental skill

Academic socialization

Acculturation of students into academic discourse

- inculcating students into new 'culture'; focus on student orientation to learning and interpretation of learning task, e.g. 'deep', 'surface', 'strategic' learning; homogeneous 'culture'; lack of focus on institutional practices, change and power
- sources: social psychology; anthropology; constructivism

Student writing as transparent medium of representation

Academic literacies

Students' negotiation of conflicting literacy practices

- literacies as social practices; at level of epistemology and identities; institutions as sites of/constituted in discourses and power; variety of communicative repertoire, e.g. genres, fields, disciplines; switching with respect to linguistic practices, social meanings and identities
- sources: 'new literacy studies'; critical discourse analysis; systemic functional linguistics; cultural anthropology

Student writing as meaning making and contested

Figure 1 Models of student writing in higher education

disciplines, notably prescriptions about the use of impersonal and passive forms as opposed to first person and active forms, and students may feel threatened and resistant – 'this isn't me' (Lea 1994; Ivanic 1998).

The recognition of this level of engagement with student writing, as opposed to the more straightforward study skills and academic socialization approaches, comes from the social and ideological orientation of the new literacy studies. Allied to this is work in critical discourse analysis, systemic functional linguistics and cultural anthropology which has come to see student writing as being concerned with the processes of meaning-making and contestation around this meaning rather than as skills or deficits. There is a growing body of literature based upon this approach, which suggests that one explanation for student writing problems might be the gaps between academic staff expectations and student interpretations of what is involved in student writing.

Requirements of student writing: staff interpretations

The interviews with staff would suggest that academic staff have their own fairly well-defined views regarding what constitute the elements of a good piece of student writing in the areas in which they teach. These tend to refer to form in a more generic sense, including attention to syntax, punctuation and layout and to such apparently

M. Lea and
B. Street

evident components of rational essay writing as 'structure', 'argument' and 'clarity'. Their own disciplinary history had a clear influence on staff conceptualizations and representations of what were the most important elements to look for in students' writing at both levels, although the epistemological and methodological issues that underlay them were often expressed through the surface features and components of 'writing' itself. It was this confusion, we argue, that led to difficulties for students not yet acquainted with the disciplinary underpinnings of faculty feedback. This confusion was compounded by the move towards multi-disciplinary courses at degree level and the modular system that was fully in place at one of the universities. As a result, although faculty understanding of student writing was often described in disciplinary terms, for example, 'In history the use of evidence is particularly important', or 'In English we are looking for clarity of expression', in practice staff were often teaching within programmes which integrated a number of disciplinary approaches and where the writing requirements consequently varied.

Despite this variation in modes of writing across disciplines and fields of study, many staff we interviewed were still mainly influenced by specific conceptualizations of their own disciplines or subject areas in their assessments of students' writing. The twin concepts of 'structure' and 'argument' came to the fore in most interviews as being key elements in student writing, terms which we examine more closely below. Even though staff generally had a clear belief in these concepts as crucial to their understanding of what constituted a successful piece of writing, there was less certainty when it came to describing what underlay a well-argued or well-structured piece of student work. More commonly, they were able to identify when a student had been successful, but could not describe how a particular piece of writing 'lacked' structure. We suggest that, in practice, what makes a piece of student writing 'appropriate' has more to do with issues of epistemology than with the surface features of form to which staff often have recourse when describing their students' writing. That is to say, underlying, often disciplinary, assumptions about the nature of knowledge affected the meaning given to the terms 'structure' and 'argument'. Since these assumptions varied with context, it is not valid to suggest that such concepts are generic and transferable, or represent 'common sense ways of knowing' (Fairclough 1992b), as the reference to 'writing problems' frequently implied.

Writing requirements: student interpretations

The research interviews with students revealed a number of different interpretations and understandings of what students thought that they were meant to be doing in their writing. Students described taking 'ways of knowing' (Baker *et al.* 1995) and of writing from one course into another only to find that their attempt to do this was unsuccessful and met with negative feedback. Students were consciously aware of switching between diverse writing requirements and knew that their task was to unpack what kind of writing any particular assignment might require. This was at a more complex level than genre, such as the 'essay' or 'report', lying more deeply at the level of writing particular knowledge in a specific academic setting.

Students knew that variations of form existed, but admitted that their real writing difficulties lay in trying to gauge the deeper levels of variation in knowledge and how to set about writing them. It was much more than using the correct terminology or just learning to do 'academic writing' – as what we term the 'academic socialization' model would suggest – and more about adapting previous knowledge of writing practices, academic and other, to varied university settings.

The conflicting advice received from academic teaching staff in different courses added to the confusion. For example, in some areas students were specifically directed to outline in detail what would follow in the main body of a traditional essay, while other tutors would comment 'I do not want to know what you are going to say'. Many different conventions were to be found around the use of the first person pronoun in student writing. Even within the same courses, individual tutors had different opinions about when or if it was appropriate to use this. Such conventions were often presented as self-evidently the correct way in which things should be done.

Students' perceptions were influenced by their own experiences of writing within and outside higher education. An example of this was the A level entrant who came unstuck when she wrote a history essay drawing on just one textual source as she regularly and successfully had done in English. Similarly, a BTEC entrant to the traditional university had worked in industry for five years and was used to extensive succinct report writing, but, when confronted with a traditional essay text in politics, as part of a course in public administration and management, he had no idea how to go about writing this piece of work.

Task B2.1.3: After you read

➤   Are you convinced by Lea and Street's argument for an academic literacies conception of student writing? Why or why not? What might some counter-arguments to their view be?

➤   Lea and Street are very critical and dismissive of the study skills and academic socialization approaches. To what extent do you think their representation of these models is comprehensive and fair?

➤   Think about the implications of each perspective for teaching academic writing in EAP classes. How might each one translate into concrete materials and tasks? Devise one task for each approach.

➤   'From the student point of view a dominant feature of academic literacy practices is the requirement to switch practices between one setting and another, to deploy a repertoire of linguistic practices appropriate to each setting, and to handle the social meanings and identities that each evokes.' What might this mean for the ways EAP teachers approach their work?

➤   The academic literacies model was based on research into L1 students' experiences. How far do you think it relates to the needs and experiences of L2 learners?

➤   How might EAP teachers work with subject specialists to overcome the mismatched expectations and misunderstandings discussed in the text?

Unit B3
Lingua franca or *Tyrannosaurus rex*?

The impact of English on other languages and on the users of those languages has been hotly debated in English language teaching and perhaps no more so than in the field of EAP. A number of key issues are raised in the text in this section.

Text B3.1
J. Swales

John M. Swales (1997) 'English as *Tyrannosaurus rex.*' World Englishes, 16, 373–82.

In this very personal paper, John Swales, one of the leading figures in EAP over the past twenty-five years, reassesses his position on the role of English in academic contexts. In the paper Swales admits to a certain equanimity about the role of English in the past, viewing it as an essentially benign movement assisting L2 students to survive and flourish in an anglophone academic world. He now, however, asks whether English has become too successful, at the expense of many other languages and the loss of alternative rhetorical practices and attitudes.

Task B3.1.1: Before you read

➤ Review the discussion in Section A concerning English as academic lingua franca or *Tyrannosaurus rex* and think about your own experiences or struggles in respect to these issues.

Task B3.1.2: As you read

➤ Consider Swales's argument and note what seem to be the main sources of evidence he draws on to support his claims and the main consequences he gives of the seemingly inexorable growth of English.

J. Swales

Triumphalist English

I want to move the concern to another area more directly relevant to my own occupations and preoccupations. This is not the loss of languages *per se*, but the loss of specialized registers in otherwise healthy languages as a clear consequence of the global advance of English. This advance is taking many forms, and has been much investigated (see Kachru, 1994, for a synopsis) so the treatment here of the relevant phenomena will be highly selective. In a recent *Scientific American*, Wayt Gibbs, in an article entitled 'Lost science in the Third World', calculates that in 1994 no less than 31 percent of all papers published in mainstream journals emanated from the USA. Japan was next with only 8 percent. Sample percentages from countries with large university systems are: Brazil, 0.6 percent, and Mexico and Egypt with around 0.3 percent. Such wrenching disproportions thus structurate (Giddens, 1984) America's role as the global academic gate-keeper. Second, the trend to English (in whatever 'nuclear' or 'interlanguage' form it manifests itself) is accelerating as computer-mediated developments such as the World Wide Web accelerate. Third, this trend continues to be reported in largely triumphalist terms by anglophone commentators, who continue, for example, to poke fun at efforts by the French government to maintain both the viability of the French language and its historically Gallic character.

Fourth, valiant and interesting attempts by critics like Phillipson and Pennycook to undermine this triumphalist rhetoric by relating it to new manifestations of neo colonialism, to the consumerist marketing of English as a 'worldly' global commodity, now seen as the lingua franca of the 'haute bourgeoisie' around the world, or to the defence of socio-political structures that rely on linguistic overclasses and under-classes for their survival, will likely fall on deaf ears in the anglophone majoritarian cultures, however much their criticism may be discussed and appreciated in smaller speech and discourse communities around the world.

I am not so sanguine. Indeed, I have belatedly come to recognize a certain deception in my 30-year involvement with English for Academic Purposes. Certainly in the 1970s I accepted the position which argued that what Third World countries needed was a rapid acceleration in their resources of human capital, which could be achieved by a hurried transmission of Western technical and scientific know-how delivered through the medium of English and supported by appropriate EAP programs. I also believed working overseas in scientific English, as researcher, materials writer and teacher, was in essence, a culturally and politically neutral enterprise, and thus one somehow dim from the oftentimes-quaint efforts of the British Council, USIS, The Alliance France and the Goethe institute to promote the glories of their national cultures in unlikely exotic and underprivileged venues. In doing so, I conveniently overlooked the links between the teaching of technical languages and the manufacture and export of technical equipment. So, when I read, say, Phillipson's counter-culture account of how British ESL created an academic and commercial base for itself, I find myself caught up in a serious reflection. I now see how ESP's 'accommodationist' and 'technocratic' stance about the value of English as a wider window on the world has paved the way for enormous resources that, both publicly and privately, have accrued to ESL.

However, as we know, it is in other areas such as the media (film, theater, television, pop music, radio, print journalism) that the concern about English domination is greater. It is doubtful, for example, whether a recognizedly world-class Swedish-language oeuvre like that of Ingmar Bergman's will be possible in the next half-century. Apart from these areas, there is also growing concern about register loss in the world of scholarship. There are several aspects that need to be considered. First, there are the attempts being made to create and foster modern scientific varieties of languages – what Philippino scholars Gonzalez and Battista call 'edulects' (quoted in Honey, 1994); more specifically, the attempts to nurture scientific or academic varieties of languages such as Swahili, Arabic, Bahasa Melayu, Hebrew and Pilipino. We can note that these are all non-Western languages with their principal homes below the Mediterranean or below the Equator, and thus a case can be made for their support for reasons of addressing North–South imbalance alone. Of course, the evolution of such registers is fraught with difficulties. To our shame, one is a relative lack of interest in them on the part of linguists and applied linguists. Another is the well-attested tendency of off-center scholars to try and publish 'their best in the West,' offering more minor works for local publication. A third, and relatively new trend, is for promotion in Third World countries (and many others) to become much more directly tied to publication in international refereed journals. This is by no means inevitably a sensible policy, because, in some fields, perhaps most crucially in agricultural and ecological sciences and in preventive medicine, the advantages of developing local research and publication traditions are clearly of benefit to many parties, from government ministers, to those concerned with environmental issues, to agricultural extension officers.

The loss of professionally-marked registers has several fairly obvious consequences and some less obvious ones. One of the latter is the loss of professional speech differentiation for the purposes of literary characterization, for entertainment and for parody. If nobody talks and writes any more like a medical professor or a research scientist, or even an avant-garde critic, because all these roles are now occupied by English, then creative national allure is itself impoverished. While I suppose that nobody would question that religious scholars need to know the languages, such as Sanskrit, Hebrew, New Testament Greek and Arabic, wherein the founding texts were originally created, nobody seems to recognize that Swedish has actually been the vehicle for much of this century for articulating the most developed forms of social democracy and the welfare state, or that, as Grafton (1994) has brilliantly showed for history, it is German scholarship that has elaborated and maintained the persuasive rhetorical device of the footnote, and as Clyne (1987) has suggested, it is German that has developed the Exkurs, inevitably and pejoratively glossed in English, as 'digression.' Ongstad, himself a Scandinavian, has observed that when a culture starts to lose its genres, it begins to die (Ongstad, 1992). As for those who would argue that fighting against an inexorable trend is just naive sentimentalism, there is Mauranen's 'cultural rainforest' argument to parallel Fishman's: 'Insofar as rhetorical practices embody cultural thought patterns, we should encourage the maintenance of variety and diversity in academic rhetorical practices – excessive standardization may counteract innovation and creative thought by forcing them into standard forms' (Mauranen, 1993b: 172).

Mauranen's back-up strategy is to accept that, in her case, scholarly writing in Finnish is not likely to long survive outside of various kinds of Finnish studies themselves. But does this mean, she asks, that if we have to use English for academic publications, we have to use it just like the anglophones? Her own research shows that Finnish rhetoric differs considerably from Anglo-American rhetoric, being more implicit, being more poetic, being less-inclined to market its text metadiscoursally, and so on (Mauranen, 1993a). Should we not try, she argues, to preserve our Finnish rhetorical traditions in another and much more widely distributed tongue? And how can we persuade the majoritarian anglophone cultures to accommodate our concerns and thus accept rhetorical – if not linguistic – diversity? While there are again many questions that arise about the transference of cultural traditions in this way and what indeed might be preserved within the matrix of another language, Mauranen's arguments should cause us to reflect soberly on anglophone gate-keeping practices.

Gate-keepers would no longer be able to get away with saying that 'these foreigners just don't know how to frame issues and arguments in ways that we feel comfortable with,' because those foreigners would no longer be trying to do those things in the first place.

Educational implications

As might be expected, a number of the foregoing reflections and concerns leak into my educational practice. My current main EAP activity is as teacher of my institute's two most advanced writing courses: Research Paper Writing; and Thesis and Dissertation Writing. These courses carry graduate credit and consist of NNS volunteers who come from all across the university. To my surprise this heterogeneity has turned out to be a great advantage. In contrast to what I know of most other advanced writing courses, in my case there is no shared content, no shared outside courses, no shared methodology and little direct competition among the participants. In consequence, everybody soon realizes that the one thing that we do share is an interest in rhetoric and discourse in all its diverse academic manifestations. The general orientation of these courses is well captured by Belcher and Braine's introduction:

> The approach to demystification of Anglophone academic discourse is . . . neither a socio-therapeutic one of open resistance to academic oppression . . . nor a psychotherapeutic approach committed to helping students find some 'unified or stable subjectivity'. It is, rather, an approach informed by a belief in the power of explicit cognitive awareness of the texts, subtexts, and contexts of academic discourse to enable individuals to join collectivist endeavors that academic communities are without loss of the 'home perspectives' that Bizzell . . . has often spoken of (1995: xv).

I would like to suggest that the approach is a kind of liberation theology, especially if it frees my students from the overarching dominance of anglophone native-speakerism, from consuming attention to the ritualistic surfaces of their texts, from an authoritative and received world view of academic and technical text as 'objective,' and from a dependence on imitation, on formulas, and on cut-and-paste anthologies of other writers' fragments.

Task B3.1.3: After you read

➤ Are you convinced by Swales's arguments? Which of his arguments do you feel are most and least persuasive?

➤ Swales observes that the spread of English 'is reported in largely triumphalist terms by anglophone commentators' who also ridicule efforts of others to protect their native language. Are countries right to defend their national language against English? What is lost with the loss of a language's academic register?

➤ Swales points to the particular plight of non-Western languages. Do you agree that these languages are more vulnerable? Why?

➤ Swales cites 'Mauranen's back-up strategy' of adopting English for academic publication but maintaining indigenous rhetorical traditions to preserve diversity. How feasible a goal do you think this is?

➤ What are the pedagogical implications of demystifying English academic rhetoric? What might Swales's 'liberation theology' look like in practice?

Unit B4
Pragmatism or critique?

The two readings in this unit represent polar views of EAP theory and practice, addressing ethical issues in teaching and whether, in assisting learners toward an academic communicative competence, we reinforce conformity to institutional hierarchies and values.

Desmond Allison (1996) 'Pragmatist discourse and English for Academic Purposes.' *English for Specific Purposes*, **15 (2), 85–103.**

Text B4.1
D. Allison

Allison's text is itself a response to earlier work by Benesch and Pennycook questioning what they saw as Swales's (1990) 'pragmatic' view of EAP and the impact of such practices on students. The text is a spirited defence of pragmatism in EAP. Drawing on the work of teachers in a variety of situations, Allison illustrates how curricular and instructional innovations often challenge existing views and function to help students succeed despite considerable contextual constraints. In doing so he argues that pragmatism is not a unified ideology which supports the *status quo* of unequal power but a contextually sensitive response to student needs and teaching conditions.

Task B4.1.1: Before you read

➤ In a journal such as the *Modern English Teacher, ELTJ, TESOL Journal, TESOL Matters, Guidelines* or the *English Teaching Forum*, find an account of an EAP teaching practice. Consider the extent to which the practice represents an innovative response to local constraints which brings about changes in curricular practices and relations and how far it reinforces existing practices and accommodates students to dominant power relations.

Task B4.1.2: As you read

➤ Make a list of the main features and aims of 'pragmatic EAP' from both Allison's statements about it and the illustrative examples he provides.

D. Allison

A pragmatic goal for EAP?

Without suggesting that all pragmatically minded people in EAP share a single goal that they would formulate identically, I am ready to follow Santos (1992) in taking comments by Swales (1990) to be broadly characteristic of pragmatic thinking and values in EAP. Swales's declared pragmatic concern was 'to help people, both non-native and native speakers, to develop their academic communicative competence' (Swales 1990: 9), and I believe that many EAP pragmatists would look favourably on such an aim in the context of their work. Swales's comments have, however, been criticised by Benesch (1993) and Pennycook (1994a, 1995b) because they are associated with a decision not to consider 'differences that arise as a result of differing ideological perspectives' in pursuing his purposes (Swales 1990: 9).

Benesch (1993) expresses her belief that 'the self-professed pragmatism of many EAP advocates . . . actually indicates an accommodationist ideology, an endorsement of traditional academic teaching and of current power relations in academia and in society' (p. 711): this ideology is one that 'aims to assimilate ESL students uncritically into academic life' (p. 714). Pennycook (1994a) represents Santos (1992) as suggesting that a tendency to stress the pragmatic at the expense of the ideological 'allows' Swales (1990) to 'sweep aside the ideological implications of discourse communities and genres' (Pennycook 1994a: 120). More generally, Pennycook charges that 'the possibilities of dealing with broader social, cultural or political contexts of discourse are denied by appeal to an ideology of pragmatism' (Pennycook 1994a: 12–121). Elsewhere, he makes clear that his criticism of the ideology of pragmatism 'does not just apply to genre-based approaches' (Pennycook 1994b: 15), but implicates EAP in general.

At least two related aspects of Swales's (1990) position, and of pragmatism in EAP, appear to have been ignored or misunderstood in these accounts. First, Swales has not disputed that a commitment to helping people develop their academic communicative competence is itself an ideological stance. I am surprised that it should appear, or be represented as less than evident, that ideology is at issue here. EAP teaching concerns clearly stand in ideological contrast, for example, with elitist 'sink or swim' traditions in which students are simply left to come to terms for themselves with all that is involved in academic discourse. EAP traditions are also clearly opposed to the reductive view that 'language teaching' is and should be limited to 'establishing the fundamental sentence patterns of the language'.

Secondly, Swales (1990) makes clear that the definitions being proposed for 'genre' and 'discourse community' are those that the author believes will effectively serve his pedagogical purpose of helping people develop their academic communicative competence. . . . Swales has developed an account of *discourse communities* and the *genres* they use that does not exclude, by definition, the possibility that differing ideological perspectives (e.g., different schools of economic theory) will sometimes compete or coexist within the same 'discourse community' (e.g., that of economists). That is a principled choice for a stated purpose, not an airy dismissal of ideological perspectives and differences. Swales (1990) takes the view that the definitions and criteria he has put forward may better serve to help incoming students (starting out as academic outsiders) to develop an understanding of what academic communication is like and how it operates.

EAP pragmatism at work

D. Allison

This section will briefly review a number of experiences reported in the EAP literature and relate them to ideological questions and values within published discourse in EAP. 'EAP pragmatism' is taken to cover the thinking and value judgements that underlie context-sensitive approaches to EAP curricular issues and that pursue the art of the possible within these contexts of understanding, action and evaluation. EAP pragmatism can be observed at work across a range of geographical, educational and cultural settings. My focus will be on undergraduate teaching. The five examples below illustrate varying degrees of curricular innovation, and of modification and challenge to prevailing practices, in the light of what has appeared possible and important to people working in different situations.

Love (1991) found that geology students and faculty at the University of Zimbabwe reported themselves as dissatisfied with the students' abilities to cope with tertiary textbooks. Love points out that the textbooks in question had not been written with an ESL readership or a local context in mind. She identified the main obstacle for students as a lack of appropriate content schemata to help them interpret geology texts, rather than an unfamiliarity with formal schemata for textbook organisation.

Love found considerable differences in the ways in which the authors set out to introduce and acculturate students to the subject. Despite these differences, Love concluded that awareness of geological processes and their products could offer a valuable frame of reference for readers of either textbook, and in principle in work with other geology texts as well. Love expresses the hope that more research of this kind can 'provide the ESP teacher with tools for assisting students to acquire literacy in their specific areas of study' (p. 102).

Although many EAP teachers and researchers will recognise the kind of circumstances in which Love was working, some features are worth specifying here. The choice of textbooks for the subject course appears to have been limited both by resources and by the fact that locally situated texts in the subject did not yet exist. . . . Immediate possibilities for change, though, were probably quite restricted. The case for working with a single core textbook is not discussed by Love (1991), but textbooks are quite commonly assumed to provide students with guidance and support. A condition, obviously, is that students can understand and work with the text, which is precisely the concern that Love's intervention seeks to address. Although Love's declared goal of 'assisting students to acquire literacy in their specific areas of study' might be interpreted by some critics as inherently accommodationist, I would suggest that we would need to know far more about pedagogic aims and strategies before any such judgement could reasonably be either warranted or refuted. A more positively speculative interpretation of such goals in EAP, however, would place them firmly within an ESL teaching tradition, going back at least to Palmer (1921), which is concerned to eliminate bewilderment among students so that learning in any form is better able to take place.

Flowerdew (1993) reports that extreme reading difficulties were identified among science students at Sultan Qaboos University, Oman, relative to prescribed course materials. After consultation with science faculty members, EAP staff eventually produced simplified versions of the core reading material so that students' comprehension opportunities were enhanced and so that their abilities could continue to develop. These materials became the required reading in support of the content lectures, thereby involving changes in educational practice that were wider than the EAP class itself. Any attempt to simplify teaching materials or tasks is, as Flowerdew's comments suggest, a strategy that requires careful evaluative scrutiny both to ensure short-term effectiveness and to assess long-term value in developing students' communicative and critical abilities. Flowerdew in fact identifies a vicious circle (a 'Catch-22' situation) with regard to students' writing, in which 'scientists did not require writing because students were unable to supply it and English teachers did not teach writing because scientists did not require it from their students' (p. 131). The damage only became apparent in later years when scientists started to demand sophisticated writing from students who lacked the necessary training and experience to produce it. Language and content staff went on to create a set of short-answer writing tasks of appropriate difficulty level and content relevance. This work initiated significant changes in curricular practice to prepare students for a more advanced and autonomous role in later work.

Johns (1993) identifies another mismatch between restricted short-term needs for undergraduate writing and substantially greater demands for subsequent writing in the case of ESL students planning to major in engineering in a university in the U.S.A. From interviews with engineering faculty and administrators, Johns established the centrality of grant writing as a professional genre. She then conducted extensive interviews with two successful grant writers. Very careful planning for a specific and powerful readership (individually targeted peer reviewers) was identified as an important lever for success in grant writing. Johns concludes that a clear pedagogic focus should be given to certain attributes of successful grant writing that had proved relevant to peer reviewers, in particular to establishing the currency, precision and scope of claim statements made in proposals. She then exemplifies work at under-graduate level that can provide students with the experience of writing on issues of moment for them to real and powerful readers whose expectations need to be discovered and taken into account. Johns describes one instance in which students wrote to university trustees and state legislators to protest over a 40 per cent increase in fees. This particular example might elicit many questions, from a variety of ideological perspectives. (Who initiated the work? Was the teacher seen as fomenting disaffection, or as diverting protest into innocuous channels? What response, if any, was elicited from target readers? How did students feel?) Readers may want to know more, and space is always a problem; nonetheless, Johns (1993) has demonstrably described EAP work that does not ignore or deny wider realities of power.

A parameter that may affect both task authenticity and the quality of student involvement is the extent to which materials and tasks take account of students' existing knowledge and culture. Barron (1991) and colleagues at the Papua New Guinea (PNG) University of Technology developed a project in Traditional Engineering that was designed to help students and educators recognise the place of engineer-ing principles and practices within (very diverse) PNG traditional cultures. Barron reports that engineering staff who participated in the project acknowledged that they had gained a greater interest in and understanding of their students' backgrounds and the potential relevance of traditional practices for their engineering courses. Barron comments on the importance of viewing EAP as a part of education in its own right. The article is an excellent example of understanding related to action in context that has been realised in a collaborative educational initiative leading to substantial curricular and attitudinal changes. Barron's work is situated within ESP traditions, and it also extends these traditions rather than perpetuating old beliefs and practices uncritically.

Starfield (1994) reports on EAP experiences at the University of the Witwatersrand (WITS) in South Africa. She points out that incoming black students were not in the fortunate position envisaged by Widdowson (1978) in which EAP students seek to transfer existing academic literacy into English, but that they had yet to acquire academic language proficiency, especially in the context-reduced modes of academic writing, since this has been lacking in their schooling. She warns that mainstream faculty perceptions of these students as experiencing linguistic and cognitive difficulties may only be reinforced by a 'traditional' EAP programme (presumably meaning EAP classes that are separate from the rest of the curriculum). The EAP teachers at WITS have consequently collaborated with faculty in order to develop an adjunct model that can more adequately contextualise their work by relating it directly to students' subject curricula. Starfield indicates that this initiative is moving towards a situation in which their Academic Support Programme can start to raise more fundamental curricular issues with the mainstream faculty.

Task B4.1.3: After you read

➤ Do you agree that pragmatism is not a single ideology but depends very much on local circumstances? Can you give an example from your own experience as a teacher or student where you sought to relate your materials or delivery to local conditions in a way which modified or changed 'usual practice' in that context?

➤ Would you accept Swales's characterization of EAP as being 'to help people, both non-native and native speakers, to develop their academic communicative competence' as fair and adequate? Can you justify your answer?

➤ How might Benesch and Pennycook re-interpret the examples Allison gives to support his view that teachers' pragmatic decisions often modify and challenge prevailing practices and relations.

➤ Select one of Allison's summarized examples and read the original account. Rewrite the summary in more detail to highlight the degree of co-operation between EAP specialist and subject tutors it describes and the extent to which the initiative changed the ways things were done to the students' advantage and how far it unreflectively 'accommodated' them to their disciplines.

Alistair Pennycook (1997) 'Vulgar pragmatism, critical pragmatism, and EAP.' *English for Specific Purposes*, 16, 253–69.

This text is a direct response to the previous one, arguing that we need to reject *vulgar pragmatism* in favour of a more critical stance. Pennycook argues that various interests have constructed 'discourses of neutrality' around English (see Unit A3) which makes it easy to see EAP as a disinterested enterprise and makes possibilities for challenge limited. In contrast, he outlines some critical directions for EAP.

Task B4.2.1: Before you read

➤ Look again at your notes on Allison's article in Text B4.1 and reflect on the strengths and weaknesses of his argument. Is pragmatism the only rational choice available to us and therefore 'non-ideological'?

Task B4.2.2: As you read

➤ Pennycook's response is framed in very different language and draws on very different arguments to those of Allison. As you read, consider Pennycook's arguments. To what extent does he address, and refute, Allison's arguments and how far are the two operating within different and incommensurate discourses?

Pragmatism and discourses of neutrality

My argument is that a position that we might characterise as 'vulgar pragmatism', a position that runs the danger of reinforcing norms, beliefs and ideologies that maintain inequitable social and cultural relations – a position that I unashamedly believe is ethically unacceptable – is made particularly available by certain 'discourses of neutrality' which construct EAP as a neutral activity, and therefore allow for a position that a pragmatist stance is an ethically viable one and that EAP is an activity for which a critical pragmatism would not have much relevance. It is these discourses, I am suggesting, that give meaning to Allison's (1996) defence of pragmatism or to Johns' (1993) argument that EAP should distance itself from the ideological stance taken in much L1 composition theory, since among other things, we already have, as her title puts it, 'too much on our plates'.

I should emphasise here that I am not trying to construct EAP as some monolithic and inherently vulgar/pragmatist enterprise. Neither is this intended in any way as a criticism of particular individuals. Rather, the point of my argument is to illuminate what I see as particular discursive positions that are readily available and what I see as a strong and unhelpful tendency amid the diversity of EAP work to opt for the pragmatic option. I am interested in the availability of a constellation of discourses around EAP that allow for the possibility of taking up a particular stance. I base these observations on my own experiences over a number of years as an EAP teacher and on my research into underlying assumptions and ideologies in English Language Teaching (ELT). These discourses focus, first, on the neutrality of language – neutral in general, neutral as a global commodity and neutral in the international domain. Next, they focus on issues of science and technology as universal and neutral rather than cultural and political; on 'issues' or 'content' as neutral with respect to the lives of our students, and on universities as sites of neutral educational exchange.

The neutrality of English as an international language

I want to suggest, first of all, then, that EAP occurs within the broader domain of the teaching of English as an international language, and that this broad context provides discourses of neutrality that help construct EAP as a pragmatic enterprise. This is based, first of all, in a view of language as neutral. This first discourse of neutrality is revealed in the very phrase English *for* academic purposes. While on one level this seemingly innocent phrase appears to do little more than articulate a sense of functionality (this is what English is being used for in this particular context), I want to argue that it also presents a particular view of language as a neutral medium through which meanings pass. This functionalist approach to language tends to construct an unproblematic relationship between 'English' and the 'academic purposes' for which it is used. As I have argued elsewhere (Pennycook 1994b), however, a poststructuralist conception of language would suggest that we need to look more critically at the contexts of language use and to view language as social practice. From this point of view, it cannot be isolated from its social, cultural and ideological contexts, so to write, speak, read, or listen can never be acts performed neutrally through some linguistic medium. For EAP classes this would mean looking beyond language simply as structure and representation in favour of a view of language as always engaged in the construction of how we understand the world.

Secondly, this view of language in general as neutral is coupled to a belief in the particular neutrality of English as an international language. This view of English as neutral derives particularly from the belief that the international is more neutral than the local, the partisan or the national. . . . The problem with this view, of course, is that it ignores the problem that English is no more neutral simply because it is no longer tied to a particular cultural context. English is deeply bound up with international capitalism and tourism, the spread of particular forms of culture and knowledge, global media, and so on. To the extent that it is almost inevitably tied to various class interests, and that in most multilingual nations this also means a certain relationship to various ethnic interests, English becomes a very unlikely candidate for neutrality.

Third, this neutral language English is frequently then constructed as a global commodity to be bought and sold on the world market. Two interesting discourses intersect here: on the one hand a view of global markets as idealised places for equitable trading, and on the other, a view of the English language and its teachers as something freely traded within this global free market economy. This discourse has implications not only for private educational institutions but also more generally as an understanding of the role of English in the world. From this position, English and English teaching are best seen as products and factories.

Critical EAP and the pluralisation of knowledge

I have already signalled in the discussion above many objections to the view of EAP as a neutral service industry to the academy, distanced from social, cultural, political and ideological concerns. These concerns point to the need for EAP to develop a more critical approach, which, if I am to concede Allison's (1996) call for an acknowledgment of pragmatism, I will nevertheless insist must be a critical pragmatism. Rather than apparently meeting the 'needs' of the students (as is often claimed after applying some form of 'needs analysis'), a belief in the educational neutrality of EAP may do a pedagogical disservice to the students. Indeed, Benesch (1996) has recently argued for the need for a critical approach to needs analysis in EAP. A curricular focus on providing students only with academic-linguistic skills for dealing with academic work in other disciplines misses a crucial opportunity to help students to develop forms of linguistic, social and cultural criticism that would be of much greater benefit to them for understanding and questioning how language works both within and outside educational institutions. By denying the political and ideological contexts of language education, a pragmatist stance adopts a conservative approach to education which at least needs to be acknowledged and justified, if not challenged. This stance leads to a self-defeating position for EAP classes. If one of the difficulties faced by EAP practitioners is marginalisation and displacement into a secondary role compared to the other disciplines, this problem cannot be overcome by accepting a role as a service department providing what other departments feel they need.

The sort of critical approach I am advocating here has some affinities with work in critical language awareness (see Fairclough 1992), which in turn is part of the larger focus on critical language study and critical discourse analysis (e.g. Fairclough 1995). The principal focus of this work is to show how discourse is both constituted by and constitutive of social relations, how any language use is determined by broader social and ideological relations and in turn reinforces those relations. Arguing for a view of discourse as social practice, Clark (1992), for example, . . . argues for the need to 'critically explore with the students the notion of academic discourse community and how it is that certain forms of knowledge and ways of telling that knowledge have evolved in the way they have' (p. 118).

Alongside the possible pluralisation of academic writing norms, we also need to consider the possibilities of the pluralisation of knowledge. If we want to give space to our students' cultures and histories, and if we want to challenge some of the standard formulations of academic knowledge, then we can start to see EAP as having a significant role in the pluralisation of our students' future knowledge. This is akin to what I have elsewhere called a 'pedagogy of cultural alternatives' (Pennycook 1997), a view of language education that stresses our need as teachers to help students to create and become aware of alternative ways of envisioning the world. . . . For EAP, this would imply developing course content that sought to critically examine the discourses that construct our and our students' understandings of our worlds. Another way forward is to develop . . . a critical understanding of English and its relationship to discourses of science, technology and education, as well as its role as national and international gatekeeper to these domains therefore becomes an integral part of an EAP curriculum.

One of the most common objections to suggesting such a critical programme is that it may deny students access to the language and discourses they need. Clark (1992) frames her discussion within the tensions between students' obligations and rights, the need on the one hand to adhere to the norms of the academic community, and on the other to challenge those norms. Thus, for example, she points to the tension between 'the ethnocentricity of demanding western-style structuring of an argument and the right of the student to include moral lessons in his writing on nuclear weapons, which he feels very strongly about' (p. 135). This tension lies at the heart of EAP: on the one hand we need to help our students gain access to those forms of language and culture that matter while on the other we need to help challenge those norms. On the one hand we need to help our students develop critical awarenesses of academic norms and practices, while on the other we need to understand and promote culturally diverse ways of thinking, working and writing.

This tension between the need to acknowledge cultural difference and the need at the same time to give people access to the cultural, linguistic and discursive conventions that matter is, of course, a classic tension in critical approaches to education. In work on critical literacy, for example, this tension emerges in the differences between those who primarily emphasise *access* to the cultures of power, and those who emphasise the exploration of difference. However, it is important to observe two points here: First, we do not need to see this as a dichotomous choice between two approaches to education, but instead can work with both. Second, as Luke (1996) has shown, we need far more complex theories about language and power than those offered by the 'genres of power' argument, since this ultimately 'runs the risk of becoming an institutional technology principally engaged in self-reproduction of the status and privilege of a particular field of disciplinary knowledge' (p. 334).

Task B4.2.3: After you read

➤ Do you agree with Pennycook? Is he right to suggest that *discourses of neutrality* pervade EAP and make it difficult to see it as anything other than 'pragmatic' or does this argument itself offer a monolithic conception of EAP? In other words, how far do you think Pennycook's critical discourse allows us to reflect on local practices and how far does it prevent a nuanced appreciation of them?

➤ Pennycook introduces several arguments to support his view of EAP. Which do you find the most convincing and why?

➤ How do you respond to Pennycook's argument about the pluralization of knowledge? How might we resolve, in our classes, the 'tension at the heart of EAP'?

➤ What parallels are there between the views of EAP outlined by Lea and Street in Text B2.1 and those presented by Allison and Pennycook?

➤ Based on the two extracts and your reflections on them, decide on some principles that should guide the teaching of English for Academic Purposes. For instance, what principles should influence course objectives, selection of materials, choice of tasks, and presentation and practice of language? How might others formulate these principles?

  ■ 'Pragmatist' EAP teachers might argue that . . .
  ■ Critical EAP teachers might argue that . . .
  ■ I would argue . . .

Theme 2: Literacies and practices

This theme follows the first in exploring the main ways that EAP understands its subject matter, addressing the methods used to investigate and describe academic texts and contexts. Despite major changes in both EAP itself and the contexts in which it operates, the field has never lost sight of its practical orientation and pedagogic responsibilities, always seeking to relate theory and research to instructional outcomes. To ensure that teaching practices recognize the particular subject-matter needs and expertise of learners EAP has developed a distinctive approach to language teaching based on identification of the specific language features, discourse practices and communicative skills of target groups.

The choice of readings in this theme introduces some of the main theories and methodologies for accomplishing these goals. Notions of *social construction, community* and *culture* and the methods of *genre analysis, corpus linguistics* and *ethnography* are the tools which currently provide our understandings of the ways individuals participate in academic life through their communicative activities. The texts that follow therefore both underline the importance to teachers of understanding how academic discourses are inextricably related to wider social, cultural and institutional issues and provide examples of how we collect information which contributes to that understanding.

Unit B5
Discourses, communities and cultures

This unit contains three readings which reflect different aspects of this broad topic. Each one, while adopting a different focus, shows how discourses are influenced by context, audience, community and culture. Myers's text shows the ways that writing for specialist and lay readers, or community insiders and outsiders, results in both different kinds of texts and views of science; Becher looks at disciplines more structurally as *tribes*, or communities with recognizable identities and particular cultural attributes; and Mauranen describes how national cultural attributes and practices can influence students' academic writing.

Greg Myers (1994) 'The narratives of science and nature in popularising molecular genetics.' In M. Coulthard (ed.), *Advances in written text analysis.* **London: Routledge.**

Text B5.1
G. Myers

In this first text, Myers traces the changes in organization, syntax and vocabulary between a research article, a popularization and a newspaper article. These different audiences and purposes mean that writers not only set the facts out differently, but actually construct different views of science. The professional article, written for a specialist scientific community, creates *a narrative of science,* following the argument of the scientist's claims. The popularizing articles, in contrast, create *a narrative of nature* by focusing on the object of study rather than the scientific activity and endows the facts with much greater authority and certainty.

Task B5.1.1: Before you read

➤ Spend half an hour watching a television science documentary or reading a newspaper feature or an article in a popular science magazine. Consider how popular science emphasizes the immediate encounter of the scientist with nature. Now read a scientific article written for a specialist audience and see how it is the concepts and procedures, rather than individuals, which are foregrounded.

Task B5.1.2: As you read

➤ Note the ways that writers of the three genres discussed by Myers use language and organization in different ways to construct different understandings of science for their different audiences.

G. Myers

I will consider the original article in *Nature* by Jeffreys and his group (JWT), a popularization in *New Scientist* (NS) by Jeremy Cherfas, and a news report in *The Economist* (EC). There have of course been a number of other popularizations as DNA finger-printing has become a widely used technique in forensic science, immigration cases, pedigree research, diagnosis of hereditary diseases and research on evolution. Here the journalistic problem was different. This was not just a shift of scientific concepts – though it was that too – it was a new technique touching on many aspects of society. I will compare the scientific and popular articles on three levels, looking at organization, syntax and vocabulary.

Organization

The introduction to the research article in *Nature* stresses a claim different from that for which it became famous – it does not mention DNA fingerprinting at all. The abstract of the JWT article gives a sense of its movement from problem to application:

> The human genome contains many dispersed tandem-repetitive 'mini-satellite' regions detected via a shared 10–15 base pair 'core' sequence similar to the generalized recombination symbol (chi) of *Escherichia coli*. Many minisatellites are highly polymorphic due to allelic variation in repeat copy number in the minisatellite. A probe based on a tandem-repeat of the core sequence can detect many highly variable loci simultaneously and can provide an individual-specific DNA 'fingerprint' of general use in human genetic analysis.

The scientific issue is foregrounded. But with a commercially applicable discovery like this, it is important to establish the researchers' awareness of the implications of their finding – otherwise someone else could patent it. JWT actually present a whole series of related findings, leading from the sequence itself, to the discovery of the probe, its application to a library and to a pedigree study. So this article does not just present simultaneous results supporting one claim. Within each section, though, it is structured with the juxtaposition of tightly linked statements, not in idealized chronological order but in a structure of argument.

There were two *New Scientist* articles on the work of Jeffreys' group soon after its publication. One, by Jeremy Cherfas, follows the structure of the *Nature* article closely, almost paragraph by paragraph, but begins and ends with the possible applications. The title, 'Geneticists develop DNA fingerprinting', emphasizes the activity of the scientists.

One early report on the technique in a general magazine was in *The Economist*. It starts with the evident need for a test to distinguish individuals. . . . Three paragraphs are devoted to this as a problem. Then Jeffreys is introduced to solve the problem. The relation of basic and applied research suggested by the original report has been reversed for Jeffreys. The discovery of a probe, while he was doing purely scientific work, led to the application in an identity test, while in *The Economist* account the need for the test leads to the probe. In fact, Jeffreys stressed in all his interviews that he had been doing 'pure' research when he hit this commercial jackpot.

Syntax

There have been many studies of the syntax of scientific articles, but most take the social function of these texts as a given, rather than as a topic for investigation. I am particularly interested in those features that seem to vary with different audiences, between the specialized scientific articles and the popularizations. We might begin with active and passive voice, since it is a heavily studied feature and we would expect to find more passive sentences in the scientific articles. . . . The contrast in grammatical voice between research articles and popularizations is not as striking as we might expect. There are active sentences with personal subjects in the research article:

> We show here that the myoglobin 33-bp repeat is indeed capable of detecting other human minisatellites . . .
>
> (JWT, *Nature*)

If we look at a wider range of research articles in this field, we will see that such sentences occur rarely, but occur at crucial points in the introduction and discussion, where the authors state their main claims. Similarly, there are many passives in the popularizations, even after the editors have gone over them. But the typical pattern is that a paragraph describing technical work begins in the active and then switches to the passive, so the personal work of the scientists is still foregrounded. This suggests that the location of shifts in grammatical voice may tell us more than a simple comparison of the numbers of passive and active sentences. The overall narrative of the research articles emphasizes the entities studied, so the explicit mention of the researchers marks an important act. Similarly, the focus on the researchers in the popularizations is maintained even when they are describing general techniques.

I have suggested that the organization of each section of the research articles involves juxtaposition of several related statements into a simultaneous order of argument, while the popularizations tend to organize the statements into a sequence. The related observation on the syntactic level is that the research articles tend to use complex sentences, and complex phrases that bring a number of clauses into the same sentence, asserting them at once. Similar (though not exactly the same) content may be conveyed in the popularizations with a series of simpler sentences. We can see this by looking for a complex sentence in a research article and comparing it to a corresponding part of the popularization, a comparison that is easier where the popularizer follows the form of the research article, as Cherfas does.

> This core region in each cloned minisatellite suggests strongly that this sequence might help to generate minisatellites by promoting the initial tandem duplication of unique sequence DNA and/or by stimulating the subsequent unequal exchanges required to amplify the duplication in a minisatellite. As polymorphic minisatellites may also be recombination hotspots (see above), it might be significant that the core sequence is similar

in length and in G content to the *chi* sequence, a signal for generalized recombination in E. *coli*.

(JWT, *Nature*)

This core identity of the different minisatellites would certainly help to promote reduplication of the region by unequal exchange. It might also actively promote recombination. Certainly the sequence resembles a region called *chi* found in the DNA of the bacterium *Escherichia coli*. The *chi* region is believed to be the signal that causes recombination . . .

(*New Scientist*)

There are many differences here – for instance, Cherfas fills in background information, and omits some evidence and some qualifications. But for our purposes, in looking for a narrative, what is interesting is that Cherfas separates out some statements in JWT's complex sentences, so that they appear one after another in shorter sentences.

There are other syntactic patterns that might be related to the narrative of nature. For instance, in my earlier study I noted the tendency for the popularizations to use question and answer patterns (a traditional technique in pedagogical literature). But there were few of them here. I have also noted the much wider range of cohesive devices in the popularizations. These strengthen the sense of following the chain of a continuous story, while the research articles could be thought of as a construction of blocks, with the connections filled in by the informed readers.

Vocabulary

We have already seen examples in which the popularization substitutes for some scientific term an explanation or a rough equivalent in the general vocabulary. Researchers who write popularizations often have to battle with editors to try to preserve some of their specialized terminology. As with any translation, associated meanings can be lost as equivalents are found for specialized terms. The coining and acceptance of a term is a crucial step in forming a disciplinary concept. For instance, when JWT uses the terms 'heterozygousity' and 'hypervariable region', the popularizers' explanations or substitutes may subtly alter the sequence of information.

the mean heterozygosity of human DNA is low ({wave}0.001 per base pair). . . . Genetic analysis in man could be simplified considerably by the availability of probes for hypervariable regions of human DNA showing multiallelic variation and correspondingly high heterozygousities.

(JWT, *Nature*)

Human DNA does not vary much between different members of the species: roughly 999 out of every 1000 base pairs (the letters of the genetic code) are the same in two unrelated individuals. There are, however, some regions that seem to be more variable, with a different structure in different individuals. . . . All of these so-called hypervariable regions have a similar structure.

(*New Scientist*)

Of every 1,000 'letters' of DNA, 999 are the same in two different people. Dr Alec Jeffreys and his colleagues at the University of Leicester have now found a way to seek out the few parts of the genetic code that vary greatly among individuals. They found that many such 'hypervariable' regions are similar.

(*Economist*)

There may be a slight difference between saying that DNA varies and saying it has a low heterozygousity. Making it into a ratio, given in a certain form, treats it as an inherent part of the description of DNA, the way litres are part of the description of an engine.

One term that makes a process into an entity, DNA *fingerprint*, is clearly a key in the JWT article. It seems like the sort of catchy journalistic name that might he added in the popularizations. But in fact Alec Jeffreys introduced it at the outset. There have been other processes in molecular biology with similar names, but this is the first to have entered the general vocabulary. Just as Jeffreys recognized early on that he had a marketable application, he realized it would need a non-technical name with the right associations, 'Probe for hypervariable regions' would not do.

Task B5.1.3: After you read

➤ What seem to be the main differences between scientific accounts written for a specialist community and popular accounts written for lay readers? What do the narratives of science and of nature consist of and what are their effects?

➤ Why are facts endowed with greater authority in popularizations while academic writers are more tentative when communicating with their peers?

➤ Why is the 'personal work of the scientists' likely to be foregrounded more in the popularizations?

➤ What implications might this study have for EAP practitioners?

Tony Becher (1989) *Academic tribes and territories: intellectual inquiry and the cultures of disciplines*. Milton Keynes: Society for Research in Higher Education and Open University Press, pp. 19–35.

This extract is taken from Becher's book, which reports a large-scale, social scientific study of activity in the disciplines, mapping communities and providing a systematic picture of the relationship of knowledge to the practices of academic communities. In this extract, Becher examines the nature of academic disciplines, characterizing them as distinctive tribes with their own cultures and practices.

Task B5.2.1: Before you read

➤ What distinguishes disciplines for you? Make a list of the features which allow us to mark off a particular academic field as a 'discipline'.

Task B5.2.2: As you read

➤ Note the various ways that Becher suggests disciplines can be characterized and the evidence used to support each characterization.

T. Becher

The nature of a discipline

The concept of an academic discipline is not altogether straightforward, in that, as is true of many concepts, it allows room for some uncertainties of application. There may be doubts, for example, whether statistics is now sufficiently separate from its parent discipline, mathematics, to constitute a discipline on its own. The answer will depend on the extent to which leading academic institutions recognize the hiving off in terms of their organizational structures (whether, that is, they number statistics among their fully fledged departments), and also on the degree to which a freestanding international community has emerged, with its own professional associations and specialist journals. In some of the typical instances of dispute, certain institutions may have decided to establish departments in a particular field but may find that the intellectual validity of those departments is under challenge from established academic opinion (as has happened in the case of black studies, viniculture and parapsychology). Disciplines are thus in part identified by the existence of relevant departments; but it does not follow that every department represents a discipline. International currency is an important criterion, as is a general though not sharply defined set of notions of academic credibility, intellectual substance, and appro- priateness of subject matter. Despite such apparent complications, however, people with any interest and involvement in academic affairs seem to have little difficulty in understanding what a discipline is, or in taking a confident part in discussions about borderline or dubious cases.

One way of looking at disciplines is through a structural framework, noting how they are manifested in the basic organizational components of the higher education system (e.g. Becher and Kogan 1980, and Clark 1983). Such a perspective tends to highlight one particular set of issues: the variation in how academic institutions elect to draw the map of knowledge; what operational distinctions need to be made between traditional established disciplines (such as history or physics) and interdisciplinary fields (urban studies, peace studies and the like), the organizational complexities of combining autonomous, self-generating units within a single managerial structure; the mechanisms for accommodating newly defined intellectual groupings and phasing out those which are no longer regarded as viable. However, in attempting to explore the relationship between disciplines and the knowledge fields with which they are concerned – as against the organizations in which they are made manifest – a more abstract approach is called for.

A wide-ranging representation of what a discipline is can be found in King and Brownell (1966). Their account embraces several different aspects: a community, a net- work of communications, a tradition, a particular set of values and beliefs, a domain, a mode of enquiry, and a conceptual structure. Other analyses are more parsimonious. Some writers focus on epistemological considerations, presenting disciplines as 'each characterized by its own body of concepts, methods and fundamental aims' (Toulmin 1972); others define them unequivocally as organized social groupings (Whitley 1976, 1984). For the most part, however, commentators on the subject give equal emphasis to both aspects. Thus Price (1970) admonishes: 'we cannot and should not artificially separate the matter of substantive content from that of social behaviour'.

It would seem, then, that the attitudes, activities and cognitive styles of groups of academics representing a particular discipline are closely bound up with the characteristics and structures of the knowledge domains with which such groups are professionally concerned. One could venture further to suggest that in the concept of a discipline the two are so inextricably connected that it is unproductive to try to forge any sharp division between them. Even so, if one is to examine the nature of their interconnections, a distinction must be made – at least in theoretical terms – between forms of knowledge and knowledge communities.

Tribalism and tradition

Despite their temporal shifts of character and their institutional and national diversity, we may appropriately conceive of disciplines as having recognizable identities and particular cultural attributes. We shall need next to consider the forms which such identities and attributes may take. . . . Among them, Clark (1963) writes:

> It is around the disciplines that faculty subcultures increasingly form. As the work and the points of view grow more specialised, men in different disciplines have fewer things in common, in their background in their daily problems. They have less impulse to interact with one another and less ability to do so. . . . Men of the sociological tribe rarely visit the land of the physicists and have little idea what they do over there. If the sociologists were to step into the building occupied by the English department, they would encounter the cold stares if not the slingshots of the hostile natives . . . the disciplines exist as separate estates, with distinctive subcultures.

An individual's sense of belonging to his or her academic tribe is manifested in a variety of ways:

> The culture of the discipline includes idols: the pictures on the walls and dustjackets of books kept in view are of Albert Einstein and Max Planck and Robert Oppenheimer in the office of the physicist and of Max Weber and Karl Marx and Emile Durkheim in the office of the sociologist.
>
> (Clark 1980)

It also involves artefacts – a chemist's desk is prone to display three-dimensional models of complex molecular structures, an anthropologist's walls are commonly adorned with colourful tapestries and enlarged photographic prints of beautiful black people, while a mathematician may boast no more than a chalkboard scribbled over with algebraic symbols.

It is, however, through the medium of language that some of the more fundamental distinctions emerge. A detailed analysis of disciplinary discourse (such as those attempted by Bazerman 1981, or Becher 1987b) can help not only to bring out characteristic cultural features of disciplines but also to highlight various aspects of the knowledge domains to which they relate. It is possible by this means to discern differences in the modes in which arguments are generated, developed, expressed and reported, and to tease out the epistemological implications of the ways in which others' work is evaluated.

On the latter point, Geertz (1983) remarks that 'the terms through which the devotees of a scholarly pursuit represent their aims, judgements, justifications, and so on, seem to me to take one a long way, when properly understood, toward grasping what that pursuit is all about'. My own research data bring out some of the connections between the terms of appraisal which are widely used in a particular discipline and the nature of the relevant knowledge field. That historians will commend a piece of work as 'masterly', and will be ready to single out the quality of 'good craftsmanship' (features that are rarely identified in other disciplines), suggests a particular emphasis on gaining command of, and shaping into an aesthetically pleasing, purposeful and well articulated product, a body of miscellaneous and formless raw material. The high premium placed on 'elegant', 'economical', 'productive' and 'powerful' solutions to mathematical and physical problems points towards a knowledge field in which it is possible to identify structural simplicity, reducing explanation to essentials, and where, in a close network of interconnected phenomena, certain discoveries hold within them the means of generating many others. The epithets 'persuasive', 'thought provoking' and 'stimulating', seemingly more common in sociology than elsewhere, suggest a particular concern with the quality of the analysis itself and with its effects on the audience, as against its substantive content. In similar vein, one might note that among physicists, 'accurate' and 'rigorous' are double-edged tributes, since no physics worthy of the name should lack either property; while in both history and sociology to use the word 'biased' is 'to betray one's naiveté', in that every inter- pretation must have this feature to some degree.

More generally, the professional language and literature of a disciplinary group play a key role in establishing its cultural identity. This is clearly so when they embody a particular symbolism of their own (as in mathematics and theoretical physics), or a significant number of specialized terms (as in many of the biological and social sciences), placing them to a greater or lesser degree beyond the reach of an uninitiated audience. But in more subtle ways the exclusion also operates in those disciplines (such as history and, perhaps, to a decreasing extent, literary studies) which pride themselves on not being 'jargon-ridden', since the communication here none the less creates what linguists would call its own register – a particular set of favoured terms, sentence structures and logical syntax – which it is not easy for an outsider to imitate.

The tribes of academe, one might argue, define their own identities and defend their own patches of intellectual ground by employing a variety of devices geared to the exclusion of illegal immigrants. Some, as we have noted, are manifest in physical form ('the building occupied by the English department', in Clark's words); others emerge in the particularities of membership and constitution (Waugh's 'complex of tribes, each with its chief and elders and witch-doctors and braves'). Alongside these structural features of disciplinary communities, exercising an even more powerful integrating force, are their more explicitly cultural elements: their traditions, customs and practices, transmitted knowledge, beliefs, morals and rules of conduct, as well as their linguistic and symbolic forms of communication and the meanings they share. To be admitted to membership of a particular sector of the academic profes- sion involves not only a sufficient level of technical proficiency in one's intellectual trade but also a proper measure of loyalty to one's collegial group and of adherence to its norms.

A note of qualification

T. Becher

In the intricate, Byzantine world of academia, nothing is as simple as it seems. If, as the argument so far has suggested, knowledge communities are defined and reinforced by 'the nurturance of myth, the identification of unifying symbols, the canonisation of examplars, and the formation of guilds' (Dill 1982), their territorial borders are simultaneously blurred and weakened by a rival set of pressures. This does not of course invalidate the exercise of identifying the distinctive cultural characteristics of individual disciplines: it merely underlines the fact that such an exercise depends on the adoption of a particular frame of reference, more specific than that relating to knowledge fields, but still sufficiently broad and general to obscure several important qualifications.

Task B5.2.3: After you read

➤ What different methods are used in the extract to identify disciplines? Can you categorize them in any way? Which of these methods do you feel is the most robust characterization?

➤ Becher argues that 'the attitudes, activities and cognitive styles of groups of academics' are closely related to the knowledge domains of their fields. What evidence does he give for this assertion and how could we study this connection further?

➤ Becher is not an EAP practitioner or applied linguist but recognizes the importance of language in defining disciplinary tribes. What would be productive ways of exploring the language of the disciplines to substantiate these claims?

➤ The 'note of qualification' at the end of the extract recognizes the 'blurring and weakening' of disciplinary boundaries and, indeed, postmodern critics would claim that disciplines do not exist at all. How far are you persuaded by Becher's claims concerning the distinctive cultural characteristics of individual disciplines?

Anna Mauranen (1993) 'Contrastive ESP rhetoric: metatext in Finnish–English economics texts.' *English for Specific Purposes*, 12, 3–22.

Text B5.3
A. Mauranen

In this extract Anna Mauranen, a Finnish academic, describes a contrastive text-linguistic study which explores a further dimension of discourses, cultures and communities. Focusing on the use of metatext, or text about text, she discovered considerable rhetorical differences between texts written by academics from different cultural backgrounds. Finnish writers use metatext much less than Anglo-American writers, and favour a more impersonal style of writing. Both these features can be seen as contributing to a more 'implicit' rhetorical strategy in the Finnish texts than is typical of texts by English-speaking economists. These differences in rhetorical preferences, Mauranen suggests, are the result of cultural factors and are likely to be more important than disciplinary preferences in academic writing practices.

Task B5.3.1: Before you read

➤ Based on your own experience as a teacher, try to think of cases where your students wrote English in a way which might have been influenced by the rhetorical preferences of their first language. How can you account for these different preferences in writing?

Task B5.3.2: As you read

➤ Consider the methodology used in the study and whether Mauranen's conclusions are justified by her results.

A. Mauranen

It seems fair to assume, or hard to contest, that culture influences writing habits in an important way. This is because writing clearly is a cultural object, existing only in the social world of humans, as a product of social activities. Writing is also very much shaped by the educational system in a writer's native culture, as has been argued by studies in contrastive rhetoric.

However, it seems that certain areas of culture are generally assumed to be universal in a way which renders cultural variation unimportant. Science is a case in point: most treatises of the history of science or the development of scientific thought rest on the tacit assumption that science advances through contributions to the common pool of human scientific thought. Even if science is seen as being developed by or within a particular nation at a particular historical time, the phenomenon of scientific thought itself is seen as emerging from a universal source.

But science, or more widely, academic research, does not exist outside writing; and so we cannot represent it, or realise it, without being influenced by the variation in the writing cultures that carry it. How does this variation then take place in writing, and how can we reconcile the universality of science with its cultural variation, if both are necessarily realised in writing, as texts? If we draw a distinction between genre and rhetoric, it can be argued that aspects of academic writing which tend to be universal are conditioned by genre, while the more variable aspects fall under the domain of rhetoric.

It can be assumed that, on the whole, similar rhetorical means are available in different writing cultures, but their frequencies and preferred uses differ. Therefore, similar means are expected to be employed in texts written by speakers of Finnish and English, but their relative frequencies are expected to differ.

Materials

A. Mauranen

The present material consists of two pairs of texts chosen for their good comparability in terms of genre (academic research reports), field (economics) and topic (two texts on forest economics models, and two on taxation models). In both pairs one text was written in English by a Finnish economist, the other by an economist who is a native speaker of English.

Defining metatext

As noted above, metatext is essentially text about the text itself. It comprises those elements in text which at least in their primary function go beyond the propositional content. . . . The function of metatext is, then, to organise and comment on the discourse, particularly the propositional content that is being conveyed. As already noted, in this article we limit ourselves to metatext which primarily serves the purpose of textual organisation. The items range from single words to sequences of sentences. Four types are focused on: connectors, reviews, previews, and illocution markers. These are presented below with examples from the material studied:

1 *Connectors.* Conjunctions, adverbial and prepositional phrases, which indicate relationships between propositions in text: *however, for example, as a result* . . .
2 *Reviews.* Clauses (sometimes abbreviated), which contain an explicit indicator that an earlier stage of the text is being repeated or summarised: *So far we have assumed that the corporate tax is a proportional tax on economic income.*
3 *Previews.* Clauses (sometimes abbreviated), which contain an explicit indicator that a later stage of the text is being anticipated: *We show below that each of the initial owners will find this policy to be utility maximising.*
4 *Action markers.* Indicators of discourse acts performed in the text: *the explanation is, to express this argument in notation, to illustrate the size of this distortion* . . .

Empirical results

The Finnish writer's text had much less metatext (22.6 per cent) than the native English writer's text (54.2 per cent). The English writer has a higher proportion of metatextual elements in each category. The incidence of longer sequences of metatext is not very high in either text, but the sequences are longer in the L1 English text, shown by the higher proportion of the sentences that appear in a sequence (17.0 per cent, as opposed to 3.2 per cent in the Finnish text). The clustering of different types of metatext was much more typical of the Anglo-American than the Finnish texts analysed. In virtually all of the sentences counted as including metatext in the Finn's text, only one metatext category was employed, typically either a connector or an expression such as *It is shown that* . . . , *We consider three compensation schemes* . . . , *As mentioned before* . . . , *Another approach is.*

Conclusions

A comparison of the text extracts from Finnish and Anglo-American texts shows that these two groups manifest certain different rhetorical preferences. Finnish economic discourse employs relatively little metalanguage for explicitly organising the text and

Extension

orienting the reader. Moreover, the writers do not make their presence explicitly felt. Finnish discourse does not explicitly indicate what the text is going to do, and in this sense does not prepare the reader for what is to come. Nor does it orient the reader very much in retrospect, either. The main theses and conclusions are largely left for the reader to infer, little explicit guidance is provided as to the work's significance or implications. These features suggest that a certain 'implicitness' is characteristic of Finnish rhetorical strategies.

In contrast, native speakers of English often use devices which anticipate both what is to follow and how text segments relate to each other. Steps in reasoning are well indicated. Anglo-American writers thus seem to condition the reader's inter-pretation by explicitly expressed guidelines. They also convey the impression of having a more acute sense of the audience than Finns seem to have, as if the readers were more present in the minds of Anglo-Americans in the process of writing. Anglo-Americans thus appear to show more awareness of the text as text, to be more oriented towards the reader, while Finns appear to have adopted the role of a solitary writer, focusing on the propositional content of the text, or the text-external reality that they are dealing with.

The careful and explicit guidance practised by Anglo-American writers, together with frequent signalling of the personal presence of the author, conveys the impression that the reader is invited to take a tour of the text together with the author, who acts as a guide. The main thesis is pointed out repeatedly, so as not to be missed, not to be misunderstood. All this is reminiscent of another genre – namely, marketing discourse. If Anglo-Americans can be said to favour marketing-type rhetorical strategies, Finns can be said to favour the 'poetic' type: they tend to make minimal inscriptions on paper, leaving plenty of scope for readers' interpretations and, in fact, demanding considerable interpretative effort from the reader. Instead of acting as a guide to his or her text, the Finn travels his path alone, leaving tracks for those who might be interested in following. The reader's task is then to find the marks, interpret them, and draw the conclusions.

Both of these strategies can be persuasive in their own way. If the writer places important information early in the text and prospects ahead with clear signalling, he or she makes the reader's task easier. The reader probably finds it easy to comprehend the message content, and is likely to see it as the writer intended. The reader may also be persuaded to believe the writer's conclusions, because he or she has already processed at least part of them once, and therefore knows to anticipate them. The main theses are then familiar to the reader towards the end of the text. In other words, a memory track has already been formed with which the conclusion can be matched. The message may therefore appear convincing, by virtue of corresponding to something already familiar.

If, on the other hand, the writer places important information towards the end of the text and does not provide very much explicit advance guidance to the reader, then he or she makes the reader's task harder, because the reader will have to make frequent inferences and supply a great deal of missing information from his or her own resources. When the end of a text is reached, the reader has supplied a considerable amount of the information required for comprehension from the knowledge already stored in his or her brain. Thus, a substantial proportion of the message as interpreted by the reader is in fact produced by him/herself. The reader may then feel a sense of ownership with the conclusions and be ready to accept them.

Both strategies are possible in both of the cultures studied, and probably reflect aspects of any normal reading process. However, they assign very different roles to readers and writers. If a reader's learned expectations are strongly in favour of one of the strategies, he or she may experience the other as less appealing, and less convincing.

The last question that ensues from this study is, then, if Finns write and argue differently from Anglo-Americans, why do they do this? Although a good answer would be the subject of another study, and certainly transcend the boundaries of linguistics, a limited answer can be speculated upon here. First of all, Finnish and Anglo-American preferences for rhetorical strategies seem to reflect very different notions of politeness. The poetic, implicit Finnish rhetoric could be construed as being polite by its treatment of readers as intelligent beings, to whom nothing much needs to be explained. Saying too obvious things is, as we know, patronising. On the other hand, being implicit and obscure can also be interpreted as being arrogant and unconcerned: the inexplicit writer can be seen as presenting himself as superior to the reader, displaying his or her own wisdom, and leaving the reader to struggle with following the thoughts, if indeed he/she is capable of such a task. If the reader cannot follow the argument, it is his/her problem.

At the outset, the marketing-type rhetoric seems to be more concerned with the reader's interests, in providing him or her with more information, guidance, and a personal approach, and in making fewer demands on him or her. However, explicitness in text leaves less room for the reader's own (possibly novel) interpretations. It also conveys a certain impression of authority, which can be seen as a positive thing, but as mentioned above, also as patronising and didactic. Both of these strategies, then, have a positive and a negative interpretation. It is likely that the typical strategy in each culture is perceived as the positive, polite one and the untypical as the negative, impolite one.

In addition to different notions of politeness, these two rhetorical strategies seem to reflect different assumptions of shared knowledge in the communication process. If the writer does not guide the reader's interpretation process very deliberately, he or she seems to assume a great deal of shared knowledge between the communicants. This is a legitimate assumption when the target audience is relatively homogeneous. In the context of Finnish culture, for example, such an assumption is often reasonable, since the entire language community is small, relatively isolated and in many important social respects (like education) a homogeneous society compared to most societies in the world (cf. also Ringbom 1987).

One might then speculate that in a homogeneous context like the Finnish one, it is natural for writing conventions to remain relatively implicit, whereas in culturally more heterogeneous contexts, like those in dominant English-speaking countries, it becomes imperative to develop writing habits which are more explicit and leave less room for interpretations which are taken for granted.

In conclusion, I would like to emphasise once more that both of the rhetorical strategies described here can be perceived as polite and persuasive in appropriate cultural contexts. There is no reason in principle, then, for Finnish economists to try to change their rhetorical strategies. However, in practice, the Finnish culture is a minority culture, and the Anglo-American culture dominates in the academic world. Awareness of these intercultural rhetorical differences is therefore particularly useful for Finnish writers, if they want to make informed choices about whether and when to conform to the expectations of the target audience.

Task B5.3.3: After you read

➤ What do you see as the strengths and weaknesses of this research? Has it persuaded you of the claim that we cannot represent or realize science without being influenced by the variation in our writing cultures? What further evidence might you need?

➤ Think about Mauranen's distinction between *genre* and *rhetoric*, one conditioning universal aspects of academic writing and the second being more culturally variable. Do you think this a useful way of conceptualizing differences in writing and what might it mean for readers of academic texts?

➤ In the conclusions Mauranen speculates on the possible reasons for these different preferences. Do you find these reasons persuasive? What other factors might influence the differences she found and how could you explore her hypothesis further?

➤ This study contributes to the research which suggests that the schemata of L2 and L1 writers differ in their preferred ways of presenting ideas, and that these cultural preconceptions can influence communication. What implications do these findings have for EAP teachers?

Unit B6
Genre analysis and academic texts

The readings in this unit provide examples of two ways that genre analysis can be undertaken and how it can be relevant to EAP practitioners. Yakhontova's text follows the previous text in examining cultural variation in academic writing, but looks more closely at a central element of much genre analysis: the rhetorical moves used to structure a text as well as some of the key surface features used to realize these. The extract from Chang and Swales, in contrast, offers a detailed linguistic analysis of certain 'informal' elements of academic writing, comparing style guide advice with their actual use in published texts.

Tatyana Yakhontova (2002) '"Selling" or "telling"? The issue of cultural variation in research genres.' In J. Flowerdew (ed.), *Academic discourse.* **London: Longman.**

Text B6.1
T. Yakhontova

In this text Yakhontova examines the important genre of conference abstracts and explores the impact of cultural variations on texts written by Ukrainian academics in their native language compared with those written by Ukrainian scholars in English and by native English-speakers.

Task B6.1.1: Before you read

Consider the purpose of a conference abstract.

➤ What is it designed to do and what kind of information do you think it is likely to contain?

➤ Do you think these features might differ across cultures?

Task B6.1.2: As you read

➤ Note the main differences between Ukrainian and English abstracts and the reasons Yakhontova gives for these differences.

Extension

T. Yakhontova

In this chapter, I will analyse cultural variation in the conference abstract on the basis of Ukrainian/partly Russian versus English texts. The choice of the conference abstract as a subject of investigation has been determined by two reasons: (1) it is a widespread and important genre that plays a significant role in promoting new knowledge within scientific communities, both national and international; (2) for Ukrainian scholars nowadays it is a kind of 'pass' to the world science market and research community that provides, if accepted, various opportunities for professional contacts and communication. . . . Ukrainian conference abstracts are usually rather lengthy (from a standard one page up to three pages) and appear in a book of abstracts separately from a conference programme; they are stored in libraries (if a conference is broad-scale enough) and are available to the reader.

Corpus and analytical framework

The analysed corpus consists of forty-five texts, of which fifteen are written in English by native speakers (EE abstracts), fifteen in Ukrainian (ten) and Russian (five) (U/R group), and another fifteen again in English, but this time written by Ukrainian and/or Russian speakers (EU/R texts). Both Ukrainian and Russian (quite different lexically) share not only some similar syntactical and stylistic features, but also (which is more significant for this study) the common ideological and intellectual heritage of the totalitarian period that is still traceable in the rhetoric of their academic discourse. Despite the state policy of Ukrainisation, Russian preserves some influence on the functioning of scholarship in eastern Ukraine, while Ukrainian dominates academic communication in the western and central parts of the country.

All the investigated abstracts belong to the field of applied linguistics. This discipline has been chosen not so much (as it might be suspected) as the area most familiar to the author, but rather as an 'Anglicised' and, to a certain extent, one of the most dynamic fields of Ukrainian scholarship. Being more open to influences from the West due to a higher level of English language awareness of Ukrainian applied linguists (as compared to that of representatives of other domains), this field also bears some ideological imprints of earlier times, and thus appears to be an interesting area for the investigation of this much-spoken-about 'transition' period characteristic not only of current sociopolitical life in Ukraine, but of its intellectual arid academic spheres as well.

Cognitive organisation of texts

The analysis of three groups of abstracts has allowed us to identify five basic moves of the conference abstract. The distribution of each of the moves in the three groups is shown below.

Moves		EE	U/R	EU/R
1	Outlining the research field	11	13	11
2	Justifying a research	14	13	11
3	Introducing the paper	12	6	11
4	Summarising the paper	12	15	14
5	Highlighting its outcome	11	15	8

Summary of the observations and findings

The English native texts and Ukrainian Russian abstracts differ significantly, if they do not oppose each other in all the features considered. On the other hand, the features within each of the two groups are consistent, that is they work together for the creation of a certain 'integral' image of a text. Thus, the EE abstracts produce the impression of clearly cut and quite 'abstract-like' texts that emphasise the originality of a particular piece of research and try to impress or even intrigue the reader. Ukrainian and Russian abstracts in these languages look like short research papers, tend to be rather global in describing their research, and are in general more impersonal than their English counterparts, emphasising not so much the novelty of the investigation, but rather its continuing and non-conflicting character. However, the EU/R group possesses such an eclectic mixture of different features (perhaps, with a slight domination of the Slavic ones) that it is difficult to outline briefly the general character of these texts.

National professional, ideological, or cultural proclivities?

The variation in the genre of the conference abstract in English and Ukrainian Russian is probably due to a number of factors that seem to overlap or complement the influence of each other. First, some features of the texts may be determined to a certain extent by the specific conditions of the organisation of a conference. In Western countries there is a tendency to plan large-scale national and international events in advance, and prospective presenters, therefore, usually have to submit their abstracts almost a year before the beginning of a conference. Under such circumstances, the research presented in an abstract is frequently incomplete and naturally resembles a general outline with such features as a short 'Summarising the paper' move. In Ukraine the period of time between the first call for papers and the deadline for abstracts is usually six months or even less. Under these different time requirements, Ukrainian academics prefer to write and talk about already achieved results. The evidence of this completeness of research can be seen in such features of the U/R and EU/R texts as a long and detailed description of the paper or a rather confident presentation of the outcome. These are, however, only partial explanations.

Western scholars are known to experience ever-increasing demands in promoting their research during the process of struggling for publishing opportunities, academic positions or additional funding. This reality of market society – the necessity to win international recognition of target addressees, to 'sell' a research product – inevitably influences academic discourse, making it persuasive and self-promotional. Such features can be traced on the different levels of the EE texts: in particular, they include the rhetorical strategies of indicating a gap, question-posing, and counter-claiming that facilitate the presentation of research as novel; strong claims for originality; clearly cut, reader-friendly structuring of texts that promotes better and quicker perception of their main points; and, simultaneously, 'eye-catching' titles, promising hints in the end of abstracts that might impress or intrigue a reviewing committee or potential audience.

In contrast, Ukrainian society has only recently started to gain market experience that affects its academic spheres, mostly in an indirect way.

As predominantly homogeneous, collaborative (at least within a limited number of research groups), and non-conflicting, Ukrainian scholarship was formed during the Soviet era, when the Communist ideology was considered to be the only method-ological foundation of research and, therefore, any explicit deviation from it was simply impossible. Thus, all research was presented as fitting this broad ideological context (though in many cases it was merely a ritual convention of Soviet academic writing). The 'imprints' of such rhetoric are traceable in the beginning of the U/R abstracts where the field of investigation and a particular research area are presented as parts of still wider and significant domains. Also, frequent reference in the Slavic texts to a current sociopolitical or economic situation is undoubtedly a 'remnant' of the Communist discourse with its constant emphasis on the superiority of societal ('communal') values over individual ones. This ideological (and ethical) factor may also account for a less personal and rather formal tone of the Slavic abstracts as compared to that of the EE texts.

On the other hand, some of these seem to be shaped by certain cultural and intellectual traditions. In particular, Galtung (1985) notices that Russia and Eastern Europe experienced the impact of the so-called Teutonic (German) intellectual style due to historical circumstances. The features of this style include special emphasis on theoretical issues, the relatively greater significance of the content of writing than its form, and weak interactive properties of written texts that require from the reader certain intellectual efforts to be properly understood. Within this tradition, knowledge is transmitted to the reader in such a way as to provide the stimulus for thought or even intellectual pleasure.

In contrast, Anglo-Saxon texts are writer-responsible, that is, they are arranged in such a way as to ensure their most adequate perception and unambiguous understanding by the reader; the English writers also favour a straightforward, rather independent style for the expression of their thoughts and ideas that may be attributed to the traditional domination of individualism and appropriate ethical values of Western society.

The influence of these different cultural contexts can be noticed in the overall generic features of the investigated abstracts. While the EE texts are reader-oriented, use helpful metadiscourse and have a distinct cognitive and formal structure, the Slavic abstracts seem to be preoccupied with the content, avoid textual organisers and any formal structuration, and reveal an inclination towards theorising and generalisations (through global statements at the beginning of the texts). These cultural backgrounds also determine the specific features of 'interestingness' that vary so strikingly in the two 'opposite', EE and U/R groups.

What is 'interesting' for different academic cultures?

Berkenkotter and Huckin (1995) investigated a large number of abstracts submitted to a particular conference (a composition convention) and came to the conclusion that a dominant rhetorical feature of conference abstracts is 'interestingness' created by the appropriate selection of a topic, convincing problem definition, and novelty. This particular framing of the discourse 'in an interesting and interestingly problematic way' (Swales, 1996b: 47) is obvious in the EE texts with their preliminary scene-settings that show the importance and novelty of the research, intriguing concluding parts, 'eye-catching' titles, and appealing language. At the same time, the formal and 'serious' Ukrainian and Russian abstracts look rather 'uninteresting' – however, only for an outsider. Those familiar with Slavic academic culture and intellectual style will identify their specific 'interestingness' created not by the specific framing of the presentation, but through a deep professional contextualisation of the research, its incorporating an appropriate theoretical background, and a detailed description of the paper and its findings that establish or emphasise the scholarly credibility of the

T. Yakhontova

author as a worthy member of his/her research communities. Thus, the Slavic abstracts appeal to their addressees by 'telling', while the promotional English texts do their 'selling job' (Swales and Feak, 1994: 214); both groups appear to be different, if not opposing each other, in the ways they realise the main goals of the genre.

Task B6.1.3: After you read

➤ Look back at your notes and consider the reasons Yakhontova suggests for the differences between conference abstracts written in English and Ukrainian. Which of these explanations seems most persuasive to you? Can you think of other possibilities?

➤ You will probably have noticed that none of the moves identified by Yakhontova occurred in every text written by the English native speakers. Is this important? What implications does this have for the model of abstracts she proposes?

➤ Examine some conference abstracts from another discipline, either on the Web or from published abstracts in your library. How far do they conform to the move pattern found by Yakhontova? Explain any differences that you find.

Yu-Ying Chang and John Swales (1999) 'Informal elements in English academic writing: threats or opportunities for advanced non-native speakers?' In C. Candlin and K. Hyland (eds), *Writing: texts, processes and practices*. London: Longman.

Text B6.2
Y.-Y. Chang and
J. Swales

In this extract Chang and Swales subject to detailed text analysis a number of informal elements found in academic writing. The authors refer to these as being of 'uncertain appropriacy' as they relate them to advice in style guides, editors' judgements, and the views of experienced writers, before studying their frequency and use in research articles in three contrasting disciplines. The paper expertly weaves these different methodological approaches together to provide a better understanding of the target features and highlights the uncertainties they present for advanced EAP students.

Task B6.2.1: Before you read

➤ What 'informal elements' do you expect to find discussed in this text? Do you, as an academic writer, see these informal elements as threats or opportunities?

Task B6.2.2: As you read

➤ Note the various methods that the authors employ to address the issue of the relaxation of rules in academic writing in English. Which methods do you feel are most effective? Are they well integrated to give a complete picture?

Y.-Y. Chang and
J. Swales

It was our hope that, through a careful and integrated examination of the handbooks, corpus and interview data collected from manual writers, journal editors, and research article (RA) authors, we could not only detect some mismatches between the prescriptive rules and expert practices, but, at the same time, reach a more appropriate understanding of disciplinary stylistic preferences. It was not our intention, however, to provide an in-depth analysis of the rhetorical functions of these features in this investigation.

Manuals survey

To compile a list of the most frequent *rules of appropriateness* for English scholarly writing to be used as the basis of data analysis in this study, a survey of forty style manuals and writing guidebooks was conducted. We focused specifically on what the guidebooks teach about how to employ *specific grammatical features* to attain an appropriate degree of formality. The sample surveyed covered manuals and guidebooks published from the 1960s to the 1990s. We put aside rules which are more trivial and focused on more general rules which represent certain broad grammatical patterns or regulate specific groups of lexical items. We thus obtained the following list of the ten most frequently mentioned features (the numbers shown in the parentheses indicate the numbers of manuals or handbooks which commented on each given feature).

1   The use of the first person pronouns to refer to the author(s) (I and *we*) (15).
2   Broad reference (11) – anaphoric pronouns (*this, those, it,* and *which*) that can refer to antecedents of varying length.
3   Split infinitives (8) – an infinitive that has an adverb between *to* and the stem of the verb.
4   Begin a sentence with – conjunctions and the conjunctive adverb *however* (5).
5   End a sentence with a preposition (5).
6   Run-on sentences and expressions (4).
7   Sentence fragments (4) – sentences which miss an essential element (i.e. subject, verb or object).
8   Contractions (3).
9   Direct questions (2).
10 Exclamations (2).

Given the association between these ten features and informal language use, it is not surprising to find disagreement over the usage of several of these items among the authors of manuals and guidebooks. Depending on their personal perception of 'objective style' and formality, authors often take different positions with regard to the usage of certain grammatical constructions. The results of the survey show that, except for the use of first person pronouns, there is no clear indication of any diachronic change.

Text study

Ten papers, all from the same journal, from each of the three disciplines (Statistics, Linguistics and Philosophy) were scanned for the ten informal grammatical features listed above. In each case, a single recent issue, in which at least one of the articles

Y.-Y. Chang and
J. Swales

was written by a faculty member at the University of Michigan, was first located. The inclusion of the local authors facilitated follow-up interviews probing into their individual and disciplinary textual expectations. In addition, to uncover the extent of the probable editorial influences in the use of these features, several e-mail interviews with the editors of the three journals were also conducted.

Three of the four most often mentioned features in our manuals survey – *first person pronoun, unattended 'this'* and *sentence-initial conjunctions* – were also found to be the most pervasive in the current corpus, all with a rather large number of occurrences. In contrast, the features discussed less often in the manuals and textbooks surveyed occurred far less frequently. *Final preposition* and *sentence fragments* were used less than fifty times; the frequency of *exclamations* was especially low, only six occurrences in total.

The results show that, except for *split infinitives* and *direct questions*, in general, among the ten informal features, those which were mentioned more frequently in the writing manuals and guidebooks also tended to have higher frequencies of total occurrences. This finding seems to reflect the tension between linguistic prescriptivism and authorial practice. On the other hand, the reason why *split infinitives*, one of the four most frequently discussed features, appeared in the data only once is probably because of the editorial control in the Statistics and Philosophy journals.

Interdisciplinary differences

Given these results, it appears that the philosophers, by employing almost all the ten features the most frequently, exhibit a more informal and interactive writing style (cf. Bloor, 1996). They achieve their intended rhetorical purposes through the manipulations of overt personal pronouns and sentence rhythm (e.g. *initial conjunctions, sentence fragments* and *contractions*). Our Philosophy informant, as a senior member in the Philosophy discourse community, provided us with a probable explanation of this writing style:

> Philosophy has to be more rhetorical in a way because it's dealing with issues where there isn't an established way of settling . . . There, if you want to give demonstrations in philosophy, you would have to be doing something more like therapy to get people over philosophical confusions.
>
> (Gibbard, interview)

Therefore, this stylistic choice of contemporary philosophers could be considered to be the closest reflection of a postmodernist view of knowledge: 'Our certainty will be a matter of *conversation* between persons, rather than a matter of interaction with nonhuman reality' (Rorty, 1979: 157; our emphasis).

On the other hand, researchers in Statistics seem to believe in the empiricist and positivist assumption that scientific studies are factual, and hence best designed to be faceless and agentless; their insistence on formal style thus still remains (cf. Biber, 1988: 192–5). To be prudent scientists, the statisticians avoid using features which reveal personal involvement or emotion (e.g. *first person pronouns, direct questions* and *exclamations*) and features which are claimed, by some authors of writing manuals and guidebooks, as reflecting incomplete thought and poor knowledge of grammar (e.g. *run-on expressions* and *sentence fragments*). The rather formal and impersonal tone in their textual presentations therefore serves to maintain an *appearance* of objectivity and neutrality since they seem to believe that knowledge is an *accurate* representation of the real world. As for Linguistics, its status as a field not comfortably categorized

Table 1 The use of the ten grammatical features in the three disciplines

Feature	Statistics		Linguistics		Philosophy		Total		% of persons
	Uses	Persons	Uses	Persons	Uses	Persons	Uses	Persons	
I/my/me	29	4	307	9	684	10	1020	23	77
Unsupported 'this'	97	9	316	10	230	10	643	29	97
Split infinitive	1	1	0	0	0	0	1	1	3
Forbidden first word	57	7	229	10	446	10	732	27	90
Initial 'and'	1	1	16	6	120	10	137	17	57
Initial 'but'	15	5	102	8	232	10	349	23	77
Initial 'so'	14	3	21	4	44	8	79	15	50
Initial 'or'	1	1	3	2	24	8	28	10	33
Initial 'however'	26	7	87	7	26	6	139	19	63
Final preposition	3	2	20	8	21	9	44	19	63
Run on	6	2	28	8	21	5	55	15	50
Sentence fragment	0	0	4	4	11	6	15	10	33
Contraction	0	0	21	5	71	6	92	11	37
Question	9	3	62	8	153	9	224	17	57
Exclamation	0	0	1	1	5	3	6	4	13

as either humanities, sciences or social sciences seems to be well reflected in its textual presentations. In general, the linguists also use all the features employed by philosophers, only that they use them less frequently, and hence exhibit a writing style less saliently informal than the philosophical style discussed above.

Conclusions

The overall use of the cluster of linguistic features investigated in this study seems to reflect tendencies towards informality in current scholarly writing, thus confirming the observations of writers such as Canagarajah (1996a), Halliday and Martin (1903: 20–1) and Pennycook (1996). However, as we have already seen, the extent to which researchers in different disciplines exhibit such tendencies seems to vary. The different distributions of these linguistic features found in this study can therefore be said to mirror different contemporary stylistic preferences in the three disciplines.

From the manuals survey, we can also see that many of the more recent manuals and handbooks already display a somewhat changed attitude about stylistic rules. [. . . But] however careful these manual/textbook writers might try to be in modifying the tone of their instructions, they still have understandable difficulty in capturing the complexity of the rhetorical choices involved in selecting and employing many of these grammatical features.

Implications for teaching academic writing

On several occasions throughout this project we asked L2 graduate student informants whether the informal features this chapter has discussed made academic writing in English easier or more difficult. Three, including an Albanian biostatistician and a Korean electrical engineer, felt that informality was a bonus. Of this group, Yao, a humanist Architecture student, was the most supportive of the trend and the most eloquent:

> In general, I think legitimizing these features makes it easier for non-native writers, since personally, it has been quite confusing for me to see how many reading materials in my field are done in some different manners from what was taught in writing classes. Sometimes, I think I unconsciously learn things through examples.

However, a clear majority of those who responded to our inquiries were concerned about the greater flexibility that greater informality might offer. The visiting medical researcher from Japan probably spoke for this majority when he wrote, 'I think these informal features make academic English more complicated.' Perhaps the shrewdest comment came from the third-year Economics student from Mainland China:

> In general, I think the use of informal language makes expressing yourself easier, because sometimes it is most natural to begin a sentence with 'But'. But it makes good writing more difficult, because it's hard to mix formal and informal language nicely.

Overall, the project reveals some palpable sense of unease with regard to potential breaches of strict formality in academic writing. And here it is useful to recall that none

Y.-Y. Chang and
J. Swales

of the informants was a language specialist, and most were intent on developing academic careers for themselves in which English would loom large as their main language of publication. In effect, they argued that learning the rules of formal academic English was already a considerable challenge and one that did not need to be further complicated by having to learn how 'to mix formal and informal language nicely'. They preferred not having to decide whether putting a particular verb into the imperative at a particular juncture would be considered 'short and snappy' or 'heavy and bossy' or whether using 'I' might or might not be considered as authorially intrusive.

★ Task B6.2.3: After you read

➤ Consider the claims being made about disciplinary preferences, trends towards informality and the difficulties these changes might present for advanced academic writers. What is most surprising here? What are your own views on these issues?

➤ What do you think is the most interesting or important finding in the article and why?

➤ Do you agree with Chang and Swales's reasons for interdisciplinary differences? Can you think of any other factors that might influence these preferences?

➤ Select one of the informal features discussed by Chang and Swales and conduct a genre analytic study of its use in five research articles in English from another discipline. How do your findings compare with those for philosophy, linguistics and statistics? Can you explain the similarities and differences?

Unit B7
Corpus analysis and academic texts

This unit focuses on corpus studies and the two readings illustrate something of the methods such studies employ and the kinds of findings they produce. Both extracts examine fairly large corpora of naturally occurring data and compare both frequencies and patterns of use among different samples. Hyland and Milton focus on L1 and L2 final year secondary students' use of hedges and boosters to express greater certainty or qualification in their writing. Simpson compares the use of high-frequency formulaic expressions in a large spoken academic corpus with other spoken registers.

Ken Hyland and John Milton (1997) 'Qualification and certainty in L1 and L2 students' writing.' *Journal of Second Language Writing*, 6 (2), 183–206.

Text B7.1
K. Hyland
and J. Milton

This reading reports a corpus study which investigates a major problem for EAP writers: the ability to convey an appropriate degree of caution and certainty in their statements. To learn more about the ways Hong Kong students present assertions in their writing, the authors compared 1,700 UK and Hong Kong students' use of doubt and certainty in a corpus of exam scripts totalling one million words. The extract illustrates how frequency studies can illuminate our understanding of students' writing and provide the basis for detailed understanding of particular features which can then form the basis of instruction.

Task B7.1.1: Before you read

➤ Think about the ways hedges and boosters are used to weaken or strengthen statements in academic writing and how your own students deploy these resources.

Task B7.1.2: As you read

➤ Attend to the way the authors explore the corpus in different ways, with quantitative data providing the basis for more qualitative understandings of student uses of these features.

K. Hyland
and J. Milton

Corpora and methodology

The data for this study consist of two large corpora. The first is a collection of essays written by Hong Kong students for the General Certificate of Education (GCE) A level 'Use of English' examination in 1994. It consists of about 500,000 words comprising 150 exam scripts in each of six ability bands. The grades in this exam range from A to F (Fail), an E roughly equating to a TOEFL score of around 450 and an A approximating to 600 (Hogan and Chan, 1993). The second corpus, also of 500,000 words, was transcribed from 770 GCE A level General Studies scripts written by British school leavers of similar age and education level as the Chinese learners.

Clearly there are many possible educational and social differences between these groups which prevents a direct comparison of their written work, and this should be borne in mind when considering the results. However, there are also considerable similarities, particularly in the subjects' ages, length of education and experience of a British curriculum structure. Similarly, the writing tasks in the two corpora are not identical, but they can be considered as being broadly comparable.

To determine the range and frequency of lexical expressions of doubt and certainty in these corpora, an inventory of seventy-five of the most frequently occurring epistemic lexical items in native-speaker academic writing was produced. The corpora were then examined to determine the frequency of these words in each grade of the Use of English corpus and in the GCE data. Fifty sentences containing each of those items (if there were fifty occurrences) were then randomly extracted from each grade and from the NS sample using a text retrieval program in order to examine items in their sentential context.

Overall frequency of devices

The analysis reveals remarkable similarities in the overall frequencies, with both student samples employing one device every fifty-five words. These figures are similar to those found in published academic writing (Adams Smith, 1984; Skelton, 1988), but may be only half as frequent as conversational uses (Holmes, 1988). In addition to agreement in total frequencies, there are considerable similarities of usage, with *will*, *may*, *would* and *always* occurring among the top six most frequently used devices of both NS and NNS writers, although with strikingly different frequencies.

Epistemic *will*, for example, occurs twice as often in the NNS sample while *would* is twice as frequent in the NS data. As both forms can be used to refer to present or future probabilities, these distributions suggest conceptual differences, with L2 writers favouring confident prediction and native speakers more tentative expression. *May*, on the other hand, occurs about twice as often in the L2 essays and appears to be the preferred marker of possibility for NNSs. The use of *think* as an epistemic verb is almost exclusively employed to express the writer's certainty in both the NS and NNS data and occurs nearly three times as often in the latter.

Overall, the L2 essays contain a more restricted range of epistemic modifiers, with the ten most frequently used items accounting for 75 per cent of the total. In fact, the top five items constitute almost two-thirds of the L2 sample, while ten devices are needed to reach this figure in the L1 scripts. The greatest differences are between *appear* (thirty-three times more often in the NS sample), *apparent(ly)* (ten times more) and *per-haps* and *possible* (each four times more). *About* and *think* each occur over four times more often in the NNS scripts. Among NNS students, there is a higher incidence of claim modification by students in the top three ability bands while the A grade essays demonstrate the greatest similarity to the LI usage.

Student expression of doubt and certainty

Analysis of the epistemic categories again indicates an uneven distribution of items between ability bands, with higher grades approximating more closely to native-speaker usage. Weaker students employ a significantly higher proportion of certainty markers while probability and possibility devices occur more often in the work of A and B learners. In fact, 40 per cent of probability markers and 45 per cent of possibility devices in the NNS corpus were found in the A and B essays.

There is a strong tendency for higher-ability students to modify their statements with more tentative expressions. While weaker students employ fewer devices overall, their writing is characterised by epistemically stronger statements. The work of A and B students on the other hand shows a more balanced distribution between quali-fication and certainty. Finally, the native speakers employ a higher proportion of tentativeness than any NNS group, with about two-thirds of the modifiers serving to withhold full commitment to claims.

Personalised vs impersonalised forms

One interesting aspect of how writers modify assertions is their use of personal and impersonal expressions. Personalised forms explicitly involve the writer in an assessment of propositional validity by use of a first person pronoun (letter denotes NNS grade):

(1) I *deeply believe* that this is not uncommon in our surrounding. (A)

(2) It *seems to me*, to be safest to stick to the wind-farms, HEP's and solar panels, because fusion is a possibility not a certainty in the future. (NS)

Impersonalised forms, on the other hand, avoid reference to the writer when com-menting on the truth of a claim and typically conceal the source of epistemic judgements by use of sentence adverbs, impersonal pronouns or passive voice:

(3) It *is certain* that reading too many comic books and neglecting the newspapers, our language ability will be inevitable slackened and undermined. (B)

(4) *Apparently*, this trend is invading Hong Kong. (D)

As we might expect, the use of these features differ markedly between the two student corpora. The NNSs appear to transfer features of a more personal register to the expository genre and exhibit less consistency in their choices, often coding epistemic comment incongruently in the academic context. NNSs are far more likely to employ a first person pronoun with an epistemic verb than native speakers and this likelihood increases as proficiency declines. Personal pronouns occur frequently with epistemic verbs in published academic writing (Banks, 1994) where they typically function interpersonally to strengthen the force of commitment to an argument or to weaken a claim by hedging its generalisability. For many learners however, attempts to boost conviction in this way are fraught with hazards:

(5) Supported by the above-mentioned arguments, *In my opinion* I *do have the confidence to believe* that wearing brand-name products is harmful to our youths. (B)

(6) *As I know*, I *am quite sure* some parents are willing to pay whenever their children ask for. (C)

So while the presence of personalised forms does not in itself indicate inappropriate tone, their frequency, incongruity and relative informality in the L2 essays suggests a comparative lack of control of this genre. L1 writers in the present study used depersonalised forms substantially more often than the Hong Kong learners and employed a greater range and frequency of epistemic verbs to comment on information. Clearly then, while such uses display an attempt to conform to the canons of objectivity and impersonality often exhorted by teachers and textbooks, the additional need to evaluate one's claims in academic genres can create serious problems of expression for L2 writers.

Epistemic clusters

A final dimension of epistemic usage is the tendency of expert writers to use devices together (Banks, 1994). Lyons (1977) employs the term 'modally harmonic' to refer to contexts where two or more forms express the same degree of modality such that 'there is a kind of concord running through the clause, which results in the double realisation of a single modality'. The NS data suggests that about 25 per cent of the modalised sentences contain at least two epistemic markers, principally functioning to weaken the strength of the claim being made:

(7) By making such laws it *might* be *possible* to remove other prejudice and discrimination. (NS)

(8) On balance it *would seem* that the only real solution to the problem *would* be to allow the papers to introduce an efficient self-governing body. (NS)

The NNS's essays on the other hand revealed far fewer epistemic clusters and we found that where they did occur their principal role was often to emphasise the strength of the accompanying proposition rather than weaken it. Moreover, many L2 students have difficulty in combining epistemic forms correctly. Frequently learners appear to misjudge the combined value of two devices and invest their claims with inappropriate conviction:

(9) It is *far beyond doubt* that Hong Kong is *certainly* an information-filled metropolis. (D)

(10) I *can tell with confidence* it is *definitely* true that the most popular form of reading material for young people today are comic books. (B)

In addition, there are many examples of modally non-harmonic clusters in the L2 essays, where forms are collocated in ways which fail to achieve a congruent degree of certainty:

K. Hyland
and J. Milton

(11) *Indeed*, there are the advantages of reading the books, but *certainly, of course, to a certain extent*. (E)

(12) If someone who cannot follow the atmosphere, he *might probably* be the laughing stock of others. (F)

The fact that many of these L2 learners combine excessively definite and certain forms and are unable to achieve an appropriate degree of assurance and probability in their writing demonstrates once again the difficulties that epistemic uses present for NNSs.

Conclusions

Overall the data show that while both student groups are heavily dependent on a narrow range of items, principally modal verbs and adverbs, the manipulation of certainty and affect in academic writing is particularly problematic for the L2 students. The Hong Kong learners employed syntactically simpler constructions, relied on a more limited range of devices, offered stronger commitments to statements and exhibited greater problems in conveying a precise degree of certainty. We believe this lack of familiarity with a convention central to many expository genres in English may be detrimental to learners' academic and professional opportunities. This is because such errors often not only influence readers' judgements of coherence and comprehensibility, but can also affect the impact of the argument, and how the academic competence of the writer is evaluated.

Task B7.1.3: After you read

➤ What is the main claim made in this text and what evidence do the authors give to support it?

➤ One of the findings in the text is that the use of these features by more proficient students approximated more closely to native-speaker usage. What conclusions can we draw from this and does it have any implications for the claims of contrastive rhetoric discussed in Unit A5?

➤ Can you explain the Hong Kong students' preference for stronger statements?

➤ Note the main epistemic features mentioned in the article and compare their frequencies in the student and Brown corpora in the Virtual Language Centre Web site (see Unit C7 for how to do this). What similarities and differences can you find, both with Hyland and Milton's results and between the two online corpora?

➤ What are the implications of these findings for EAP pedagogy?

Text B7.2
R. Simpson

Rita Simpson (2004) 'Stylistic features of academic speech: the role of formulaic speech.' In U. Connor and T. Upton (eds), *Discourse in the professions.* **Amsterdam: Benjamins.**

Simpson employs some key corpus analysis techniques to identify high-frequency formulaic expressions in the spoken MICASE corpus (see Unit C7) and compares them with three comparison corpora. Following a careful identification of target patterns, she conducts frequency counts and comparisons then examines some typically academic formulas more closely in context to determine their functions in academic speech.

 Task B7.2.1: Before you read

➤ Consider what formulaic expressions you would expect to find frequently in academic speech and whether they might differ from those in other spoken contexts.

 Task B7.2.2: As you read

➤ Once again, note Simpson's use of both quantitative and qualitative methods to gain a better understanding of this feature and the different interpretations it allows her to make about spoken academic discourse.

R. Simpson **The corpora**

This research is based on MICASE, a spoken language corpus of approximately 1.7 million words (200 hours) of contemporary university speech recorded at the University of Michigan between 1997 and 2001. Speakers represented in the corpus include faculty, staff and all levels of students, and include both native and non-native speakers. The data collection for the corpus involved recording entire speech events sampled across student levels and academic divisions including a variety of non-classroom academic speech events as well as the more traditional academic speech genres such as lectures, seminars, and class discussions.

The quantitative part of this study begins with a comparison of the frequencies of formulaic expressions across several different corpora of speech. Three corpora were chosen for comparison purposes: the Corpus of Spoken Professional American English (CSPAE), the Bank of English National Public Radio subcorpus (NPR), and the Switchboard Corpus (SWB). These corpora were chosen because they were the only sizable corpora of spontaneous spoken American English available at the time of the study. Of these three corpora, the one that is most similar to MICASE in terms of speech genre is CSPAE. This is a two-million-word corpus consisting of one million words of speech from White House press conferences and one million words of faculty committee meetings. The NPR corpus consists of over three million words of news radio broadcasts from National Public Radio. Switchboard is a corpus of casual phone conversations, approximately thirty minutes each, recorded between strangers who

R. Simpson

were recruited specifically for the purpose of constructing the corpus and were given suggested topics of conversation. As it is the only corpus containing casual conversation, it is important for comparative purposes; but since it represents an unusual, contrived situation, it is less than ideal as an example of naturally occurring speech.

Analytical procedures

The methods of analysis used in this study are firmly grounded in a corpus-based approach. This approach involves, first of all, a text analysis program that can generate frequency statistics for sequences of words in the corpus, and secondly, a concordance program that shows all the occurrences of a particular phrase in its surrounding context. Using these methods allows for a detailed comparison of different genres based on quantitative evidence, and also permits more in-depth qualitative analysis of certain items chosen on the basis of those quantitative findings. Ultimately, the most revealing insights into professional discourse – or any particular language genre – will be gained from a closer look at the texts, the speakers, and the situational variables; quantitative analysis alone can never provide a satisfactory picture, especially when one of the goals of the research is to make the findings applicable to language teaching.

The units of analysis for this study were frequently occurring expressions of three, four or five words, which I refer to as high frequency formulate expressions. The minimum frequency used as a cutoff point was twenty tokens per million words (or thirty-four total tokens in MICASE).

In addition to this minimum frequency level as a basis for selecting which formulaic expressions to analyze, I applied the notions of structural and idiomatic coherence to further narrow the set of expressions investigated. Structural coherence refers to the syntactic composition of the word string; idiomatic coherence is essentially an intuitive notion. So only strings that constitute complete syntactic units, sentence stems, or that intuitively look, sound, and feel like idiomatically independent expressions were included in the set. Examples of syntactically complete units include prepositional phrases (*at the end, in the past*), noun phrases (*a lot of people, the first thing, something like that*), verb phrases (*to make sure, look at this*), or entire clauses (*I can't remember, does that make sense*). Examples of sentence stems include: I *think that*, I *don't have*, and *do you know*. And examples of idiomatically independent expressions include discourse marker strings such as *well you know*, or focusing expressions such as *the thing is*, or *it turns out* (*that*).

The entire list of three-, four-, and five-word strings in MICASE occurring at least twenty times per million words or a total of at least thirty-four tokens in the entire corpus included almost 1,800 expressions (1,611, 157, and eleven three-, four-, and five-word strings, respectively), but of these, only 224 expressions were classified as structurally coherent or idiomatically complete. . . . The final part of the analysis involved identifying, on the basis of the above comparisons, a few expressions that appeared to be quintessential academic formulae, and examining them in context from a pragmatic perspective.

Cross-corpus comparative frequencies

As already stated, the first step in this research was to find out which expressions occur most frequently in MICASE, and of these, which expressions are more frequent than

Extension

in the three comparison corpora. Table 1 shows the twenty most frequent three-, four-, and five-word expressions found in MICASE using the criteria discussed above. A number of these expressions, however, are also very frequent in other spoken corpora. So, in order to find out which expressions are typical of academic speech in particular, and not just characteristic high frequency expressions in any speech genre, I looked for the expressions that were significantly more frequent in MICASE than in all three of the comparison corpora, and these are listed in Table 2.

Table 1 Most frequent three, four and five-word formulaic expressions in MICASE

Expression	Total tokens	Frequency (million)	Expression	Total tokens	Frequency (per million words)
I don't know	1519	882	in other words	229	133
a little bit	669	389	at the end	229	133
in terms of	550	319	something like that	220	128
I don't think	503	292	and so on	216	125
I think that	482	280	do you know	212	123
you can see	368	214	what I mean	194	113
and I think	328	191	I don't have	179	103
do you think	258	150	the same time	173	101
I don't know if	256	149	but I think	173	101
the same thing	235	137	in this case	165	96

Table 2 Top twenty expressions significantly more frequent in MICASE than in all three comparison corpora

Expression	Frequency (per million words)			
	MICASE	CSPAE	NPR	SWB
you can see	214	41	26	36
and so on	125	59	28	23
what I mean	113	9	4	49
in this case	96	34	34	8
I was like	85	1	3	31
look at it	85	63	7	52
you don't know	84	31	11	43
so you have	82	19	7	35
point of view	77	55	28	24
you know what I mean	75	2	1	33
all of these	71	38	24	12
the first one	67	33	8	32
so we have	65	36	5	35
what I'm saying	64	23	4	27
look at this	60	32	8	6
and in fact	59	19	17	24
in the book	59	7	12	3
it doesn't matter	57	5	5	26
do you see	47	24	9	14

Analysis of selected expressions in context

In this section I turn to a small selection of phrases for a more detailed analysis of their contextual environments in order to further elucidate their functions in academic speech. These expressions were chosen on the basis of the results of the quantitative analysis as well as the range and salience of the functions they seem to be performing.

I'm gonna (going to) go

The first expression in this section is one that initially seemed unlikely to appear on a list of academic formulaic expressions; it is not obvious at first glance why I'm *gonna go* would be comparatively more frequent in academic speech. However, a look at the fifty examples from MICASE shows that nearly half of the uses of this expression have to do with discourse or task management, as in the expressions I'm *gonna go over/ through/into (something)*, meaning to discuss or present something in the class. The examples below illustrate this use:

(1) I'm *gonna go* through and give some examples.

(2) if I have time I'm *gonna go* over question three and five from the problem set.

Other similar uses have more to do with task management or the immediate sequencing of the unfolding discourse, as in these examples:

(3) I'm *gonna go* to roman numeral twenty-eight.

(4) I'm *gonna go* back and say something that I forgot to say.

the thing is

This expression in its discursive sense functions pragmatically as a focuser, prefacing and drawing attention to the ensuing comment or statement. However, a closer examination of the contexts in which the phrase occurs reveals a more complex pragmatic profile. First, it is often used when negating, contrasting, or qualifying – and simultaneously emphasizing – a crucial point:

(5) so I'm moving with the velocity here. but *the thing is* I'm not moving with the average velocity, right?

(6) *the thing is* here we are not doing the T-star version we're not going further and going through that cuz . . .

It is also used for explaining a problem, complication, or complex situation:

(7) *the thing is* that, that you have to make the sculpture so it can be free standing. that's a kind of a problem. you've gotta get it balanced right.

(8) *the thing is*, maximum size is, i- is rather a nebulous thing and it's rather difficult to determine.

171

Extension

Perhaps the most interesting usage is illustrated by the longer excerpt in (9), in which this expression is used while arguing a point interactively. Excerpt (9) is an example from a composition class of a student struggling with a small detail about rules of punctuation, in which she questions arid challenges the instructor. He in turn responds to her question 'Are you sure?' by launching into a slightly more detailed explanation, and prefaces the crux of the argument with *the thing is*, in order to draw attention not only to the content of the following point, but also to his conviction about the importance and validity of his explanation.

(9) Instructor: uhuh. this stuff goes inside, unless you've got a citation to
     include in your sentence |Student: okay.| this stuff goes outside.
        Student: of quotations?
        Instructor: right.
        Student: always?
        Instructor: always.
        Student: see that's totally new to me. are you sure?
        Instructor: |LAUGHS| it isn't actually. |Studs: LAUGH| um, here's why
     uh you can, {arrow} *the thing is* if you add a comma here and it's your
     comma and not Foucault's comma, you know you still need the comma
     so, it's alright. right? th- y- that's like it's sliding. it's it's – technically
     you're adding something to Foucault's text.

Discussion

The research for this study began by identifying a list of all three-, four-, and five-word formulate expressions in MICASE occurring above a specified frequency range. Following from that, approximately one-fourth of the expressions from that list were found to be significantly more frequent in MICASE than in three comparison corpora of other speech varieties, and thus particulary characteristic of academic speech. Finally, this research has examined the high frequency, characteristically academic formulaic expressions from a functional pragmatic perspective, showing that the most common functions can be broken down into two broad categories – functions related to the organization and structuring of discourse, and functions related to interactivity. There is a constant interplay between these two overarching charac-teristics of academic speech, which is by nature an information-rich genre, but in which interaction between the participants is also of paramount importance, and the formulaic expressions identified here serve to highlight these dual pragmatic features.

   All of these expressions are valuable items for EAP students to learn both for listening as well as speaking. And, since they occur across the whole range of academic divisions, they need not be presented in subject-specific classes or contexts. These phrases are used as discourse structuring or organizing devices; for demonstrating, emphasizing, and hedging; for interactional purposes; and also sometimes as fillers. They are often crucial linking phrases between segments of the propositional content of utterances. As such, they contribute to idiomaticity and fluency in multiple ways, and are thus important items to include in an EAP curriculum.

Task B7.2.3: After you read

➤ What criteria does Simpson use to identify the target patterns and what are the main findings that this identification of formulaic expressions produces?

➤ Are the formulaic expressions identified by Simpson likely to be common in written discourse too? Enter some of the expressions from Table 1 into the Virtual Language Centre concordancer and compare the frequencies. Explain your results.

➤ Take five of the most common patterns identified by Simpson and see which are favoured by professors and which by students in monologic speech by searching the online MICASE site (see Unit C7 for guidance).

➤ The extract reports two of the high-frequency patterns which Simpson subjects to greater collocational analysis, *I'm gonna* and *the thing is*. Select *two* more expressions and examine their use in the online MICASE corpus. Can you identify their main functions?

➤ How might EAP teachers use these findings for instruction?

Unit B8
Ethnographically oriented analysis and EAP

Elaine Chin (1994) 'Redefining "context" in research on writing.' *Written Communication*, **11, 445–82.**

Interest in the social aspects of learning and writing has led researchers to examine more closely the contexts in which writing takes place. In this extract Chin sets out to detail the relationship between context and composing in an ethnographic study of a postgraduate journalism course. Using a variety of qualitative methods, she suggests how these students experienced their course.

 Task B8.1.1: Before you read

> Consider how the physical context of writing might influence students' experience of a course, their writing and their perceptions.

 Task B8.1.2: As you read

> Look for what Chin sees as the positive and negative aspects of the course for students and the evidence she uses for these evaluations. Note the different way that the study is presented compared with corpus research findings.

In this article, I present one aspect of an ethnography, that is, how students' interaction with, and 'reading' of the contexts for the production of writing affected their composing. The next few sections provide a brief account of the study. They include a description of the field site, a description of the participants, and a summary of the methods used in data collection and analysis.

The setting

The journalism program selected for this study is one of several graduate programs in the Department of Communication and Mass Media Studies at 'Bayview University'. Although Bayview supports a number of professional programs like the journalism program, its primary mission is research. This research orientation characterizes the Department of Communication and Mass Media Studies as well, although the graduate-level journalism program and a related professional development program for returning journalists play important roles in the life of the Department. It is important to keep the general institutional character of Bayview in mind as the ethos of this organization determined to a great extent the general history of the Department and the subsequent design and assignment of the departmental offices and classroom space.

The master's degree in journalism is completed within three terms. Students who enroll in the master's program typically have had little or no experience working in newsrooms. In fact, students with two or more years of newsroom experience are usually not accepted into the program. Bayview's journalism program is not significantly different from other graduate journalism programs in the United States. It combines practical training in newswriting and reporting with course work in media and communication theory, media law, media ethics, and other related topics. In theory, this program is designed to provide liberal arts or science majors with the skills and knowledge needed to enter the world of print journalism.

The participants

During the year of this study, thirteen students accepted Bayview's offer of admission. Because exposure to American media is an important factor in people's learning the discourse of American journalism, I did not ask the foreign students to take part as subjects in the study, although their insights and informal, off-the-record comments provided a different but valuable perspective on the year's activities. Six of the nine Americans, four women and two men, volunteered to participate in this study. All six had undergraduate degrees in either the humanities or the sciences. Only one of the men had taken some undergraduate journalism courses as part of his college major; the rest had never taken any courses in journalism.

The faculty stated that these students had been admitted because they were seen to be excellent students (all were in the top 20 per cent of their graduating classes and had respectable GRE scores); good writers, as was evident in the writing samples they submitted; and highly motivated. That the faculty were impressed by these students' past academic achievements and work experience was regularly communicated to the students themselves. Each of the students had worked in some capacity for a publication or media organization prior to their time at Bayview (e.g., college newspapers, college literary magazines, local radio stations, in-house newsletters, etc.). Both of the men had had some experience working for a city daily, although this experience was limited and short in duration.

Methods for data collection and data analysis

My data consist of field notes, samples of students' writing, and transcribed audiotaped interviews with my informants. The majority of the field notes were written during classes I observed. During the academic year in which the subjects were enrolled, I observed four reporting and writing courses and a lunchtime journalism seminar (approximately 110 total hours of observation time for all four courses), and occasionally attended three communication theory courses, a media ethics course, a media law course, and two other specialized journalism writing courses (magazine and opinion writing). I also attended any event that students covered for their assignments (e.g., public functions such as speeches, city council meetings) and social gatherings to which all of the students were invited.

Interviews were conducted with all six students, the faculty most closely involved with the students' training, and reporters and editors who read some of the students' stories. There were five occasions in which I interviewed students individually and three occasions when I interviewed students in groups of two or four. The faculty were interviewed twice during the year. All interviews were audiotaped, and selected interviews were transcribed.

In addition, I collected audiotapes of students' responses to questions that asked them to reflect upon the process of writing each article. These responses were usually audiotaped immediately after the students had finished writing an article. These nine sets of questions changed over the course of the year as I refined my study. The students were encouraged to be expansive in their answers to these questions and to talk about any issues concerning their program-related experiences that they found to be troubling or problematic.

Samples of the students' writing were collected throughout the year. These samples included the news articles written for classes and for publications and their other school writing assignments. For some of the news articles, students also gave me their drafts, their notes, and other documents or references to documents, such as government reports, used in preparing an article; audiotapes of interviews they had conducted with news sources; clips of their articles that appeared in campus newspapers or in other publications; and the final copy of stories they submitted to their instructors.

Cultural categories were developed as they arose from my observations and interviews. Story, objectivity versus fairness, reporting versus writing, were some of the categories that emerged from my analysis of the data. To verify the validity of these categories, I checked them against the literature on journalism and asked experienced journalists to comment upon them. I then used these categories in coding sections of the interview and field note data. A modified version of the *Double Helix* data management program was used to apply the codes and to identify patterns within the data.

A critical rereading of the Department as a context for writing

Although few of the students would deny that they benefited from the material support provided by Bayview's Department of Communication and Mass Media Studies, these benefits were offset by the sense of exclusion they developed as members of this Department, and in particular by the liminal state they came to occupy within the Department itself. The students soon came to understand that they existed in the outer boundaries of the Department. They developed this belief through their reading of the Department's 'social text', specifically through their reading of the Department's design and use of physical space, the allocation of important material resources crucial to reporting work, and the economic value assigned to research versus professional work. None of the students ever talked about the Department as being their academic 'home'.

If we review the physical design of the Department, we can see a sharp distinction made between the space occupied by the journalism/master's program and that controlled by the communication-research/doctoral programs. The Department of Communication and Mass Media Studies occupies one wing of a larger complex of buildings housing other academic departments. Within this wing are two floors. The top floor is devoted to the graduate program in journalism and a professional development institute for mid-career journalists and visiting scholars. The bottom floor is home to the graduate programs in mass media and communication. The assignment of faculty offices follows this general pattern of a division between research and professional training. Faculty most closely involved with the training of the master's students have offices on the top floor, whereas those engaged in media research have offices on the bottom floor.

The Department assigned the journalism students to one carrel area so that they would have opportunities to develop close ties with one another. However, it also served to isolate them from the rest of the Department. Unlike the doctoral students whose offices occupy areas adjacent to or immediately outside of a faculty member's office, the journalism students' carrels are in a space physically removed from the faculty or from other students in the Department. Although the location of the carrels made it easy for students to travel between their office space and the computer lab or the classrooms where most of their course work took place, it also established a pattern of traffic that maintained a separation between the journalism students and the rest of the Department. Only administrators of and participants in the visiting journalists' program had keys to the areas where the visiting journalists had carrels or to the lounge where they gathered for seminars or informal meetings.

In addition, although the journalism students seemed to enjoy many of the material benefits the Department had to offer, they did not have ready access to the one resource crucial to the work they had to do as reporters – telephones. All thirteen students used the hall phone, sharing it with each other and with anyone else entering the building who wished to use it. In addition, students could call only those cities and towns within a twenty-mile radius from Bayview. All other non-local calls to communities outside of this radius could be made only if students knew a special long-distance access code. The journalism students were not given this access code. This situation presented particular problems for the journalism students when they were assigned to write news stories that involved their interviewing or contacting sources who resided or worked outside of the calling radius.

To solve the problem of long-distance calling, students were often forced to carry around pockets full of change (for those without a calling card) or to run home between classes to make their calls. This system rarely worked well for the students as their news sources were rarely available when students were able to call them. For example, not only did Mike have to shuttle between the Department and his dorm room on campus, which was about a half-mile away, but he found that he spent an inordinate amount of time leaving messages for people who did not return his calls. The pressure to complete an assignment within a short space of time contributed to the students' sense of frustration about the lack of phones. During this same conversation, Mike also commented on how Katherine and Stan also admitted to having missed some of their classes to interview sources for their news writing assignments. This practice of missing theory classes to do reporting work did not sit well with the instructors for those courses.

The material context for writing within which these master's students worked directly affected their ability to do journalistic work. In particular, their reporting for their newswriting classes was hampered by the restrictions put upon their access to phones. But the context for writing had another effect upon the students' learning to write the news. From reading the physical design of the Department and experiencing the frustrations of trying to do reporting without adequate facilities, the students came to believe that their activities were less valuable to the Department than those required for doing research. Although no explicit statements were ever

Extension

made to students about this hidden economy, each of the students admitted in their conversations with me that they understood such an economy existed.

Conclusion

The argument I have made throughout this article has focused on the ways in which writing involves both the bodily experience of occupying spaces and times that constitute the material world from which writers compose as well as the meanings writers construct about what it means to inhabit such worlds and to do writing in them. By problematizing context, I have tried to define a different vision for studying writing that takes into account the personal, the political, and the sociohistorical dimensions of human activity so that writing can be seen as an experience encompassing both material and mental worlds. This article, then, represents one attempt to define writing as *practice* and to suggest how such an orientation may change what we try to understand in our research on writing.

In conceiving of writing as practice, we can begin to build descriptions of writing *in situ* that help us make sense of writers' decision making that may seem to defy the logic of what a rhetorical situation demands. As teachers of writing, it affords us different ways of thinking about students' 'failures' or 'errors' in writing. What may appear to be a failed attempt at producing competent prose, as judged by 'experts' of a genre, may in fact be students' attempts to use strategies that maximize their efforts within the confines of a specific social environment. There may indeed be a logic to seemingly incompetent performance that escapes our analysis if we look at writing performance strictly in terms of how well it emulates expert practices. To understand the 'logic' underlying writers' approaches to writing tasks will require us to examine aspects of the composing process that have not been usually considered important to composing itself.

Task B8.1.3: After you read

➤ What are the main claims made in this text, both about the nature of context and this course in particular?

➤ This reading is a selected extract from a much longer paper which is itself just part of a doctoral dissertation about learning to become a journalist. What other aspects of the course and the teaching–learning context would interest you and what methods might be used to obtain this kind of information?

➤ What might the department learn from this study to provide a more helpful context for writing and learning?

Theme 3: Design and delivery

EAP has moved a considerable distance from its early conceptions of student needs, classroom relevance and exclusive text-focused instruction to develop innovative, and perhaps unique, teaching methodologies and practices. The main concerns remain essentially unchanged in that teachers have always focused on needs analysis, text analysis and developing syllabuses and instructional practices which assist learners to communicate effectively in their study situations. These core practices are, however, now more centrally informed by more complex understandings of what exactly constitutes student needs, about the nature of academic specific language and how this might be best organized and assessed, and about the effectiveness of different methodologies and materials for learning.

The texts in this theme are therefore more practical than those in the preceding themes in that they address aspects of planning and delivering courses. The readings encourage you to consider issues surrounding some of the main decisions you will make as a teacher. They focus on issues of power and rights implied in the EAP concept of *need*; on the pros and cons of collaborating with subject specialist teachers in course design and implementation; on using socioliterate, genre and corpus teaching approaches; and on the importance of feedback on writing.

Unit B9
Needs and rights

The fact that students respond to courses and assignments in different ways has led EAP practitioners to question the adequacy of academic genres and skills as the sole basis of English for EAP instruction. To reflect the complexity of students' academic experiences, teachers have begun to explore student expectations and difficulties with their courses and study their responses to classroom discourse, texts and assignments. The reading in this unit raises some key issues in conceptualizing 'needs' and illustrates one way in which teacher intervention can accommodate wider issues in assisting students to negotiate and benefit from their subject courses.

Text B9.1
S. Benesch

Sarah Benesch (1999) 'Rights analysis: studying power relations in an academic setting.' *English for Specific Purposes*, **18, 313–27.**

Benesch provides an example of how EAP can make students aware of power relations in academic settings and ask how decisions about their education are made. The article focuses on a paired EAP writing/psychology lecture course at a US college in which half the forty-five students in the psychology class were immigrant students enrolled in Benesch's EAP course. Benesch describes how she conducted a 'rights analysis' by attending and audio-taping the psychology lectures, taking observation notes of classroom interactions, recording students' oral and written reactions to the course and regularly meeting the psychology teacher. This data helped her to identify students' difficulties and underlying institutional constraints and to establish ways for her students to express their concerns and explore possibilities for challenging limitations.

Task B9.1.1: Before you read

➤ Re-read Unit A9 and reflect on how EAP can not only develop students' linguistic and cognitive skills but also encourage them to ask questions about the nature and quality of their educational experience. Consider how you might promote this kind of questioning in your own teaching context and the value of doing so.

Task B9.1.2: As you read

➤ Think about the constraints and challenges that the psychology lectures posed for Benesch's students and how she addressed these. Reflect on any parallels this situation might have with your own experiences of teaching and the relevance and feasibility of the solutions Benesch adopted to your own context.

Needs analysis and 'rights analysis'

S. Benesch

Needs analysis has been the principal method for determining what to include in ESP/EAP curricula, providing descriptions of academic skills and genres NNS students may encounter in future courses or that they will encounter in particular courses (Johns and Dudley-Evans 1991; Robinson 1991). While this research offers detailed explanations of classroom activities and at-home assignments, it does not explain how students respond to those tasks, including their objections and suggestions. Needs analysis presents NNS students' academic experience from an institutional perspective and assumes student compliance with course requirements (Benesch 1996). It describes what is expected of students, not what might happen if their wishes were elicited and acted on.

The present study balanced the descriptive approach of needs analysis with a critical approach to the target situation, where the teacher/researcher aims to transform existing conditions to encourage student engagement (Canagarajah 1993; Pennycook 1994; Peirce 1995; Benesch 1996). To emphasize the contrast between descriptive and critical EAP, I am calling the analysis carried out in the present study 'rights analysis'. Rights analysis recognizes the classroom as a site of struggle. It studies how power is exercised and resisted in an academic setting, aiming to reveal how struggles for power and control can be sources of democratic participation in life both in and outside the classroom.

The term 'rights' highlights power relations and theorizes EAP students as potentially active participants rather than compliant subjects. Rights are not a set of pre-existing demands but a conceptual framework for questions about authority and control, such as: what are students permitted to do in a particular setting? How do they respond to rules and regulations? How are decisions about control and resistance made? Rights analysis does not assume that students are entitled to certain rights or that they should engage in particular types of activities but that the possibility for engagement exists. It acknowledges that each academic situation offers its own opportunities for negotiation and resistance, depending on local conditions and on the current political climate both inside and outside the educational institution.

The findings of needs analysis in this study yielded a limited number of activities: listening to lectures, taking notes, reading a textbook and studying for multiple-choice exams. These were incorporated into the EAP syllabus to allow students to feel comfortable and prepared in the psychology class.

Feedback: students' responses to professorial authority

Student feedback about both classes came in several forms: complaints, class discussions and written responses assigned in my class. I may have encouraged feedback by telling the students, when our class met after the first psychology lecture, that

I would ask Professor Bell to write on the board in the future. Perhaps following my lead, during the next meeting of the EAP class, one student asked if I could tell Professor Bell to assign pages to read in the textbook, in preparation for the next lecture. I communicated this request to him but, like writing on the board, it was observed only intermittently.

Rather than continuing to act as intermediary, I asked the students to write any suggestions they had for Professor Bell. Bell made it clear that no structural changes would be made, such as setting aside time for discussion of lecture or textbook material. He reasserted the current policy: students were permitted to ask questions before, during or after lectures. However, though Bell reiterated the invitation to ask any question, the situation was not as clearcut as he made it seem. Due to the pressure to cover a certain amount of material, he did not always welcome questions and at times discouraged them.

Coverage is control

Coverage is a common concern of postsecondary teachers. How can we cover all the material, they ask, if we let students talk? How will they learn if we do not lecture? Bell expressed these concerns, telling me: 'I can't even spare ten seconds. It's ridiculous.' In this class, teacher talk was regulated by the departmental syllabus, the textbook and the lectures. Though Bell upheld the coverage tradition, he recognized that it was not working well. Many students, native and non-native, could not keep up with the pace of the lecture.

Coverage can be viewed both pedagogically and politically. From a pedagogical viewpoint, there has been a great deal of L1 and L2 research demonstrating the importance of student talk and writing in learning new material. When teachers invite students to use expressive talk and writing to make sense of academic concepts, the students understand the material better than if they simply listen to lectures and read textbooks. Yet, despite the preponderance of evidence pointing to the need for an increase in student talk and writing, coverage of a certain amount of material, through lecturing and testing, continues to dominate college teaching in the US.

Taking a political perspective, it may be that lecturing persists because that mode of discourse is an expression of institutional control over faculty and students alike. If, in each of their courses, students must memorize large of amounts of information, there is no chance for them to challenge the *status quo*. They are so busy listening to lectures, taking notes, reading textbooks, memorizing material and taking tests, that they have no time to occupy themselves with larger social issues or questions about the relationship between their daily lives and their education.

For their part, the teachers are so consumed with covering the material that they have little time to get to know the students, listen to their questions, or invite them to write about and discuss the course material. In other words, coverage is control; it controls both teachers and students. Teaching and learning are regulated by the tradition of the textbook-driven lecture course, a manifestation of institutional power. The EAP students tried to follow that pace, using questions to understand new concepts and, as I show in the next section, to slow down lectures and to participate as legitimate members of classroom life. Questioning was an area of struggle over who controlled classroom discourse and time; questions became a way for students to resist non-stop lecturing after their requests to obtain more discussion had been rejected.

Questions: negotiating power

S. Benesch

At the beginning of the semester, I noticed that students who were talkative in my class were quiet in psychology. I therefore encouraged the EAP class to sit together in the first two rows of Bell's classroom, to feel as entitled to speak as the NS students and to ask questions whenever they wanted. Some of the EAP students discussed their fears of making mistakes and being misunderstood by Bell and the other students because of their pronunciation. Those who were less timid tried to persuade the others to speak. Gradually, nine out of the twenty-one students became active questioners and four more asked occasional questions. A support system developed: when students had difficulty expressing themselves in the psychology class or when they were not understood, other EAP students jumped in to help with pronunciation, vocabulary or phrasing. The camaraderie did not go unnoticed by Bell who, during our final discussion at the end of the semester, commented on the sense of community between the EAP students.

Yet, although Bell acknowledged the importance of questions, he faced a dilemma. He felt compelled to lecture about a certain amount of material, even though it appeared in the textbook, and too many questions from students prevented that coverage. So, he could either allow questions and rush through his lecture, or refuse to answer them. To avoid rushing, Bell violated his own policy of accepting questions at any time by dismissing them unpredictably. He sometimes refused their requests to write on the board, indicate the pages in the text where the lecture material appeared, or contextualize the material being presented in light of what came before and what would come after. So, EAP students who had achieved a level of ease talking in front of NS students faced uncertainty over whether their questions would be answered. I encouraged them to continue asking, but to prepare themselves for not getting answers.

Still, students' desire for less lecture and more student talk persisted; it did not disappear simply because Bell did not agree to provide it. The solution some found was to use questions to create the time they needed to process material or just to take a break. It may be that there was an implicit or even explicit understanding between students to ask questions when the information became overwhelming. A hand raised during a lecture could be interpreted as a signal to the teacher to stop talking so that students could process what had just been presented. It was a way to control the flow of information and prevent the introduction of new concepts.

Another function of questions had to do with NNS students asserting their right to be in that classroom and to be heard. During a time of anti-immigrant attitudes at the national and local levels, the class offered opportunities for NNS students to speak in front of natives, to participate as legitimate members of the college. They did not hide in the back of the room, silently taking notes. In fact, in this section of psychology, many of the EAP students participated more comfortably than native students in both sections of psychology Bell taught, probably because they knew each other and because the EAP class provided support for their participation. Bell remarked that the pleasure my students took in each others' company created a more congenial atmosphere than the one in the other section.

A final observation about students' questions is that even when they were permitted, the questions were only to be ones related directly to the material Bell covered in his lecture. The students were not invited to formulate questions about psychology based on their own experience and intellectual curiosity. Had the psychology curriculum been governed in part by students' questions about psychology and not only the lectures themselves, they would have had opportunities to discuss the subjects that concerned them. Instead, the textbook, departmental syllabus and lecture format drove the curriculum, offering students a set of facts to be memorized and, as Bell pointed out on the first day of class, to forget.

Conclusion

With class size growing at the college where the study took place, as it is at many publicly-funded US colleges, lecture courses and the delivery of large amounts of information are likely to continue to dominate. The present study departed from the usual focus in EAP of discovering academic requirements and preparing students to fulfill them. My role as a critical teacher/researcher was to study power relations and to discover possibilities for greater student engagement.

The students in the present study did not have to be taught resistance. They responded to displays of unilateral bureaucratic power with questions and complaints, as Foucault (1980) predicts. From the first day the EAP class met they had complaints about the university writing test, the registration process and the college's limited transportation and parking. By the second meeting, there were complaints about the speed of the psychology lectures and the lack of reading assignments on the course outline. Even the students who were less vocal could be said to have been resisting; their silence may have been a form of protest. Yet the complaints and silence were not aimed in a way that could bring about change, so I encouraged them to write proposals and to ask questions in Bell's class. They created a community that affected the entire psychology class, leading to a higher degree of participation in that section of psychology than in the other one Bell taught.

The difficulty Bell had getting through all the material he wanted to cover, due to the number of questions my students asked, raises the issue of the role of EAP. What are the implications of an EAP class encouraging students to intervene in the teaching of the content class, through questions and suggestions, in addition to listening attentively and taking clear lecture notes? I believe that EAP can help students fulfill certain academic expectations while challenging others. Needs analysis reveals institutional requirements and expectations; rights analysis reveals possibilities for change. The starting point for EAP can be the institutional requirements but a vision of student engagement can provide the momentum for change. This dual focus of compliance and resistance allows students to choose which aspects of the course they want to accept and which they might challenge. As Auerbach (1991) and Peirce (1989) point out, if we do not make students aware of these kinds of choices, we are choosing compliance for them.

Task B9.1.3: After you read

➢ Rights analysis is conceptualized as a framework for identifying issues of power in EAP classes. It also suggests that both power and opportunities to confront it will differ depending on the local situation. Based on your own experience, what factors are likely to influence these issues in particular contexts?

➢ Benesch identifies the issue of 'coverage' as a source of control, influencing classroom content, interactions and relationships. Underlying this imperative to present all the material in a syllabus is a model of education which values both 'cost-effective' modes of delivery and products which are measurable through assessment. These features reach beyond the local context to characterize educational settings in many countries. Can you identify any general principles which might inform the ways we address these issues in specific situations?

➤ The article focuses on questioning as a way for these students to challenge classroom authority and engage with the psychology lecture. What other options do you see as available to the teacher and students in this context?

➤ Benesch concludes with the statement 'if we do not make students aware of these kinds of choices, we are choosing compliance for them'. Do you agree with this statement and what does it mean for the ways teachers work? How far is it the EAP teacher's job to encourage learners to engage with the sociopolitical aspects of their learning?

Unit B10
Development and implementation

In planning course objectives, tasks and assignments in EAP some engagement with the subject department is essential. This helps to contextualize instruction, make the EAP course as relevant and supportive as possible, create greater equality between subject and language courses, and facilitate two-way interaction to ensure that L2 learners' concerns are considered. It is important that this relationship should not position the EAP teacher in a subservient 'service' role, simply propping up the goals of the subject course, but offer opportunities for real collaboration in constructing curricula which link theory with practice. The reading in this unit is unusual in that it provides an illustration of an unsuccessful collaborative venture and seeks to explain the reasons for this failure in terms of the dominant philosophies underpinning science and EAP.

Text B10.1
C. Barron

Colin Barron (2003) 'Problem-solving and EAP: themes and issues in a collaborative teaching venture.' *English for Specific Purposes*, **22 (3), 297–314.**

This text describes an unsuccessful collaboration between subject teachers and EAP teachers on a course for second-year science students at the University of Hong Kong. Barron discusses the problems in terms of a framework of methodology, epistemology and ontology and suggests that co-operation broke down as a result of inability to reconcile what appear to be incommensurable discourses. The extract is included as his analysis of this situation has wider implications for EAP–subject collaboration. He discusses collaboration in terms of three levels:

- *Methodological:* issues of different teaching methods and managing the process of collaboration.
- *Epistemological:* issues of subordinating EAP teachers to subject content.
- *Ontological:* issues of the status of disciplines and their boundaries, and their different philosophies.

Task B10.1.1: Before you read

➤ Do you agree that collaboration between EAP and subject tutors should be a key part of academic courses? What potential difficulties and advantages do you think this collaboration presents and how do you think it might best be accomplished?

Task B10.1.2: As you read

➤ Identify the problems that arose in implementing the course and the perception of the course by EAP teachers, the science tutors and the students themselves.

Collaboration appears to offer action based on negotiation between disciplinary cultures. The prevailing view in EAP is that collaboration is a continuum, from low interaction between teacher, i.e. co-operation, to high interaction, i.e. team teaching (Dudley-Evans and St John, 1998). Barron (1992) arranges four ways on the continuum that English teachers and teachers of other subjects may collaborate, based on the amount of involvement by the subject-specific teacher (Fig. 1).

Figure 1 Co-operative teaching ventures (Barron, 1992)

Most collaborative ventures in EAP take place at the co-operation level 'because of a lack of reciprocity between the parties' (Benesch, 2001). For Dudley-Evans and St John (1998), co-operation 'involves the language teacher taking the initiative in asking questions and gathering information about the students' subject course'. Co-operation is thus 'characterized by informal trade-offs and by attempts to establish some reciprocity in the absence of rules' (Mulford and Rogers, 1982). Collaboration involves formative negotiations and occurs between two teachers (Dudley-Evans and St John, 1998).

These views of collaboration are static, assuming that the parties are already part of an organised relationship. They under-represent the developmental nature of collaboration (Gray, 1989) and they ignore the different philosophical backgrounds that the parties bring with them to collaboration. In place of a static continuum, I offer Gray's definition of collaboration:

> a process through which parties who see different aspects of a problem can constructively explore their differences and search for solutions that go beyond their own limited version of what is possible.
>
> (Gray, 1989, p. 5)

This is a dynamic, evolutionary view of collaboration, which does not require different levels because the different kinds of collaboration are interdependent. That is why the title of this paper includes the word 'collaborative' and not 'co-operative'.

A dynamic collaboration brings together these different perspectives to create a richer, more comprehensive perspective than any single one could construct alone. The common conceptualisation that results is known as the *problem domain* (Trist, 1983). The problem domain brings together the different sets of knowledge of each of the parties and the different ways of knowing how to go about the problem. It involves a common understanding with the following five principles (Gray, 1989):

- The parties are interdependent.
- Solutions emerge by dealing with differences constructively.
- Joint ownership of decisions.
- Collective responsibility for the future direction of the problem domain by the parties.
- Collaboration is an emergent process.

The problem domain is the place where the parties establish a common ground for talking about methods, knowledge, language and ideology. The prevalence of co-operative ventures reported in the EAP literature indicates that the problem domain is dominated by the content teachers and the EAP teachers occupy a subordinate position – 'the butler's stance' (Raimes, 1991). The lack of reciprocity between content teachers and EAP teachers has led to considerable opposition to collaborative ventures by EAP teachers, a situation which prevails at the University of Hong Kong. The reason, Benesch (2001) suggests, is that EAP teachers 'position themselves as compliant objects in the relationship'. My discussion of EAP and Science above suggests that the ontological superiority that Science teachers give to their scientific facts is not conducive to free negotiation.

A science problem in Hong Kong

1 *Areas of negotiation*

The course for second-year Science students at the University of Hong Kong is an illustration of how negotiation and collaboration can break down when some teachers, both EAP and Science, maintain the superiority of their respective objective facts. We had negotiated with teachers of one of the compulsory courses that the second-year Science students at the University of Hong Kong take, called 'Science Concepts and Notions', and agreed on the method and the content. SCN aims to provide an overview of scientific concepts. We thought this course would provide the necessary scientific conceptual basis for the problem. We decided on a single, broad problem: 'A science problem in Hong Kong' and an outcome, a poster, which was assessed by teachers of both departments. The assessment of the posters was the only time when the EAP and Science teachers were together in the same room. But we had not taken into account ontological differences between teachers.

2 Aims and methodology

The specific objectives of the course are to develop the students' skills in communicating in English, problem-solving and information technology. These are the three skills which employers in Hong Kong rate as their top three requirements of graduates (Wan, 2000). The more general objective of the project is to demonstrate to the students that science is all around them, not just an academic subject located within schools and universities. The students work in small groups and collaborate by assigning tasks and activities to different group members. They go out into Hong Kong, undertake different kinds of methods, including conducting questionnaires, interviewing and talking to people, observation and collecting data, and bring their information back with their solutions. This integrates language and knowledge with community.

3 Concerns of EAP teachers and Science teachers

The simple rubric created problems because it challenged EAP and Science teachers at all levels. There was a general methodological issue because the unstructured nature of Problem Based Learning requires that both language and knowledge are generated as the problem unfolds. Some of the EAP teachers found this a challenge because they wanted the whole course and materials at the beginning of the semester. Their instrumental view of language as arising from a series of functions is resistant to change once the functions have been specified. The problem of change during the course was exacerbated by the Science teachers, who made changes to the course without informing us.

There was a major epistemological concern regarding what counts as knowledge. Some of the EAP teachers expressed this concern as 'Where's the English?' By this comment they identified language as a subject that can be isolated in the classroom and taught by controlling carrier content. Neither language nor content was under the control of the EAP teachers. The content mattered because the students were generating it. The EAP teachers' comment expressed their concern about losing their disciplinary identity. What counted as knowledge for the Science teachers was strictly scientific facts. The different perspectives that the students were expected to investigate in their problems – scientific, social, economic, environmental, etc. – were, according to some of the Science teachers, irrelevant. Some of the Science teachers told the students that they would assess their posters only for 'scientific content'. Any 'other irrelevant content' would at best be ignored, or, worse, result in a lower grade. This was one of several instances when the Science teachers made decisions without informing the EAP teachers and which we eventually learnt from the students.

The ontological differences between the two disciplines were evident at a meeting held to discuss the problems with the course. It was here that the EAP teachers' linguistic facts came up against the Science teachers' facts. The EAP teachers barely had a say as the science representative instructed those present how to investigate chocolate using only scientific means. His invocation of the ontological principle to privilege his scientific facts over all other facts repelled the EAP teachers even more. Both sides retreated with their ontological facts, further apart than before the meeting. It was a vivid example of how two disciplines with apparently similar realist backgrounds are in fact incommensurable with no basis for negotiation and collaboration. With their emphases on the status of their respective knowledges, controlling content and managing the task, both sets of teachers were not concerned about reciprocity and 'participating in an arrangement where both parties contribute and influence each other equally' (Benesch, 2001), but with maintaining the integrity of their disciplines.

This is an issue for functionalism in EAP, not for EAP generally. Its imitation of Science in its recognition of objective entities gives it a timelessness that is unable to account for the rhythm of language. It is this rhythm which accounts for changes across time as it intertwines with knowledge, and provides the sense of community as students and teachers cross disciplinary boundaries.

4 Students' actions

The students clearly perceived the ontological clash because they stated overwhelmingly in their evaluations of the course that the link between the two departments should be terminated. Some expressed this by stating that the course was very time-consuming. Some expressed it by stating that they specifically wanted grammar and vocabulary exercises, reinforcing the functionalist view that there are language facts distinct from scientific facts, even in an English-medium university. Some students expressed the distinction more clearly as a wish for a business English course, distancing themselves and English from Science by looking into their future workplaces in business organisations. This view is confirmed by a study on the attitudes of Science students at the University of Hong Kong towards Science carried out by a group of students on this course. They found that 64 per cent of the students in the faculty did not want to be scientists and for 58 per cent of them Science was not their first choice (Chan, Luk, Hui, and Hui 2001).

The majority of the students also stated that they liked the group work and problem-solving. This is to be expected in students who go around Hong Kong in small groups, doing things together (Scollon, Bhatia, Li, and Yung 1999). Their collaboration overcame the disciplinary battle going on under the surface and they rose to the occasion magnificently. The poster exhibitions at the end of the semester were highly interactive events that generated an infectious buzz which one teacher described as being like a carnival. The quality of the 105 posters was high, with few exceptions. They covered a wide range of topics, illustrating the students' concerns about the environment and topical issues such as the dangers of mobile phones. The students demonstrated that they had engaged in collaboration, reflexivity and active engagement. They had solved problems. For example, they discovered how to make a poster. Here are some students' comments:

A poster is different from a display board.

Most of the posters are presented in a good way.

We tried to make more decoration to make it more attractive.

They had planned and to an extent become independent through the creation of individual posters. One of the students commented:

I think in this exhibition we can see a lot of creativity.

C. Barron

The students' comments show that they had critically thought about the project and had resolved issues through collaborative group efforts. The success of the posters at the end was a powerful reminder of what problem-solving requires.

- Generativity – the students had used both Cantonese and English to generate knowledge in a community of speakers.
- Personal relevance – they had integrated scientific discourse and language in a problem that mattered to them.
- Personal autonomy – they had developed ownership of a problem, which they chose.
- Active engagement – they had made posters and had collaborated inside and outside the classroom.
- Reflectivity – they had become independent in seeking knowledge and how to present it; 'the teacher's role should be to challenge the learner's thinking – not to dictate or attempt to proceduralize the learning' (Savery and Duffy, 1998).
- Integration – they had fostered interdisciplinarity, sharing concepts and ideas across disciplines.

What the constructivism of the students showed through their posters is that knowledge and language are not timeless, but intertwine in time to create something that is much more than the sum of the individual parts.

Conclusion

The course has identified one positive feature. There is an EAP disciplinary identity, which has ontological, epistemological and methodological bases. It has also revealed a fundamental issue which may be masked in successful collaborative ventures. This is an issue for functionalism. Because it shares a realist background with Science, a functionalist EAP cannot engage as an equal partner in collaboration with scientific disciplines because its objective facts are not accepted at the same ontological level of generality as those of Science. Shared methodologies and even shared knowledge will not necessarily lead to successful collaboration. There has to be also a flexible ontological background that is open to negotiation and change. The alternative to the absolutism of the realism of science and the functionalism of applied linguistics is, perhaps surprisingly, constructivism. It offers a good possibility for collaboration at both the disciplinary and intercultural levels because it relies on reciprocity. The risk of failure is just too great.

Task B10.1.3: After you read

➤ Summarize the different ontological positions which Barron claims EAP and Science represent. How far are these 'incommensurate discourses' and to what extent do you agree that they were responsible for the failure of this course?

➤ Barron suggests adopting a 'dynamic, evolutionary view of collaboration' where equal partners mutually respect each other and engage in free negotiation without preconceptions. How does this model compare with that of Dudley-Evans and St John which was discussed in Unit A10. To what extent does Barron offer a realistic perspective on collaboration and should we be satisfied with something less ideal?

➤ While Barron presents the course as a failure of co-operation between the EAP teachers and the science teachers, do you see any positive outcomes of the course? What lessons might be drawn by the teachers concerning how to manage their relationships with the Science department and organize the course more successfully in future?

➤ 'Shared methodologies and even shared knowledge will not necessarily lead to successful collaboration. There has to be also a flexible ontological background that is open to negotiation and change.' Given the deep-seated problems identified by Barron, how far is collaboration between EAP and science teachers actually possible? What can be done to overcome these obstacles?

Unit B11
Methodologies and materials

While students' learning experiences are influenced by needs analysis, course design and materials, it is methodologies, and the teacher's understandings of language and learning which lie behind these, which are at the heart of EAP instruction. This unit contains three readings each of which focuses on a different way of approaching literacy instruction in academic contexts. The first text, by Ann Johns, illustrates her 'socioliterate approach' in which students draw on their experiences with genres and discourse communities to better understand relevant texts. In the second text Lynne Flowerdew describes a course for engineering students which is organized around a genre analysis of student reports. Finally Mark Warschauer discusses ways that computer-mediated communication can be used in writing classes to reflect different methodological orientations.

Ann Johns (1997) *Text, role and context.* **Cambridge: Cambridge University Press, chapter 6.**

Text B11.1
A. Johns

Ann Johns advocates a socioliterate approach to EAP teaching to help students learn to view texts as purposeful rather than arbitrary, as situated rather than autonomous and as constructed within broader social contexts of classrooms, disciplines and the wider world. The method encourages student inquiry into texts, their own literate lives and the literacy practices of others, focusing on genres, practices and contexts. By seeing how texts work and considering the social factors that influence texts students are helped to see how this understanding can enhance their own writing, reading and participation in academic tasks. In this extract Johns describes how she encourages her undergraduates to go beyond the classroom to study and reflect on the views and practices of their subject discipline tutors thorough interviews, literacy journals and participant observation.

Task B11.1.1: Before you read

➤ Think about what students might be asked to do in order to research texts and contexts beyond the classroom. Note down some of the tasks that students might be asked to do.

Task B11.1.2: As you read

➤ Record the different tasks Johns discusses and think about which might be most suitable for your own classes as a way of enhancing their understanding of disciplinary practices.

Research beyond the classroom

Interviews with discipline-specific faculty and expert students

Much student research on texts and processes can be completed in literacy class-rooms, but students also need to go outside: to observe, to question, and to develop hypotheses. One productive way for students to test their hypotheses about texts, roles, and contexts, and about writers' and readers' purposes, is to interview discipline specific (DS) faculty members. In preparing their interview questions, students must first ask themselves what their purposes are. Do they want to find out about a specific class and the nature of the assignments? Do they want to ask questions about specialist text form and content, about vocabulary and argumentation? Do they want to hear about the socioliterate practices of the instructor: his or her discipline and disciplinary practices, favorite classes, and requirements? Sometimes the students are interested in several of these general topics; however, I encourage them to focus on one topic and to pursue it in depth during the interview.

Each group of four or five students decides on a topic, then the groups begin to develop a series of questions to pose to the faculty expert. They share their questions with other student groups as they work on refining them. In some cases, the students conduct a practice interview with their literacy teacher or a student volunteer before the DS faculty interview takes place, in order to reduce the possibility for misunderstanding or insult and to ensure that the information desired will be elicited by the questions posed. These activities provide excellent opportunities for rehearsing question posing, a skill that is both necessary and difficult for many students (McKenna, 1987). When practicing the interviews, students can work on pronunciation, intonation, vocabulary choice, and pragmatic considerations such as topic nomination and turn taking. As the students practice, the literacy teacher acts as informant and facilitator, providing commentary and critique when necessary.

When the students are ready to conduct their interviews, each group visits the faculty member. In most cases, the roles are planned: certain students ask the questions, others take notes, and others tape record (if permitted). After the interviews, the group meets to write up their findings for a report to their literacy class.

Disciplinary practices interviews

The possibilities for interview topics relating to texts, tasks, and other classroom issues are many. One example that focuses on the faculty member's professional interests as they relate to his disciplinary community is provided here. These are the questions the students prepared.

1 Why did you study this subject (e.g., biology)?
2 What is your educational background? Why did you choose to complete your degrees at the educational institutions you attended?

3 When did you complete your thesis or dissertation? What was the title? (And sometimes: What does the title mean?) May we see a copy? What methodology did you use? Is this a common methodology in your discipline? Have you published something from your dissertation? May we see a copy?

4 Are you still interested in your dissertation topic, or are you now involved in other research topics?

5 How do you use your dissertation or current research in teaching your classes, if at all? Which classes are most related to your research interests and dissertation topic? Why?

6 Are any of your students doing research with you? What are their roles in the research process? Do they co-author the papers?

7 Would you encourage today's students to pursue your research interests? Why or why not?

8 What are the important research or reaching topics in your discipline today? How can we find out about them?

Using their notes and their recordings, the student groups wrote up their interview results as a brief research report, citing as sources quotations from the faculty member as well as elements from the dissertation or class textbooks. It should be noted that a dissertation itself can provide a number of possibilities for student research: They can discuss who reads it (the 'committee'), how it is structured, the content and form of the hypotheses, data collection, and the use of nonlinear information such as formulas, charts, and graphs. This student exposure to disciplinary rather than pedagogical texts and experiences can lead to useful discussions and discoveries.

Emboldened by their interview successes, students often approach other faculty to conduct similar, less formal discussions, and, not incidentally, ask specific questions about their own future study and involvement in a disciplinary community.

Text-as-artifacts interviews

Other students are more concerned about their current literacies than they are about the rules and practices of a disciplinary community. In these cases, another type of scripted interview, about pedagogical artifacts, can take place. As has been noted, the textbook is the most typical classroom reading for many undergraduates, and for some graduate students as well; thus these can be chosen as artifacts for interviews.

The following set of interview questions were posed to a faculty member in his office by four members of my literacy class.

1 Why was X textbook chosen for X class? Was it chosen by you? If so, why do you prefer it to the other textbooks available? Was it chosen by another member of the faculty or a department committee? What were the reasons for their choice?

2 What do you see as the function of the textbook in the class? Is it a reference? Does it provide the most important reading?

3 What particular aids in the textbook are most important for student use in this class? Why? How do they relate to the classroom goals?

4 What are the central concepts, topics, or ideas for the classroom that this textbook includes? What parts of the textbook are not as important for the course? Why?

5 How would you read or study for this class, using this textbook? (Students may assist the faculty member in this discussion by turning to a chapter and asking the

Extension

faculty member to show how she or he would approach the reading and study of the text.) Would you take notes, gloss the margins, or use another method? What would you take notes on? Why would you study in this way?

6 Do you read textbooks to keep up with your discipline? If not, what do you read? How does what you read as a professional differ from a textbook reading? (And, for the braver students: Why don't students read the kinds of texts you read?)

Students find this kind of interview useful, even if they are not enrolled in the faculty member's class. It helps them to understand the textbook as genre and to see its potential relationships to classroom practices. In some cases, students find that faculty have not thought much about their textbooks, and this can be frustrating or revealing. In other cases, the faculty turn the tables: They ask students to talk about the textbooks and how the students read them. Whatever happens, these sessions can become learning experiences for all concerned.

Participant observation

Our students are, and will continue to be, participants in academic endeavors. Another research goal, then, is to convert them from students into participant observers, to change what is often a passive role into an active one. What does this mean for the student researchers? Doheny-Farina and Odell (1985, p. 508) describe participant observation in the following manner:

> the researchers must adopt a dual role – that of both participant and observer. As participants, researchers try to develop an empathetic relationship with the individuals they are studying. Researchers must try to see things from these individuals' point of view, becoming – at least vicariously – participants in the life of the group to which the individuals belong. Researchers, however, must also be able to distance themselves, to look at phenomena from an outsider's point of view.

For students, this juxtaposition of participant in academic classrooms and observer (budding researcher) is ideal. It enables them to participate fully, yet it requires them to attempt to 'see things from |the faculty or expert student| point of view'.

The following features of participant observation, adapted from a discussion by Spindler (1982), can be applied to the roles that students take as researchers:

1 Observation is contextualized: The significance of events is seen in the framework of the immediate setting. |Students observe and participate in a class or a lecture. They observe the elements of a rhetorical situation in which discourses serve important purposes.|

2 If possible, observation is prolonged and repetitive. Students should have more than one experience with a classroom culture in order to pose hypotheses. |If enrolled in a class, they attend class regularly; they are able to make prolonged and repetitive observations that assist them in recording what they see and making hypotheses about the meanings embedded in the situation. Though repeated observation is not always possible, one participant observer experience can still be valuable to students and literacy class discussion.|

3 Hypotheses and questions emerge as the researcher observes a specific setting. |Students begin to develop hypotheses not only about the classroom or other

academic cultures, but about texts and other discourses and their own evolving literacies.|

4   Researchers make inferences about the 'native' |faculty or disciplinary community| view of reality. |These can be inferences about a faculty member's discipline and research, goals and objectives for the content class, about testing, or about ways of grading.|

5   Student researchers make observations about their own emerging literacy practices.

Of course, our students can only be novice participant observers. Most will never qualify as full-blown educational ethnographers. However, encouraging them to both observe and record what they see is enabling as they begin to understand the relationships between their literacy experiences and the contexts they are observing.

Task B11.1.3: After you read

➤   The idea of asking students to research their courses and their subject tutors is a fairly novel one. What are your views on this? What do you see as its potential advantages, what problems might arise and what preparatory work needs to be done to avoid these problems?

➤   What are the main differences between the various data-gathering methods which Johns suggests students might undertake and what kinds of information are they likely to yield?

➤   Can you see connections between Johns's approach and the readings in the previous two units? How might student research into disciplinary and faculty literacy practices feed into needs and rights analysis, and how might it relate to EAP–subject collaboration?

➤   Select one of the approaches to out-of-class-literacy inquiry that Johns describes and design a task that requires students to employ this method to research disciplinary practices. Why did you choose this task and what will students gain from it?

Lynne Flowerdew (2000) 'Using a genre-based framework to teach organisational structure in academic writing.' *ELTJ*, 54 (4), 369–75.

This extract provides an example of how genre analysis can inform EAP pedagogy in a very direct way. Flowerdew discusses a course for final-year engineering under-graduates at a Hong Kong university which draws on an analysis of fifteen exemplar texts, suggesting that 'apprentice' texts provide more realistic models for learners. She proposes a number of tasks based on her analysis which highlight key features of the genre such as the Problem–Solution pattern, move realizations and lexical phrases.

Task B11.2.1: Before you read

➤ Re-read the section on genre-based teaching in Section A and consider what this approach offers students and teachers in EAP contexts. What features would you expect a course on engineering reports to highlight?

 Task B11.2.2: As you read

➤ Note the different tasks Flowerdew recommends and consider how far these might help students to identify salient features of this genre and the extent to which they might assist learners to write effective reports of their own.

The main aim of this course is to help students to write up their final-year engineering project reports. With this in mind, it was decided to use good models of these as materials on the course. It would probably be more motivating for students if they could be exposed to good 'apprentice' generic exemplars which can provide a realistic model of writing performance for undergraduate students. Another reason is that good models of these reports are easily accessible from the subject lecturers, who can also give advice on which reports they consider to be the best.

Generic structure

Although the introduction to a selected exemplar report can be regarded as proto-typical for the genre, in the sense that it exhibits all the main move structures, I did find quite a lot of variation between this example and fifteen other Introductions taken from other mechanical engineering reports. Sometimes scope and aim were reversed, or scope was embedded in the purpose statement, while in others there was no 'overview of tasks' section at the end. This report contains a literature review in Chapter 2, but in a number of others the literature review was incorporated into the Introduction. Sometimes definitions were given in the Introductions, although in this report, each of the key terms mentioned in the scope were given an extended one-paragraph definition in a following section entitled 'Background Information'.

Prototypical move structures for the discussion section of research articles and M.Sc. dissertations are reported on in Hopkins and Dudley-Evans (1988), Swales (1990) and Dudley-Evans (1994). Swales (1990: 172–3) lists the following eight most frequent moves: background information, statement of results, (un)expected outcome, reference to previous research, explanation, exemplification, deduction and hypothesis, and recommendation, which can occur in a cyclical manner throughout the discussion section. In the Results Analysis, the statement of results move was always present in each cycle, i.e. each subsection, while the explanation and deduction moves were usually present.

Unlike the Introductions, the Results Analysis sections showed more conformity in move structure patterning when compared across the fifteen reports. However, it was unusual to find a modifications move in this section, as any modifications were usually reported on in the various discussion cycles, or referred to only very briefly, as they had been extensively dealt with in a previous progress report. Furthermore, it was very rare to find any reference to previous research or the exemplification move in all fifteen reports. The recommendation move for future improvements to the design was present, but it occurred in the Conclusion section, and typically constituted only one or two sentences.

Problem–Solution pattern

The Problem–Solution pattern was in evidence in both sections of the report. In the Introduction, the background and value of study moves can be considered to have been subsumed under 'Situation', and the justification for project move as encompassing the Problem – Response + Evaluation (a + sign is used to indicate that the Evaluation is embedded in the Response, i.e. *As a result, we need an efficient, low-cost water treatment system to keep the water quality below the tolerance limits*).

The modifications move, which constitutes a sub-section within the Results Analysis section, incorporates a sequence of Problem–Solution statements. The first paragraph in the modifications section highlights the fact that the design of the sea water treatment system only provides a partial response, since it is negatively evaluated in some aspects, and sets up another problem to be solved: *The original air injection system integrated with the filter could not provide enough oxygen to the culture.* However, the proposed response to this problem, in turn, sets up another problem to be solved: *We added an external air pump to improve the situation. However, we could not inject air into the tank directly, as foam might form.* This second problem is finally resolved as follows: *As a result, we added an air pump into the foam removal unit allowing external air to be injected into the unit.* This analysis has shown that for pedagogical purposes it may well be advisable to consider textual patterning in addition to the generic structure, as the two are distinct yet complementary aspects of discourse structure.

Pedagogical suggestions

This section describes a suite of exercises, based on the preceding analysis, to sensitize students to key features of the organizational structure of their final-year project reports. The suggestions for exercises that examine the organization of content by breaking down the genre into the finer features of move structure include the following: identifying move structures to reconstruct a section of text; comparing several examples to show the variation in move structure; identifying the type and ordering of information within each sub-section, and understanding how that relates to information in previous sections; using flowcharts or gap-filling exercises to represent the Problem–Solution pattern, and creating discussion topics related to the reports. Some language focus exercises are also given, as these can provide clues for decoding the moves.

Reconstructing a text

One common type of exercise is to have groups of students reconstruct a text from a set of jumbled paragraphs by identifying the salient move structures. When I did this for the introduction, I was surprised to find that students had difficulty in ordering the information, and always put the aim move first. I consequently modified the jumbled paragraph exercise to give the students a little more help, and found that they were able to reassemble the text when I asked them to identify the Problem–Solution pattern first and then build the other paragraphs around them. I also reminded students that the usual ordering of information is from general to specific.

Comparing texts

As many practitioners have pointed out, it is important to avoid presenting genres as a rigid model for reproduction. This can be achieved by presenting students with a variety of examples, and is particularly important for the introductions, in which considerable variation was noted among the fifteen reports. Students could be asked to compare several examples, identify the move structures, and comment on the differences in the organization, inclusion, exclusion, or embedding of those move structures.

Identifying content

A suggested exercise for encouraging students to examine the type and ordering of information within each sub-section of the Results Analysis is to provide them with Swales' (1990) list of possible move structures for discussion sections, together with brief glosses, and/or alternatively a text exemplifying these. Students can then be asked to comment on which are the obligatory and common ones occurring in final-year project reports. Students should notice that of the eight moves mentioned by Swales as occurring in research articles, only three – statement of results, explanation, and deduction – regularly occur in this report.

Relating content in different sections

Students can be made aware of the relationship between one part of a text and another if they are asked, using the sub-headings for clues, to identify items in the Results Analysis that were previously mentioned in the scope move in the Introduction, and then asked to comment on any differences.

Identifying the Problem–Solution pattern

The Problem–Solution pattern in the modifications sub-section of the Results Analysis can be elucidated by having students complete a flowchart which represents the chain of problems and partial responses in the first paragraph. Alternatively, either the Problem or the Solution statements can be blanked out for students to complete with any suitable suggestions, based on their own background knowledge, e.g. *In order to remove carbon dioxide from the culture,* _____.

Creating a discussion topic

As a discussion extension exercise for the Introduction, I have found it is motivating for students to talk around the topic. This has the further advantage of making the lesson less text-based and less teacher-centred, by providing greater opportunity for spoken interaction among students. For example, students could discuss the health consequences for customers and the legal consequences for the restaurant owners, of keeping fish in contaminated sea water. There have already been reports of a few cases of cholera infection due to the consumption of contaminated seafood in restaurants. These have had a negative impact on tourism, and resulted in the prosecution of a number of restaurant owners.

Language focus

L. Flowerdew

In addition to recognizing prototypical move structures and their variations, students also need to be made aware of the variety of key lexical phrases (Nattinger and DeCarrico 1992) which are representative of the move structures. Exercises are suggested for the following language points: examining the lexical phrases used for discourse organization, identifying expressions that state causal relationships, and identifying typical phrases for making deductions.

Students can be asked to underline the key lexical phrases in the Introduction, which they feel help to identify particular move structures, and which they could use in their own reports. They can then be given, or asked to provide, alternatives, and encouraged to discuss which would be more appropriate in academic writing. Although students are aware of such phrases and use them in their writing, very often they are not presented in an acceptable form. For example, for the aim move the following phrases are commonly found in student writing: *The project is aimed to . . . The report's aim . . . This project tries to . . . This report is focused on . . .*

In the Results Analysis, students can identify the typical phrases for offering explanations, such as *This was mainly due to . . .* Students tend to overuse and misuse expressions such as *This is because . . . This is due to the fact that . . .* when the context requires a more mitigating expression using a modal verb. It is therefore of the utmost importance to introduce these phrases within a contextualized framework rather than as a list of exponents which students could mistakenly regard as interchangeable. In this report it is also noticeable that the expression *This means that . . .* is always used for making deductions. In the subsection on ammonia concentration, for instance, it is used when a causal expression would be a more appropriate way to explain the significant increase in ammonia concentration. Students therefore need to be exposed to a greater variety of appropriate lexical phrases for these two key rhetorical functions of the Results Analysis section.

Conclusion

This article has surveyed issues in genre-based materials related to the teaching of the organizational structure of academic writing. I have indicated that it is necessary to consider the generic move structure as well as the Problem–Solution pattern, as these two features co-occur. I have also stressed the importance of acknowledging the variation within genres of the types and ordering of move structures, and the variation in linguistic realizations of those move structures which is determined by contextual factors (for example, an explanation could be couched either strongly or tentatively, depending on the context). Based on these observations, I have made suggestions for some exercises to sensitize students to some key organizational aspects of the genre under discussion.

Task B11.2.3: After you read

➤ Flowerdew suggests that good exemplars of the target student genre are likely to make better models for writers than expert texts. Do you agree with this and what arguments would you use to support your view?

> The writer notes that her analysis revealed variation in the move structures of the introductions in this sample of texts. Should teaching tasks and materials reflect this variation to sensitize students to the choices available to them, or should they present a more uniform picture to help learners gain control of the genre first? Give reasons for your decision.

> How could variation in the steps or moves of a genre best be taught? Devise a series of tasks to familiarize students with the different patterns in this genre.

> Flowerdew introduces a discussion element into her activities. How important do you think this is in helping students to understand a genre, does it need to be related to topic only (rather than language) and how could you use it to raise awareness of genre features?

Mark Warschauer (2002) 'Networking into academic discourse.' *Journal of English for Academic Purposes,* **1 (1), 45–58.**

In this extract Warschauer discusses the role of information and communication technologies (ICT) in EAP pedagogy, examining how three teachers in Hawaii have attempted to integrate technology into their writing classes. He argues that technology does not comprise a single method but shows how the Internet can be harnessed to support diverse pedagogies, focusing in particular on the grammatical correctness of formalism, the development of cognitive processes of constructivism, and the awareness of discourse and community of social constructionism.

 Task B11.3.1: Before you read

> Consider what the Internet might offer EAP teachers and learners. What skills and language competences do you think are best developed through the use of computer-mediated communication and what kinds of task does it best lend itself to?

 Task B11.3.2: As you read

> Think about the three different approaches discussed in the extract and consider the advantages of each for students. How can each approach benefit learners and develop their academic communication skills or awareness of communities?

From 1996–1998, I carried out ethnographic research on the use of ICT in language and writing classes in Hawaii. The entire study has been published elsewhere (Warschauer, 1999); in this article I focus on discussing three classrooms where academic English-language writing was being taught. The teachers in the three classrooms each moulded their instruction to their own beliefs about the nature of learning to write. The cases present an interesting illustration of the relationship between ICT use and theories of academic writing. I will briefly introduce the first two cases, of technology supporting formalism and constructivism, and then discuss at greater length the case of technology use in support of social constructionism.

A formalist approach at a private college

Mary Sanders at Miller College – a private religious institution – epitomized the formalist approach to the teaching of writing. Mary believed that ESL students needed to master the formal structures of what she considered the standard academic essay, and she emphasized those structures in her ESL writing course.

All of Mary's assignments were geared toward furthering students' mastery of correct forms, whether at the level of the sentence, paragraph, or essay. And Mary was able to mold the use of ICT to support this purpose of her instruction. The class met twice a week in a computer laboratory and twice a week in an ordinary classroom. The sessions in the computer laboratory began with an online quiz, sent from the teacher to the students via e-mail, that called for identifying and correcting grammatical errors. Additional practice grammar exercises were made available to students on the World Wide Web; a total of sixty grammatical exercises were assigned during the semester. The students worked in small electronic groups throughout the semester, e-mailing paragraphs back and forth that their classmates corrected for grammar and spelling and e-mailed back. The students decided in advance their topic sentences for each paragraph and e-mailed these to their classmates for correction and feedback.

The students also corresponded with *keypals* (i.e. electronic pen pals) at other universities, an activity used by many teachers to promote writing fluency. However, in this class, writing to keypals principally served the goal of achieving formal accuracy. The keypal activity began with a weekly essay that students wrote and e-mailed to Mary for her grammatical revision. Mary then e-mailed the essay back to the students who made the required grammatical corrections, added a sentence or two of introduction, and sent the correct essays as letters (of a sort) to their keypals.

Although the forms of computer use in Mary's classroom paralleled those uses advocated by constructivists and social constructionists the underlying content was strictly formalist. Mary was able to wield technology to her exact purposes. And she achieved her desired results. Students in her course learned to write acceptable five-paragraph essays. There is of course the broader question of whether the five-paragraph essay actually matches a desirable genre of academic writing.

A constructivist approach at a community college

If Mary Sanders was a strict adherent to a formalist approach to the teaching of writing, Joan Conners was equally firm in her adherence to a constructivist approach. Joan taught a course called 'Advanced Expository Writing' at Bay Community College. Joan's main classroom goal was to immerse students in a writing environment so they could learn as much as possible from their own experience. Her assignments focused on topics that were either highly personal (an autobiography or a biography) or practical (a brochure or Web page for a community organization). There were no assignments that taught students how to make academic arguments through the use and citation of scholarly sources.

M. Warschauer

Like Mary, Joan was able to deploy ICT to her own ends. Virtually the entire course was conducted via computer-assisted discussion. Each day, students came in and communicated with each other and the teacher using real-time online discussion, following instructions and prompts provided by the teacher. This served Joan's goal of providing the maximal amount of practice in the writing process. In addition, the nature of their assignments – discussing the meaning of readings, brainstorming about their own thoughts and ideas, posting and critiquing their drafts of essays – all further served the writing process goals. In the second half of the semester, students worked in groups on a technology-based service learning project, developing either a brochure or a Web site for a local community organization. For Joan, this too was part of the writing process, which in her opinion is increasingly marked by multimedia authoring skills rather than by text-production *per se*.

Joan, like Mary, was able to mold the use of technology to further her own beliefs about writing. For Joan, writing is a highly personal and communicative act. She used technology to help students find their own voice, gain practical writing experience, and develop their writing and multimedia authoring skills, without much attention to whether the genres of their writing matched those of academic scholarship. She, too, was pleased with the results, and, from my observations, students progressed in the kinds of personal and practical writing that Joan valued.

A social constructionist approach at a research university

Luz Santos's ESL writing class at Aloha University differed in several ways from those described above. While Mary and Joan taught undergraduates, Luz taught a graduate course. Mary and Joan's institutions were principally concerned with teaching, while Luz taught at a research university. Finally, while Mary and Joan were older full-time faculty members, Luz was a younger doctoral student who taught part-time.

Luz's approach to writing mirrored those of prominent social constructionists such as Bartholomae (1986), who wrote that a student of academic writing 'has to learn to speak our language, to speak as we do, to try on the peculiar ways of knowing, selecting, evaluating, reporting, concluding, and arguing that define the discourse of our community' (p. 4). Learning to write was thus a matter of the student reinventing the university itself. Luz sought to help this process along by giving students the opportunity to gradually learn and become accustomed to the ways of knowing, selecting, evaluating, reporting, concluding and arguing that defined both their own academic discipline and graduate life overall.

In essence, then, Luz viewed learning in her class as a form of apprenticeship, as she slowly drew her students into a new academic discourse community. This type of teaching/learning approach has been characterized as legitimate peripheral participation (Lave and Wenger, 1991). As a component of this strategy, Luz organized a good deal of discussion, with students assigned questions and issues to talk about with their classmates, their subject matter instructor, and the writing instructor. With classmates, students explored together the nature of academic writing in the USA and how it differed from their own languages. With the writing instructor, students had the opportunity to ask a mentor about her own experiences and ideas regarding academic writing in English and the broader academic life of a graduate student. With their subject instructors, students were asked to discuss narrower issues about writing in their own discipline, for example to inquire about the most important journals and the most common reference style.

Like Joan and Mary, Luz was able to successfully deploy technology to her ends. For Luz, ICT served the purpose of helping her students network into new academic discourse communities. Specifically, ICT served the function of facilitating three forms of apprenticeship learning: (1) *collaborative apprenticeship* (with students providing scaffolding for each other); (2) *tutor–tutee apprenticeship* (in which students learn from a mentor); and (3) *direct engagement* with the broader academic community outside the classroom.

1 Collaborative apprenticeship

In a process of collaborative apprenticeship, students work together, under the guidance of a teacher, to support their own learning and development. Luz, like Joan, made use of computer-assisted classroom discussion to support this type of learning. However, unlike Joan, Luz employed this kind of discussion only occasionally, rather than regularly. Secondly, the topics of discussion were different. Luz chose topics that closely related to life as a graduate student and academic writer in the United States. She used computer-assisted discussion when she felt that participatory discussion on these topics would be especially valuable, since the students – most of whom were Asian, and many of whom had been socialized to be quiet in class – tended to participate more fully in the computer-assisted discussion than in face-to-face classroom talk.

2 Tutor–tutee apprenticeship

Tutor–tutee apprenticeship between a mentor and learners was facilitated by the use of student–teacher e-mail. This provided an additional venue to raise and discuss issues related to academic writing and academic life. This interaction took place in part through formal e-mail journals that were submitted every two weeks. Journal assignments dealt with topics such as the nature of the writing process, the structure of an academic paper, students' own writing experience, students' experiences with subscribing to academic e-mail lists, and students' thoughts and questions about the role of e-mail and the World Wide Web in academic communication and networking.

An example of the effect of this type of electronic apprenticeship is seen through the case of Miyako, a first-semester master's student in Asian Studies. My personal interviews with Miyako indicated that she was feeling somewhat overwhelmed by the newness of being a master's student and wasn't quite certain what graduate school was really all about. Miyako was very quiet in class and thus didn't raise these issues orally. However, she participated avidly in e-mail, sending messages about once a week to Luz as well as many additional messages to classmates. She often used her messages to Luz to raise questions, doubts, and concerns about academic life in the USA and, over the course of the semester, this process appeared to contribute a good deal to Miyako's coming to grips with her new role as a graduate student.

Now, if one sees academic writing only as the final putting down of words on paper, it may seem that what Miyako accomplished through this exchange was far removed from learning how to write. However, if we accept the social constructionist viewpoint, learning academic writing involves a lengthy process of discovering what university life is about and what one's own role in it is. From this perspective, Miyako may not have finished writing her master's thesis in Luz's class, but she may well have taken some important early steps in learning how to write it.

3 Engagement with the broader academic community

Luz also sought ways to assist students in engaging the broader academic community. Technology served this process in a number of ways, especially through student assignments related to the creation of Web pages and participation on academic e-mail lists. Luz required each of her students to create their own professional Web page. Luz tried to emphasize the role that Web pages could have in projecting a professional presence by including a curriculum vitae, a description of research interests, or the students' published or unpublished papers.

Luz also required that students subscribed to and participated in e-mail discussion lists related to their academic interests. Students were taught ways of searching the Internet for appropriate lists, and some did manage to find useful lists either through searches or consulting with other students or faculty. Few students however were bold enough to actually send messages to lists. One exception was Atsuko, a first-semester master's student in Teaching English as a Second Language. Atsuko, like Miyako, was a shy, soft-spoken Japanese student. And like Miyako, Atsuko also took well to the electronic environment. She e-mailed Luz regularly to discuss her work and twice posted messages to academic e-mail lists to seek support for her writing assignments.

Conclusion

Technology does not constitute a method; rather, it is a resource that can be used to support a variety of approaches and methods. As the examples of Mary, Joan, and Luz demonstrate, technology can be used to support diametrically different approaches to the teaching of academic writing. Luz's use of technology is particularly interesting because it represents an approach that consciously tried to scaffold students' entry into the world of academic discourse. This can be a challenging task because the language of the academy is not 'a monolithic discourse that can be packaged and transmitted to students' (Zamel, 1995).

For the students in Luz's course, technology was an important part of this process, in several ways. Learning about technology gave them better access to the tools needed for success in academic discourse. And the students were able to put the tools to immediate effect in writing about their own experiences, questions, thoughts, and concerns. They could put out their own experiences in a written form that other students and the teacher could reflect on and respond to. In at least some cases, this proved to be a powerful tool for assisting students in invention and reinvention, discovery and exploration, reflection and negotiation – enhancing students' opportunities to think critically about the academy and their role in it. Computer-mediated communication was not the only means by which the process of critical reflection occurred, but it did seem to be an effective medium for facilitating this process.

Task B11.3.3: After you read

➤ There are pros and cons of each approach discussed in the extract, but which advantage or disadvantage most closely corresponds with your own views of teaching academic writing?

➤ Summarize the goals, tasks and outcomes of each approach and evaluate what the students might learn from each of them.

➤ Warschauer mentions a number of specific tools of computer-mediated communication in the extract including e-mail, keypals, synchronous discussion, multimedia authoring and discussion lists. Which, as far as you can see, seemed to work best for students? Select two of these and compare their relative strengths and weaknesses.

➤ 'Technology does not constitute a method; rather, it is a resource that can be used to support a variety of approaches and methods.' Warschauer's research certainly supports this claim, but how might ICT be used in a dialogic, skills or academic literacies approach? Select one methodological orientation and suggest how technology might contribute to this.

Unit B12
Feedback and assessment

Assessment has both a teaching and testing function and its teaching role is most clearly realized in teacher feedback. Teachers are now very conscious of the potential feedback has for helping to create a supportive teaching environment, for conveying and modelling ideas about good writing, for developing the ways students talk about writing, and for mediating the relationship between students' wider cultural and social worlds and their growing familiarity with new literacy practices. The text in this final unit explores different styles of subject tutor and EAP teacher responses to students' writing. It focuses in particular on the messages these responses convey about the academy, about writing, about the discipline and about students' own identities as learners and writers.

Text B12.1
R. Ivanic,
R. Clark and
R. Rimmershaw

Roz Ivanic, Romy Clark and Rachel Rimmershaw (2000) '"What am I supposed to make of this?" The messages conveyed to students by tutors' written comments.' In M. Lea and B. Stierer (eds), *Student writing in higher education: new contexts.* **Buckingham: Open University Press.**

This text explores a selection of responses to student writing from five subject tutors and four EAP teachers at two universities, one in the UK and one in South Africa. The authors aim to identify some of the ways that tutors provide feedback and some of the messages carried by these types of response. They suggest that responses are used to explain a grade, correct students' work, compare students' writing to an 'ideal' answer, engage in dialogue with the student, offer advice on later essays, and give advice on rewriting the current essay. They also argue that these responses send messages to students about themselves, about academic writing and about disciplinary and university values. The text offers some interesting observations on disciplinary enculturation and carries important implications for EAP instruction.

 Task B12.1.1: Before you read

➤ Consider what different purposes feedback on student writing might serve and the types of signals these can send to students. Divide these into positive and negative messages and think about how the positive can be emphasized.

Task B12.1.2: As you read

➤ Note the different categories of response that the authors identify and reflect on what kinds of comments might realize these different purposes.

Different styles of response

R. Ivanic,
R. Clark and
R. Rimmershaw

Responses vary enormously in quantity. The quantity depends, of course, partly on how much time tutors have. However, we suggest that the amount of time and detail tutors put into their responses to students' work depends primarily on their values, their beliefs about the nature of university education, about the role of writing in learning, and about the role of their responses in all this. They will have developed particular working practices to support these beliefs. Those tutors who give minimal responses perhaps see the task of reading students' writing as largely administrative, and/or do not consider students to have the sort of role in the academic community which merits engaging in dialogue with them. Those who give a lot of feedback must believe that reading and responding to students' work serves more than just administrative purposes. We will develop this idea in the rest of this section and the next.

The tutors' circumstances, values, beliefs and working practices become particularly interesting when we consider the relationship between specific textual comments and general comments, and where the comments were written. Very few subject teachers organize their courses in such a way that they have time to see their students' writing in progress, enormously desirable though this would be. In all but the rarest of cases, subject tutors are looking at a final product of the writing process, and are reading with the primary aim of grading. This may explain the fact that, on the whole, subject tutors seem to focus more on general comments. All of them put a grade at the end, and all except subject tutor A wrote something to support that grade.

Subject tutors vary enormously, however, in whether and how much they respond to the details of what the students have written. Subject tutors A and B appear not to see any purpose in reading and responding to their students' writing other than to contribute to the assessment process. Subject tutors D and E, by contrast, provide a large quantity of numbered responses to the text itself – so many, in fact, that they are written on a separate sheet. The sheer quantity of these specific comments on the text indicates that these tutors believe that they should be engaging with what the students have written, as well as assessing it. The four EAP tutors vary enormously in the balance between general and specific comments, and in the place of these comments.

Six categories of response

1 *Explain the grade in terms of strengths and weaknesses*

This function appears in all the subject tutors' comments, for reasons we have already discussed. All the tutors are making both positive and negative comments, although paying far more attention to the negative – perhaps to ensure the students know the weaknesses of their work so that they do not challenge a relatively low grade. The EAP tutors in our sample do not put a grade on the work to which they are responding.

R. Ivanic,
R. Clark and
R. Rimmershaw

2 Evaluate the match between the student's essay and an 'ideal' answer

This function and the next are both based on the underlying belief that the tutor is the arbiter of what is right. There is, we suggest, a continuum from the sort of academic assignment which clearly has an ideal answer to the sort of open-ended assignment in which a wide range of answers are possible. The majority of assignments in the social sciences are probably at the open-ended pole of the continuum: this is certainly the case for the assignments in our sample. However, even for open-ended assignments, tutors often indicate that what the student has written falls short in some way of what they would have judged as 'good' or 'ideal'.

3 Correct or edit the student's work

Compared with the two previous categories, very few of the subject tutors' comments in our sample are aimed at correcting or editing the students' work. It is, in fact, quite common to find subject tutors who see it as their business to edit and correct students' work as well as justifying grades, but we have not included any in our sample. Similarly, there are many EAP tutors who do *not* see this as their primary aim when responding to students' work.

4 Engage in dialogue with the student

Although this sounds as if it should be the major function of tutors' responses, we have found it to be surprisingly rare. Subject tutor D shows an interest in engaging in debate over content with the student, but it is always couched in terms of a veiled or outright disagreement with what she has written. It is all too common for tutors to correct or edit students' work on the basis of their assumptions; far more productive, and less dangerous, we suggest, to take the view that students usually are trying to mean something, that we do not necessarily know what that intended meaning is, that our job is to find out what it is and help them find a way of expressing it (see Zamel 1985).

5 Give advice which will be useful in writing the next essay

Some subject tutors' comments very explicitly have this aim. Subject tutor B's sentence, 'You need to pay more attention to the structure of your essays', and subject tutor C's sentence, 'Avoid the use of personal pronouns and expressions like 'In my view' in all academic work', are typical cases of this. They are giving blanket statements of advice about what the student must do to improve next time. One of the problems with this is that advice such as this does not give any indication of *how* the student is to achieve what he is recommending. Another problem is that the advice that one tutor gives may not apply when writing for another tutor.

6 Give advice on rewriting this essay

All the EAP tutors in our sample are responding to drafts of essays. By contrast, none of the subject tutors in our sample were responding to drafts of essays, so strictly speaking this category is irrelevant for them. However, subject tutors sometimes respond *as if* the student were going to rewrite the essay. This kind of advice – very

R. Ivanic,
R. Clark and
R. Rimmershaw

specific, but too late – is very common. Specific advice on one essay can only be useful for writing the next (probably quite different) one if the student is able to generalize from it.

Conclusion

We suggest that tutors' overarching purpose in responding to student writing has a powerful shaping effect on the nature of their comments. An implication of our study is that tutors do not always give a great deal of thought to what they are attempting to achieve through their responses to students' writing. Some are neglecting the opportunity to fulfil some of the possible functions. Some are slipping from one function to another, without signalling as much to the student. Looking at this from the point of view of the students on the receiving end, we do indeed wonder what they are supposed to make of it. It is not surprising that they find such responses confusing, do not appreciate their purposes and are unable to benefit fully from them.

The possible messages students may receive from different types of response

Messages about themselves

The ideology of educational institutions in most countries is that tutors are superior to students, and everything tutors write will inevitably be affected by this power differential. Unless they take positive action to challenge this belief (their own and their students') that they are superior, their comments, like everything else they do, will reproduce and reinforce it. Like all ideologies, this effect works insidiously, below the level of consciousness: not all tutors intend to reinforce their positions of power over students. Ideally, tutors' comments could help to build students' sense of membership of the academic community, rather than emphasizing their role on the margins of it or, worse, seeming to exclude them from it. Carefully worded responses can encourage students, and give them a sense that what they are writing is valued.

Messages about academic writing

The very fact that tutors grade what students have written conveys messages about it: that student writing is an object to be measured, that writing is the only way, or at least an important way, of proving our knowledge, intelligence and effort, and that tutors have the sole right and responsibility for assessment. Even while writing is being used as a means of assessment, the way tutors respond to it can convey messages about its value and functions.

- By giving only a grade or evaluation tutors give the firm message that writing is no more than an object to be measured.
- Focusing on form rather than content conveys the message that grammatical accuracy and appropriateness are the qualities which matter most in writing.
- By giving mainly evaluative comments, tutors reinforce the view that students' academic writing is an imperfect version of professional academic writing.
- Evaluative comments also convey the message that tutors are arbiters of writing standards. This is just as true of positive evaluations as it is of negative evaluations.

R. Ivanic,
R. Clark and
R. Rimmershaw

Extension

Messages about university values and beliefs

Styles of response differ in the messages they convey about the values and beliefs which operate within the institution. Some present conventions as absolute values of the academic community as a whole – comments such as 'Don't use "in my view" in academic work'. Others present conventions as determined by disciplinary or departmental culture – comments such as 'In history we don't. . . .' Yet others present conventions as determined by 'neutral' functional considerations – comments such as 'A new para would be helpful here'.

Tutors' comments convey messages about students' and tutors' roles and relationships, about the nature of knowledge, and about academic conventions and orthodoxies. As we have shown, different types of response reveal different beliefs about the role of a student in the academic community, ranging from being a fully fledged member with authority and knowledge-making rights, to being on the margins, scarcely a member of the community at all.

Some responses give the impression that there are right and wrong answers, right and wrong perspectives, or right and wrong views. Such comments convey an objective view of knowledge. Comments can reveal beliefs about the relative value of knowledge and wisdom: whether the work of academics is to create and reproduce a body of knowledge and information, or to analyse and discuss issues with wisdom and understanding. More specifically, comments contain covert messages about such things as what counts as sufficient justification for a particular point, what counts as an acceptable argument, what counts as an adequate explanation. These micro-messages are more likely to be discipline-specific, but some may be framed as values of the academic community as a whole.

More generally, responses can also convey ideological messages about the extent to which the institution is monolithically authoritative or open to diversity and change. We suggest that responses which do not admit or encourage alternative content and/or forms have the covert effect of valuing orthodoxy.

Implications for EAP provision

All the points listed above are relevant to EAP tutors when they respond to student writing. In addition, EAP tutors might develop courses which help students to become 'ethnographers' of the new communities they are entering. This would include helping them to develop strategies for finding out what criteria will be operating in the assessment of their writing, what styles of response their tutors use, and what they are supposed to make of them. One way of doing this is for students to look at past essays from particular courses, respond to and 'evaluate' them, and then look at and discuss the tutor's comments and evaluation.

The kinds of comments we have identified from both subject tutors and EAP tutors suggest that much useful feedback can be given on writing *as communication* by an interested reader without drawing on subject expertise, so EAP tutors could build on this by facilitating peer feedback on student writing. Not only could this approach reduce the time involved in one-to-one work, it would also send messages about community membership and ownership of conventions to students who participate.

EAP tutors need to do a great deal more than just judging students' writing as right or wrong by some mythical criteria of communicative competence. It is important to recognize variety in academic practices: those of us working in this area should be concerned with the actual tasks which students are currently engaged in, and should examine these practices critically, both for ourselves and with our students.

R. Ivanic,
R. Clark and
R. Rimmershaw

Task B12.1.3: After you read

➤ Do you agree with Ivanic *et al.*'s analysis relating response practices and tutor attitudes? Does the quantity of commentary equal greater engagement, for instance? What other factors could influence the amount of feedback that teachers give and the ways they give it?

➤ Do you think that students and tutors would agree with this analysis? Reflect on the methodology used in this study and what could be added by including tutor and student voices. Devise a set of interview questions that might be useful in this research.

➤ Consider your own response practices. Which categories do your own comments most usually fall into and what messages could these comments be sending to students?

➤ The authors suggest greater use of peer response to encourage a sense of community, but studies show that students often feel reluctant to criticize their peers (Carson and Nelson, 1996) or may not value their comments (Zhang, 1995). How might EAP teachers encourage greater participation in peer review?

➤ How might EAP teachers use these findings to help subject staff develop more supportive feedback practices? Draw up a list of points that might be used for this purpose in a staff development workshop.

SECTION C
Exploration

Theme 1: Conceptions and controversies

Section C of this books helps you to go beyond reading and thinking about the work of others raised in Section A, and discussed in more detail through the core readings in Section B, to being an active researcher yourself. Here we return to Theme 1 and to the conceptions of EAP and the controversies which surround this conception which were elaborated earlier. My purpose here is to provide further samples and material to illustrate the ways that academic discourses and communicative practices are inextricably related to wider social, cultural and institutional issues and to encourage an exploration of these issues through a series of open-ended and locally relevant activities.

You will find that each unit in this theme is structured around data, activities and feedback to encourage you to develop independent views on the issues you have previously examined. These tasks revisit questions of generality or specificity, of study skills or academic literacy, of EAP as lingua franca or vehicle for linguistic imperialism, and of pragmatism or critique. Some tasks simply ask you to *consider* these issues, but these are often a prelude to *research* and *follow-up* activities which help structure more detailed exploration.

Unit C1
Specific or general academic purposes?

The term 'academic English' presupposes that there is a 'core' to the different ways that language is used in the academy, but as we saw in Section A, this is more often assumed than established. The debate concerning the degree of specificity that it is possible, or even desirable, to achieve is crucial to defining EAP. It is also central to our pedagogic practices and in deciding how far we should try to go in describing, explaining and teaching specific discourses in our courses. Underlying this debate are fundamentally different views of language and learning which the following tasks encourage you to explore.

Task C1.1

CONSIDER

The texts below have been extracted from textbook blurbs, prefaces and research papers, but all relate to the issue of specificity in various ways.

> If we are to prescribe content, we need to ask, whose content? For the non-native speaking first-year students in my university, to offer modules on marketing, accounting, and nursing is to depart from the very tradition of a liberal arts education. On the other hand, for very specialised international graduate students, a content approach might be the most appropriate. . . . immigrant students need general English; that is, they need more than ways to adapt to course requirements for a few years.
>
> (Raimes, 1991: 420)

> *Approaches to Academic Reading and Writing* is intended for use as a guide for advanced learners of English as a foreign language whose goal is mastery of written English as it is used in an academic environment. . . . The purpose of the text is twofold: to guide students toward intensive analytical reading of academic prose, and to provide them with the writing skills necessary to academic writing assignments, from short essay exam answers to complex research papers.
>
> (Seal, 1997: book cover blurb)

We would argue that discoursal studies of the disciplinary surface can be particularly valuable for discussion, for metacognition and for rhetorical consciousness-raising. The revelations about actual discoursal practice additionally show something about how discoursal and linguistic choices are socially constructed in particular fields.

(Swales and Leubs, 2002: 149)

ESP must be seen as an *approach* not as a *product*. ESP is not a particular kind of language or methodology, nor does it consist of a particular type of teaching material. Understood properly, it is an approach to language learning, which is based on learner need. . . . ESP, then, is an approach to language teaching in which all decisions as to content and method are based on the learner's reason for learning.

(Hutchison and Walters, 1987: 19)

➤ How would you describe the views of language or learning which lie behind each of these extracts?

➤ Which one fits most closely with your own views?

➤ How would you respond to those you disagree with? Use examples from your own experience to support your case.

 Task C1.2

CONSIDER

Hyland's text in Section B1.2 refers to a number of studies which suggest that the writing tasks students have to do at university are specific to discipline. Chemists write laboratory reports, computer scientists write program manuals, English majors write essays, and so on. While there are problems in clearly demarcating disciplines to make generalizations about student writing needs, this is a useful way of focusing on the typical text types, or genres, that disciplines require. Coffin *et al.* (2003), for instance, argue that different kinds of writing assignments can be related to four main groupings of disciplines, and this categorization and the types of texts associated with them are shown in Table C1.1.

Look at the 'typical genres' given for broad groupings of disciplines in Table C1.1.

➤ Do the disciplinary clusters they suggest correspond to your own under-standings of disciplinary similarities and differences? What principles do you think Coffin *et al.* have used to make these distinctions? What changes would you make to these groupings and what disciplines might you add or remove from them?

➤ Do the lists of typical genres associated with these fields seem to be related to the disciplinary categories? What genres would you add or remove from these categories?

➤ Can you think of ways in which this categorization of disciplines and genres might be useful to EAP teachers?

Table C1.1 Disciplines and their typical written genres

Sciences	Social sciences	Humanities/arts	Applied fields
Examples			
Physics, geology, biology, chemistry	Sociology, politics, economics, media studies, psychology	English, history, languages, classics, fine arts, religion	Business, music, health and social welfare, engineering
Typical genres			
Lab reports, project proposals and reports, fieldwork notes, essays, theses	Essays, project reports, fieldwork notes, theses	Essays, projects, critical analyses, translations	Essays, case studies, theses, projects

Source: Coffin *et al.* (2003: 46).

RESEARCH NOTE

➤ Select *two* disciplines from different categories in Coffin *et al.*'s groupings and carry out a small survey of the types of writing that students are expected to produce in them. To do this you could adopt one of the following methods:

■ Draw up some questions and interview several tutors in those disciplines.
■ Devise a short questionnaire to be completed by subject tutors.
■ Collect course documents from those disciplines that set out assignment requirements.

FOLLOW-UP

➤ Now evaluate the implications which your research has for the issue of disciplinary specificity.

■ Do your findings support the view that the typical genres written by students are discipline-specific or are there features and practices which can be generalized across fields?
■ What do your conclusions mean for EAP teaching?

Task C1.3

CONSIDER

Hyland points out in Text B1.2 that terms such as 'essay', 'report' and 'dissertation' are actually very vague and the particular texts that are expected or written under these labels may vary considerably. What counts as a 'report' in accountancy is likely to be significantly different from one in civil engineering or clinical psychology. In particular, there may be variations in how students are expected to present evidence, structure information, make claims, discuss results, and use diagrams and illustrations. Students working in interdisciplinary or modular programmes, in fact, may have to relearn the appropriate conventions every time they sit down to write an assignment.

➤ If conventions vary according to discipline and course, even within text types which have the same name, what kinds of problems are students likely to experience when writing for several distinct audiences?

➤ What teaching strategies might help students to deal with these tensions? List some ideas that you have used or believe would be useful.

RESEARCH NOTE

➤ Collect a piece of student writing from each of two different courses or two research articles from different disciplines and conduct a small study on disciplinary differences.

◼ Identify one feature (lexical, grammatical or rhetorical) which seems to be used differently in both.
◼ Determine how it is used differently. Is it the frequency which is different? Or the position at which it occurs in the discourse or the sentence? Or the connection it has with the surrounding text? Or is it some other difference?

FOLLOW-UP

➤ Write an EAP task which highlights this difference and encourages students to see how to use the feature appropriately in their own field.

 Task C1.4

CONSIDER

For many subject lecturers and students, 'academic English' is a uniform and transferable set of writing skills which can be applied to any assignment in any discipline. Textbooks often make similar assumptions and convey the impression that successful academic writing and reading means following universal rules and skills. It is, however, difficult to identify what might be included in such a common core. Table C1.2 is one attempt to offer a set of principles for 'general expository academic prose' based on the arguments of three writing experts concerning the nature, values and features of academic writing (Johns, 1997: 58–64).

Table C1.2 Features of 'academic writing'

- Texts are explicit, with clear discussion of data and results
- Texts follow an inductive 'top down' pattern, with clear topic sentences and an introduction to help readers see where the text will lead
- Texts contain metadiscourse such as *to summarize, in conclusion, firstly, secondly*, etc., to help guide readers through the argument
- Texts are emotionally neutral and strive to appear objective
- Texts contain hedges like *probably* and *might* to avoid sounding too confident
- Texts are intertextual in that they draw on, and may be similar to, other texts in terms of their structure, form and patterns of argument
- Texts adopt the right tone to show appropriate confidence and modesty
- Texts acknowledge prior work and avoid plagiarism
- Texts comply with the genre requirements of the community or classroom

Source: Johns (1997).

➤ How far do you think these familiar features of academic writing represent a 'core'?

➤ Are there any features of academic writing that you would add or omit from this list?

➤ Johns goes on to point out that each of these points may be further refined and developed differently within each discipline, so that some fields, such as literature, may actually subscribe to none of them. How would you make use of this list to alert students to differences and help them challenge stereotypes in the discourse of their own fields?

RESEARCH NOTE

➤ Select one item on Johns's list and compare its use in an academic research article in a TESOL or applied linguistics journal with the advice given in an academic style guide or writing textbook. Examine how far the frequency of the feature and the meaning(s) it conveys in the article correspond with the importance it is given in the pedagogic text and the advice it offers.

FOLLOW-UP

➤ Devise a teaching task for a group of students you are familiar with which draws on the results of your study. Write the task and the rubric to clearly set out the issue and what you want students to do. Then write a reflection on the usefulness of the task as a means of raising students' consciousness of how the feature is used.

Unit C2
Study skills or academic literacy?

Essentially, the three broad approaches to EAP discussed in Unit A2 emphasize three different elements of the teaching context:

- *Skills.* Teaching the generic set of skills and strategies such as 'referencing', 'note taking' and 'essay writing' that can be taught then applied in a particular learning situation. Language is broken down into sets of oral and written skills that need to be mastered, largely through control of particular grammar and functions.
- *Socialization.* Orienting learners to the genres, norms and practice of particular disciplines, familiarizing them with the ways it constructs knowledge and what it values in writing and communication. The notion of 'access' is central, although it is often seen as something students need to adjust to.
- *Literacies.* Assisting learners to engage in, understand and critique the discursive practices and epistemologies of their fields, recognizing the complexity and specificity of those fields and their effects on individual identities. The emphasis here is on ways of doing things and 'how' we know the world.

In practice there is considerable overlap between the second and third approaches, with the socialization model dominant in teaching practice and the academic literacies model increasingly important in research. In this section the tasks seek to make these approaches more concrete in terms of researching classroom practices and participant perceptions.

Task C2.1

CONSIDER

The following extracts are taken from EAP teaching materials and exemplify different approaches to language teaching and learning. Read the extracts and answer the questions which follow.

(1) Find two assignment titles that you are working on from different courses at the moment. They may be courses in the same subject areas or 'fields of study' (e.g. both broadly history courses), or they may be from different areas altogether (e.g. European Studies and English).

Take a blank piece of A4 paper. At the top of the page write the two assignment titles that you have chosen.

Now look at the list of questions below. As you work through the list write down your answer in relation to the assignment titles that you have chosen. . . .

(a) Are the two assignments from the same subject area?
(b) How do you think they seem similar?
(c) How do you think they seem different?
(d) Would you describe the kind of writing that is being asked for as an essay or as something else – for example a report, a commentary, a summary?
(e) Will you need to quote from sources in writing this assignment?
(f) How will you reference other authors in this assignment?
(g) What sources (books, articles, reports, hand-outs) will you need to help you write the assignment?
(h) Will you use any of the following in preparation: lecture notes; books and articles by recognised authors on the same topic; official reports; primary sources (a poem, a novel, an original historical document); secondary sources (what somebody else has written about the above, for example a book on literary criticism); graphs, charts and diagrams?

(Crème and Lea, 2003)

(2) Working with a partner, put the following sentence variations in order from 1 (strongest claim) to 6 (weakest claim). Some disagreement is reasonable. Can you think of other verbs or verb phrases that could complete the sentences? How would you evaluate the strength of claim for your alternatives?

Unsound policies of the International Monetary Fund (IMF) _____ the financial crisis.

- a. contributed to
- b. caused
- c. may have contributed to
- d. were probably a major cause of
- e. were one of the causes of
- f. might have been a small factor in

As you can see, each of the options 'fits' in that each makes sense; however, only one may actually be the 'right' choice for a particular context.

It is not easy to predict precisely what you might need to do in a data commentary, but here are some of the more common purposes.

■ Highlight the results.

■ Assess standard theory, common beliefs, or general practices in light of the given data.

■ Compare and evaluate different data sets.

■ Assess the reliability of the data in terms of the methodology that produced it.

■ Discuss the implications of the data.

Typically, of course, a data commentary will include at least three of these elements.

(Swales and Feak, 2004)

(3) From the following titles/headings, what can you predict about the passages which follow them?

1   Science student numbers rising
2   The overselling of candidates on television
3   Summary
4   What economics is
5   The challenges of studying abroad
6   Study abroad: a manual for overseas students
7   Abstract
8   The emergence of the tiger economies
9   Immigrants positive for economy
10 War of technology giants
11 Using your compact disc player

Choose a magazine or book. By overviewing the cover page(s), predict as much as you can about the contents. Check how accurate your predictions were by looking at the list of contents. From the list of contents, select one article or chapter. Overview this in no more than two minutes. After you have finished, read all of the article or chapter to see how accurate your predictions were.

(Garbutt and O'Sullivan, 1996)

➤ To which of the three models: skills, socialization or academic literacy, does each extract most closely correspond? Justify your answer.

➤ What are the goals of the task? What is it trying to achieve?

➤ Which one do you think would be most effective with an appropriate EAP group? Why?

➤ Say how you might use this material in a class you are familiar with. How would you contextualize the material and prepare students for the task?

➤ How would you present it?

➤ What tasks would you use to follow up the activity and consolidate student learning?

RESEARCH NOTE

➤ Is there a dominant approach in EAP at the present time? Conduct a survey of the resources available at your institution and in the catalogues of the leading textbook publishers such as Pearson, Routledge, Cambridge, Oxford, Prentice Hall, etc. As far as you can, categorize the materials according to their predominant approach to EAP and present your results as a short report to your department colleagues.

FOLLOW-UP

➤ What do your findings tell you about EAP as it is currently practised?

➤ Is there a trend or movement towards a particular pedagogic approach?

➤ Do tasks always follow a consistent approach in each textbook?

➤ Are there overlaps or hybrids of these approaches?

 Task C2.2

The academic socialization model of EAP assumes that students need to learn the norms and conventions in their new academic discipline or culture. An academic literacies approach suggests that attempting to mimic disciplinary approved forms of discourse can create serious problems for many students. Because they have to use language in unfamiliar ways their choices of expression are restricted and their own opinions, experiences and identities are devalued. This can mean that students have to present a persona that feels alien to them, as one of Ivanic's interviewees points out:

> I felt I was getting closer to portraying an Identity I feel comfortable with in my writing, but this year the more the pressure mounts, and the more I'm asked to do and produce in a certain way, no, I have an overwhelming feeling I'm moving away from it. I think that's one of the reasons I'm getting disheartened.
>
> (Ivanic, 1998: 228)

This can result in students just feigning an identity, putting on a show for their tutors and examiners that they don't believe themselves.

CONSIDER

➤ Do you agree that academic writing forces students to adopt new roles and identities which may be unwanted and which they might resist? Or do you think students simply adopt these identities temporarily with little investment then discard them later? In other words, do you think students actually contest the demands made on them or shrug them off? Discuss these issues in an essay, drawing on your own experiences to illustrate your views.

➤ How far can teachers provide conditions for students to recognize and challenge the ways they are positioned by academic discourses? What kinds of activities could facilitate this? What might the positive and negative consequences be of helping students to 'write as themselves', for their writing, for their sense of engagement in their studies, and for their work in their subject courses? Discuss these issues in a short report to be presented at a teachers' conference.

RESEARCH NOTE

➤ Now, moving from essay to action, conduct a small-scale study into these issues of identity and self-presentation. Secure the agreement of two students in different disciplines, preferably one undergraduate and one postgraduate, and interview them concerning their views and discourses practices. Draw up a list of questions to learn more about:

- Their perceptions of their academic courses, what they enjoy and dislike about them, what they find difficult, what they would like to see changed, and so on.
- Their reflections on the kinds of writing they are asked to do, the guidance they get, how it is assessed, the feedback they get on it, the satisfaction they feel from it, and so on.
- Their views on academic writing conventions in English more generally, whether they feel constrained or empowered by it, whether they are comfortable and familiar with it, how far it expresses what they want to say, and so on.

FOLLOW-UP

➤ What do your interviews tell you about these students' perceptions and practices?

➤ Can you explain any differences in terms of discipline or graduate/ undergraduate status?

➤ What implications might there be for classroom practice?

Task C2.3

These different ways of conceptualizing EAP raise interesting and important questions for theory and research, focusing attention on what teaching and learning involves in relation to wider contexts and how it is understood by participants.

Equally important, however, these perspectives imply different ways of teaching, different tasks, and different ways of engaging students in their learning. This task requires you to reflect more specifically on these approaches and how they might influence what you do in the classroom.

CONSIDER

➤ Devise a unit of work (of, say, three or four lessons) to teach a particular feature, skill or genre using the approach you currently subscribe to. The unit should be about five or six pages and consist of the following sections:

   ▪ A brief description of relevant aspects of the context, including the students' subject course(s), proficiency, prior learning (and so on).
   ▪ A rationale for the unit. This is a set of objectives or learning outcomes – what do you want the unit to achieve?
   ▪ A lesson plan for each of the units, with a brief outline of the tasks students will engage in and a description of the materials they will use.
   ▪ Teacher notes on how to deliver each lesson.

FOLLOW-UP

➤ Write a reflection on the materials you have produced, commenting on how successful you think they might be, their strengths and shortcomings, and how the students might respond to them.

Unit C3
Lingua franca or *Tyrannosaurus rex*?

The use of English as the international language of research and scholarly communication is now well documented. While some fields seem less susceptible to the dominance of English than others, there is no denying the influence of the language on international publishing and on the growth of EAP. The effects of this influence are less well documented, however, and are subject to less agreement. Some writers believe that EAP should be regarded as a means of assisting L2 learners and academics to participate in global networks of research and scholarship, while others see it as the handmaiden of Anglo-American cultural and economic hegemony. The tasks in this section encourage you to research and explore aspects of this issue.

Task C3.1

CONSIDER

One measure of the grip of English on published research is the Science Citation Index (SCI), available online through the Web of Science. This database includes over 8,700 journals in some 100 disciplines, covering the most prestigious, high-impact research journals in the world. This resource has provided commentators with evidence for the supremacy of English in publication (e.g. Garfield, 1983), but as Swales (1990) points out, there is a tendency for the database to select mainly those journals which emanate from the northern hemisphere and which publish in English. The dominance of English may therefore be overstated and, indeed, the ISI has admitted as much. This is, however, an indicator of the most celebrated and influential journals and provides a useful resource for examining the influence English has on a global, rather than local, stage.

The use of English in international publication is very uneven. Some research bodies, such as those responsible for the sciences in France, for example, make considerable efforts to preserve national language publishing, and we might suppose that research fields of more local interest such as literature, architecture and religious studies would be more likely to escape the spread of English. In the humanities and social sciences, rather than the natural sciences, there still seems to be a considerable amount of publication in languages other than English, often in national journals not widely available outside the country of publication.

RESEARCH NOTE

In this activity you will use the ISI database to do a small-scale study of the distribution of English in publishing in different fields. This database contains a (free) searchable list of journals in a number of academic domains such as arts and humanities, engineering and technology, life sciences and clinical medicine. Follow these steps:

➤ Go to the Thompson ISI Web site journal page (http://www.isinet.com/journals/).

➤ Scroll down to the 'Searchable databases' and select the 'Arts and humanities citation index'.

➤ Hit the 'View subject category' option then select a discipline and view the journal list.

➤ From this list note down the country of publication and, from the title and other information, decide whether the journal is published in English or not, recording your results.

➤ Now go back to the 'Searchable databases' and do the same from the 'Biophysics and biochemistry citation index' then again from the 'Chemistry citation index'.

FOLLOW-UP

➤ What do your notes show? Present a table to compare your findings and discuss the main results.

➤ Is there a greater concentration of English in some academic fields than others? Why do you think this is?

➤ What might be some of the limitations of measuring the role of English in academic publishing using this method?

  Task C3.2

CONSIDER

Another issue is the extent to which L2 academics participate in this global exchange of research communication. In a well known study of publications in aquatic sciences and fisheries Baldauf and Jernudd (1983) estimated (on the basis of the institutional affiliation of first author) that some 80 per cent of English-language papers originated in countries where English is either the national or official language. The study by Wood (2001) mentioned in Section A, however, offers a different perspective. Using an admittedly rough-and-ready definition of non-native

English-speaker, he found L2 writers to be well published in *Science* and *Nature* over a one-year period, contributing almost half of all papers. Discipline, individual preference and institutional pressure may help account for such variations, and for some academics it might actually be more prestigious to publish locally in non-English language journals. Tsou (1998), for example, suggests that political reasons often mean it is better for Chinese scientists to publish their work in the *People's Daily* than in Western journals.

RESEARCH NOTE

This task involves conducting a journal survey to determine the extent to which non-metropolitan and L2 authors contribute to major journals.

➤ Select a leading journal from each of any two disciplines of your choice in the sciences and social sciences or humanities.

➤ Go to either your library or the Web and look at the contents pages of your selected journals for all the issues published in a one-year period.

➤ Record the following details: (1) The country of the institutional affiliation of the first author (usually the main author). (2) Whether the first author was likely to be a native speaker of English. (Use Wood's rough-and-ready criteria that a non-native English-speaker is a first author whose whole name indicates that that he/she is not a native speaker of English, despite being affiliated to an institution probably not in that person's home country.)

➤ Now compile a chart for each journal to show the number of articles, the number of likely NS and NNS of English as first authors, and the percentage of papers written by each group.

FOLLOW-UP

➤ Write a report to present and discuss your results. Explain any variations between the proportions of L1 and L2 writers and the similarities or differences across the two journals and disciplines. How far do the results support the arguments of Phillipson, Pennycook and Canagarajah discussed in Section A on this topic? What are the limitations of this study and how might they be overcome?

Task C3.3

CONSIDER

There are various reasons for the relatively low publication rates of L2 writers in English-language journals, but one is the imposition of a single, standard 'academic' variety on users. Kachru (1985) has famously divided the English-using world into three concentric circles:

- The 'inner circle' of native English-speaking countries.
- The 'outer circle' of former British and US colonies where nativized varieties of English are widely used in key areas.
- An 'expanding circle' where English is fast becoming a dominant second language.

Although there are differences among these in the use of English, Kachru insists that outer-circle users are as entitled as inner-circle users to assert ownership of English and to claim that their variety has equal status to others. In academic contexts, however, the gatekeepers of the inner-circle journals insist that L2 speakers conform to what amounts to a single variety.

Participation in global research communities therefore requires a knowledge not only of English but the *right kind* of English. As we noted in Unit C2, this variety may be alien and challenging to L1 English speakers as well as L2 writers, but most researchers have stressed the additional difficulties faced by L2 academics. In interviews with Hong Kong scholars, for instance, Flowerdew (1999) discovered that these researchers felt disadvantaged *vis-à-vis* native speakers of English by a range of problems when writing for publication in English. These included less facility of expression; longer writing time; a smaller vocabulary; a restricted writing style; difficulties in making appropriately strong claims; and the influence of L1 practices on their writing. For these reasons many avoided qualitative articles and tried to stick to more statistical and quantitative papers.

RESEARCH NOTE

This task addresses the kinds of problems that might face L2 speakers of English trying to publish in English-language journals and solutions that might begin to address these problems.

➤ Recruit a non-native English-speaking academic or research student who is willing to be interviewed on the subject of writing in English.

➤ Construct a list of questions to discover his or her views on the need to write in English for publication or study and the problems this presents for him or her.

➤ Write a report for the Research Support Office of a university setting out these views and perceptions and detailing how an advanced 'writing for publication' EAP course might address these issues.

FOLLOW-UP

In response to these issues, the Japanese Association of Language Teachers (JALT) journal pairs L2 authors with L1 mentors to polish their work. Elsewhere the importance of publishing for institutional prestige and government funding exercises means that EAP programmes for L2 researchers are increasingly common (e.g. Sengupta *et al.*, 1999). Use the results of your study as needs analysis data for a one-to-one course with your interviewee. Identify the main difficulties he or she experiences in writing in English and devise a series of tasks which address these needs.

Task C3.4

It is clear that this issue is a highly controversial one, with arguments on both sides. Some observers see an international language as an enabling or empowering resource for outer and expanding circle academics and students, a way by which they can access knowledge from around the world and a means of engaging in global debates. Others regard it as an extension of American and British political, cultural and economic interests.

CONSIDER

➤ What are your own views based on what you have read and the small research activities you have completed in this unit?

➤ What arguments would you use to convince someone who held an opposing view?

RESEARCH NOTE

Rehearse these arguments by participating in an online discussion with other EAP and ESP professionals. Online conference and discussion groups allow you to post and receive e-mails on topics of interest to the group, and relevant ones can be found at the following addresses. You will need to register or 'subscribe', although all are free, and you may like to just observe before you participate, but they are a good source of discussion and information for teachers.

- *BAAL List.* Information at: http://www.sfs.nphi.uni~tuebingen.de/linguist/.
- *EST-L (English for Science and Technology).* E-mail: listserv@asuvm.inrc.asu.edu.
- *Linguist List.* Information at: http://www.baal.org.uk/baalf.htm.
- *Writing discussion group.* List: listpro@Hawaii.edu. Information at: http://kalama.doe.Hawaii.edu/hern95/pt035/writing/wholalist.html.
- *TESL-L (Teachers of English as a second language list).* List: listserv@cunyum.cuny.edu. E-mail: eslcc@cunyum.bitnet.

FOLLOW-UP

➤ Look at the transcript of your discussion, or a thread of a previous discussion on this issue, and make a list of the main arguments for and against each position. Write a short essay setting out these arguments, commenting on whether you agree or disagree with them and stating which ones you find most persuasive.

Unit C4
Pragmatism or critique?

Critical perspectives on EAP encourage us to consider wider aspects of learning, teaching and knowledge, challenging the traditional view that teachers should subordinate their instruction to the demands and arrangements of colleagues in subject departments. These views force us to consider how such one-sided practices uphold unequal relations which may marginalize students in their disciplines and position EAP teachers as lower-status members of the academic hierarchy, acting in a 'service' role to experts in subject disciplines.

Task C4.1

EAP teachers are often trying to strike a balance between respecting the cultural and rhetorical differences of their students while assisting them towards control of dominant discourse conventions. Pennycook (1994: 317) sees this as a tension between emphasizing *access* to the cultures of power and emphasizing the exploration of *difference*.

> While on the one hand . . . I need to help students meet the criteria for 'success' as they are defined within particular institutional contexts, as a critical educator I need also to try to change how students understand their possibilities and I need to work towards changing those possibilities. I am not, therefore, advocating a *laissez-faire* approach to language forms that encourages students to do as they like, as if English language class-rooms existed in some social, cultural and political vacuum. Rather I am suggesting that first, we need to make sure that students have access to those standard forms of the language linked to social and economic prestige; second, we need a good understanding of the status and possibilities presented by different standards; third, we need to focus on those parts of language that are significant in particular discourses; fourth, students need to be aware that those forms represent only one set of particular possibilities; and finally, students also need to be encouraged to find ways of using the language that they feel are expressive of their own needs and desires, to make their own readings of texts, to write, speak and listen in forms of the language that emerge as they strive to find representations of themselves and others that make sense to them, so that they can start to claim and negotiate a voice in English.

CONSIDER

➤ Are these contradictions and difficulties of the EAP teacher's role ones you recognize yourself?

➤ How far is this a dilemma of the teacher's own making and how far is it driven by students' perceptions of the situation? Who seems to be driving the issues?

RESEARCH NOTE

➤ Formulate a set of questions which address the issues raised in Pennycook's statement above and interview a number of EAP students. Focus on their university experiences and their perceptions of their needs.

➤ Now interview a number of EAP teachers, asking them similar questions to determine their understandings of their sociopolitical role and their stance on 'pragmatism', 'accommodationism' and 'critical EAP'.

FOLLOW-UP

➤ Compile your data and compare the responses. Do your interview subjects agree? Do they see it as the EAP teacher's job to 'work towards changing those possibilities' that the academy offers learners? Write up your results to clearly show the implications.

 Task C4.2

Harwood and Hadley (2004) express concern that critical EAP has not been much concerned with practicalities and, with a few notable exceptions, has left teachers without ways of implementing a critical stance. They observe that:

> there is a tendency for critical pedagogy to concern itself with 'lofty theory' or impenetrable jargon, couched in 'the language of proletarian protest', which is likely to result in alienating many potential converts. Indeed, not only is the discourse of critical pedagogy often fashionably 'radical', it is also dangerously dogmatic and judgemental, falling into the very trap it accuses mainstream pragmatist pedagogy of falling into. It can be so vociferous in its criticism of Pragmatic EAP's perpetuation of the dominant discourses, for instance, that it pressurizes students into rejecting all mainstream practices – thereby, as Clark (1992, p. 135) neatly puts it, 'moving from one kind of prescriptivism to another', being as undemocratic and unreflexive as its pragmatic equivalent.

So, on one hand, pragmatic EAP can be seen as prescriptive by assuming that students should conform to established discourse conventions, while on the other, critical EAP can seem reactionary by 'pressurizing students to deliberately flout established practices without good reason'.

CONSIDER

➤ How persuasive do you find this critique of the critical position?

➤ What teaching practices might help make this 'lofty theory' more practical?

➤ Devise a series of tasks to teach an aspect of academic writing for an EAP class which address both *access* and *difference*.

➤ How far do your tasks address Harwood and Hadley's call for 'grounded' critical EAP?

Task C4.3

CONSIDER

Theresa Lillis (2001) has argued that academic writing is 'mysterious' in that its practices are poorly understood by teachers and students alike. Not only does academic discourse vary enormously from field to field, but subject lecturers themselves are often unsure of and disagree about what constitutes good academic writing (Lea and Street, 1999; Lea and Stierer, 2000). Subject tutors often believe that academic discourse is a homogeneous, easily identifiable practice which can be taught in a straightforward way by EAP support units which exist to 'fix up' learners' difficulties in grasping the conventions of this practice. This view is implicit in the disparate and sometimes conflicting advice that students get on their writing from assignment guidelines and department handbooks (e.g. Candlin and Plum, 1999; Lea and Street, 1999) and from subject tutor feedback on written assignments (Ivanic *et al.*, 2000). The mysteries of academic writing, and what tutors actually want from students, remain obscured by a general assumption that learners will 'pick up' what is wanted, perhaps by osmosis over time or from their EAP classes.

RESEARCH NOTE

➤ Collect together the information and advice given by your institution or particular departments to students in handbooks, course guides, Web sites, and so on.

➤ Examine the advice it provides. Is it transparent, consistent and likely to be helpful to learners?

FOLLOW-UP

➤ Rewrite this advice in a form that helps learners to more clearly understand what plagiarism is and how they may avoid it. This can take the form of teaching materials or a small out-of-class project.

 Task C4.4

It is becoming increasingly clear to EAP practitioners that in order to assist their students they also need to raise subject tutors' awareness of discourse variation and the complexities of academic discourse. If we regard academic communication as specific to disciplines and courses and as requiring new forms of literacy from students, then we have to assist tutors to convey these demands effectively to students.

CONSIDER

➤ Do you agree that EAP teachers should also seek to work with subject tutors in this way? How might they do this?

RESEARCH NOTE

➤ Conduct a small research project and devise tasks to raise tutors' awareness of academic literacy issues.

■ Devise an interview schedule designed to gather information about tutors' perceptions of academic writing, their conceptions of the conventions involved and expectations of student performance, and their practices when giving feedback or counselling students on their writing.

■ Use this to interview two tutors, preferably in different departments, and note down their views and practices.

FOLLOW-UP

➤ Based on the data you have collected from your interview and document survey, devise a short course, either face-to-face or online, for subject tutors to raise their awareness of academic literacy issues and to assist them in improving their interactions with students on these issues.

Theme 2: Literacies and practices

The tasks in Theme 2 focus on a number of conceptual and methodological issues central to EAP practice. Here we return to the key ways in which EAP comes to grips with understanding and describing the texts and behaviours which form its central subject matter. Attention is drawn in these activities to the ways language works in academic contexts with different audiences and for different purposes. They are designed to encourage you to explore the role of discourse in constructing knowledge, the affordances offered by the concepts of community and culture in understanding academic language use, the value of genre and corpus analyses in understanding spoken and written texts, and the connections between language and its contexts of use.

Unit C5
Discourses, communities and cultures

While academic discourse is an identifiable register, choices of language and text within that register vary considerably across disciplines and sub-disciplines. Scholarly discourse emerges from specific communities which have different ideas about what is worth communicating, how it can be communicated, what readers are likely to know, how they might be persuaded (and so on). Disciplines can be seen as distributed along a cline, with the 'hard knowledge' sciences and 'softer' humanities at opposite ends as shown in Figure C5.1.

Figure C5.1 The continuum of academic knowledge

We can understand the cline like this:

- The sciences see knowledge as a cumulative development from prior knowledge and accepted on the basis of experimental proof. Science writing reinforces this empirical basis by highlighting a gap in knowledge, presenting a hypothesis related to this gap, and then experiments and findings to support this hypothesis.
- Disciplines in the humanities rely more on case studies and introspection and claims are accepted or rejected on the strength of argument.
- Between these the social sciences have partly adopted methods of the sciences but in applying these to less predictable human data give greater importance to explicit interpretation.

Task C5.1

CONSIDER

➤ How far do you think this cline and the explanations given above adequately represent the work of the disciplines?

RESEARCH NOTE

➤ Conduct a small-scale research project to develop and strengthen your own position on this question by identifying two disciplines from different points on the continuum and collecting information about their practices and approaches. Depending on your situation and access to such information, this might involve:

▪ Collecting curriculum documents and course descriptions (from the Web or elsewhere).
▪ Examining textbooks.
▪ Studying course assignments.
▪ Interviewing students and expert practitioners.

FOLLOW-UP

➤ Write up your findings in a short report for your fellow students or teaching colleagues.

Task C5.2

Text B5.1 by Myers illustrates how context, particularly author purpose and intended audience, can play a significant role in constructing scientific facts. As Myers (1990: 4) points out, a major consequence of the social constructionist view is:

> That an understanding of the discourse of any discipline depends on a detailed knowledge of that discipline – not just a knowledge of its content, since the construction of that content is what is at issue, but a knowledge of its everyday practices.

While we need to recognize our limitations as outsiders to the disciplines we study, all inquiry needs to be situated. That is, we have to recognize that the content of knowledge cannot be separated from the social processes that produce it, and for EAP practitioners this means understanding texts in their social contexts.

CONSIDER

➤ Think about the quote from Myers above. How would you go about studying the everyday practices of the disciplines? Is it even possible for an outsider to access such understandings?

RESEARCH NOTE

This activity seeks to sensitize you to some of the possibilities and challenges in this process by conducting a mini-analysis of a particular text.

▪ Decide on a particular genre to study. This could be a lecture, a course assignment, an examination, a research article, review, student essay, and so on.
▪ Decide what you want to discover about this genre, e.g. how is it produced and delivered and/or how is it received? How do users prepare for it? Is it collaboratively or individually constructed? What attitudes do users have to it? (And so on.)
▪ Employ at least *two* methods to study these aspects. These could include interviews, observations, shadowing case study subjects, asking participants to complete diaries, etc.
▪ Analyse your results.

FOLLOW-UP

➤ Write up your findings and discuss what you have learnt about the genre.

➤ Your report should include a reflection on the problems and challenges involved in this activity.

 Task C5.3

One of the earliest, and most explicit, discussions of discourse community in EAP was by John Swales (1990: 21–32), who emphasized their essentially *functional* and *purposive* character. For him, a discourse community:

▪ Has a broadly agreed set of common public goals – whether implicit or tacit.
▪ Has mechanisms for intercommunication among members – a crucial feature as members must interact with *each other*.
▪ Uses its participatory mechanisms primarily to provide information and feedback – membership implies uptake of the group's communications to exchange information.
▪ Possesses and uses one or more genres to further its goals – communities have certain expectations about the role of texts, their organization and their use.

■ Employs specific lexis – uses everyday vocabulary in specialized ways or develops its own lexis and acronyms (*SLA, ELT, EAP, IELTS*, etc.).
■ Has a threshold level of members with a suitable degree of expertise – implies mechanisms for changing memberships with a reasonable ratio of experts to novices.

Such communities are obviously not confined to academic contexts and Swales gives an example of a hobby group with an interest in Hong Kong stamps.

CONSIDER

➤ We all belong to several 'communities' or groups which share certain communicative purposes and common genres. Note down one community that you belong to and describe how it meets each of Swales's characteristics by completing the chart in Figure C5.2.

Name of group:
Goals
How members interact (with each other/with outsiders)
Written genres
Spoken genres
Specialized lexis
Common acronyms
How members join/leave
What counts as expertise
Other defining features

Figure C5.2 Characteristics of a discourse community (Swales, 1990)

➤ Now reflect on this activity and note down any difficulties you had in doing it. What do these difficulties imply for Swales's characterization and how would you modify it to fit the community you have selected?

➤ Which are the most important genres in the community you have considered? Why are they the most important?

RESEARCH NOTE

➤ Conduct a small survey of both experts and novices in this community. You might do this either by interviewing two or three individuals from each group or by gathering together several participants to form a focus group.

➤ Your questions should seek to discover what your subjects see as their discipline's main characteristics, its aims and purposes, its most important genres, its leading figures and events, etc., as well as their views of their own participation in the community.

FOLLOW-UP

➤ Prepare an oral presentation for a conference describing your research, with hand-outs and overhead slides or PowerPoints. Discuss your methodology and participants and compare the views of the two groups, discussing any similarities and differences.

 Task C5.4

While the impact of the first language on students' second language writing and speaking will obviously vary, and can be positive, it can also be a crucial feature distinguishing learner performance. Much of the comparative research is limited by small samples and is restricted to student essays, but some of the main findings of contrastive rhetoric are summarized in Table C5.1.

Table C5.1 Some differences between L1 and L2 student academic essays

- Different organizational preferences
- Different approaches to argument (justification, persuasive appeals, credibility)
- Different ways of incorporating material (use of quotes, paraphrase, allusion, unacknowledged borrowing, etc.).
- Different ways and extent of getting readers' attention and orienting them to topic
- Different estimates of reader knowledge
- Different uses of cohesion and metadiscourse markers (used to organize text, e.g. *however, but, next, finally*, etc.)
- Differences in how overt linguistic features are used (generally less subordination, passives, modifiers, lexical variety and specificity in L2 writing)
- Differences in objectivity (L2 texts often contain more generalizations and personal opinions)
- Differences in complexity of style

Source: from Connor (1996); Grabe and Kaplan (1996: 239); Hinkel (2002).

CONSIDER

➤ Based on your experience as a teacher, do you agree with the characterization of L1 and L2 students identified in Table C5.1?

➤ Which features are likely to have the greatest impact on how you respond to an essay as an EAP teacher?

➤ Do you think these would be the same features as a subject tutor would find most noticeable?

➤ Are they the features which most influence the comprehensibility of the essay or its acceptability as an academic essay?

RESEARCH NOTE

➤ Take two of these differences and decide how you might identify them in student essays.

➤ Now collect a small sample of texts written by L2 students and examine them to discover whether the writers have used these features appropriately for the context and topic.

➤ If possible, now do the same with a sample of L1 student essays.

FOLLOW-UP

➤ Compare your results with the L2 sample. What do your findings tell you about the ways students use these features and about the value of such comparisons more generally?

Unit C6
Genre analysis and academic texts

It may seem that teachers' work loads are already heavy without adding the need to analyse texts as well, but this is not an optional extra removed from the everyday business of 'teaching'. Research is a practical activity central to an awareness of how texts work and to ensuring that language remains at the heart of EAP teaching. This is because genre analysis helps reveal the conventional ways that people convey their purposes and how this differs across disciplines. Broadly, research in genre analysis attempts to:

- Identify how texts are structured in terms of functional stages or moves.
- Identify the features which characterize texts and realize their communicative purposes.
- Examine the understandings of those who write and read the genre.
- Discover how the genre relates to users' activities.
- Explain language choices in terms of social, cultural and psychological contexts.
- Provide insights for teaching language.

Genre analysis is therefore a key resource for EAP teachers as it provides both a description of communicative activity and support for making it explicit to students. The activities in this section encourage an awareness of genre-specific texts for teaching.

 Task C6.1

CONSIDER

Look at the two extracts below taken from the introductions to two research articles.

- ➤ Can you identify the two disciplines?

- ➤ In what ways are the extracts similar and different?

- ➤ What might these differences tell us about the ways claims are established and knowledge is constructed in these two fields?

(1) To determine if the increases in elastic shear moduli seen with MAP2c could be due solely to bundling of ac tautin filaments, the relative light scatter of solutions of actin filaments were measured. It was noted that at dilute molar ratios of MAP2c to actin there was no increase in light scatter. Higher molar ratios increased the scattering. These results suggest that dilute concentrations of MAP2c may have caused actin gelation by organizing the actin filaments into an isotropic network

(2) I want us to consider 'Saintly Co-operation'. One day, while you are waiting to deposit your Social Security check in a bank, you are approached by an eccentric tycoon. She has a million dollars but very little time. She offers you ten dollars if you assure her that you will deposit her million dollars in her bank account. She's in a hurry and can't get any details about you that would enable her to track you down if you failed to keep your promise. What do you do? Is it rational for you to put the money in her account? After all, you are still doing better (namely, ten dollars better) than if you had given no assurance at all. But can we really consider this clearly moral, indeed saintly, decision as rational?

RESEARCH NOTE

➤ Collect two examples of students' writing from two different disciplines, or if you are unable to do this, go to the library and select two research articles from different disciplines.

- Compare the two texts, noting their similarities and differences in terms of length, purpose, audience, and structure.
- Now look carefully at the language and organization of the two texts. Can you identify a series of stages (e.g. an introduction, body and conclusion)? What are the key language features? You may like to use Table C6.1 to help you.

FOLLOW-UP

➤ Compare your findings, and completed table of features, with those of another student. Can you construct tentative hypotheses for the similarities and differences that you have found?

Table C6.1 Organizational stages

Feature	Text 1	Text 2
Main grammar features		
Sentence types		
Use of modal verbs		
Tense choices		
Use of long noun groups		
Vocabulary choices		
Use of technical words		
Use of descriptive words		
Use of attitude words		
Cohesion		
Use of conjunctions		
Use of reference		
Other		
Layout		
Diagrams		
Examples		
Sub-heads		

Task C6.2

CONSIDER

Hyland (2000) suggests that the structure in Table C6.2 below is widely used for research article abstracts.

➤ Collect a number of abstracts from articles in two disciplines and decide how well they fit this structure. What variations can you find? To what extent are these related to discipline?

➤ Following your move analysis, look at the following features of the texts which often tend to be prominent in abstracts as a result of their frequency or importance:

  ▪ *Tense.* What tenses tend to predominate in each move? Can you explain why writers might favour these choices?
  ▪ *Voice.* Is passive or active voice favoured in these texts? What reasons might you give to explain these choices?

- *Verb choices.* Can you categorize the verbs in each move by their main purpose?
- *Hedges.* While writers highlight what is new and interesting, they are also reluctant to overstate their findings and so tone them down with hedges. Can you identify these?
- *Noun groups.* The use of nominal groups allows writers to package complex events or entities as single things so they can be thematized and discussed. Can you find nominal groups in the texts?
- *Promotional matter.* Introductory moves rarely provide simple background but seek to emphasize the importance, topicality, or relevance of the study to the discipline. In what ways is this done in your sample?

Table C6.2 Move structure of research article abstracts

Move	Function
1 Introduction	Establishes the context of the paper and motivates the research
2 Purpose	Indicates the purpose and outlines the intention behind the paper
3 Method	Provides information on design, procedures, assumptions, data, etc.
4 Results	States the main findings, the argument or what was accomplished
5 Conclusion	Interprets or extends the results, draws inferences, points to implications

RESEARCH NOTE

➤ Collect about eight to ten samples of a short genre such as book acknowledgements, book blurbs, encyclopaedia entries or the introductions to student written assignments.

➤ Identify the move structure of the genre in review in terms of the main purpose that the writers seem to be expressing and the salient grammatical features, using the list above.

FOLLOW-UP

➤ Write up your results as a poster for a teachers' conference setting out your purpose, sample, method and findings.

Task C6.3

CONSIDER

To guide analysis, in an initial examination of a text before looking more closely at its rhetorical and linguistic features, Paltridge (2001: 51) suggests the following questions. This helps to orient us to a text and link it with its social context.

- What is the text about?
- What is the purpose of the text?
- What is the setting of the text? (e.g. in a textbook, newspaper, etc.)
- What is the tone of the text? (formal, informal, etc.)
- Who is the author of the text?
- What is his/her age? Sex? Ethnic background? Social status?
- Who is the intended audience of the text?
- What is the relationship between the author and intended audience?
- What rules or expectations limit how the text might be written?
- What shared cultural knowledge is assumed by the text?
- What shared understandings are implied?
- What other texts does this text assume you have knowledge of?

➤ How might the answers to these questions differ across different academic texts such as textbooks, student assignments and seminar presentations?

➤ Are all of these questions relevant to academic genres? Which might be less important?

➤ Are there other questions that it might be useful to add to this list?

RESEARCH NOTE

➤ Select a text from any non-academic source. This could be in a newspaper, magazine, leaflet, political broadcast, or from anywhere.

➤ Work through Paltridge's list of questions to get an initial impression of the text and its general characteristics.

➤ Use your notes to write a short description of the text.

➤ Now repeat the procedure with an academic text and compare your findings with those for the non-academic text.

FOLLOW-UP

➤ Do you think this was a useful exercise? How might you use this approach with students?

➤ Could you answer all the questions? Which ones were you unable to answer and why?

➤ Which questions offered the most interesting insights into the academic text?

➤ What further information would you need to answer these questions and how could you get this information?

Task C6.4

CONSIDER

Bhatia (1993) suggests some basic steps for conducting genre analysis, summarized below, which provide a useful checklist to ensure that analysis doesn't lose sight of the link between texts and contexts.

1   Select a text of the genre you intend to teach and compare it with other similar texts to ensure that it broadly represents the genre.

2   Place the text in a situational context, i.e. use your background knowledge and text clues to understand where the genre is used, by whom, and why it is written the way it is.

3   Study the institutional context in which the genre is used (visit the site, interview users, look at rule books, manuals, etc.) to better understand the conventions which text users often follow.

4   Select a level of analysis (look at vocabulary, grammar, types of cohesion, move structure, etc.) and analyse the key features.

5   Check your analysis with a specialist informant to confirm your findings and insights.

RESEARCH NOTE

➤ Following Bhatia's steps above, select a written genre that you would like to know more about and identify a site where it is used. This need not be an academic genre and the site could be an office, a factory, a school, a social club, the home, or elsewhere.

▥ Focusing on step 3 of Bhatia's guidelines, arrange to visit the site and conduct a small-scale research project into the ways the genre is employed and understood in that site.

Interview users, collect documents, observe how examples of the genre are created, developed and used, and who is engaged in this process.

 Write up your results in a short communication skills audit report for employers or group leaders at the site, setting out a clear description of how communication is accomplished.

FOLLOW-UP

➤ In what ways did the visit help you to understand the genre?

➤ Did it confirm or disprove the intuitions you had about the text following the orientation questions?

 Task C6.5

CONSIDER

Genre analysis has gradually begun to accept the idea that visuals are often as important as verbal elements of academic texts. There has been a shift in our systems of representation from verbal to the visual in a whole range of genres, from ads to journalism, as well as in research and education. A social semiotic approach to multimodality seeks to describe the potentials and limitations (or 'affordances') for making meaning which inhere in different modes. According to Kress (2003: 1) writing and image are governed by different logics: writing by time and image by space. So in writing meaning is attached to 'being first' and 'being last' in a sentence, while in a visual it is position which is important. Placing something in the centre, for instance, gives it different significance from placing at the edge, while placing something above can make it 'superior' to what is below.

These multimodal representations are most obvious in academic discourse in the sciences, where visuals do more than merely illustrate or supplement information, and where learning to read them is a part of learning scientific discourse. Myers (1997) suggests that teachers and students should ask three questions about visuals:

➤ *Why is the visual there?* Examine the captions and the in-text reference and ask what they direct us to do with the picture. Is it a gloss, an interpretation or a background statement?

➤ *How does the picture refer?* Photographs, cartoons, maps, portraits, diagrams, graphs, etc., work in different ways, and awareness of this can encourage reflection on their assumed naturalness and the ways symbols are created and used in the discipline. There are three ways of referring, with some overlap:

    Indexical references linked directly with the thing referred to, as a fingerprint is an index of a finger.

- *Iconic* references based on resemblance to the thing referred to, such as a photograph or drawings of DNA as a helix.
- *Symbolic* references based on arbitrary conventions, such as letters used to symbolize elements in the periodic table.

➤ *How real is it?* Kress and van Leeuwen (1996) observe that there is a visual modality, like our use of *might* or *could* or *probably* in language. Thus realistic images, such as the grainy detail of an x-ray or autoradiogram, stake a claim to being statements of evidence and suggest greater certainty than the simplicity of a line diagram.

We could add to this the size of the visual and its position on the page or screen in relation to the text, the colours it employs and the orientation of its elements to the reader.

RESEARCH NOTE

➤ Take a textbook chapter which makes use of visual materials and consider the part these are playing in the text. Look at the types of visuals and how they are organized, their positions on the page, the relations between text and visuals and between the visuals themselves.

➤ Ask the following questions of the chapter and write up your responses as a report for a team developing EAP materials in your department or section:

- What would the book lose if the visuals were deleted?
- What information do they add?
- Why choose this form of presentation (such as a diagram rather than a photograph)?
- What different captions are possible?
- Why is the visual placed in that particular portion in the text?
- What conventions do readers use to interpret it?

FOLLOW-UP

➤ Select one or more visuals and devise a task to sensitize students to their use and meaning.

Unit C7
Corpus analysis and academic texts

With the availability of online corpora and concordancers and falling prices of text analysis software, corpus analysis can no longer be regarded as an esoteric aspect of EAP teaching and research. It is now fairly easy for teachers to collect or buy collections of texts, store them on a PC, and analyse them using widely available and relatively inexpensive software.

The main commercial corpora are the British National Corpus (information at http://info.ox.ac.uk/bnc/index.html) and the International Computer Archive of Modern English (http://nora.hd.uib.no/corpora.html). The first comprises 100 million words representing a wide cross-section of spoken and written British English and a smaller sampler of one million words. The second includes three parallel corpora each of one million words of written English: the Brown Corpus (American), the Lancaster–Oslo/Bergen corpus (British) and the Kolhapur Corpus (Indian). Corpora are also often packaged with concordance programs, such as Wordpilot 2002 (http://compulang.hypermart.net/download.htm), Wordsmith Tools (http://www.lexically.net/wordsmith/) and MonoConc (www.athel.com). There are also a number of searchable EAP-relevant corpora on the Web. These include a reduced version of the BNC at http://thetis.bl.uk/lookup.html and the Corpus of Business Letters at http://ysomeya.hp.infoseek.co.jp/. KWICFinder (http://miniappolis.com/KWiCFinder) enables the whole Web to be used as a text corpus.

 Task C7.1

CONSIDER

One of the best online corpora is the VLC Web Concordancer, which is hosted by the Polytechnic University of Hong Kong at http://www.edict.com.hk/concordance/. This is a simple to use concordancer with a range of corpora to choose from, including several containing student writing and academic texts from computer studies, business and applied linguistics. Figure C7.1 shows the opening screen.

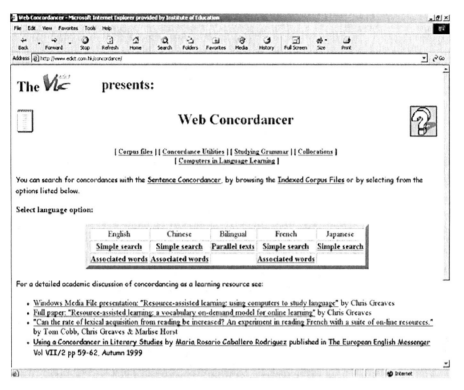

Figure C7.1 Opening screen of the Web Concordancer

PRACTICE

➤ To use it, go to 'English – Simple search' and type in a word or phrase to search for, select a *corpus* and hit <Enter> to start the search. You can select any of the corpus files to search from the selection list. The associated search allows you to also specify an associated word which will be found in proximity to the key word (e.g. *less* and *more*, or *possible* and *that*). The concordancer also allows you to search for all instances starting with, containing or ending with the search words or letters, and to sort results according to the right or left collocate, which is a useful way of seeing common collocates. A full help file is available by clicking the ? symbol on the opening screen.

➤ Select a general corpus and look at the concordance lines for *persist* and for *persevere* which have similar referential meanings but different connotative meanings. Note their frequencies, common collocates and connotative meanings.

➤ Now look up the phrase 'it is because' in the merged corpus of student writing. Can you see what is wrong with these examples? (Check their context by double clicking on the word.) Look up the same phrase in any of the files which were not written by students (e.g. the Brown or LOB corpora). How many examples can you find? Why is this?

➤ Search for the word *besides* in the merged student corpus and compare the frequency and use of this item with examples from the LOB corpus. What similarities and differences are there?

➤ Using the Web Concordancer and the Brown corpus, find the difference between *spend on* and *spend in*. Does your interpretation of the data correspond with dictionary definitions of the two?

RESEARCH NOTE

➤ Now explore academic vocabulary using the concordancer. Lists of academic vocabulary such as Coxhead's (2000) *Academic Word List* seek to provide learners with items common across a range of disciplines and genres. Such lists usually group words together which belong to the same 'word family' (Bauer and Nation, 1993). However, such families often contain homographs, or words which have two or more unrelated meanings. Use an academic corpus and note the distinct meanings you find for the following homographs. Are there differences in the most common meanings in different corpora?

issue	*correspond*	*abstract*
consist	*row*	*major*
project	*object*	*appreciate*

➤ Swales and Feak (2000: 126) believe that 'there is a probabilistic rule that favours *the* before a following "*of* phrase" but favours indefinite articles before following phrases governed by other prepositions'.

■ Use the *associated word concordancer* (sort right) to test this rule.
■ What counter-examples can you find?
■ Are there enough to propose a 'probabilistic rule'?

➤ Marco (2000) found that the frame *the * of* is particularly common in research articles, where it is used with nouns to express existence (*the occurrence of, the absence of*), process (*the beginning of, the onset of*) and quantity (*the amount of, the frequency of*).

■ Which is the more common structure: *the . . . of* phrases or *a . . . of* phrases?
■ Which nouns are most common in the *the . . . of* pattern and do they vary by genre?

FOLLOW-UP

➤ Design a conference poster to present your results from one of these corpus studies you have completed. Be sure to include a description of your method together with the quantitative data, illustrating frequencies, and your interpretations of the results.

TASK C7.2

CONSIDER

Spoken corpora are far less commonly available than written corpora, as they involve hours of painstaking transcription to transfer them into machine-readable text. The BASE (British Academic Spoken English) corpus of lectures and seminars developed at the Universities of Warwick and Reading, and the HKCSE (Hong Kong Corpus of Spoken English), developed at the Hong Kong Polytechnic University, which contains an academic section, are two major projects of this kind. MICASE, the Michigan Corpus of Academic Spoken English at http://www.hti.umich.edu/m/micase/, is unique in being the only spoken discourse corpus on the Web. It comprises 152 transcripts from sixteen different speech events across four academic fields at a US university totalling 1.8 million words. The corpus is divided into independently searchable sub-corpora identified by speech event, academic area, discipline, type of participant, interactive mode, gender, age, academic role, native-speaker status and first language. This means that users can explore the broad range of spoken discourses which occur in academic settings by students and faculty, both native and non-native English speakers, from the main academic fields.

There are two ways of searching the corpus: Browse and Search. The Browse function allows users to search for particular words or phrases according to specified speech event types (listed on the left) and speaker attributes (on the right). These return frequency information and references to the files in which the search items occur.

The second approach, Search, works more like a sophisticated concordancer, enabling users to search the corpus for words or phrases in specified contexts and returning concordance lines with references to files and various search criteria. Figure C7.2 shows how it is possible to search for a word or phrase in any speech event or speaker attribute category, using the wild card character * and with an optional neighbouring word or phrase, with up to two speaker attributes appearing in the results display. Figure C7.3 shows returns for *the important* by gender and academic position sorted on the word to the right of the node word.

MICASE has been extensively studied and is beginning to yield interesting information about the nature of spoken academic English (e.g. Fortanet, 2004; Simpson, 2005; Swales, 2004). A list of publications is available at http://www.lsa.umich.edu/eli/micase/publications.htm.

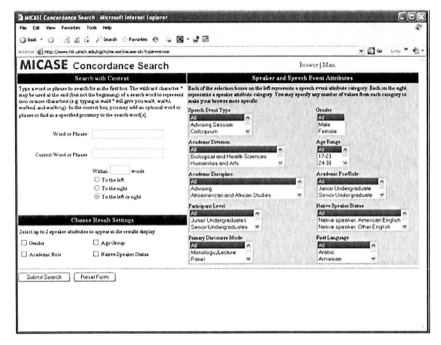

Figure C7.2 MICASE search screen

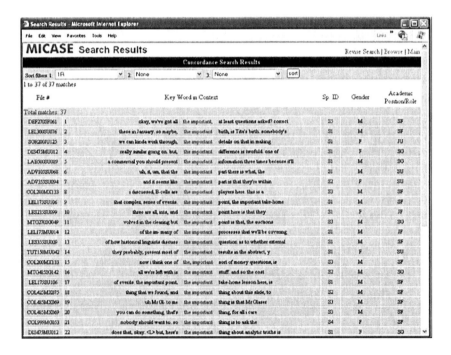

Figure C7.3 Concordance lines in MICASE for 'the important' by gender and role

PRACTICE

The following tasks offer a brief familiarization with the MICASE search facilities and corpus:

➤ How many times does *sorry* occur? Do men or women use it the most? What functions does it serve for speakers in this corpus?

➤ Is the word *possible* more often a noun or an adjective?

➤ Look at the word *second* in large lectures in humanities and arts and in large lectures in sciences and engineering. What can you say about the different uses in these areas?

➤ *If* occurs frequently in most corpora and textbooks often tell students there are three conditionals: the first (*if* + *will* or *shall*), the second (*if* + *would* or *should*), and the third (*if* + *would have* or *should have*). This is roughly accurate but does not fully describe all uses. Which of these forms is the most common in the corpus? (Remember, this is a spoken corpus and you may need to search for contracted forms of *will, would, should,* etc., which are likely to be common.)

➤ The temporal use of the word *just* tends to be stressed in ESL pedagogical materials but this is not the primary function of the word in academic speech. Can you determine its main function?

➤ We often tell our students that the words *data* and *criteria* are plural forms, but is this really the case in actual usage? Do speakers use them as singular or plural and are there any examples of *criterion* and *datum* in the corpus? Is it always possible to tell which is intended? (Kibbitzer 1 on the MICASE site has more on this topic.)

RESEARCH NOTE

Hyperbole, or exaggeration for the sake of effect, is far more common in speech than in academic writing, where writers are more careful to negotiate their claims. Often this takes the form of overgeneralization ('Everybody wants to be an engineer') or exaggeration in number ('I've had thousands of student inquiries this morning'). Ohlrogge and Tsang (Kibbitzer 3 on MICASE) show that numbers are nearly always used literally but that overgeneralization with non-specific personal pronouns such as *everyone, everybody, no one* and *nobody* occurs frequently in MICASE and fairly regularly as hyperbole.

➤ Which of these forms is most common overall in the corpus?

➤ Choose two speaker categories and compare their use of overgeneralization. Can you explain your result?

➤ Choose two contrasting event types (e.g. a lecture and a tutorial) and compare the use of overgeneralization in each setting. What conclusions can you draw?

FOLLOW-UP

➤ Write up your results as a short paper for undergraduate students showing the extent and types of hyperbole used in different contexts. Point out the kinds of exaggeration that they can expect and how they might identify and interpret them.

Task C7.3

CONSIDER

➤ Now you have gained some familiarity with the MICASE and Web Concordancer programs, use one of these resources to conduct a research project of your own. Reflect on *two* features of academic writing or speech which your students have difficulty with or about which you are curious to learn more.

RESEARCH NOTE

➤ Now conduct a corpus investigation into these features, examining their frequencies and collocations to show how they are used in particular contexts.

FOLLOW-UP

➤ What implications could your findings have for teaching? Design a set of materials and tasks which make use of your findings or data to help students understand more about one of these features.

➤ Write up your investigation and reflections in a short evaluation report for fellow EAP teachers unfamiliar with corpora and their applications.

Task C7.4

CONSIDER

A practical difficulty of corpus analysis is obtaining a corpus of the appropriate genre and disciplines we are interested in. Using an optical scanner to digitize published texts, such as research articles or textbooks, is time-consuming, tedious and possibly illegal, and while Web-based material offers access to journalistic, business and government texts, it may not always yield the genres we are looking for. It is, however, fairly easy for teachers to create a learner corpus by asking their students to submit assignments electronically, on disk or by e-mail attachment, and their permission to store these for academic study. A representative collection of work can then be gradually assembled and key features of the genres students write analysed in order to understand their developing control of a genre and identify where they seem to be having difficulty.

RESEARCH NOTE

➤ Collect an academic corpus which might help inform your teaching. You can do this by collecting student assignments electronically or by drawing on Web sources such as online newspapers, chatroom transcripts, bulletin board threads, articles from online journals such as *New Scientist, The Economist*, the BBC or ABC sites, and so on.

- Specify the principles and methods that you used to assemble these texts and identify a feature that you would like to analyse.
- Convert the files to ASCII (text-only) format and upload them to the Web Concordancer site. To do this go to the site, click the link entitled 'Uploading and searching your own personal corpus' and follow the instructions there.
- Use the Web Concordancer to investigate your selected feature.

FOLLOW-UP

➤ Write a report on your findings and discuss how you might make use of them in an EAP class.

Unit C8
Ethnographically oriented analysis and EAP

Exploring the activities which surround the creation and use of texts allows us to fill out and enrich a focus on texts themselves. It helps us to see that texts are varied; that they can be negotiated and resisted; that they can change; and that people have different ideas about their use and how they can be written. In other words, studying contexts allows us to situate texts in the practices users employ to create knowledge and communicate in different disciplines and helps students to see these as embedded in institutional life, communities and cultures.

Qualitative research methods perhaps offer an unfamiliar and confusing array of choices to novice researchers. The main challenge is that the researcher is at the heart of the research and that what you see, hear and participate in is central to data collection and analysis. Methods are best learnt by using them, in particular situations and in various combinations. A good source on ethnography is Holliday (2002) and user-friendly introductions to qualitative methods and analysis can be found in McDonough and McDonough (1997) and Richards (2003). The following tasks set out the main methods of collecting qualitative data and ask you to conduct small-scale studies to give you some experience and confidence in conducting research using them.

 Task C8.1

CONSIDER

Elicitation: questionnaires and interviews. These are the main methods of obtaining information and attitudes from informants. Both allow researchers to tap people's views and experiences, but questionnaires are widely used for collecting large amounts of structured and easily analysable self-report data, while interviews offer more flexibility and greater potential for elaboration and detail. The two may be used productively in parallel. Interviews may usefully precede questionnaires as exploratory studies for identifying issues and focusing questions more precisely. Alternatively, questionnaires can highlight general issues about what goes on in a context which can be explored later by more in-depth methods.

Questionnaires have been used to collect self-report data on writing and reading practices (what users believe they do), and to discover the kinds of writing that a community requires from particular genres, such as what subject teachers demand of students. Questionnaires vary in how open-ended responses are, but they have the advantages of being relatively quick and easy to administer, of allowing the views of many informants to be collected, and of providing results that can be easily compared and understood. Because the information is controlled by the researchers' questions, they also allow considerable precision and clarity, although it is remarkably easy to design ambiguous questions, encouraging us to trial questions first (see Brown, 2001; Dörnyei, 2003).

RESEARCH NOTE

➤ Design a questionnaire, which includes both open and closed question types, to learn more about one of the following topics:

■ What assignments subject specialists set their students, what their perceptions of good writing are, and what behaviours attract good grades.

■ What exposure students get to English outside the classroom.

■ How your fellow students go about preparing, researching and writing a course assignment.

➤ Pilot the questionnaire with three or four friends and modify it according to their responses to this activity.

➤ Distribute the questionnaire to a target group and collate the results.

FOLLOW-UP

➤ Write up your results in a short article for a teaching journal, setting out your findings and what they mean for pedagogic practice.

➤ Based on your experience with this mini-project, list what you see as the advantages and disadvantages of using questionnaires for EAP research.

➤ Write a short essay on why pilot studies are a necessary part of research.

CONSIDER

Interviews offer more interactive and less predetermined modes of eliciting self-report information, enabling participants to discuss their understandings of events in their own words and in more detail than through questionnaires. Interviews can be conducted with individuals or with small groups (focus groups). A focus group is a form of qualitative research in which people are asked about their attitudes to a product, concept, practice or event in an interactive group setting where participants are free to talk with other group members. These methods have been widely used in EAP research, either as the main source of gathering data or in combination with other techniques to obtain what Geertz (1973) called a 'thick description' to explain the context of the practices and discourse that take place within a context so that these practices become meaningful to an outsider. They can range from simply working through a list of predetermined questions, much like a spoken questionnaire, to a relatively unstructured format where the interviewer is guided by the responses of the interviewees to allow unanticipated topics to emerge.

RESEARCH NOTE

➤ Devise an interview schedule to follow up your questionnaire study above with a semi-structured or naturalistic interview or focus group to get more detailed responses on what seem to be key issues.

FOLLOW-UP

➤ Reflect on the different practices you have employed in conducting research in this unit and write a short report for a novice researcher on one of the two topics below:

- In what ways is the use of naturalistic or semi-structured interview techniques helpful as a research methodology and what difficulties can they cause for the researcher?
- What do you see as the value of mixing methodologies such as interviews and questionnaires?

 Task C8.2

CONSIDER

Introspection: verbal and written reports. Verbal report data rest on the belief that many tasks, such as the processes of writing, reading, giving feedback, and so on, require conscious attention and that at least some of the thought processes involved can be recovered, either as retrospective recall or simultaneously, with the task as a think-aloud protocol. Think-aloud techniques have been useful in revealing the strategies of writers, showing that writing is not simply a series of actions but a series of decisions which involve setting goals and selecting strategies to achieve them. But they have also been criticized as offering an artificial and incomplete picture of complex cognitive activities, while the act of verbalizing may slow task progress and interfere with the way people perform the task or the explanations they give. But despite these criticisms the method has been widely used (e.g. Smagorinsky, 1994), partly because the only alternative is to make guesses about thinking solely from subjects' behaviour, and this is far less reliable.

RESEARCH NOTE

➤ Record yourself thinking aloud while performing a language learning or teaching task (such as marking a paper, writing an essay or engaged in reading and note taking).

➤ At the end of the task transcribe the tape.

➤ Does the activity tell you anything you weren't previously aware of about your behaviour? List the aspects of your activities you were previously unaware of.

FOLLOW-UP

➤ Which of the activities you listed in the previous task could you profitably research further? How would you go about this?

➤ Write up your reflections on your think-aloud activity with extracts from the data in a short report for your teaching colleagues as a professional development exercise, pointing out what you have learnt and how your findings might be useful for them.

CONSIDER

Diary studies offer an alternative, and more straightforward, way of gaining introspective data. They provide a first-person account of writing practices through regular candid entries in a personal journal which is analysed for recurring patterns or important events. They can be kept by students, teachers, expert text users or researchers themselves, and are often followed up with interviews. Participants can be asked, for instance, to enter all their thoughts about using a genre and what they did when using it, such as how they collected data or the ways they considered their readers. When a substantial amount of material has been produced the diary is examined for patterns, which are then interpreted and discussed with the writer. Diaries can therefore provide valuable insights into both social and psychological aspects of behaviour that might be difficult to collect in other ways. They are, however, time-consuming and may be resisted by participants.

RESEARCH NOTE

➤ Keep a teaching or learning diary for two weeks. Set aside some specific times each day to record fairly freely your experiences in a particular class, recording what materials you used, how you presented them, what tasks students engaged in, how you followed them up, and so on. Also record your impressions of how successful the activities were in terms of learning, student engagement, interactivity, etc.

➤ After two weeks reflect on the entries and look for patterns of habit, frequency, preference, etc. Do any salient features emerge? For example:

■ Do you spend more time on some activities than others?
■ Do you engage in some tasks and ignore others?
■ Do you feel more positive about some types of behaviour?
■ Do your learners regularly opt to do tasks in certain ways or with particular others?
■ Which activities, materials, interactions, etc., do your students prefer?

➤ How do you interpret these in terms of your teaching/learning in this class? Write up how you conducted the study and what you learnt from it.

➤ How might you follow up the study to further address interesting issues in more detail?

FOLLOW-UP

➤ For many people keeping a diary is not easy and can be a time-consuming and burdensome task, perhaps even leading to negative attitudes to what is reported on. Based on your experience of keeping a diary, what strategies do you think might help to involve diarists in a study and increase their motivation to participate?

➤ Thinking aloud while performing a task can be equally difficult for EAP learners. Why might this be the case? List the problems a researcher might confront in collecting data in this way and how these difficulties might be overcome.

 Task C8.3

CONSIDER

Observations. While elicitation and introspective methods provide reports of what people say they think and do, observations gather direct evidence of this. Observation of students is something EAP teachers engage in constantly and, as a result, is a mainstay of classroom research, although the focus of research observation can be much broader and include ourselves as teachers; the behaviour of students engaged in learning tasks; the language-using context (room layout, group arrangements, writing stimuli, uses of source materials, etc.); and the actions of expert writers in relevant target contexts.

Unlike everyday 'noticing', observation for research purposes involves systematic and conscious recording as a way of seeing these actions in a new light, often based on prior decisions about what to observe. Noting down everything is impossible and so some observers decide to check (tick) pre-defined boxes when an expected action occurs. Obviously this approach is easier and yields more manageable data than on-the-spot descriptions, but it is not an ethnographic method, as pre-selection may ignore relevant events that the analyst did not anticipate. For novice researchers a clear structure is easier to apply and yields more manageable data, increasing the likelihood that a new perspective might be gained on a familiar situation. An example of this kind of pre-observation coding based on a study of peer interaction is shown in Figure C8.1.

Peer review task observation   Student: *Vincent*   Class: *4*   Date: *Wed 19*   Time: *2–2.20*

	Frequencies	Total
Student talks in L1	*1111*	*4*
Student uses reference material		
Student writes on feedback sheet	*1*	*1*
Student talks to teacher		
Student questions peer		
Student offers suggestion		
Student offers praise	*11111*	*5*
Student offers criticism		
Student reads essay aloud	*11*	*2*
Student listens to peer	*11111*	*5*
Student engages in off-task activity	*11*	*2*

Figure C8.1 Coding from a structured observation sheet (Hyland, 2003: 266)

Burns (1999: 81) favours structured observation and provides the following guidelines:

- Decide a focus relevant to the research. Don't try to record everything.
- Identify a specific location for the observation (classroom, common room, library).

■ Identify the group or individual to be observed (class, peer group, teacher–student conference).
■ Record the events (video, audio or checklist).
■ Be as objective and as precise as possible and avoid evaluative descriptions.
■ Record complete events or incidents for a more inclusive or holistic picture.
■ Develop a recording system that fits in with other events in the context of observation.

An alternative approach is to write or video-record a full narrative of events, trying to capture all relevant aspects of the event. Such open-ended notes can be more receptive to different features of a situation but are likely to be influenced by whatever draws the observer's attention. They may, in other words, still be selective but in a less obvious way than a more structured procedure (Allison, 2002). An example of this approach is the following extract from observation notes of an L2 writing class (Hyland, F., unpublished data).

Class B   *11.00 a.m.–12.00 p.m.*

11.10 a.m.
T tells the students to choose a question.

11.13 a.m.
T asks if they have decided but there is no response. She asks those who are doing question 1 to put up their hands. There is no response to this or to question 2. Many people choose question 3. Jo and Di on table A then say they are doing question 1. Polly says so is she. Polly is told to move to table A and all the other students are told to work in a group or pairs.

T says that the second thing that you do is to brainstorm ideas. She tells them to do this in a group but to write down their own ideas. She tells them to move. Polly moves to table A and the two Thai girls on table A move to table B.

11.15 a.m.
Tables A, B and C are talking in English. On table D students are reading their theme booklets. T sits with table A and listens as Mo talks about the question in relation to Thailand and the other students listen. T says, 'You have to understand exactly what the question says.' They discuss this together. Polly gets some paper.

Table C start talking in Chinese. They whisper and one takes notes. They switch from Chinese to English and back again. Lydia speaks more English than the others. The students on table D start to talk in English. They are discussing ideas. Li says, 'Advantages and disadvantages. Anything else?' Table B are still talking in Thai. Mo says, 'Speak English,' and they switch. 'Plan OK, plan,' one says, and they get out some paper. They laugh and talk in English. They also write from time to time.

11.20 a.m.
By now all tables are talking and English is dominating. Table D is quieter than the others and Li and BJ are doing nearly all the talking.

T is still sitting with table A and they are talking about the difference between general ideas and specific examples. T is telling the students they will need to start in general terms. The students interrupt and ask questions. All three students are contributing.

11.24 a.m.
T leaves table A and stands in front of table D. The students talk quietly. She moves away to table C and asks, 'How are we doing here?' She sits down. Fa is consulting his dictionary. T jokes with him, telling him to put it away as it makes her blood pressure rise. He goes red and does so. Lam reads the question aloud. T asks them what compare means. They are unable to tell her immediately and start to read the relevant sheet to find out. T asks them what they are going to do and Lam says they will talk about similarities. T asks to see their list. They say that they are sorry but they don't have one. T says that this is slack but she laughs as she says it. Lam gets out a piece of paper. They decide to think of a definition.

Groups D and A are talking a lot, with contributions from nearly all students. Li is leading table D. Table B are leaning forward and writing. They look absorbed.

RESEARCH NOTE

➤ Consider the narrative classroom observation notes in the extract and identify potentially useful categories which might help characterize the lesson. What productive lines of inquiry does the description suggest? How might these be followed up?

➤ Decide on an aspect of EAP instruction that interests you and arrange to observe a class to study it. Either:

▪ Brainstorm the behaviours that might provide insights about the feature and devise a systematic observation scheme to use to tick off such behaviours when they occur; or
▪ Observe the class and write as comprehensive field notes as possible.

FOLLOW-UP

➤ Examine your data from the second task above for significant patterns and write up your findings in the form of a conference paper to be presented to fellow EAP professionals. State the purpose of the research, how you carried it out, what you found and what it might mean for teaching and learning.

> What difficulties did you encounter and how would you overcome them if you were to repeat the research in the future?

> Do you think your observation data captured the behaviour you were studying? Why or why not and what other methods would you use to get a fuller picture of the activity?

 Task C8.4

Data analysis is a crucial aspect of research. How you approach the data you have collected is important to how you understand the situation you have researched and perhaps how you will understand it as a basis for action. But it is important to see data collection and analysis as a single process. Figure C8.2 shows how the two are interrelated, ongoing and often cyclical or iterative. Researchers think about their data as they are collected: what they mean, how they can be usefully supplemented, how to exploit interesting points, and so on.

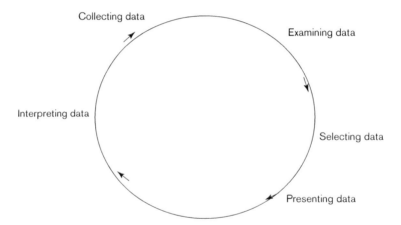

Figure C8.2 The analytical process. *Collecting data*: gather raw information by one or more means. *Examining data*: study material to understand the events and experiences it represents. *Selecting data*: distinguish important factors, group similarities, simplify complexities. *Presenting data*: represent selected data in an easily understood form (outline, table, etc.). *Interpreting data*: clarify relationships and explain the situation

Clearly the data that have been collected will differ both in what they look like and in the amount of structure that the collection method has already imposed on them. Data can be gathered by tightly structured methods such as controlled observations, structured interviews or multiple-choice questionnaires. In the former the observer simply ticks every occurrence of a certain behaviour while multiple-choice questions and transcripts of controlled interviews produce precisely targeted categories that can be coded and counted. More open-ended data, including most interview responses, observation field notes, verbal protocols and diary entries, call for more interpretation, and data will need to be reduced and grouped into categories in some way. Some researchers find software packages such as ATLAS, Winmax or N6 to be useful in combining and categorizing qualitative data, but they are not cheap. (Overviews and links can be found at http://sophia.smith.edu/~jdrisko/qdasoftw.htm.)

CONSIDER

➤ Look again at the different methods you used in Tasks C8.1, C8.2 and C8.3 and consider the kinds of data you collected using them.

➤ Identify the main problems you encountered analysing your data and describe how/whether you resolved them. What would you do differently when analysing these kinds of data in the future and how might the changes improve the analysis?

FOLLOW-UP

➤ Select any *two* of the methods you used in Tasks C8.1, C8.2 or C8.3 and write a set of *guidelines* which would help a novice researcher to use these methods and analyse the data they produce effectively.

Task C8.5

CONSIDER

➤ Look at the following questions and decide on a method of collecting data you might use to answer each one of them. Justify your answers.

- What are the effects of peer comments on revisions?
- What do subject teachers regard as an effective text in a particular context?
- What is the typical move structure of a particular genre?
- What difficulties do students experience in lectures?
- What difficulties do subject tutors have in encouraging student involvement in seminars?
- How do writers go about planning and preparing to write a particular genre?
- How do subject tutors decide on course assignments and their assessment?
- What writing tasks are typically required of participants in a target context?
- Does using a word processor make any difference to the process of student writing?
- Does a student's culture or L1 make a difference to their participation in group activities?

FOLLOW-UP

➤ Select one question from the list and consider how a variety of different methods could make a contribution to answering it. What could each one bring to the research to provide a more comprehensive picture?

Task C8.6

An important element of all research, qualitative or otherwise, is how it will impact on the participants, which means that researchers have to consider the ethical implications of their study. Key issues here are respect for 'personhood', associated with the idea of *informed consent, explicitness* and *avoiding harm*. These take on particular significance when conducting research in one's own context, as care needs to be taken to avoid exploiting relationships with students or colleagues through lack of negotiation or confidentiality. How could you avoid coercing students or colleagues into participation? Would researching students compromise your role as an independent teacher? How could you avoid misunderstandings which might arise as a result of this dual role and the power imbalance between teacher and student? How can you gain students' co-operation while making it clear that their non-participation will have no adverse consequences for them? Below are listed some key guidelines for ethical research (Hyland, 2003; see also Cohen *et al.*, 2000; Hitchcock and Hughes, 1995).

- *Gain approval* from participants – for documents, quotations, observations, transcripts – anything!
- *Explain clearly.* Ensure those involved understand the aims, methods and intended dissemination.
- *Clarify consequences.* Guarantee that subjects are not penalized for involvement/non-involvement.
- *Maintain confidentiality.* Ensure participants' anonymity.
- *Involve participants.* Encourage others with a stake in the work or contributing to it.
- *Get feedback.* Allow contributors to see and discuss your accounts of their behaviour.
- *Report progress.* Keep the work visible and remain open to suggestions from colleagues.
- *Negotiate release of information.* Different agreements may be needed at different levels.
- *Retain rights.* If participants are satisfied with fairness and accuracy, then accounts should not be vetoed later.

CONSIDER

➤ Imagine you want to study the effects of feedback on two groups of writers using an experimental method. One group will receive feedback on their drafts and the other only a grade, then each group will be tested on its improvement. What ethical issues does this raise? How could you modify the research to address these issues?

➤ One potential ethical dilemma arises when informing subjects of what the research is about may influence the data. How might you address this issue in an ethical way?

➤ Return to the research tasks you carried out in Task C8.1 and consider what ethical issues they raise using the list above. Reflect on one of these studies and write up what these issues are and how you addressed them or would address them in the future.

➤ Look at the consent form, Figure C8.3, for experimental research involving human participants. This form relates to a study of behaviour in groups and not EAP practice, but, using it as an example, draw up a consent form for your own study which explains the research, ensures participants' approval and sets out their rights and responsibilities.

Description of Study:

This experiment examines the intellectual performance of groups. As a participant, you will be asked to work with the other members of your group to solve a series of problems that tests both your intelligence as well as your creativity. Your group will be compared to other groups to determine the quality of your group's performance.

To provide some incentive for doing well, only the members of groups that perform well will become eligible to win a raffle to be held when all the experimental sessions have been completed. That is, if your group wins, (a) your name will be written on an entry slip; (b) the slip will be placed in the raffle box; (c) at the end of the study one name will be drawn from the box; (d) and that person will be awarded a prize of $50. If your group does not perform as well as the other group, then your name will not be placed in the raffle box.

Informed Consent Statement:

I have read the above statement, understand the nature of my participation in the research, and I freely agree to participate. I recognize my right to withdraw my consent and discontinue participation in the project without fear of any prejudice, and recognize that my activities and data generated by my participation will remain strictly confidential. I also understand that at the conclusion of the study I can choose to destroy any records of my participation, and that if I desire I can request a copy of the final report describing the research's conclusions.

By signing this form I indicate that I understand my role in the research and agree to participate. I also understand that in the event of any physical and/or mental injury resulting from my participation in this research project, Virginia Commonwealth University will not offer compensation.

Figure C8.3 Consent form for a psychology research project involving human participants

RESEARCH NOTE

➤ Collect what information and guidelines you can from different sources on the ethical conduct of research involving human subjects. You might find these on the Internet, in research manuals, in the guidelines provided by professional bodies and universities, and so on.

➤ Do you find the guidelines appropriate to your own needs? In what ways would you modify them?

➤ Summarize and simplify the guidelines into a few rules that would be helpful for a novice researcher.

➤ Give an example of how each rule might apply in practice. What would be unethical according to the guidelines?

 Task C8.7

CONSIDER

Ethnographically oriented methods are widely used for researching the ways genres are used in academic contexts. To understand practices in this way can help learners to demystify forms and patterns which might otherwise be seen as arbitrary and conventional. It helps *explain* why people use language in the ways they do, and such understanding can enable learners to avoid seeing genres as simply templates for communication. Asking the questions below can give a clearer idea of what a genre is and why it is as it is.

➤ What writing strategies does a group of writers employ in accomplishing a writing task?

➤ Is writing usually done collaboratively or individually? Who takes the lead role and how is this decided? Who writes, edits and gives final approval to the text?

➤ Who reads it and what is their relationship and relative status to the writer?

➤ How is writing related to reading and speech in specific contexts?

➤ What are users' attitudes to the genre?

➤ Which genres carry the most prestige in different contexts and how is this shown?

➤ What other texts influence the genre? Is it a response to other texts?

➤ What do this audience typically look for in a text in this genre and how do they read or listen to it?

➤ What do writers/speakers need to know about the target audience to produce successful texts?

➤ What do text users regard as the function and purpose of the genre?

➤ What do they see as its key features? Do these features differ from one text to another?

➤ What do readers/hearers regard as an effective example of the genre?

➤ Can they provide text examples?

RESEARCH NOTE

This task encourages you to research a context in this way.

➤ Select an individual, group, target context or EAP class you would like to know more about as a possible case study and investigate this case drawing on the questions in the list above.

➤ Formulate a general research question which embraces several of the questions above and draw up a research design to investigate it including a time schedule.

➤ Outline who the participants will be, the research site, the kinds of data you will need, how you will collect them, and how you will analyse them. Specify any ethical issues involved and how you will deal with them.

➤ Carry out the research and write up your findings.

FOLLOW-UP

➤ Reflect on what you have learnt about the context and what you have failed to learn. What improvements or changes would you make to a similar future study to overcome any shortcomings or to expand the scope of your data?

➤ Now develop a task to raise students' awareness of this dimension of texts.

  ▪ Write a rubric and instructions for the task.
  ▪ Set out the aims and objectives, the questions to be asked and the methodological steps to be taken.
  ▪ What outcome(s) do you expect and what difficulties do you anticipate students will face?

This theme focuses on the practicalities of planning courses, writing and evaluating teaching and learning materials, devising classroom activities and assessing students' work. It is, then, concerned with the practical implementation of English for Academic Purposes programmes drawing on the conceptions discussed in Theme 1 and the methodological approaches of Theme 2. Here the tasks encourage you to reflect on and conduct research into issues of learner needs and the decisions involved in teaching based on those needs, what it means to develop a coherent, targeted course and to sequence learning activities, and the implications of adopting particular teaching methods, materials and ways of monitoring learning.

Unit C9
Needs and rights

Needs analysis is a key feature of any EAP course, but the definition of 'needs' in given contexts and the sources, methods and types of data that feed into contemporary needs analyses have developed considerably in recent years. While an understanding of the skills, assignments and discourses students are likely to encounter in their academic classes remains important, this is now often combined with efforts to discover how students respond to their assignments and courses and tutors' reactions to students' writing and participation.

Table C9.1 Some common needs data collection methods (Hyland, 2003)

Type of information	Data collection method
Students' goals and priorities	Brainstorming, group discussions, interviews, student diaries
Learning preferences	Interviews, group discussions, questionnaires, observations, diaries
Background information (age, gender, prior learning, L1, L1 literacy, occupation, years in country)	Enrolment documents, individual interviews, questionnaires, observations
Current L2 proficiency (English literacy and writing experiences)	Placement or diagnostic tests, individual interviews, classroom observations, self-assessment
Target behaviours	Interviews with learners, interviews with 'experts', literature reviews, genre analyses, observation of target tasks, observations of target sites, questionnaires, case studies

Task C9.1

Some of the main types of needs information and data collection methods are listed in Table C9.1. The choice of data collection methods we use obviously depends on the time and resources available and on the proficiency of the students. Different collection procedures produce different kinds of data which can be analysed using different methods and these, in turn, address different areas. It is always a good idea, if possible, to collect and analyse data from several sources to achieve a reliable and comprehensive picture which can provide an informed basis for course design.

CONSIDER

➤ Given constraints of time and other resources it is often impossible to gather as much information about learners and their needs as we would like. Therefore:

■ Decide what kind of information you consider it is most important to collect to conduct a needs analysis for a given community of EAP learners.

■ Suggest how this information would be useful in designing an effective course.

➤ As preparation for a structured needs analysis interview with EAP tutors, draw up a list of questions to ask them about their difficulties in teaching a particular group of students and their perceptions of those students' needs. You might consider issues such as current resource provision, class size and composition, students' grasp of particular target communication skills, specialized vocabulary or genres, their access to texts and materials, and so on.

➤ Now modify the questions so they can be used in interviewing a subject tutor.

RESEARCH NOTE

➤ Select an EAP textbook or a set of course materials and try to reconstruct the results of the needs analysis it was based on. How do you think these data were collected?

➤ Contact and 'shadow' a student as he or she prepares for an assignment by collecting data and conducting literature searches. Record, in note, audio or video format, the methods he or she uses in this process.

FOLLOW-UP

➤ Collate your data and organize your findings. Categorize the different steps or practices the student adopted. Do your findings of these activities suggest any instructional practices which might help improve these processes?

 Task C9.2

CONSIDER

Perhaps the most commonly used instrument for collecting needs data is the questionnaire. This is partly because its structured format makes it easy to administer and gives the teacher considerable control in framing issues for large groups and in analysing the results. The lack of opportunities for immediate follow-up and clarification, however, means that we need to be confident that items can be interpreted unambiguously and that instructions for completing them are clear (Brown, 2001; Dörnyei, 2003).

RESEARCH NOTE

➤ Look again at the framework in Table C9.1 and use it to devise a needs analysis questionnaire for a group of new students you are about to teach. You might want to include questions which address the following areas, although the choice is yours:

- The situation in which students need to write or speak in English.
- The types of writing, reading, listening or speaking they will have to do.
- What students hope to learn from the course.
- Self-assessment of current language abilities in English.
- Views on textbooks or methods of learning.

➤ Pilot the questionnaire with a small group of students and modify it based on your results.

➤ Now modify the questionnaire for the subject tutors of the new arrivals.

FOLLOW-UP

➤ Discuss what issues you addressed in each questionnaire, what changes you made to the tutor questionnaire and why you made the changes.

Task C9.3

A learning situation analysis is an important feature of EAP course design as various features of the local teaching context can impact on how a course is conceived and implemented. Some key aspects of the local context are listed in Table C9.2 on page 280.

CONSIDER

Consider this quote from Dudley-Evans (2001: 133):

> For ESP courses to be successful and to have a lasting effect to study or work using English, the environment in which English is taught versus that in which it is used must be assessed. For example, if learners are used to rote learning, it may be that a problem-solving approach . . . will be alien to their learning styles and contrary to their expectations. This does not mean that the problem-solving approach cannot be used, but it would be more effective if the factors that militate against its use are known and allowed for.

Every pedagogic situation offers possibilities and limitations for learning. The term 'affordances' refers to the potential for action posed by objects in the environment and these are always balanced by constraints and the need for teachers to trade off the two. Can you identify a constraint in your current teaching or learning context that presents an obstacle to the kinds of approach you would prefer to use? What measures could you take to introduce the approach in a way which allows for such 'militating factors'?

Key factors in a learning situation analysis are the classroom and institutional cultures, but any analysis must acknowledge that what might work well in one context may fail in another, even though the students may have similar language needs. The kinds of needs data it is possible to collect are often constrained by the type of course that is planned. One important difference is:

- Whether the course is a short pre-sessional programme aimed at helping students to develop their academic language skills in preparation for their chosen degree course.
- In-sessional programmes which support students who are studying for a degree or other course.

➤ What would be the effect of these different contexts on the ways you collect data? And the types of data you can collect?

➤ Modify the questionnaire you designed in Task C9.2 to address these issues.

Table C9.2 Some features of the teaching/learning context

The society	Whether it is a foreign or second-language context Attitudes to English in society (resistant, pragmatic, indifferent, etc.) The kinds of teaching methods and materials that are culturally appropriate The kinds of roles normally associated with teachers and learners
The institution	Influence of 'stakeholders' (learners, subject tutors, sponsor, government, etc.) The 'culture' of the institution (attitudes to innovation, teacher autonomy, etc.) Morale of staff and students within the institution
The resources	The number, background and professional competence of teachers involved Teachers' knowledge and attitude to the syllabus, materials and methods Availability of materials, aids, library facilities, etc. Technological and reprographic resources (computers, photocopiers, etc.) Physical classroom conditions (pleasant, noisy, cold, etc.)
The course	The length of the course and what it can reasonably hope to achieve Whether the course is intensive or extensive and frequency of sessions Whether the course is EGAP or ESAP Whether the course is linked to other courses in the curriculum Whether the course is concurrent with students' needs or prior to them Whether there is an external examination
The class	Whether the group has been selected on the basis of language proficiency Whether the group is homogeneous in terms of goals, age, interests, etc. Whether the group is homogeneous in terms of disciplinary specialization

RESEARCH NOTE

➤ Investigate the context in which you are now studying and describe its main features using the list in Table C9.2. Focus on who the students are, what resources are available, how material is being delivered and practised, the type of course that it is and where it is being conducted.

FOLLOW-UP

➤ Based on the data you collected from this research, draw up a plan for a learning situation analysis for the next course of this kind. Specify how you will collect the data, who you will collect it from and how you will analyse it.

Task C9.4

CONSIDER

Benesch argues that rights analysis must supplement needs analysis and suggests that it should include an examination of 'who sets the goals, why they were formulated, whose interests are served by them, and whether they should be challenged'. Her argument is that rights are not pre-established entitlements worked out for the benefit of students by EAP teachers, but have to be discovered in each particular setting, seeing what is possible and beneficial, by a particular group of students. This bears a strong resemblance to a *negotiated syllabus* (Clarke, 1991) which has a long history in English language teaching (Breen and Candlin 1980) and is widespread in postgraduate education in the UK. A negotiated syllabus means that the content of a particular course is a matter of discussion between teacher and students, according to the wishes and needs of the learners in conjunction with the expertise, judgement and advice of the teacher.

RESEARCH NOTE

➤ Look again at your current learning context and conduct a rights analysis of this context using, where possible and appropriate, the methods Benesch adopted in Text B9.1:

- ▦ Attending lectures and making observation notes.
- ▦ Recording the lectures and discussing problems with students.
- ▦ Collecting written responses from students about their concerns and difficulties.

FOLLOW-UP

➤ Write a report of your study describing what you did and what you discovered, and make recommendations for changes in practice based on this.

Unit C10
Development and implementation

Course development starts with needs and rights analyses and uses the information to state the broad goals and the more specific outcomes on which a course is based. These in turn form the basis of a systematic plan of what needs to be learnt, selecting and sequencing the content and tasks that will lead to the desired learning outcomes. Conducting needs analyses, setting goals and objectives and devising and evaluating syllabuses are therefore part of a closely integrated process. It is important to repeat, however, that these decisions do not automatically flow from needs data or instructional objectives but involve making judgements throughout the progress of the course. A syllabus publicly declares what the teacher regards as important to students and so reflects a philosophy of teaching, including beliefs about language and learning.

 Task C10.1

Objectives can be stated in a number of ways, for example they can specify:

- What the instructor intends to do.
- The course content of skills or knowledge to be taught.
- The general patterns of behaviour that will result (e.g. to develop critical thinking).
- The specific behaviours which learners will be able to demonstrate at the end of the course.

CONSIDER

➤ Consider the four ways of expressing objectives listed above and decide which is likely to be the most useful in an EAP course. How would you justify your alternative formulation of these imperatives? State the criticisms you would make of the other methods.

➤ Look at an EAP textbook and try to reconstruct the aims and objectives of the course for which it might be used.

RESEARCH NOTE

➤ Conduct a search of EAP courses advertised or promoted on the Internet. Note whether the courses are described using explicit objectives and how these objectives are expressed. Which is the most common way of stating objectives?

FOLLOW-UP

➤ Write up your results as a report for students seeking a suitable course. Account for your findings and make recommendations based on the clarity and explicitness of the objectives.

Task C10.2

Objectives which specify what learners should do as the result of instruction are sometimes called 'performance objectives', and some planners (e.g. Mager, 1975) advocate that such objectives should specify three essential components:

- *Performance:* what learners will be able to do.
- *Conditions:* the parameters within which they can do it.
- *Criteria:* the level of competence expected.

So, for example, an objective from an intermediate EAP course might be: 'By the end of the course students will be able to take notes on a short lecture in a classroom simulation with 80 per cent of the key points included.' This kind of precision allows objectives to be graded for different proficiency levels by modifying the conditions and criteria, although many teachers may find this kind of specification too constraining.

Performance objectives can also be expressed as 'competence statements' which are then broken down into observable performance criteria (judged by an assessor), as in this example:

Competence	Can deliver a short oral presentation
Criteria	Uses appropriate staging and structures a presentation clearly
	Delivers statements clearly
	Links main ideas cohesively and logically
	Uses appropriate vocabulary
	Uses appropriate level of formality

However, while many teachers and learners like the structure and guidance this framework affords, the idea that teaching implies objectively measurable behaviours does not suit everyone and perhaps few teachers specify what they set out to do in this way, despite the advantages of doing so (see Brindley, 1989).

CONSIDER

➤ Think of a course you are teaching or have taught and state the objectives of the course as competence statements. Select two of these competences and specify the criteria you would use to evaluate them.

RESEARCH NOTE

➤ Conduct a survey to discover the views and practices of your fellow EAP teachers or classmates concerning the use and expression of course objectives.

  ▪ Do they believe that setting measurable objectives is a useful practice?
  ▪ What kinds of objectives do they prefer to use and why?
  ▪ Do some prefer not to specify course outcomes prior to the course in this way and, if so, why do they adopt this approach?

FOLLOW-UP

➤ Can you see a consensus on these issues or are there disagreements? Write up your findings, listing the arguments for and against the different approaches your respondents have discussed.

 Task C10.3

Table C10.1 is an example of course objectives adapted from the Australian Certificate of Spoken and Written English (CSWE), which has the goal of assisting migrants to participate in further education. Assessment occurs throughout the course and is based on ability to perform tasks which measure communication skills.

CONSIDER

➤ Select one of the objectives in Table C10.1 and:

  ▪ Specify criteria that will allow you to determine if students have met that objective.
  ▪ Sketch a unit of work which will provide the instruction towards meeting that objective.

Table C10.1 Aim and objectives of a text-based EAP course

Aim

To assist adult learners of non-English-speaking backgrounds to develop the literacy skills required to undertake further education

Objectives

Students will be able to:

- Undertake the roles and responsibilities of a learner in a formal learning environment, accepting a degree of responsibility for learning and participating effectively in learning situations

- Use a range of learning strategies and resources both within and outside class, using computers for writing and establishing an appropriate study pathway

- Write a report of 1,000 words on a topic relevant to the learner using appropriate staging and organizing factual information into coherent paragraphs with appropriate vocabulary and grammatical structures

- Write a discussion of 1,000 words on a topic relevant to the learner using appropriate staging and organizing material into paragraphs which express coherent arguments for and against, including supporting evidence to support claims. The writing will display appropriate conjunctive links, vocabulary and grammar

- Write a short formal letter of 100 words using appropriate staging and layout and using paragraphs which express objective information about situations/events, providing information and supporting evidence to substantiate a claim and request action. Texts will display appropriate conjunctive vocabulary and grammar

---

Task C10.4

Creating a course is clearly a matter of juggling different demands and constraints, yet it need not involve starting fresh each time. An important part of the process, like needs analysis and teaching itself, is to learn from prior experience and from the experiences of others. Modification and evolution are helpful approaches to course design. Colleagues, the Internet and research and teaching literature are therefore useful sources of information, particularly when designing courses intended for EGAP contexts.

CONSIDER

While we may be able to modify an existing syllabus for our current purposes, this must be done with caution, partly because a syllabus is more than a list of tasks and objectives. Consider this quote from Breen (1984: 49):

> Any syllabus will express – however indirectly – certain assumptions about language, about the psychological process of learning, and about the pedagogic and social processes within a classroom.

➤ Examine a textbook or syllabus and identify these features. Could you modify the syllabus or textbook to better reflect your own views on these issues?

RESEARCH NOTE

The following types of EAP syllabus were introduced in Unit A10:

lexico-grammatical	task-based	text-based
functional	process	content-based

➤ Choose *one* of these six types of EAP syllabus and conduct a literature search to find out more about this type of syllabus and the ways it has been used in EAP course design contexts.

FOLLOW-UP

➤ Based on your research, what do you see as the main advantages and problems of this type of syllabus in EAP contexts and what could you do to overcome the problems?

➤ Work with colleagues to design a syllabus of this kind for a group of students you are currently teaching or are likely to teach in the future.

 Task C10.5

The next stage of designing an EAP syllabus is to determine the content, tasks and assignments which will meet the objectives established for the course. Ideally this will include a balance of skills and text knowledge and a variety of topics, task types, genres and input, with discussions, talk and data gathering as input. Depending on the orientation and length of the course, it is good practice to make provision for five main kinds of knowledge and skills (Hyland, 2003):

- *Genre:* ensuring relevant genres are included and deciding how these will be introduced.
- *Context:* familiarizing learners with target contexts and the roles and relationships they imply.
- *System:* ensuring that students will acquire the elements of the language system they need to understand target genres.
- *Content:* selecting and sequencing the content domains students will learn 'through'.
- *Process:* making provision for students to develop their writing and speaking skills with different types of practice.

CONSIDER

➤ Think about the needs of a group of students you are familiar with. Brainstorm what skills and communicative resources they might need in their target contexts.

➤ Which of the five kinds of knowledge and skills would you prioritize for these needs and what principle would you use to sequence content, tasks or genres for learning? Explain your decisions.

RESEARCH NOTE

➤ Examine a collection of EAP textbooks or sets of course materials and try to identify which of the five kinds of knowledge and skills mentioned above it seems to privilege. Is there a single approach or does it combine several?

➤ Note how material is sequenced using this method, how the remaining elements are incorporated and the ways tasks draw on several kinds of knowledge and skills.

FOLLOW-UP

➤ Present your results in a conference poster format using both text and graphs (or tables) to show how these different materials you have analysed represent different approaches to EAP pedagogy.

Task C10.6

An important way of incorporating critical principles into an EAP classroom is to involve students directly in their learning through democratic decision making and negotiation of the syllabus. With their origins in classical liberalism and humanist philosophies, current approaches have responded to developments in communicative language teaching and process syllabuses (Breen and Candlin, 1990). Underlying process syllabuses is the key idea of negotiation between teachers and learners. Breen and Littlejohn (2000: 19–29) give six key reasons for this kind of negotiation in the language class:

▪ Negotiation is a means for encouraging responsible membership of the classroom community, taking on active and democratic identities and facilitating understanding of different views.
▪ Negotiation helps construct and reflect learning as an emancipatory process by calling on students to make decisions, encouraging autonomous action and valuing their input.

- Negotiation can activate the social and cultural resources of the classroom group, providing a sense of shared decision making and sense of ownership.
- Negotiation enables learners to exercise their active agency in learning by providing them with opportunities to articulate and refine their prior understandings and purposes as references for new learning.
- Negotiation can enrich classroom discourse as a resource for language learning by avoiding teacher-channelled communication, diversifying input and encouraging learners to engage in authentic discussion and express their own beliefs and theories about learning.
- Negotiation can inform and extend a teacher's pedagogic strategies by allowing learners' diversity of knowledge and ways of working to be explicitly drawn on, and through the teacher's modelling of negotiation and discussion strategies.

CONSIDER

➤ Are you persuaded by these principles of the need for adopting negotiation in the EAP classroom? Which of the above arguments do you think is the most important? How far would you be prepared to relinquish control over syllabus planning and pedagogy to students?

RESEARCH NOTE

➤ Undertake a piece of action research to assess the feasibility of sharing decision making in relation to the unfolding EAP curriculum of your class and to determine which classroom decisions might be open to negotiation. According to Breen and Littlejohn (2000b: 31) the kinds of decisions open to negotiation might include:

- *Purposes.* Which immediate and long-term needs for learning should be focused on?
- *Content.* What topics, themes, genres and specific uses of the language should be the focus?
- *Ways of working.* What resources, texts, materials, tasks and procedures, balance of in- and out-of-class learning, etc.
- *Evaluation.* What should be the outcomes of the learning and how should it be assessed?

➤ Conduct discussions with your students and find ways for them to participate actively in the next unit of work in the course.

➤ Devise a unit of work for the class based on these negotiations and, if possible, teach it.

FOLLOW-UP

➤ Write up your action research as a research article, showing what you set out to do, how you conducted the research, the issues involved and the outcomes. Evaluate the research and discuss the affordances and constraints of this approach to classroom decision making for EAP teachers more generally.

Task C10.7

There are numerous ways a syllabus can be organized, including negotiation with learners on their own preferences. All approaches, however, require a principle of arranging content, genres or structures into a coherent sequence which ensures students can progress smoothly from one developmental step to the next. In a content-based syllabus, for instance, themes or topics are selected according to their relevance or interest to learners and sequenced by the level of difficulty or by real-world progression in target contexts. In a text-based course it might be possible to sequence genres according to their rhetorical demands or their immediate value to learners. Table C10.2 shows the steps for creating a text-based course outlined by Burns and Joyce (1997).

Table C10.2 Steps in developing a text-based syllabus

1 Identify the overall contexts in which the language will be used
2 Develop course goals and objectives based on this context
3 Note the sequence of language events within the context (what students do with the language)
4 List the genres used in this sequence
5 Outline the sociocognitive knowledge students need to participate in this context (e.g. in an EAP context this involves knowledge of classroom practices, expectations concerning participation, the institution, classroom roles and responsibilities, etc.)
6 Gather and analyse samples of texts
7 Develop units of work related to these genres (ordering tasks, providing explicit input, giving guided practice and ensuring there are opportunities to perform independently)

Source: Burns and Joyce (1997).

CONSIDER

➤ Use this framework to plan an EAP course for students you are currently teaching or anticipate teaching in the future. In particular you should:

- Specify the target context and genres likely to be useful.
- Contact the content department to gain access to sites of learning, materials and informants for collecting data.
- Consider what data-gathering and analysis procedures are likely to be most useful to you.

RESEARCH NOTE

➤ Now conduct the research needed to develop a text-based syllabus, collecting data from relevant sources such as lectures, seminars, tutor-identified examples of good student writing, textbooks and other reading materials.

FOLLOW-UP

➤ Collate your data and decide on a course structure, identifying the genres you will include. Do not develop individual tasks but sketch units of work or cycles to show what students will do, the sequence they will do them in, and what the outcomes will be. Write this up as a course document.

 Task C10.8

CONSIDER

EAP specialists stress the importance of involving subject tutors in the development of EAP courses. This is partly to help tutors adjust their teaching and assignments to take account of students' literacy needs, and partly to encourage their awareness of literacy practices among students more generally. This involvement can, however, be an uphill struggle, and Johns (1997: 71–6) lists a number of reasons why tutors may be unwilling to change their approaches to teaching or become involved in EAP courses:

- Institutions often do not adequately reward or provide incentives for good teaching and so send signals that students' needs and learning are less important than research and other activities.
- Tutors often have ill-informed or underdeveloped views of academic literacy, seeing it as a single, unified set of vocabulary and grammar skills (see Unit A1).
- EAP and academic literacy are not matters of intellectual interest in most academic departments.
- EAP is not recognized as a single, established international discipline and its practitioners have diverse backgrounds and work in a variety of units, centres and departments and so lack professional cohesion.
- EAP often conflicts with subject disciplines by valuing pedagogy and language acquisition above the importance of subject content.

RESEARCH NOTE

➤ Draw up a list of questions to address these issues and conduct interviews with a number of subject specialists to get their views on them. How do they see academic literacy? What is their opinion of EAP teaching? What do they see as the greatest obstacles to closer co-operation with EAP staff?

➤ You could usefully follow this up by conducting interviews with EAP teachers to discover their perceptions of subject tutors' attitudes and barriers to co-operation.

FOLLOW-UP

➤ Consider the results of the interviews and identify what seem to be the greatest challenges to closer co-operation between EAP and subject discipline staff. Write up your findings, with specific recommendations for more integrated pedagogical practices, in a report for a meeting between the two groups to explore ways of working more closely together.

Task C10.9

The greatest form of subject tutor–EAP teacher involvement is through team teaching, which in many ways also represents the ideal in collaboration. One approach to team teaching has been described by Johns and Dudley-Evans (1980, reprinted in Swales, 1985) and this suggests a model which can be adapted in other contexts. Throughout the programme the EAP and subject teachers attended each other's sessions, with the teaching in both classes carefully evaluated and improved. To summarize this project, the stages were as follows:

▪ *Planning.* Joint discussions to establish students' literacy difficulties and needs and to assist the subject instructor in making his or her teaching approaches and assignments more accessible to the L2 students.
▪ *First term.* Focus on lectures: helping students identify the argument and main points, classifying types of evidence, using technical and sub-technical vocabulary.
▪ *Second term.* Focus on examination essays. The subject tutor set the questions and discussed criteria for good responses which the EAP teachers then assisted students in understanding by working on the meanings of question types, discussing course expectations, structuring answers and presenting arguments.

CONSIDER

➤ Look again at the three types of engagement with the disciplines discussed in Unit A10. For a course you teach (or have taught) consider the feasibility of each type of co-operation and show how you would work with a subject tutor(s) to achieve it. How would you collect information, allocate tasks, inform students, etc.?

RESEARCH NOTE

➤ Investigate some of the possible pros and cons of team teaching or other kinds of collaboration between literacy and content specialists.

   ▪ If possible, negotiate access to a team-taught course, observe the ways it works and interview the participants to gather their views on it.
   ▪ If this is not possible, interview teaching colleagues and peers to gather data on their impressions and previous experiences of collaborative teaching.

FOLLOW-UP

➤ Using the Johns and Dudley-Evans course design sketched above and your research notes from the study you have just conducted into collaborative teaching, plan a team-teaching version of a course you have taught. Map out a plan to show how you would work together, what the course would look like, and how you would overcome potential difficulties.

Unit C11
Methodologies and materials

Methodologies and materials are the realization of a teaching plan in the delivery of a course. Their importance is measured in the extent to which they contribute to students' learning experiences and in developing control over target genres. Most discussions, however, tend to focus on classroom methodologies as ready-made, off-the-shelf solutions to teaching and learning issues, foregrounding generic treatments and ignoring specific contexts and teacher perceptions. Teaching, however, is massively shaped by personal views and interpretations. A teacher's self-awareness – knowing why we teach the way we do – is central to our effectiveness as teachers, our job satisfaction and our professional development.

Task C11.1

Personal reflection on teaching methods and our own beliefs and practices is a useful starting point in understanding and critically evaluating how we approach our classroom practices. Table C11.1 is an abridged example of such a reflection by a teacher, Costas Gabrielatos (full version at: http://www.developingteachers.com/ articles_tchtraining/mymethodologypf_costas.htm). Setting out our approaches in this way can help us overcome the limitations of packaged methodologies to develop a coherent pedagogy based on our experience and views of language and learning.

CONSIDER

➤ How far do you agree with the items on Gabrielatos's list? Are there points you would add or remove? Do they apply equally to EAP and to general ELT course design?

FOLLOW-UP

➤ Reflect on your own teaching practices and what they tell you about your views of teaching and learning. Do you have favourite ways of presenting material, engaging students, encouraging participation, working with texts, and so on?

Identify and list the ways you seek to achieve your teaching goals through your choice of methods and student tasks.

➤ Now try to identify what you are trying to achieve by these methods. Do they suggest particular beliefs about how people learn to use language through instruction?

Table C11.1 Personal reflections on methodology

How my views of language translate into methodology

- Helping learners investigate and produce language in context (both real and imaginary)
- Examining language in its natural environment (texts/discourse)
- Helping learners become aware of and accept the fuzzy aspects of language, as well as its organizing principles, and create a basic framework on which to build
- Helping learners to manipulate form to produce intended meaning, and interpret form to infer meaning
- Helping learners realize the existence of different registers and genres, and become aware of the factors that influence variety in language use, so that they can make informed choices
- Helping learners see the link between the language and the culture behind it

How my views on learning and teaching translate into methodology

- Trying to make learning interesting, by dealing with topics relevant to learners' interests and needs, but also exposing them to new issues/angles/views
- Fostering an investigatory approach to learning. Helping learners develop study and observation skills, so that they can keep learning autonomously
- Providing opportunities for both reflection and interaction, by mixing individual and group work, offering and inviting feedback, and encouraging collaboration and peer feedback
- Finding the right balance between support and challenge

 Task C11.2

Consciousness-raising tasks play a major role in EAP pedagogies, as teachers often see their main role as making features of target texts salient to learners as a preliminary to focusing instruction on those features. These tasks are always based on research into target texts or contexts and seek to encourage students' reflection on their attitudes to academic writing and their understanding of the language used in academic genres. Two examples are reproduced here from a textbook for graduate students by Swales and Feak (2000). First, see Figure C11.1.

CONSIDER

➤ What do you think Swales and Feak are trying to achieve with Task C11.1?

➤ What are its main strengths and weaknesses?

➤ Select a genre relevant to a particular group of students familiar to you and design a task which encourages learners to reflect on their own use of a feature.

The second task from Swales and Feak (Figure C11.2 on page 296) draws on genre research (by Chang and Swales, 1999 – see Text B6.2) to consider several informal features often used by experienced academic writers but generally forbidden by style guides.

American academic English, in comparison to other research languages, has been said to:

	1	be more explicit about its structure and purposes.
___	2	be less tolerant of asides or digressions.
___	3	use fairly short sentences with less complicated grammar.
___	4	have stricter conventions for sub-sections and their titles.
___	5	be more loaded with citations.
___	6	rely more on recent citations.
___	7	have longer paragraphs in terms of number of words.
___	8	point more explicitly to 'gaps' or 'weaknesses' in the previous research.
___	9	use more sentence connectors (words like *however*).
___	10	place the responsibility for clarity and understanding on the writer rather than the reader.

■ Reflect upon your own first academic language. Place a checkmark (✓) before those points where academic writing in your L1 and American academic English differ. If you do not think the difference holds for your language, leave it blank.

■ Are there other differences that you think ought to be mentioned?

■ If you are writing for an American audience how much do you think you need to adapt to an American style? Do you think you need to fully 'Americanize' your writing, or can you preserve something of your own academic culture in your academic writing?

Figure C11.1 Example of a reflective consciousness-raising task (Swales and Feak, 2000: 16)

CONSIDER

➤ What are the aims of this task? What is it trying to achieve?

➤ Do you think it is likely to be more effective than the previous task in drawing attention to salient features of writing? Justify your answer.

RESEARCH NOTE

➤ Select a genre and conduct an analysis of a key feature using a representative text or set of texts.

FOLLOW-UP

➤ Now design a task which draws on this analysis, employing authentic examples or frequency information, to raise students' awareness of how this feature is used.

Element	No. of occurrences	Average per paper	No. of authors using element
Imperatives	639	21.3	30
I/my/me	1020	34.0	23
Initial *but*	349	11.6	23
Initial *and*	137	4.6	17
Direct questions	224	7.5	17
Verb contractions	92	3.1	11

Take a photocopy of what you consider to be a good but typical paper from your own specialized area, and with a highlighter, highlight all occurrences of the six informal elements that you find. Count and tabulate your findings.

■ In general, how does your field compare to those in the table? What explanations for any differences occur to you?
■ Which of these elements would you feel comfortable using yourself?
■ Have you come across or been told other prescriptive rules? Do you think such rules have validity?

Below are some comments from the informants. From your perspective, decide whether you agree or disagree and why. Then, if possible, discuss your reactions with a partner.

■ Imperatives

  1 I think it is uncommon. I often use it only in references, never in the full text. I feel it is risky to use it in text. (Visiting medical scholar from Japan)

■ *I/my/me*

  2 One good thing of having co-authors is that I can use *we* as many times as I want. (Korean Ph.D. student in psychology)
  3 Only usable for senior scholars. (Chinese Ph.D. student in chemistry)

■ Initial *and* and *but*

  4 If I used these, my advisor would edit them out! (Chinese Ph.D. student in science)
  5 Although I am not sure it is grammatically correct, since many authors use it effectively, I feel it is quite tempting to follow. (Thai Ph.D. student in architecture)

Figure C11.2 Example of a consciousness-raising analysis task (Swales and Feak, 2000: 16)

 Task C11.3

CONSIDER

'Scaffolding' is a key aspect of many methodologies and refers to means of providing support for learners as they build their understanding of texts and their linguistic competence to create them. This involves providing input and instruction which both support and challenge students, gradually increasing their competence as they move towards a point where they can write a target text without assistance. By creating learning situations that are cognitively and interactionally demanding for learners, it is possible to push them to higher levels of performance than they could reach by working alone (e.g. Ohta, 2000).

RESEARCH NOTE

➤ Return to the analysis you made of the genre in Task C6.4, or if you prefer, undertake an analysis of another (academic) genre.

- Analyse the text to identify the move structure and its key lexico-grammatical features.
- Set out the moves and list the aspects of grammar and vocabulary that you believe are central to this genre.

FOLLOW-UP

➤ Now plan a unit around this analysis.

➤ Devise a series of tasks which carefully scaffold student learning by gradually reducing teacher support and moving students towards greater independence.

➤ Use the teaching–learning cycle discussed in Unit A10 to guide you with this activity, showing how your tasks relate to the stages of the cycle.

Task C11.4

Computers offer a range of different opportunities for language instruction, including word processing, CALL programmes, concordancing, synchronous (live chat) and asynchronous (e-mail) computer-mediated communication. But like any other learning activities, the use of computers in an EAP course is effective only when it is integrated into a sustained, coherent methodology that offers learners some control over their learning and guidance from teachers. The choice of programs, sites, texts and tasks should therefore be carefully based on students' target needs and current abilities.

CONSIDER

One difference between online and traditional classes is that students are present only when they are actually participating in an electronic forum, when they are contributing to the online discussion rather than simply 'lurking' in the background. A major challenge for teachers using computer-mediated communication is therefore how to encourage their students to contribute to electronic discussions and to form an online community. This involves introducing topics which motivate involvement with the ideas expressed by their peers and interaction socially with their peers themselves.

➤ What kinds of topics might best foster such a community? Can you think of any ice-breaking activities to get people acquainted and interested in each other?

➤ Devise two activities for a synchronous chat class and two for an asynchronous e-mail activity, setting out clear goals and instructions for the tasks and describing what the students are expected to do before, during and after that activity.

RESEARCH

➤ Either using the corpus you collected for task C7.4 or by compiling another, show how you would draw on the data in this corpus to teach a particular feature or target genre.

➤ Rather than write materials based on your analysis, devise tasks which encourage students to conduct their own studies of the corpus to see how the feature(s) are used.

➤ Trial the tasks on one of your classmates or another EAP teacher/teacher trainee, asking him or her to carry out the tasks by following the rubric you have written.

FOLLOW-UP

➤ Write an evaluation of the tasks based on the trial and the comments of your co-operating partner for a materials writing team. Point out the pros and cons of the activity and suggest recommendations for improvement.

 Task C11.5

CONSIDER

Course books are probably the most widely used source of EAP materials and can often enhance learning while saving teachers considerable time and effort in producing in-house materials. Course books can, however, suffer from cultural biases, *ad hoc* grammar explanations, vagueness about users and their proficiencies, lack of specificity about target needs and invented and misleading text models. Table C11.2 summarizes these pros and cons. The huge volume of commercial resources to choose from simply adds to these difficulties.

RESEARCH NOTE

➤ Construct a questionnaire to explore users' perspectives on a commercial textbook used in your institution. You may need to write one questionnaire for teachers and one for students. Design the instrument to learn about how both teachers and students use the materials, what they like and dislike about it, whether they find it engaging and instructive, how far they need to use other materials to supplement it, whether they prefer in-house or published materials, and so on.

FOLLOW-UP

➤ Write a research report to describe your study and what you have discovered about the ways commercial materials are used and perceived in that institution. What are your most interesting findings and what recommendations might you make for practice to ensure more effective use and agreement between tutors and learners?

Table C11.2 The advantages and disadvantages of textbooks

For	Against
Framework – gives course a sense of structure	Inadequacy – fails to address individual needs
Syllabus – guide to content to be covered	Irrelevance – content may not relate to needs
Resource – ready-made and tested texts and tasks	Restrictive – inhibits teachers' creativity
	Homogeneity – fails to address in-class variety
Reference – source of language information	Deskilling – teachers just mediate materials
Economy – cheaper than in-house materials	Inauthentic – texts and readings often invented
Convenience – easy to use, store and carry	Intuitive – models based on author's intuitions
Guidance – support and ideas for novice teachers	Cultural inappropriacy – unsuitable content
	Cost – may be a financial burden to students
Autonomy – facilitates out-of-class work	
Face validity – students see course as credible	

Source: Hyland (2003: 96).

Task C11.6

Before examining any textbook or other published materials, it is helpful to consider what purpose you want the book for and how you intend to use it in your particular context. This will involve considering the type of book needed, its orientation, role, proficiency level and suitability for teachers and the institution. It is useful to address these issues using a series of questions such as these:

➤ Does the textbook fit the general orientation and pedagogical ethos of the course?

➤ What role is the textbook required to play? A source of readings, models, information, content or exercises? All of these?

➤ Will it be core to the programme or will it supplement other materials?

➤ Who are the learners? Their proficiency, their expectations of textbooks, their budgets, etc.

➤ What are the learners' goals? Their immediate and target needs.

➤ What are the institutional, financial, cultural or educational constraints?

➤ Who are the teachers? What training, skills and experience do they have?

CONSIDER

➤ Now devise a set of criteria for evaluating an EAP Web site, textbook or other set of published materials for a particular purpose and group of students. You may want to choose items from a list that includes:

  ▪ How far the materials relate to the course goals and students.
  ▪ The degree of disciplinary and cultural appropriacy.
  ▪ The local availability and cost.
  ▪ The design, layout and visual appeal.
  ▪ The extent and quality of support materials.
  ▪ The organization, sequencing and progression of exercises.
  ▪ The extent of scaffolding offered and degree of recycling of skills and content provided.
  ▪ The academic content.
  ▪ The methodology.

➤ Which of these criteria are most important for you? Reduce your list to six features.

RESEARCH NOTE

➤ Now use your criteria to evaluate an EAP Web site (such as one of those listed at the College Writing Centres site at http://www.cyberlyber.com/writing_centers_and_owls.htm) or an EAP textbook.

FOLLOW-UP

➤ Create a Web page for a course you are teaching using the Web page template in MS Word or the Composer program in Netscape. These are easy to use and tutorials can be found online. Decide on what you want to include and how you want your students to use the pages through hyperlinks. Use the criteria you devised above to evaluate the site.

Task C11.7

CONSIDER

The processes of creating new materials and modifying existing ones are very similar. Hutchison and Waters (1987) suggest a framework for materials design which includes both adaptation and creation (Table C11.3). This model reflects the instructional roles of materials and emphasizes the fact that materials lead to a task. The resources of language and content that students need to successfully complete this task are supplied by the input.

Table C11.3 A model of materials design

➤ *Input.* Typically a written text, an audio dialogue, video, picture, etc. This provides:

- A stimulus for thought, discussion and writing
- New language items or the re-presentation of earlier items
- A context, a topic and a purpose for writing
- Genre models and exemplars of target texts
- Opportunities for learners to use and build on prior knowledge

➤ *Content focus.* Topics, situations, information and other non-linguistic content to generate meaningful communication

➤ *Language focus.* Opportunities for analyses of texts and for students to integrate new knowledge

➤ *Task.* Materials should lead towards a communicative task, in which learners use the content and language of the unit

Source: adapted from Hutchison and Waters (1987: 108–9).

RESEARCH NOTE

➤ Take a unit from any writing textbook and identify the four components of materials in Table C11.3.

➤ Adapt the unit for the needs of a particular group of learners that you know and develop one additional task from it.

FOLLOW-UP

➤ Select a text as a model exemplar of a genre you wish to teach and devise a series of tasks to exploit it for a group of EAP learners.

Unit C12
Feedback and assessment

It is possible to identify ten broad principles from the literature as a guide to good practice in language assessment (e.g. Bachman, 1990; Bachman and Palmer, 1996; Douglas, 2000; Weigle, 2002):

- The assessment *criteria* should be made explicit to students in terms they can understand as early in the course as possible. These are then used to support students and become target outcomes for the course.
- The assessment *methods* and conditions under which they will be assessed should be explained to learners (the kinds of tasks, whether timed writing, portfolio, etc.).
- The assessment should employ criteria-referenced scales which describe competences so the focus is on learning outcomes, what students can do, rather than ways of teaching.
- The assessment should be valid by being directly related to the genres students have studied; this also implies relevance, usefulness and a basis in real academic practices.
- The assessments should be reliable in that all assessors agree on the criteria and how they will be applied. This implies rater training to aim at consistent scoring.
- There should be regular diagnostic assessments to monitor progress and suggest the teaching intervention which may be needed.
- Where possible, students should be involved in diagnostic assessments so they can develop techniques for reflection and for peer and self-assessment. This is done most effectively through assembling a portfolio collection or providing a checklist of criteria for learners to appraise their own performance (or their peers).
- Achievement assessment should take place at the end of a cycle of learning to ensure students' best performance.
- Students should receive feedback on all assessment tasks in order to point out their strengths, their progress and what they need to do to improve further.
- The assessment should be reported in terms that are understandable to potential users of the results (e.g. students, teachers, administrators, subject specialists, etc.).

Task C12.1

CONSIDER

➤ Do you agree with all these points? List in order of priority what you consider to be the five most important of the principles set out above for EAP teachers and justify your decisions.

➤ Think about the practical implications of each of the five principles you have chosen. What steps would you need to take to ensure that an assessment task met these principles?

RESEARCH NOTE

➤ Conduct a piece of action research to gather student and tutor perceptions of language assessment. Using interviews, questionnaires or focus groups, discover what they think the purpose of assessment is, whether tasks and marking are fair and transparent, how results are used, what fears or misgivings they have about current procedures, what alternatives they would prefer, and so on.

FOLLOW-UP

➤ Collate the data you have collected and write it up for a presentation to your colleagues at a professional development seminar. Discuss the results and account for similarities or differences among the two groups and make recommendations for practice based on your findings.

Task C12.2

CONSIDER

Two key elements of any assessment task are the *rubric* and the *prompt*. The former refers to information about how the assignment should be done and the latter the input to be processed to complete the task. Douglas (2000: 50) suggests that the *rubric* may include:

▪ The specification of the objective: describing what the task or each part of the task will assess, e.g. 'This is a test of your ability to identify the main points in a short lecture.'
▪ The procedures for responding, e.g. 'Answer all the questions in complete sentences,' 'Complete the table using information from the graph.'
▪ The task format, including the relative importance of the sub-tasks and distinctions between them, e.g. 'The questions relate to the case study materials provided,' 'The writing task is based on your understanding of the text and so you should attempt section one first.'

- The time allotted or the submission deadline, e.g. 'The assignment should be handed in to the office in week 10 of the course.'
- The evaluation criteria: the relative weighting given to each part of the task and information on how it is to be marked, e.g. 'Part one carries 60 per cent of the marks,' 'You will get extra marks for using original examples.'

In the real world this information is typically implicit but in assessment contexts it needs to be spelt out and should be as clear and as comprehensive as possible.

RESEARCH NOTE

➤ Select six tasks from EAP textbooks, in-house examinations or other materials and analyse them. Identify the rubric information and decide which categories they include.

FOLLOW-UP

➤ Do you think the rubric information is adequate?

➤ Do you think it is excessive?

➤ What might be added to help students complete the task without overwhelming them with details?

➤ Design a task and write a rubric for it showing how it meets the criteria set out above.

 Task C12.3

The prompt, in contrast to the rubric, stimulates the response to the task. Kroll and Reid (1994: 233) suggest there are three main formats:

- A *base prompt:* states the entire task in direct and simple terms:

  1 What are the advantages and disadvantages of interviews as a data collection method in the field of business studies?
  2 Discuss the view that sociology is not a science.

- A *framed prompt:* presents a situation as a frame for the interpretation of a task:

  1 You have been invited by your old school to give a short presentation on an important development in your field for a group of final-year students. The audience knows a little about the general area but almost

nothing about the topic. They have asked for a fifteen-minute presentation with PowerPoint slides. Prepare and deliver the presentation.

2   You are an official of the Ministry of Education. You have been asked to write an article for a student magazine in support of the view that university students should be required to pay the full cost of their education through their own resources or government loans. You expect your audience to disagree with you, so present the argument as a problem which your position will solve.

■   *A text-based prompt:* presents a text to which the student responds or uses in his or her writing.

1   Read the book review published in *The Plant Cell* and answer the questions below:

   1   Explain the purpose of each paragraph in the review. Use Motta-Roth's scheme if possible.
   2   Which sentences contain complimentary elements and which contain critical elements? Where in the text do the criticisms occur?
   3   How serious do the cited weaknesses seem to be?
   4   Hyland (2000) concludes that praise is global but criticism is specific. Does this hold true for this review?
   5   How has the author sought to soften his criticisms?

   (Swales and Feak, 2004: 187)

2   Use the notes, article extracts, newspaper columns and other materials in the file to write an argument essay to either support or oppose the use of corporal punishment by parents.

CONSIDER

➤   Go back to the six tasks you selected for C12.2 and look carefully at their prompts. What kinds of prompt are used? Can you identify both *contextual* and *input* data in the prompt? Is this information adequate?

FOLLOW-UP

➤   Write a rubric and prompt for both a writing and listening task ensuring that learners have sufficient information to complete the tasks successfully.

Task C12.4

While most assessment tasks still require a single piece of writing to be done in a fixed time with no choice of topic or opportunities for revision, such tasks can seriously disadvantage L2 writers. One alternative is portfolios: multiple writing samples, written over time, and selected from various genres to either showcase a student's best work or display a collection of both drafts and final products to demonstrate improvement. Each piece of work initially contributes diagnostic information to teachers and students, then finished work is selected for inclusion in the portfolio to receive a final achievement grade. Portfolios have the advantages of increasing the validity of assessments through multiple samples and ensuring that evaluation washes back into teaching (Hamp-Lyons and Condon, 2000). As a result of assembling their texts over time, students are able to observe changes in their work, compare different genres and writing experiences, and reflect on their writing and the criteria employed for judging it. It is therefore an assessment which promotes greater responsibility for learning.

Portfolios can offer a more accurate picture of students' writing in relatively natural and less stressful contexts which reflect the practice of academic writing assignments. Texts can include drafts, reflections, readings, diaries, observations, teacher or peer responses, as well as finished texts, thus representing multiple measures of a student's ability. Table C12.1 shows an example of a portfolio structure for EAP students, illustrating how a portfolio draws on a range of genres and how it can encourage students to reflect on these genres and on their writing practices and attitudes. Such reflections are often seen as a major strength of portfolios as they make visible what students see in their work, in their development, and what they value about writing. On the other hand, portfolios are more complex than dealing with a single piece of writing because of the heterogeneous nature of what is assessed and the difficulties of ensuring reliability across raters and rating occasions. In fact, portfolios place huge cognitive and time loads on raters, which means they may take short cuts in making decisions (Hamp-Lyons and Condon, 2000).

CONSIDER

➤ What do you see as the main advantages and disadvantages of this form of assessment?

RESEARCH NOTE

➤ Conduct a small survey to collect students' and EAP teachers' views on adopting portfolio assessments. Find out whether they have had experience of them and what they see as their pros and cons.

Table C12.1 A portfolio assessment for an undergraduate academic writing class

A timed in-class argumentative essay

> Reflection questions for brief response: What is the structure of this essay? What do you particularly like about the essay? What are you most dissatisfied about?

A research-based project (including drafts and materials leading to the final paper)

> What difficulties did you encounter writing this? What did you learn from writing it?

A critical summary (of an article)

> Why did you select this article to summarize? What is the structure of your summary? Why is it organized like this?

A writer's choice (any text of your choice written by you at any time)

> What is this? When did you write it? Why did you choose it? What does it say about you?

An overall reflection of the portfolio (a letter to the EAP teacher integrating the entries)

> What were the goals of this class? How does each entry help to achieve these goals?

FOLLOW-UP

➤ Write a report for your head of department recommending either the adoption or non-adoption of this method of assessment and setting out reasons based on your research.

Task C12.5

Portfolios differ widely as they reflect the goals of different courses and the needs of different learners, but all require careful thought from the outset. When designing a portfolio assessment, a number of questions can be addressed as a concrete starting point:

➤ What do we want to know about the writer? Progress? Genre awareness? etc.

➤ What texts will best achieve this purpose? What genres? Drafts or final only? etc.

➤ Who will choose the entries? Teachers only? Students only? Teacher and student together?

➤ What should the performance criteria be and how will these be linked to course objectives?

➤ Should each entry receive an initial grade or the portfolio be graded only as a whole?

➤ What part will students' reflections and self-assessments play in the assessment?

➤ How will consistent scoring and feedback be achieved? What rater training is needed?

➤ How many people will grade it and how will scoring disagreements be resolved?

➤ How will the outcomes of the evaluation process wash back into students' learning?

CONSIDER

➤ Look again at the example portfolio rubric in Table C12.1 and the list of questions for designing a portfolio above.

▪ Devise a portfolio that would be an appropriate course assessment for a particular course and group of students you are familiar with.

▪ Set out the context – who the learners are, the nature and length of the course, the objectives and so on.

▪ List the items you would require students to include and the reflection questions they should respond to.

FOLLOW-UP

➤ Provide a written justification for your choice of items and outline how you would address the questions in the list above.

 Task C12.6

The research into teacher-written feedback is often scathingly negative, suggesting that much of it is devoted to surface errors and that this is discouraging, over-controlling, and unhelpful. Knoblauch and Brannon (1981: 165), for example, summarize their survey of the L1 research on teacher feedback like this:

> commenting on student essays might just be an exercise in futility. Either students do not read the comments or they read them and do not attempt to implement suggestions and correct errors.

Zamel (1985: 86) suggests a similar picture in ESL contexts:

> ESL writing teachers misread student texts, are inconsistent in their reactions, make arbitrary corrections, write contradictory comments, provide vague prescriptions, impose abstract rules and standards, respond to texts as fixed and final products, and rarely make content-specific comments or offer specific strategies for revising the texts.

CONSIDER

➤ Do you agree with these observations about teacher feedback? What research methods could you use to study feedback to substantiate or refute these claims?

➤ List three things you could do as a teacher to make your written feedback more effective in improving students' writing and explain how they would influence students' revisions.

RESEARCH NOTE

➤ Conduct a study to understand the ways feedback is given, understood and used by a group of teachers and students in a particular context. Use the following methods:

▪ Devise a number of questions and interview both EAP teachers and students for their views on the value of feedback, their preferences and their practices.
▪ Discuss particular examples of feedback with both teachers and students.
▪ Look at examples of teacher comments on drafts and how students have used these comments in their subsequent revisions.

FOLLOW-UP

➤ Write up your work as a research paper, setting out a brief review of the issues discussed in the literature, your methodology and findings, and what the findings mean for pedagogic practice.

Task C12.7

Numerous factors can influence the errors students make and, once again, teachers will need to consider individual differences and students' particular preferences for feedback. Teachers need to have a strategy for targeting particular errors, prioritizing problems for feedback and review. In deciding which errors to target in feedback, the following criteria may be useful:

▪ *Genre-specific errors*: those particular to the current target text type.
▪ *Stigmatizing errors*: those which most disturb the particular target community of readers.
▪ *Comprehensibility errors*: those which most interfere with the clarity of the writing.
▪ *Frequent errors*: those consistently made by the individual student across their writing.
▪ *Student-identified errors*: those the student would like the teacher to focus on.

CONSIDER

➤ Which of the types of error listed above should receive most urgent attention? Why?

➤ Which are likely to be the easiest and most difficult to address through teacher-written feedback?

➤ Will your answer depend on the students or local context? How and why?

RESEARCH NOTE

➤ Interview students to discover their preferences for error correction. What kinds of errors, if any, do they want teachers to focus on, and how explicit do they want teachers to be in responding to them?

FOLLOW-UP

➤ Write up your results as a report for your teaching colleagues, setting out your findings, drawing conclusions and making recommendations for practice.

Glossary

ACADEMIC LITERACY
An extension of the 'new literacy studies' model to academic contexts, viewing literacy as integral to the meanings of the particular institutions in which academic practices take place and to the identities of individual students and participants.

ACADEMIC WORD LIST
A compilation of 570 word families which occur more frequently in academic writing and which are believed to be essential for students pursuing higher education irrespective of their chosen field of specialization (Coxhead, 2000).

ASSESSMENT
The ways used to collect information about a learner's language ability or achievement in order to modify instruction and assist learners' progress towards control of their skills and understandings.

AUDIENCE
The writer's construction of his or her readers, whose predicted beliefs, understandings and values are anticipated and appealed to in the conventional features and structure of a text.

COHERENCE
The ways a text makes sense to readers through the relevance and accessibility of its configuration of concepts, ideas and theories.

COHESION
The grammatical and lexical relationship between the different elements of a text which hold it together.

COLLOCATION
The regular occurrence of a word with one or more others in a text. The term can also refer to the meaning a word can take on as a result.

COMPUTER-MEDIATED LEARNING
Any form of teaching and learning in which computers are directly involved at both ends, such as e-mail, asynchronous discussion boards, synchronous group conferencing or pair chatting and video-conferencing.

CONCORDANCE
A list of unconnected lines of text called up by a concordance program with the search word at the centre of each line. This list allows patterns of use to be seen and explored.

CONSTRUCTION OF
KNOWLEDGE

The view that knowledge is not a privileged representation of reality but a conversation between individuals based on theoretical and cultural perceptions and agreed through discoursal persuasion.

CONTEXT

Factors outside a stretch of language being analysed and considered relevant to its interpretation. These are generally thought to include the situation, cultural knowledge, participant relationships, other texts and parts of the same text. Texts are said to help to shape context, and contexts to influence the conventions, values and knowledge a text appeals to.

CONTRASTIVE RHETORIC

The view that the rhetorical features of L2 texts may reflect different writing conventions learned in the L1 culture, and the cross-cultural study of these differences.

CORPUS

A collection of texts, usually stored electronically, seen as representative of some subset of language and used for linguistic analysis.

CRITICAL DISCOURSE
ANALYSIS (CDA)

An interdisciplinary approach to the study of texts, which views language as a form of social practice and attempts to reveal the ideological underpinnings of discourses and features that have become naturalized over time so that they are treated as common, acceptable and natural.

CRITICAL EAP

A perspective which states that EAP should not simply respond to the needs of content courses but seek to critique existing educational practices and institutions and encourage students to shape their academic goals and the ways they reach them.

CRITICAL LANGUAGE
AWARENESS

The view that language education should seek to assist learners towards a critical consciousness of the discourse practices found in the various communities to which they belong. The goal is to create new practices and conventions which can contribute to social emancipation.

CULTURE

An historically transmitted and systematic network of meanings which allow us to understand, develop and communicate our knowledge and beliefs about the world.

DISCOURSE

Language produced as an act of communication. This language use implies the constraints and choices which operate on writers or speakers in particular contexts and reflects their purposes, intentions, ideas and relationships with readers and hearers.

DISCOURSE ANALYSIS

(1) The study of how stretches of language in context are seen as meaningful and unified by users. (2) How different uses of language express the values of social institutions.

DISCOURSE COMMUNITY	A rather fuzzy concept used to account for how particular rhetorical features of texts express the purposes and understandings of particular groups. The term carries a core meaning of like-mindedness of membership which is widely used to help explain discourse coherence.
DISCURSIVE PRACTICES	A CDA term which refers to the acts of production, distribution and interpretation which surround a text and which must be taken into account in text analysis. These practices are themselves embedded in wider social practices of power and authority.
DRAFTING	The recursive process of text creation, rewriting and polishing; getting ideas on paper and responding to potential problems for readers.
ENGLISH FOR GENERAL ACADEMIC PURPOSES (EGAP)	A view of EAP which involves isolating and teaching the skills, language forms and study activities believed common to all disciplines.
ENGLISH FOR SPECIFIC ACADEMIC PURPOSES (ESAP)	A view of EAP based on the distinctiveness of literacy demands as a result of discipline or course characteristics.
ETHNOGRAPHY	A research approach which seeks to gather a variety of naturally occurring data to provide a highly situated, minutely detailed and holistic account of writers' behaviour.
FEEDBACK	The responses from teachers, peers or computers which students receive on their language performance and which is designed to support learning, convey and model ideas about good performance, develop a linguistic metalanguage and encourage familiarity with new literacy practices.
GENRE	Broadly, a way of acting using discourse. The term usually refers to a set of texts that share the same socially recognized purpose and which, as a result, often share similar rhetorical and structural elements to achieve this purpose.
GENRE ANALYSIS	A branch of discourse analysis which seeks to understand the communicative character of discourse by looking at how individuals use language to engage in particular communicative situations.
GENRE CHAINS	The ways spoken and written texts routinely cluster or are linked together, involving systematic transformations from one genre to another.
GENRE NETWORKS	The fact that genres are often loosely arrayed in a system as each interacts with, draws on, and responds to another in a particular setting.

GENRE SETS	The part of the entire genre constellation that a particular individual or group engages in, either productively or receptively.
GOALS (or aims)	Refer to general statements about what an EAP course hopes to accomplish; the global target outcomes around which the course is organized.
HEDGING	Linguistic devices used to indicate either the writer's lack of commitment to the truth of a statement or a desire not to express that commitment categorically by allowing alternative voices into the text.
IDENTITY	In EAP this is typically seen as the way a student or academic conveys a sense of self as a result of the cultural and social experiences he or she brings to academic communication. Essentially it is socially constructed 'voice' based on specific rhetorical choices.
IDEOLOGY	A body of ideas that reflects the beliefs and interests of an individual, a group or a social institution which finds expression in language.
INTERACTION	Refers to the social routines and relationships which surround acts of communication or the ways that these are expressed in a text. The former have been studied to elaborate the influence of context on writing processes, and the latter to show how texts can reflect an individual's projection of the understandings, interests and needs of a potential audience.
INTERDISCURSIVITY	The wider rhetorical and generic factors which make the use of one text dependent on knowledge of other texts through borrowing conventions and forms to create new texts.
INTERTEXTUALITY	The fact that every utterance reacts and responds to other utterances in that domain. This is often seen as what Fairclough calls *manifest intertextuality*, or the borrowed traces of earlier texts through quotes, paraphrase or citation.
LINGUISTIC IMPERIALISM	The process where a powerful language displaces others in some function(s) in a given context.
LITERACY PRACTICES	Literacy viewed as an integral part of the ways particular groups of people produce, transform and make sense of the world using language.
MATERIALS EVALUATION	Assessment of course materials, particularly those designed in-house, to determine their effectiveness in meeting student needs. Often conducted by involving students in the process via a brief questionnaire.
MEMBERSHIP	The ability to display credibility and competence through familiarity or exploitation of discourse con-

ventions typically used in a community. This can identify one as an 'insider', belonging to that community and possessing the legitimacy to address it.

MULTIMODAL DISCOURSE
Discourse which employs and integrates more than one mode of presentation, such as words and graphics. See above.

NATIVE SPEAKER
Traditionally a person who has proficiency in and intuition about a language by virtue of having acquired a language in infancy. Now very much a challenged and contested term owing to widely varying positions of bilingualism.

NEEDS ANALYSIS
The techniques for collecting and assessing information to establish the *how* and *what* of an EAP course by examining the *present situation*, or information about learners' current proficiencies and ambitions, and *the target situation*, or their future roles and the linguistic skills and knowledge they need to perform competently in their disciplines.

NEW LITERACY STUDIES
The view that written language is socially and historically situated and that literacy practices reflect broader social practices and political arrangements.

NEW RHETORIC PERSPECTIVE
Approach to genre analysis that foregrounds the social and ideological realities that underlie the regularities of texts and which employs the use of ethnographic methods to unpack the relations between texts and contexts.

OBJECTIVES
The description of specific achievable behaviours that learners will be expected to perform at the end of a course.

OUTER CIRCLE
A term coined by Braj Kachru to refer to countries where English is an official or widely used administrative language, e.g. India, Nigeria, Singapore.

PORTFOLIO
An assessment method based on a collection of multiple writing samples selected either to showcase a student's most successful texts or to reveal a process of writing development. They can be used to structure writing courses, encourage reflection and provide more comprehensive and equitable assessment.

POWER
The ability to impose one's will on others. In discourse studies it refers to the fact that this ability to influence and control is, at any given time, expressed through discourse and is unevenly distributed and exercised.

PROCESS APPROACH
A teaching approach to writing which emphasizes the development of good practices by stressing that writing is done in stages of planning, drafting, revising and

editing which are recursive, interactive and potentially simultaneous.

PROCESS SYLLABUS

A framework for decision making between teachers and learners in a classroom setting. Classroom decisions are therefore seen as potentials for negotiation rather than a fixed programme of learning.

PROTOCOL RESEARCH

A research technique widely employed in writing research as a means of getting at the processes which underlie writing by eliciting the verbalized thoughts of writers.

QUALITATIVE RESEARCH

A body of empirical research techniques which explores relationships through loosely structured, mainly verbal data rather than measurements. Analysis is interpretative, subjective, impressionistic and diagnostic and draws on case study, observation, interviews and ethnography. Results are not usually considered generalizable, but are often transferable.

REGISTER

A term from Systemic Linguistics which explains the relationship between texts and their contexts in terms of field (what), tenor (who) and mode (how). Registers refer to broad fields of activity such as legal papers, technical instructions, advertisements and service exchanges.

RHETORICAL CONSCIOUSNESS RAISING

The drawing of the learner's attention to features of the target language, exploring lexical, grammatical and rhetorical features of discourse to use this knowledge to construct their own examples of a genre.

RIGHTS ANALYSIS

An approach to course design and instruction which supplements traditional needs analysis to recognize the challenges that students face in order to assist them to articulate their difficulties with their subject courses and participate more actively as members of an academic community.

SCAFFOLDING

A teaching practice which emphasizes interaction with peers and with experienced others in moving learners from their existing level of performance to a level of independent performance.

SCHEMA

A model of interpretation which suggests that readers make sense of a text by reference to a set of organized, culturally conventional understandings of similar prior experiences.

SOCIAL CONSTRUCTIVISM

The view that knowledge and understanding are created through the discourses of social communities.

SOCIOLITERACY

A teaching approach advocated by Ann Johns (1997) which assists learners to understand their own literate lives and the literacy practices of others. It involves students researching the ways register features interact with social purposes and cultural forces in known genres before they study academic genres.

STUDY SKILLS
The abilities, techniques and strategies which are used when reading, writing, speaking or listening for study purposes.

SYLLABUS
A framework for the potential content of teaching, stating what is to be achieved in the course, identifying what will be worked on in reaching the overall course aims and providing a basis for evaluating students' progress.

SYSTEMIC FUNCTIONAL LINGUISTICS (SFL)
The theory of language developed by Michael Halliday which emphasizes that language is the expression of meaning. The forms writers choose to express meanings in specific situations are influenced by the complex elements of those situations.

TASK-BASED INSTRUCTION (TBI)
An approach to language teaching where learners seek to complete activities which simulate real-world problem solving, learning a language focusing on meaning rather than form.

TEACHING AND LEARNING CYCLE
A resource for planning classroom activities informed by a view of learning as a series of linked stages which provide the support needed to move learners towards a critical understanding of genres.

TEAM TEACHING
The closest form of collaborative engagement between EAP and subject discipline staff involving both teachers working together in the same classroom.

TEXT
A chunk of authentic spoken or written language produced for the purposes of communication in real situations.

WRITING CONFERENCE
A two-way interaction between teacher and student(s) where meaning and interpretation are constantly being negotiated by participants, and which provides both teaching and learning benefits.

Further reading

UNIT 1 SPECIFIC OR GENERAL ACADEMIC PURPOSES?

Coffin, C., Curry, M., Goodman, S., Hewings, A., Lillis, T., and Swann, J. (2003). *Teaching academic writing.* London: Routledge. A practical book designed to help university lecturers reflect on the writing tasks they set their students and on the feedback they give them, but also a very useful introduction for EAP teachers assisting students to write in their disciplines.

Dudley-Evans, T., and St John, M.-J. (1998). *Developments in English for Specific Purposes: a multi-disciplinary approach.* Cambridge: Cambridge University Press. A readable overview of the major developments in EAP and ESP. Chapter 3 underlines the contextual basis of EAP and briefly introduces the distinction between EGAP and ESAP.

Flowerdew, J., and Peacock, M. (eds) (2001). *Research perspectives on English for Academic Purposes.* Cambridge: Cambridge University Press. A collection of articles on academic discourse covering the main approaches and touching on issues of specificity and generality in EAP discourses.

Hyland, K. (2002/2004). *Disciplinary discourses.* London: Longman and Ann Arbor, MI: University of Michigan Press. A detailed study of the relationships between the disciplines and their unique discourses, showing how rhetorical conventions both shape and are shaped by the disciplines.

UNIT 2 STUDY SKILLS OR ACADEMIC LITERACY?

Barton, D., Hamilton, M., and Ivanic, R. (eds) (2000). *Situated literacies.* London: Routledge. An interesting series of studies in both academic and non-academic contexts which illustrate and explain the view that written language must be seen as located in particular times and places and is indicative of broader social practices.

Becher, T. (1989). *Academic tribes and territories: intellectual inquiry and the cultures of disciplines.* Milton Keynes: Society for Research in Higher Education and Open University Press. A very readable and influential qualitative study based on interviews with 220 academics in twelve disciplines mapping the relationship between the social aspects of knowledge communities and the epistemologies of the disciplines.

Jones, C., Turner, J., and Street, B. (eds) (1999). *Students writing in the university: cultural and epistemological issues.* Amsterdam: Benjamins. A collection of papers from a British perspective on issues of language and power in university writing, exploring issues such as what counts as knowledge, how it is rhetorically constructed, and the extent these conventions can be taught and challenged.

Lea, M., and Stierer, B. (eds) (2000). *Student writing in higher education.* Buckingham: Open University Press. A series of studies from a broadly 'academic literacies' perspective examining writing and assessment as contextualized social practices.

Lillis, T. (2001). *Student writing: access, regulation, desire.* London: Routledge. A qualitative study of ten non-traditional university students' experience of academic writing. The book challenges the 'skills' view of academic writing to produce a framework for understanding how language and literacy are represented in higher education and how meanings and choices are made.

UNIT 3 LINGUA FRANCA OR *TYRANNOSAURUS REX*?

Block, D., and Cameron, D. (2002). *Globalization and language teaching.* London: Routledge. While not specifically concerned with EAP, the book presents a series of papers documenting and reflecting on the impact of globalization on language policies and practices around the world, addressing various questions from a variety of perspectives.

Canagarajah, S. (2002). *The geopolitics of academic writing.* Pittsburgh, PA: University of Pittsburgh Press. This book critiques current scholarly publishing practices, revealing inequalities in the way academic knowledge is constructed and legitimized through the functioning of text conventions, community member interactions and publishing practices which often relegate the work of Third World scholars to the perimeter of academic discourse.

Davies, A. (2003). *The native speaker: myth and reality.* Clevedon: Multilingual Matters. An examination of one particular issue introduced in this unit, that of the concept of the native speaker and the kinds of knowledge this implies, concluding that the basic opposition between native and non-native speakers of a language is one of power.

Pennycook, A. (1994). *The cultural politics of English as an international language.* London: Longman. Pennycook covers a range of issues which impact on the growth of English as an international language and the global spread of teaching practices. Taking a critical view and examining case studies of Malaysia and Singapore, the book argues that English can never be removed from the cultural and economic contexts in which it is used.

UNIT 4 PRAGMATISM OR CRITIQUE?

Benesch, S. (2001). *Critical English for Academic Purposes.* Mahwah, NJ: Erlbaum. A clearly written discussion of critical pedagogy in EAP, covering theoretical issues and grounding these in the demands of real teaching contexts.

Bizzell, P. (1992). *Academic discourse and critical consciousness.* Pittsburgh, PA: University of Pittsburgh Press. A collection of papers exploring Bizzell's influential views on education for critical consciousness. While written in the 1980s, these papers raise key issues in an accessible and stimulating way.

Clark, R., and Ivanic, R. (1997). *The politics of writing.* London: Routledge. Examines writing as a social practice, both inside and outside educational contexts, to explore the various contexts and purposes of writing and how these influence identity, power and educational practice.

Pennycook, A. (2002). *Critical applied linguistics: a critical introduction.* Mahwah, NJ: Erlbaum. A tour through the leading figures and ideas of social theory as far as they are related to applied linguistics, providing an overview and exploring critical questions in language education, literacy, discourse analysis and other language-related domains.

Theme 2: Literacies and practices

UNIT 5 DISCOURSES, COMMUNITIES AND CULTURES

Casanave, C. (2004). *Controversies in second language writing.* Ann Arbor, MI: University of Michigan Press. A very readable overview of some controversial issues in academic discourse, including contrastive rhetoric and the notion of communities.

Connor, U. (2004). Special issue on *Contrastive rhetoric* of *Journal of English for Academic Purposes, 3* (4). A collection of state-of-the-art papers re-evaluating the idea of culture and writing in academic contexts and applying contrastive studies to student writing in different contexts.

Flowerdew, J. (ed.) (2002). *Academic discourse.* London: Longman. A collection of articles on academic discourse from writers in different parts of the world and covering some key approaches to discourse analysis: genre analysis, corpus linguistics, contrastive rhetoric and ethnography, with each illustrated by empirical studies.

Swales, J. (1990). *Genre analysis.* Cambridge: Cambridge University Press. A tremendously influential book which not only gave an enormous theoretical impetus to EAP but set a research and teaching agenda for EAP and genre analysis for the following decade. Still an excellent introduction to academic discourse.

UNIT 6 GENRE ANALYSIS AND ACADEMIC TEXTS

Hyland, K. (2004). *Genre and second language writing*. Ann Arbor, MI: University of Michigan Press. This book links theory and practice to explain genre theories and their importance for understanding texts and contexts, and how they can be employed in designing courses, tasks, assignments and assessments.

Johns, A. (ed.) (2002). *Genre in the classroom: multiple perspectives*. Mahwah, NJ: Erlbaum. A collection of articles providing a clear and readable understanding of the issues and problems of applying genre-based pedagogies. The papers draw on theory, research and practical experience to illustrate what the three schools of genre can offer teachers.

Kress, G., and Van Leeuwen, T. (1996). *Reading images: the grammar of visual design*. London: Routledge. A systematic and comprehensive account of the grammar of visual design. Drawing on a range of examples, the book explores the role of colour, perspective, framing and composition to show how images communicate meaning.

Swales, J. (2004). *Research genres*. New York: Cambridge University Press. A sequel to Swales's influential *Genre analysis*, this very readable book provides an account of today's research world, focusing on its genres and the role of English in it, before looking in more detail at dissertations and defences.

UNIT 7 CORPUS ANALYSIS AND ACADEMIC TEXTS

Baker, P. (2006). *Corpora in discourse analysis*. London: Continuum. A comprehensive, clearly written and well illustrated introduction to corpus techniques for research into discourse.

Hunston, S. (2002). *Corpora in applied linguistics*. Cambridge: Cambridge University Press. A very accessible and detailed account of the techniques of investigating a corpus and applying corpora in a range of research and pedagogic activities.

McEnery, A., Xiao, R., and Tono, Y. (2005). *Corpus-based language studies*. London: Routledge. A 'how to' textbook with exercises and cases covering different theoretical approaches to the use of corpus data and supported by readings from leading figures in the discipline.

Partington, A. (1996). *Patterns and meanings: using corpora for English language research and teaching*. Amsterdam: Benjamins. A series of case studies focusing on a particular problem area of language use such as phraseology, metaphor, idiom, etc., which are used to explain in detail how concordance technology works.

Sinclair, J. (1991). *Corpus, concordance, collocation*. Oxford: Oxford University Press. The classic text on using corpora to understand and describe language use. Sinclair discusses how to create a corpus and interrogate it for language insights.

UNIT 8 ETHNOGRAPHICALLY ORIENTED ANALYSIS AND EAP

Allison, D. (2002). *Approaching English language research*. Singapore: Singapore University Press. While not entirely devoted to qualitative methods, this book offers a gentle, practical introduction to researching language in various ways.

Pole, C., and Morrison, M. (2003). *Ethnography for education*. Maidenhead: Open University Press. A well written book which clearly shows the potential of ethnography for research in educational settings, discussing data analysis and illustrated with real research projects.

Prior, P. (1998). *Writing/Disciplinarity: a sociohistoric account of literate activity in the academy*. Mahwah, NJ: Erlbaum. An in-depth study of sociohistoric theory and ethnographic methods in relation to graduate writing and its role in their enculturation into particular fields of study.

Richards, K. (2003). *Qualitative inquiry in TESOL*. London: Palgrave Macmillan. An engaging and clearly written research methods textbook for undertaking qualitative, naturalistic and action research projects in TESOL, suitable for novices and advanced students.

Swales, J. (1998). *Other floors, other voices: a textography of a small university building*. Mahwah, NJ: Erlbaum. A brilliant application of qualitative research principles to the observation of three academic cultures on different floors of a small university building. Through close observation, interviews and detailed analyses of texts Swales shows the fine detail of literate lives in a computer help centre, a herbarium and Swales's own English language institute.

Theme 3: Design and delivery

UNIT 9 NEEDS AND RIGHTS

Brown, J. D. (1995). *The elements of language curriculum: a systematic approach to program development*. Boston, MA: Hienle and Hienle. Describes and exemplifies the elements in language curriculum design in a clear and well organized way.

Holliday, A. (1994). *Appropriate methodology and social context*. Cambridge: Cambridge University Press. Using an ethnographic framework to explore the complex and diverse cultures of classrooms, student groups and teacher communities in different countries and educational environments, Holliday argues that these factors have to be acknowledged in the design and implementation of appropriate methodologies.

Jordan, R. (1997). *English for Academic Purposes: a guide and resource book for teachers*. Cambridge: Cambridge University Press. A lightweight, though wide-ranging, introduction to EAP for teachers. Includes needs analysis and course design and takes a skills-based approach to the field.

Richards, J. (2001). *Curriculum development in language teaching*. New York: Cambridge University Press. A systematic, step-by-step introduction to the key elements involved in developing and evaluating language courses.

UNIT 10 DEVELOPMENT AND IMPLEMENTATION

Breen, M., and Littlejohn, A. (eds) (2000). *Classroom decision-making: negotiation and process syllabuses in practice*. Cambridge: Cambridge University Press. A practice-based collection of accounts from teachers in a range of contexts who, using the structured framework of process syllabuses, have introduced shared decision making with students into their classes.

Feez, S. (1998). *Text-based syllabus design*. Sydney: NCELTR/Macquarie University/AMES. A practical handbook for implementing a genre-based syllabus with lower-proficiency learners. Includes discussion of needs analysis, course design, and planning lessons.

Hyland, K. (2003). *Second language writing*. New York: Cambridge University Press. A systematic discussion of the key issues in second-language writing including course design, needs analysis, lesson planning, tasks, texts, materials, assessment and the use of technology in pedagogy.

Schleppegrell, M., and Colombi, M. (eds) (2002). *Developing advanced literacy in first and second languages: meaning with power*. Mahwah, NJ: Erlbaum. A collection addressing the linguistic challenges faced by students in various disciplines when engaging in academic tasks requiring advanced levels of reading and writing. The book spans a range of orientations and approaches, most obviously SFL, genre theory and socio-cultural perspectives, and raises issues for teacher education.

UNIT 11 METHODOLOGIES AND MATERIALS

Johns, A. M. (1997). *Text, role and context: developing academic literacies*. Cambridge: Cambridge University Press. Johns's discussion of a socioliterate approach to EAP, where students are asked to draw on their experiences and their own research with genres and discourse communities to interpret, critique and produce texts.

Swales, J., and Feak, C. (2004). *Academic writing for graduate students: essential tasks and skills*, 2nd edn. Ann Arbor, MI: University of Michigan Press. This successful, research-based guide to writing for graduate students shows how research-based tasks for disciplinary heterogeneous classes can be implemented. Full of good teaching ideas.

Thurstun, J., and Candlin, C. (1998). *Exploring academic English: a workbook for student essay writing*. Sydney, NSW: NCELTR. A book of structured activities which provide ideas for assisting students to research patterns in concordances and compose their own written texts.

Warschauer, M., and Kern, R. (eds) (2000). *Network-based language teaching: concepts and practice.* Cambridge: Cambridge University Press. An interesting and very readable collection of papers which explore the uses of synchronous and asynchronous network communication in language learning.

Wichmann, A., Fligelstone, S., McEnry, T., and Knowles, G. (eds) (1997). *Teaching and language corpora.* London: Longman. An edited collection illustrating how corpora can be used in a range of different contexts to produce teaching tasks and materials and how they can be used by students in the study of language.

UNIT 12 FEEDBACK AND ASSESSMENT

Douglas, D. (2000). *Assessing languages for specific purposes.* Cambridge: Cambridge University Press. The first book to examine the issues surrounding the implementation of speaking, listening, reading and writing tests for ESP and EAP. The book discusses principles and procedures which teachers can use to develop tests in classroom settings.

Ferris, D. (2003). *Response to student writing.* Mahwah, NJ: Erlbaum. While mainly focusing on teacher response to error, this book synthesizes and critically reviews the literature on feedback on student writing and discusses the implications of that research for classroom practice in the areas of peer response, teacher-written feedback and error correction.

Hamp-Lyons, L. (ed.) (1991). *Assessing second language writing in academic contexts.* Norwood, NJ: Ablex. An edited collection looking at the role of summative assessment in L2 academic writing environments.

Hyland, K., and Hyland, F. (eds) (2006). *Feedback in second language writing: contexts and issues.* New York: Cambridge University Press. A collection addressing current thinking and practice in feedback, exploring socio-cultural, interpersonal and pedagogic issues and including research on teacher-written feedback, oral conferencing, peer feedback, computer-mediated feedback and self-evaluation.

Weir, C. (2005). *Language testing and validation: an evidenced-based approach.* London: Palgrave Macmillan. An innovative book of relevance to EAP test designers dealing with all elements of language testing and based on the latest approaches to test validation.

References

Allison, D. (1996). 'Pragmatist discourse and English for Academic Purposes.' *English for Specific Purposes*, 15, 85–103.

Allison, D. (2002). *Approaching English language research*. Singapore: Singapore University Press.

Aston, G. (1997). 'Involving learners in developing learning methods: exploiting text corpora in self access.' In P. Benson and P. Voller (eds), *Autonomy and independence in language learning*. London: Longman.

Atkinson, D. (2004). 'Contrasting rhetorics/contrasting cultures: why contrastive rhetoric needs a better conceptualization of culture.' *Journal of English for Academic Purposes*, 3 (4), 277–90.

Azhari, M., Shahidi, A. R., and Saadatpour, M. M. (2005). 'Local and post-local buckling of stepped and perforated thin plates.' *Applied Mathematical Modelling*, 29 (7), 633–52.

Bachman, L. (1990). *Fundamental considerations in language testing*. Oxford: Oxford University Press.

Bachman, L., and Palmer, A. (1996). *Language testing in practice: designing and developing useful language tests*. Oxford: Oxford University Press.

Bakhtin, M. (1986). 'The problem of speech genres.' In C. Emerson and M. Holquist (eds), *Speech genres and other late essays*. Austin, TX: University of Texas Press.

Baldauf, R., and Jernudd, B. (1983). 'Language of publications as a variable in scientific communication.' *Australian Review of Applied Linguistics*, 6, 97–108.

Ballard, B., and Clanchy, J. (1991). 'Assessment by misconception: cultural influences and intellectual traditions.' In L. Hamp-Lyons (ed.), *Assessing second language writing in academic contexts*. Norwood, NJ: Ablex.

Barron, C. (1992). 'Cultural syntonicity: co-operative relationships between the ESP Unit and other departments.' *Hong Kong Papers in Linguistics and Language Teaching*, 15, 1–14.

Bartholomae, D. (1986). 'Inventing the university.' *Journal of Basic Writing*, 5, 4–23.

Barton, D. (1994). *Literacy: an introduction to the ecology of written language*. Oxford: Blackwell.

Barton, D., and Hamilton, M. (1998). *Local literacies*. London: Routledge.

Bates, M., and Dudley-Evans, T. (1976). *Nucleus: general science*. London: Longman.

Bauer, L., and Nation, P. (1993). 'Word families.' *International Journal of Lexicography*, 6 (4), 253–79.

Baynham, M. (2000). 'Academic writing in new and emergent discipline areas.' In M. Lea and B. Stierer (eds), *Student writing in higher education: new contexts*. Buckingham: Society for Research in Higher Education and Open University Press.

Bazerman, C. (1994). 'Systems of genres and the enactment of social intentions.' In A. Freedman and P. Medway (eds), *Genre and the new rhetoric*. London: Taylor & Francis.

Becher, T. (1989). *Academic tribes and territories: intellectual inquiry and the cultures of disciplines*. Milton Keynes: Society for Research in Higher Education and Open University Press.

Belcher, D. (1994). 'The apprenticeship approach to advanced academic literacy: graduate students and their mentors.' *English for Specific Purposes*, 13 (1), 23–34.

Benesch, S. (2001). *Critical English for Academic Purposes*. Mahwah, NJ: Erlbaum.

Benson, P., and Voller, P. (eds) (1997). *Autonomy and independence in language learning*. London: Longman.

Bereiter, C., and Scardamalia, M. (1987). *The psychology of written composition*. Hillsdale, NJ: Erlbaum.

Berwick, R. (1989). 'Needs assessment in language programming: from theory to practice.' In R. K. Johnson (ed.), *The second language curriculum*. Cambridge: Cambridge University Press.

Bhatia, V. (2002). 'A generic view of academic discourse.' In J. Flowerdew (ed.), *Academic discourse*. Harlow: Longman.

Bhatia, V. (2004). *Worlds of written discourse: a genre-based view*. London: Continuum.

Bhatia, V. K. (1993). *Analysing genre: language use in professional settings*. London: Longman.

Biber, D. (1988). *Variation across speech and writing*. Cambridge: Cambridge University Press.

Bisong, K. (1995). 'Language choice and cultural imperialism.' *ELT Journal*, 49 (2), 122–132.

Blue, G. (1988). 'Individualising academic writing tuition.' In P. Robinson (ed.), *Academic writing: process and product*. ELT Documents 129. Basingstoke: Modern English Publications.

Blyler, N., and Thralls, C. (eds) (1993). *Professional communication: the social perspective*. London: Longman.

Bourdieu, P. (1991). *Language and symbolic power*. Oxford: Polity Press.

Braine, G. (1989). 'Writing in science and technology: an analysis of assignments from ten undergraduate courses.' *English for Specific Purposes*, 8, 3–15.

Braine, G. (1995). 'Writing in the natural sciences and engineering.' In D. Belcher and G. Braine (eds), *Academic writing in a second language: essays on research and pedagogy*. Norwood, NJ: Ablex.

Breen, M. (1984). 'Process syllabuses for the language classroom.' In C. Brumfit (ed.), *General English syllabus design*. Oxford: Pergamon.

Breen, M. (1987). 'Contemporary paradigms in syllabus design.' *Language Teaching*, 20 (3), 157–74.

Breen, M., and Candlin, C. (1980). 'The essentials of a communicative curriculum in language teaching.' *Applied Linguistics*, 1 (1), 89–112.

Breen, M., and Littlejohn, A. (eds) (2000). *Classroom decision-making: negotiation and process syllabuses in practice*. Cambridge: Cambridge University Press.

Brewer, J. (2000). *Ethnography*. Buckingham: Open University Press.

Brindley, G. (1989). *Assessing achievement in the learner-centred curriculum*. Sydney, NSW: NCELTR Publications.

Brinko, K. T. (1993). 'The practice of giving feedback to improve teaching.' *Journal of Higher Education*, 64 (5), 574–93.

Brinton, M., Snow, M., and Wesche, M. (1989). *Content-based second language instruction*. Boston, MA: Heinle & Heinle.

Brown, J. D. (1995). *The elements of language curriculum*. Boston, MA: Heinle & Heinle.

Brown, J. D. (2001). *Using surveys in language programs*. Cambridge: Cambridge University Press.

Bruffee, K. (1986). 'Social construction: language and the authority of knowledge: a bibliographical essay.' *College English*, 48, 773–9.

Burns, A. (1999). *Collaborative action research for English language teachers*. Cambridge: Cambridge University Press.

Burns, A., and Joyce, H. (1997). *Focus on speaking*. Sydney, NSW: National Centre for English Language Teaching and Research, Macquarie University.

Cadman, K. (2002). 'English for academic possibilities: the research proposal as a contested site in postgraduate genre pedagogy.' *Journal of English for Academic Purposes*, 1 (2), 85–104.

Canagarajah, A. S. (1996). '"Nondiscursive" requirements in academic publishing, material resources of periphery scholars, and the politics of knowledge production.' *Written Communication*, 13 (4), 435–72.

Canagarajah, A. S. (1999). *Resisting linguistic imperialism in English teaching*. Oxford: Oxford University Press.

Canagarajah, A. S. (2002). 'Globalization, methods, and practice in periphery classrooms.' In D. Block and D. Cameron (eds), *Globalization and language teaching*. London: Routledge.

Candlin, C. N., and Hyland, K. (1999). 'Integrating approaches to the study of writing.' In C. N. Candlin and K. Hyland (eds), *Writing: texts, processes and practices*. Harlow: Pearson, pp. 1–18.

Candlin, C. N., and Plum, G. A. (1999). 'Engaging with challenges of interdiscursivity in academic writing: researchers, students and teachers.' In C. N. Candlin and K. Hyland (eds), *Writing: texts, processes and practices*. Harlow: Pearson, pp. 193–217.

Candlin, C. N., Kirkwood, J. M., and Moore, H. M. (1975). 'Developing study skills in English.' In ETIC *English for academic study: problems and perspectives*. London: British Council.

Carson, J., and Nelson, G. (1996). 'Chinese students' perceptions of ESL peer response group interaction.' *Journal of Second Language Writing*, 5 (1), 1–19.

Cherryholmes, C. (1988). *Power and criticism: poststructural investigations in education*. New York: Teachers College Press.

Chick, K. (1996). 'Safe-talk: collusion in apartheid education.' In H. Coleman (ed.), *Society and the language classroom*. Cambridge: Cambridge University Press.

Christie, F. (1987). 'Genres as choice.' In I. Reid (ed.), *The place of genre in learning: current debates*. Deakin, Vic.: Deakin University Press.

Christie, F., and Martin, J. R. (eds) (1997). *Genre in institutions: social processes in the workplace and school*. New York: Continuum.

Clark, R., and Ivanic, R. (1997). *The politics of writing*. London: Routledge.

Clarke, D. (1991). 'The negotiated syllabus: what is it and how is it likely to work?' *Applied Linguistics*, 12 (1), 13–28.

Coffin, C., Curry, M., Goodman, S., Hewings, A., Lillis, T., and Swann, J. (2003). *Teaching academic writing: a toolkit for higher education*. London: Routledge.

Cohen, A. D., and Cavalcanti, M. C. (1990). 'Feedback on compositions: teacher and student verbal reports.' In B. Kroll (ed.), *Second language writing: research insights for the classroom*. Cambridge: Cambridge University Press.

Connor, U. (1996). *Contrastive rhetoric*. Cambridge: Cambridge University Press.

Connor, U. (2002). 'New directions in contrastive rhetoric.' *TESOL Quarterly,* 36, 493–510.

Coxhead, A. (2000). 'A new Academic Word List.' *TESOL Quarterly*, 34 (2), 213–38.

Crème, P., and Lea, M. (2003). *Writing at university: a guide for students,* 2nd edn. Maidenhead: Open University Press.

Crystal, D. (2003). *English as a global language*. Cambridge: Cambridge University Press.

Cunningsworth, A. (1995). *Choosing your coursebook*. Oxford: Heinemann.

Currie, P. (1993). 'Entering a disciplinary community: conceptual activities required to write for one introductory university course.' *Journal of Second Language Writing*, 2, 101–17.

Curtis, S., and Schaeffer, J. (2005). 'Syntactic development in children with hemispherectomy: the I-, D-, and C-systems.' *Brain and Language*, 94 (2), 147–66.

Cutting, J. (2002). *Pragmatics and discourse: a resource book for students*. London: Routledge.

Devitt, A. (1991). 'Intertextuality in tax accounting.' In C. Bazerman and J. Paradis (eds), *Textual dynamics of the professions*. Madison, WI: University of Wisconsin Press.

Dey, I. (1993). *Qualitative data analysis: a user-friendly guide for social scientists*. London: Routledge.

Dörnyei, Z. (2003). *Questionnaires in second language research: construction, administration, and processing*. Mahwah, NJ: Erlbaum.

Douglas, D. (2000). *Assessing languages for specific purposes*. Cambridge: Cambridge University Press.

Dudley-Evans, T. (1993). 'Variation in communication patterns between discourse communities: the case of highway engineering and plant biology.' In G. Blue (ed.), *Language, learning and success: studying through English*. London: MEP and Macmillan.

Dudley-Evans, T. (2001). 'English for Specific Purposes.' In R. Carter and D. Nunan (eds), *The Cambridge guide to teaching English to speakers of other languages*. Cambridge: Cambridge University Press.

Dudley-Evans, T., and St John, M.-J. (1998). *Developments in English for Specific Purposes*. Cambridge: Cambridge University Press.

Ellis, R. (1999). 'Input-based approaches to teaching grammar: a review of classroom-oriented research.' *Annual Review of Applied Linguistics*, 19, 64–80.

Ellis, R. (2003). *Task-based language learning and teaching*. Oxford: Oxford University Press.

Entwistle, N., and Ramsden, P. (1983). *Understanding student learning*. London: Croom Helm.

Ewer, J. R., and Latorre, G. (1969). *A course in basic scientific English*. London: Longman.

Fairclough, N. (1992). 'Introduction.' In N. Fairclough (ed.), *Critical language awareness*. London: Longman.

Feez, S. (1998). *Text-based syllabus design*. Sydney: Macquarie University and AMES.

Feez, S. (2002). 'Heritage and innovation in second language education.' In A. M. Johns (ed.), *Genre in the classroom*. Mahwah, NJ: Erlbaum.

Ferris, D. (1997). 'The influence of teacher commentary on student revision' *TESOL Quarterly*, 31 (2), 315–39.

Ferris, D. (2003). *Response to student writing*. Mahwah, NJ: Erlbaum.

Firth, A. (1996). 'The discursive accomplishment of normality: on lingua franca English and conversation analysis.' *Journal of Pragmatics*, 26, 237–59.

Flowerdew, J. (1993). 'Concordancing as a tool in course design.' *System*, 21 (2), 231–44.

Flowerdew, J. (1999). 'Problems of writing for scholarly publication in English: the case of Hong Kong.' *Journal of Second Language Writing*, 8 (3), 243–64.

Flowerdew, J. (2001). 'Attitudes of journal editors to nonnative speaker contributions.' *TESOL Quarterly*, 35 (1), 121–50.

Flowerdew, J., and Miller, L. (1992). 'Student perceptions, problems and strategies in second language lecture comprehension.' *RELC Journal*, 23, 60–80.

Flowerdew, J., and Miller, L. (1996). 'Lectures in a second language: notes towards a cultural grammar.' *English for Specific Purposes*, 15 (2), 121–40.

Flowerdew, J., and Peacock, M. (eds) (2001), *Research perspectives on English for Academic Purposes*. Cambridge: Cambridge University Press.

Fortanet, I. (2004). 'The use of "we" in university lectures: reference and function.' *English for Specific Purposes*, 23 (1), 45–66.

Freedman, A. (1994). '"Do as I say"? The relationship between teaching and learning new genres.' In A. Freedman and P. Medway (eds), *Genre and the new rhetoric.* London: Taylor & Francis.

Freedman, A., and Adam, C. (2000). 'Write where you are: situating learning to write in university and workplace settings.' In P. Dias and A. Pare (eds), *Transitions: writing in academic and workplace settings.* Creskill, NJ: Hampton Press.

Garbutt, M., and O'Sullivan, K. (1996). *IELTS strategies for study: reading, writing, listening and speaking at university and college.* Sydney, NSW: National Centre for English Language Teaching and Research, Macquarie University.

Garcez, P. (1993). 'Point-making styles in cross-cultural business communication: a microethnographic study.' *English for Specific Purposes*, 12, 103–20.

Garfield, E. (1983). 'Mapping science in the Third World.' *Science and Public Policy*, 10 (3), 112–27.

Gee, J. (1990). *Social linguistics and literacies: ideology in discourse.* Brighton: Falmer Press.

Geertz, C. (1973). 'Thick description: toward an interpretative theory of culture.' In *The Interpretation of Cultures.* New York: Basic Books.

Geertz, C. (1983). *Local knowledge: further essays in interpretive anthropology.* New York: Basic Books.

Gibbs, W. (1995). 'Lost science in the Third World.' *Scientific American*, August, 92–9.

Glaser, B., and Strauss, A. (1967). *The discovery of grounded theory.* Chicago: Aldine.

Glaze, W. H. (2000). 'The universal language.' *Environmental Science and Technology*, 24, 369A.

Goffman, E. (1959). *The presentation of self in everyday life.* London: Penguin.

Goldstein, L. M., and Conrad, S. M. (1990). 'Student input and negotiation of meaning in ESL writing conferences.' *TESOL Quarterly*, 24 (3), 443–60.

Gollin, S. (1998) 'Literacy in a computing department: the invisible in search of the ill-defined.' In C. Candlin and G. Plum (eds), *Researching academic literacies: framing student literacy.* Sydney: NCELTR, Macquarie University.

Gosden, H. (1992). 'Research writing and NNSs: from the editors.' *Journal of Second Language Writing*, 1 (2), 123–39.

Grabe, W., and Kaplan, R. (1996). *Theory and practice of writing.* Harlow: Longman.

Graddol, D. (1997). *The future of English.* London: British Council.

Graddol, D. (1999). 'The decline of the native speaker.' In D. Graddol and U. Meinhof (eds), *English in a changing world. AILA Review 13.* Oxford: Catchline.

Graddol, D. (2001). 'English in the future.' In A. Burns and C. Coffin (eds), *Analyzing English in a global context.* London: Routledge.

Granger, S. (ed.) (1998). *Learning English on computer.* London: Longman.

Gray, J. (2002). 'The global coursebook in English language teaching.' In D. Block and D. Cameron (eds), *Globalization and language teaching.* London: Routledge.

Haas, C. (1994). 'Learning to read biology: one student's rhetorical development in college.' *Written Communication*, 11 (1), 43–84.

Hall, D., and Kenny, B. (1988). 'An approach to a truly communicative methodology: the AIT pre-sessional course.' *English for Specific Purposes*, 7, 19–32.

Halliday, M. A. K. (1989). *Spoken and written language.* Oxford: Oxford University Press.

Halliday, M. A. K. (1994). *An introduction to functional grammar*, 2nd edn. London: Arnold.

Halliday, M. A. K., Macintosh, A., and Strevens, P. (1964). *The linguistic sciences and language teaching.* London: Longman.

Hammersley, M. (2001). 'On Michael Bassey's concept of fuzzy generalization.' *Oxford Review of Education*, 27 (2), 219–25.

Hammond, J., and Macken-Horarik, M. (1999). 'Critical literacy: challenges and questions for ESL classrooms.' *TESOL Quarterly*, 33, 528–44.

Hamp-Lyons, L. (1997). 'Introduction.' *English for Specific Purposes*, 16 (1).

Hamp-Lyons, L., and Condon, W. (2000). *Assessing the portfolio: principles for practice, theory and research.* Cresskill, NJ: Hampton Press.

Harmer, J. (2001). *The practice of English language teaching.* Harlow: Pearson.

Harwood, N., and Hadley, G. (2004). 'Demystifying institutional practices: critical pragmatism and the teaching of academic writing.' *English for Specific Purposes*, 23 (4), 355–77.

Hawking, S. (1993). *Black holes and baby universes and other essays.* New York: Bantam.

HEFCE (1999). *Performance indicators in higher education in the UK.* Bristol: HEFCE.

Henry, J. (2004). 'Imperial: half of students will be foreign.' *News Telegraph*, November.

Herbert, A. J. (1965). *The structure of technical English.* London: Longman.

Hinkel, E. (2002). *Second language writers' text.* Mahwah, NJ: Erlbaum.

Holliday, A. (1994). *Appropriate methodology and social context.* Cambridge: Cambridge University Press.

Holliday, A. (2002). *Doing and writing qualitative research.* London: Sage.

Holliday, A., and Cook, T. (1982). 'An ecological approach to ESP.' *Issues in ESP. Lancaster Papers in ELT*, 5, 123–43.

Horowitz, D. M. (1986). 'What professors actually require: academic tasks for the ESL classroom.' *TESOL Quarterly*, 20 (3), 445–62.

Hughes, A. (1989). *Testing for language teachers.* Cambridge: Cambridge University Press.

Hunston, S. (2002). *Corpora in applied linguistics.* Cambridge: Cambridge University Press.

Hutchison, T., and Waters, A. (1987). *English for Specific Purposes.* Cambridge: Cambridge University Press.

Hyland, F. (1998). 'The impact of teacher written feedback on individual writers.' *Journal of Second Language Writing*, 7 (3), 255–86.

Hyland, F. (2000). 'ESL writers and feedback: giving more autonomy to students.' *Language Teaching Research*, 4, 33–54.

Hyland, K. (2000/2004). *Disciplinary discourses: social interactions in academic writing.* London: Longman/Ann Arbor, MI: University of Michigan Press.

Hyland, K. (2001). 'Bringing in the reader: addressee features in academic articles.' *Written Communication*, 18 (4), 549–74.

Hyland, K. (2002). 'What do they mean? Questions in academic writing.' *TEXT*, 22 (4), 529–57.

Hyland, K. (2003). *Second language writing.* New York: Cambridge University Press.

Hyland, K. (2004). *Genre and second language writing.* Ann Arbor, MI: University of Michigan Press.

Hyland, K. (2006). 'Disciplinary differences: language variation in academic discourses.' In K. Hyland and M. Bondi (eds), *Academic discourse across disciplines.* Frankfurt: Peter Lang.

Hyland, K., and Tse, P. (2004). '"I would like to thank my supervisor." Acknowledgements in graduate dissertations.' *International Journal of Applied Linguistics*, 14 (2), 259–75.

Hyland, K., and Tse, P. (2007). 'Is there an academic vocabulary?' *TESOL Quarterly*.

Hyon, S. (1996). 'Genre in three traditions: implications for ESL.' *TESOL Quarterly*, 30 (4), 693–722.

Ivanic, R. (1998). *Writing and identity: the discoursal construction of identity in academic writing.* Amsterdam: Benjamins.

Ivanic, R., Clark, R., and Rimmershaw, R. (2000). '"What am I supposed to make of this?"

The messages conveyed to students by tutors' written comments.' In M. Lea and B. Steirer (eds), *Student writing in higher education: new contexts*. Buckingham: Open University Press.

Iverson, C. (2002). 'US medical journal editors' attitudes towards submissions from other countries.' *Science Editor*, 25, 75–8.

Jenkins, S., Jordan, M. K., and Weiland, P. (1993). 'The role of writing in graduate engineering education: a survey of faculty beliefs and practices.' *English for Specific Purposes*, 12, 51–67.

Johns, A. M. (1988). 'The discourse communities dilemma: identifying transferable skills for the academic milieu.' *English for Specific Purposes*, 7, 55–9.

Johns, A. M. (1997). *Text, role and context: developing academic literacies*. Cambridge: Cambridge University Press.

Johns, A. M. (ed.) (2002). *Genre in the classroom: multiple perspectives*. Mahwah, NJ: Erlbaum.

Johns, T., and Dudley-Evans, T. (1980). 'An experiment in team teaching of overseas postgraduate students of transportation and plant biology.' *Team Teaching in ESP*. ELT Documents 106, pp. 6–23.

Jordan, R. (1997). *English for Academic Purposes*. Cambridge: Cambridge University Press.

Jordan, R. (2002). 'The growth of EAP in Britain.' *Journal of English for Academic Purposes*, 1 (1), 69–78.

Jordan, R. R. (1989). 'English for Academic Purposes (EAP).' *Language Teaching*, 22 (3), 150–64.

Knapp, P., and Watkins, M. (1994). *Context – text – grammar: teaching the genres and grammar of school writing in infants and primary classrooms*. Sydney: Text Productions.

Knoblauch, C., and Brannon, L. (1984). *Rhetorical traditions and the teaching of writing*. Portsmouth, NH: Boynton/Cook.

Kress, G. R. (2003). *Literacy in the new Media Age*. London: Routledge Falmer.

Kress, G., and Van Leeuwen, T. (1996). *Reading images: the grammar of visual design*. London: Routledge.

Kress, G. R. and Van Leeuwen, T. (2002). *Multimodal discourse: the modes and media of contemporary communication*. London: Arnold.

Kroll, B., and Reid, J. (1994). 'Guidelines for designing writing prompts: clarifications, caveats and cautions.' *Journal of Second Language Writing*, 3 (3), 231–55.

Lamb, T. (2000). 'Finding a voice: learner autonomy and teacher education in an urban context.' In B. Sinclair, I. McGrath and T. Lamb (eds), *Learner autonomy, teacher autonomy: new directions*. London: Longman.

Lantolf, J. P. (1999). 'Second culture acquisition: cognitive considerations.' In E. Hinkel (ed.), *Culture in second language teaching and learning*. Cambridge: Cambridge University Press.

Larsen-Freeman, D. (2000). *Techniques and principles in language learning*. Oxford: Oxford University Press.

Lave, J., and Wenger, E. (1991). *Situated learning: legitimate peripheral participation*. Cambridge: Cambridge University Press.

Lea, M., and Stierer, B. (2000). *Student writing in higher education: new contexts*. Buckingham: Society for Research in Higher Education and Open University Press.

Lea, M., and Street, B. (1999). 'Writing as academic literacies: understanding textual practices in higher education.' In C. N. Candlin and K. Hyland (eds), *Writing: texts, processes and practices*. Harlow: Pearson.

Lea, M., and Street, B. V. (2000). 'Student writing and staff feedback in higher education.' In M. Lea and B. Stierer (eds), *Student writing in higher education: new contexts*. Buckingham: Society for Research in Higher Education and Open University Press.

Leki, I. (1990). 'Coaching from the margins: issues in written response.' In B. Kroll (ed.), *Second language writing*. Cambridge: Cambridge University Press.

Li, S. L. and. Pemberton, R. (1994). 'An investigation of students' knowledge of academic and subtechnical vocabulary.' In *Proceedings, joint seminar on corpus linguistics and lexicology*. Hong Kong: University of Science and Technology Press.

Lillis, T. (2001). *Student writing: access, regulation, desire*. London: Routledge.

McDonough, J., and McDonough, S. (1997). *Research methods for English language teachers*. London: Arnold.

McGrath, I. (2000). 'Teacher autonomy.' In B. Sinclair, I. McGrath and T. Lamb (eds), *Learner autonomy, teacher autonomy: new directions*. London: Longman.

Mager, R. (1975). *Preparing instructional objectives*. Palo Alto, CA: Fearon.

Marco, M. (2000). 'Collocational frameworks in medical research papers: a genre-based study.' *English for Specific Purposes*, 6 (1), 31–43.

Markus, H., and Kitayama, S. (1991). 'Cultures and the self: implications for cognition, emotion and motivation.' *Psychological Review*, 98, 224–53.

Martin, J. R. (1992). *English text: system and structure*. Amsterdam: Benjamins.

Master, P. (1995). 'Consciousness raising and article pedagogy.' In D. Belcher and G. Braine (eds), *Academic writing in a second language: essays in research and pedagogy*. Norwood, NJ: Ablex.

Mendoca, C., and Johnson, K. (1994). 'Peer review negotiations: revision activities in ESL writing instruction.' *TESOL Quarterly*, 28 (4), 745–68.

Messick, S. (1996). 'Validity and washback in language testing.' *Language Testing*, 13, 241–56.

Miles, M., and Huberman, A. (1994). *Qualitative data analysis: an expanded sourcebook*. Thousand Oaks, CA: Sage.

Miller, C. (1994). 'Genre as social action.' In A. Freedman and P. Medway (eds), *Genre and the new rhetoric*. London: Taylor & Francis.

Miller, T. (1998). 'Visual persuasion: a comparison of visuals in academic texts and the popular press.' *English for Specific Purposes*, 17 (1), 29–46.

Milton, J. (1999). 'Lexical thickets and electronic gateways: making text accessible by novice writers.' In C. N. Candlin and K. Hyland (eds), *Writing: texts, processes and practices*. London: Longman.

Mittan, R. (1989). 'The peer review process: harnessing students' communicative power.' In D. Johnson and D. Roen (eds), *Richness in writing: empowering ESL students*. New York: Longman.

Munby, J. (1978). *Communicative syllabus design*. Cambridge: Cambridge University Press.

Myers, G. (1990). *Writing biology: texts in the social construction of scientific knowledge*. Madison, WI: University of Wisconsin Press.

Myers, G. (1997). 'Words and pictures in a biology textbook.' In T. Miller (ed.), *Functional approaches to written text: classroom applications*. Washington, DC: US Information Service.

Nation, I. S. P. (2001). *Learning vocabulary in another language*. New York: Cambridge University Press.

Nattinger, J., and De Carrico, J. (1998). *Lexical phrases and language teaching*. Oxford: Oxford University Press.

Navarro, F. A. (1995). 'L'importance de l'anglais et du français sur la base des références bibliographiques de travaux originaux publiés dans la *Presse médicale* (1920–1995).' *La Presse médicale*, 24, 1547–51.

Nunan, D. (1992). *Research methods in language teaching*. Cambridge: Cambridge University Press.

Ohta, A. (2000). 'Rethinking interaction in SLA: developmentally appropriate assistance in the zone of proximal development and the acquisition of L2 grammar.' In J. Lantolf (ed.), *Sociocultural theory and second language learning.* Oxford: Oxford University Press.

Pakir, A. (1999). 'Connecting with English in the context of internationalization.' *TESOL Quarterly*, 33, 103–14.

Pally, M. (ed.) (1999). *Sustained content teaching in academic ESL/EFL.* Boston, MA: Houghton Mifflin.

Paltridge, B. (2001). *Genre and the language learning classroom.* Ann Arbor, MI: University of Michigan Press.

Partington, A. (1996). *Patterns and meanings: using corpora for English language research and teaching.* Amsterdam: Benjamins.

Pennycook, A. (1994). *The cultural politics of English as an international language.* London: Longman.

Pennycook, A. (1996). 'Borrowing others' words: text, ownership, memory and plagiarism.' *TESOL Quarterly*, 30, 201–30.

Pennycook, A. (1997). 'Vulgar pragmatism, critical pragmatism, and EAP.' *English for Specific Purposes*, 16 (4), 253–69.

Phillipson, R. (1992). *Linguistic imperialism.* Oxford: Oxford University Press.

Plum, G. (1998). 'Doing psychology, doing writing: student voices on academic writing in psychology.' In C. Candlin and G. Plum (eds), *Researching academic literacies; framing student literacy.* Sydney: NECLTR, Macquarie University.

Pogner, K.-H. (1999). 'Discourse community, culture and interaction: on writing by consulting engineers.' In F. Bargiela-Chiappini and C. Nickerson (eds), *Writing business: genres, media and discourses.* London: Longman.

Pole, C., and Morrison, M. (2003). *Ethnography for education.* Maidenhead: Open University and McGraw-Hill.

Prior, P. (1998). *Writing/Disciplinarity: a sociohistoric account of literate activity in the academy.* Mahwah, NJ: Erlbaum.

Raimes, A. (1991). 'Instructional balance: from theories to practices in the teaching of writing.' In J. Alatis (ed.), *Georgetown University roundtable on language and linguistics.* Washington DC: Georgetown University Press.

Ramanathan, V., and Atkinson, D. (1999). 'Ethnographic approaches and methods in L2 writing research: a critical guide and review.' *Applied Linguistics*, 20 (1), 44–70.

Reid, J. M. (1993). *Teaching ESL writing.* Englewood Cliffs, NJ: Regents and Prentice Hall.

Richards, J., Platt, J., and Platt, H. (1992). *Longman dictionary of language teaching and applied linguistics.* Harlow: Longman.

Richards, K. (2003). *Qualitative inquiry in TESOL.* London: Palgrave Macmillan.

Robinson, P. (1991). *ESP today: a practitioner's guide.* New York: Prentice Hall.

Rorty, R. (1979). *Philosophy and the mirror of nature.* Princeton, NJ: Princeton University Press.

Rutherford, W. (1987). *Second language grammar: learning and teaching.* London: Longman.

Sarangi, S., and Roberts, C. (1999). *Talk, work and institutional order: discourse in medical, mediation and management settings.* Berlin: Mouton de Gruyter.

Seal, B. (1997). *Academic encounters: content focus human behaviour.* Cambridge: Cambridge University Press.

Sengupta, S., Forey, G., and Hamp-Lyons, L. (1999). 'Supporting effective English communication within the context of teaching and research in a tertiary institute: developing a genre model for consciousness raising.' *English for Specific Purposes*, 18 (supplement 1), S7–S22.

Sheldon, L. (1987). *ELT textbooks and materials: problems in evaluation and development.* London: Modern English Publications and British Council.

Silva, T. (1993). 'Toward an understanding of the distinct nature of L2 writing: the ESL research and its implications.' *TESOL Quarterly*, 27, 665–77.

Simpson, R. (2004). 'Stylistic features of spoken academic discourse: the role of formulaic expressions.' In U. Connor and T. Upton (eds), *Discourse in the professions: perspectives from corpus linguistics.* Amsterdam: Benjamins, pp. 37–64.

Sinclair, J. (1991). *Corpus, concordance, collocation.* Oxford: Oxford University Press.

Smagorinsky, P. (ed.) (1994). *Speaking about writing: reflections on research methodology.* Thousand Oaks, CA: Sage.

Spack, R. (1988). 'Initiating ESL students into the academic discourse community: how far should we go?' *TESOL Quarterly*, 22 (1), 29–52.

Stamenović, D. (2005). 'Effects of cytoskeletal prestress on cell rheological behavior.' *Acta Biomaterialia*, 1 (3), 255–62.

Stanley, J. (1992). 'Coaching student writers to be effective peer evaluators.' *Journal of Second Language Writing*, 1 (3), 217–33.

St John, M.-J. (1996). 'Business is booming: business English in the 1990s.' *English for Specific Purposes*, 15, 3–18.

Street, B. (ed.) (1993). *Cross-cultural approaches to literacy.* Cambridge: Cambridge University Press.

Street, B. V. (1995). *Social literacies: critical approaches to literacy in development, ethnography and education.* New York: Longman.

Swales, J. (ed.) (1985) *Episodes in ESP: a source and reference book on the development of English for Science and Technology.* Oxford: Pergamon.

Swales, J. (1990). *Genre analysis: English in academic and research settings.* Cambridge: Cambridge University Press.

Swales, J. (1997). 'English as *Tyrannosaurus rex.*' *World Englishes*, 16, 373–82.

Swales, J. (1998). *Other floors, other voices: a textography of a small university building.* Mahwah, NJ: Erlbaum.

Swales, J. (2004a). 'Evaluation in academic speech: first forays' In G. Camiciotti and E. Bonelli (eds), *Academic discourse: new insights into evaluation.* Berne: Peter Lang.

Swales, J. (2004b). *Research genres.* New York: Cambridge University Press.

Swales, J., and Feak, C. (1994). *Academic writing for graduate students: essential tasks and skills.* Ann Arbor, MI: University of Michigan Press.

Swales, J., and Feak, C. (2000). *English in today's research world: a writing guide.* Ann Arbor, MI: University of Michigan Press.

Swales, J., and Feak, C. (2004). *Academic writing for graduate students*, 2nd edn. Ann Arbor, MI: University of Michigan Press.

Swales, J., and Luebs, M. (2002). 'Genre analysis and the advanced second language writer.' In E. Barton and G. Stygal (eds), *Discourse studies in composition.* Cresskill, NJ: Hampton Press.

Tajino, A., James, R., and Kijima, K. (2005). 'Beyond needs analysis: soft systems methodology for meaningful collaboration in EAP course design.' *Journal of English for Academic Purposes*, 4 (1), 43–66.

Tardy, C. (2004). 'The role of English in scientific communication: lingua franca or *Tyrannosaurus rex?*' *Journal of English for Academic Purposes*, 3 (3), 247–69.

Thralls, C., and Blyler, N. (1993). 'The social perspective and pedagogy in technical communication.' *Technical Communication Quarterly*, 2 (3), 249–70

Tomkins, R., Ko, C., and Donovan, A. (2001). 'Internationalization of general surgical journals.' *Archives of Surgery*, 136, 1345–52.

Tomlinson, B. (ed.) (1998). *Materials development in language teaching.* Cambridge: Cambridge University Press.

Tribble, C., and Jones, G. (1997). *Concordances in the classroom: a resource book for teachers.* Houston, TX: Athelstan.

Trimble, L. (1985). *EST: a discourse approach.* Cambridge: Cambridge University Press.

Trowbridge, L., and Bybee, R. (1990). *Becoming a secondary school science teacher,* 5th edn. Columbus, OH: Merrill.

Truscott, J. (1996). 'The case against grammar correction in L2 writing classes.' *Language Learning,* 46, 327–69.

Tsou, C.-L. (1998). 'Science and scientists in China.' *Science,* 280 (5363), 528–9.

Vygotsky, L. (1978). *Mind in society: the development of higher psychological processes.* M. Cole, V. John-Steiner, S. Scribner and E. Souberman (eds). Cambridge, MA: Harvard University Press.

Wallace, C. (2002). 'Local literacies and global literacy.' In D. Block and D. Cameron (eds), *Globalization and language teaching.* London: Routledge.

Ward, L. (2004). 'High hopes for foreign students.' *The Guardian,* April.

Warschauer, M., and Kern, R. (eds) (2000). *Network-based language teaching: concepts and practice.* Cambridge: Cambridge University Press.

Watson-Gegeo, K. (1988). 'Ethnography in ESL: defining the essentials.' *TESOL Quarterly,* 22, 575–92.

Weigle, S. (2002). *Assessing writing.* Cambridge: Cambridge University Press.

Weir, C. (2004). *Language testing and validation: an evidence-based approach.* Basingstoke: Palgrave Macmillan.

Wells, G. (1992). 'The centrality of talk in education.' In K. Norman (ed.), *Thinking voices: the work of the National Oracy Project.* London: Hodder & Stoughton.

Wertsch, J., del Rio, P., and Alvarez, A. (eds) (1995). *Sociocultural Studies of Mind.* Learning in Doing: Social, Cognitive and Computational Perspectives. Cambridge: Cambridge University Press.

West, M. (1953). *A general service list of English words.* London: Longman.

White, R. V. (1988). *The ELT curriculum.* Oxford: Blackwell.

Widdowson, H. (1983). *Learning purpose and language use.* Oxford: Oxford University Press.

Widdowson, H. (1990). *Aspects of language teaching.* Oxford: Oxford University Press.

Wilkins, D. (1976). *Notional syllabuses.* Oxford: Oxford University Press.

Wilson, D. (2002). *The Englishization of academe: a Finnish perspective.* Jyvakskyla: University of Jyvakskyla Language Centre.

Wood, A. (2001). 'International scientific English: the language of research scientists around the world.' In J. Flowerdew and M. Peacock (eds), *Research perspectives on English for Academic Purposes.* Cambridge: Cambridge University Press.

Wu, M. H. (1992). 'Towards a contextual lexico-grammar: an application of concordance analysis in EST teaching.' *RELC Journal,* 23 (2), 18–34.

Zamel, V. (1985). 'Responding to writing.' *TESOL Quarterly,* 19 (1), 79–101.

Zamel, V. (1993). 'Questioning academic discourse.' *College ESL,* 3, 28–39.

Zhang, S. (1995). 'Reexamining the affective advantage of peer feedback in the ESL writing class.' *Journal of Second Language Writing,* 4 (209), 222.

Author index

Subject index

academic literacy, 12, 16, 21–2, 32, 67, 90, 103, 108, 115, 118–23, 133
action research, 79, 288–9, 303
adjunct course, 86–7, 133
appropriation (of student texts), 104
assessment, 3, 35, 72, 87, 99–102, 140–1, 182–5, 188, 197, 208–12, 256, 279, 302–7, 311, 315; formative, 99, 104, 187; summative, 99
audience, 13, 43, 46, 49, 92, 100–3, 114, 131–2, 139, 146, 150–1, 155, 240–1, 247, 250, 274, 305, 311, 314
authenticity, 78, 83, 90, 95, 97–8, 105, 132, 288, 295, 317
autonomy, 76, 80, 94, 104, 191, 280

case study research, 22, 51, 65, 70, 115, 219, 240, 242, 275, 316
coherence, 167, 169, 311, 313
cohesion, 50, 96, 244, 251, 290, 311
collaboration, 14, 76–8, 83, 86–7, 89, 91, 110, 132, 155, 186–92, 197, 291, 292, 294, 317
collocation, 62–4, 255, 311
computer assisted language learning (CALL), 297
computer mediated learning (CMC), 202–7
concordance, 58, 61–4, 89, 93–4, 169, 173, 254–7, 297, 311
conferencing (teacher–student), 104–5, 268, 311
contrastive rhetoric, 44–5, 148, 167, 244, 312
co-operation, 76, 86–8, 133, 186–92, 291
corpora, 18, 37–8, 58–6, 93–4, 138, 154, 158–9, 163–5, 167–74, 179, 239, 254–61, 298, 312
critical discourse analysis, 312
critical EAP, 32–6, 91, 135, 137, 176, 235, 312
culture, 8, 17, 19–23, 28–33, 35, 39, 42–4, 70, 71, 77, 105, 109, 117, 119–21, 125–6, 130–6, 139, 145–8, 151–6, 208, 212, 226, 229, 233, 246, 271, 280, 287, 294, 298, 300, 312, 314, 317

diary studies, 67, 70, 242, 265–6, 270, 306
disciplinary socialization, 16, 19–22, 28, 30, 118–23, 223, 225–6
disciplines, 3, 9–25, 30–4, 38–41, 50, 59, 69–71, 76, 86–90, 103, 109–17, 120, 122, 137, 139, 143–8, 157–9, 189–97, 204, 212, 218–21, 226–7, 240–1, 246–9, 252, 257, 280, 290, 300
discourse community, 15, 20–1, 31, 37–42, 46, 49, 67, 76, 79, 94, 104, 109, 112, 130, 136, 139, 144, 151, 154, 159, 194–5, 197, 204–6, 209, 211–3, 221, 242–4, 278, 313
drafts, 19, 56, 103, 109, 206, 210, 306, 313

editing, 109, 210, 315
e-mail writing, 27, 93, 207, 260, 297–8
English for General Academic Purposes, 9–11, 20, 37, 59–60, 109–17, 217–18, 280, 285, 313
English for Specific Academic Purposes (ESAP), 11–15, 17, 38, 49, 82, 86, 109–17, 120, 179, 217–18, 243, 280, 313
English for Specific Purposes, 1, 2, 147, 218, 233, 279
essay, 22, 56, 60, 78, 90, 100, 102, 109, 115, 120, 122–3, 147, 203, 208, 210–11, 217, 218, 220, 223–4, 227, 233, 234, 245, 263, 279, 305, 307
ethics, 30, 175
ethnography, 34, 65–9, 138, 174, 202, 262, 267, 313, 315–16

feedback, 43, 66, 69, 70, 99, 101–5, 118–22, 179, 181, 199, 203, 208–9, 211–13, 216, 227, 233, 237–8, 242, 264, 272, 274, 294, 302, 304, 307–10, 313
functional approach, 35, 49, 83, 86, 121, 172, 191, 242, 286

genre, 5, 15, 19, 31, 33–7, 39, 42, 46–52, 58, 64, 75, 78, 84–6, 90–2, 95, 97, 103, 114–15, 130, 132, 138, 148–50, 152–7,